S0-DHV-789

Woman's World
Cook Book

Edited by
MELANIE DE PROFT
Director, CULINARY ARTS INSTITUTE

from THE AMERICAN WOMAN'S COOK BOOK
Edited by
RUTH BEROLZHEIMER

Published by
CULINARY ARTS INSTITUTE

1961

Copyright© 1961

by

BOOK PRODUCTION INDUSTRIES INC.

Certain material in this Book taken from the

AMERICAN WOMEN'S COOK BOOK

Copyright© 1956

by

BOOK PRODUCTION INDUSTRIES, INC.

Manufactured in the United States of America

FACTS ABOUT FOOD
USE OF RECIPES

TO BECOME A GOOD COOK requires more than the blind following of a recipe. This is frequently illustrated when several women living in the same community, all using the same recipe, obtain widely differing results. It is the reason so many cooks say, "I had good luck with my cake today," or "I had bad luck with my bread yesterday." Happily, luck causes neither the success nor the failure of a product. To become a good cook means to gain a knowledge of foods and how they behave, and skill in manipulating them. The recipe by itself, helpful as it is, will not produce a good product; the human being using the recipe must interpret it and must have skill in handling the materials it prescribes.

Some of the lessons which the person desiring to become a good cook should learn are given in the following pages. They will not be learned all at once; but if they are mastered gradually, luck will play a less important part in culinary conversation.

Methods of Cooking Food

BAKE—To cook by dry reflected heat. See Oven Temperatures for Baking, page 5.

BARBECUE—To roast an animal slowly either whole or cut in pieces, on a spit or rack over direct heat, basting with a special highly-seasoned sauce.

BOIL—To cook in liquid, at a temperature of 212° F. at sea level. The boiling point decreases about 1° F. for every 500 feet of elevation. At the correct boiling temperature large bubbles rise rapidly and continually, so that all of the liquid is agitated.

BRAISE—To brown meats or vegetables, in a small amount of hot fat, and then cook slowly, in a covered utensil, on top of stove or in oven with a very small amount of liquid.

BROIL—To cook by direct heat.

CANDY—To cook fruit in heavy sirup until plump and transparent, then drain and dry; to cook vegetables in sugar or sirup and fat; to glaze.

CARAMELIZE—To heat dry sugar or foods containing sugar until a brown color and characteristic flavor develops.

CODDLE—To cook slowly just below the boiling point.

FIRELESS COOKING—To cook by heat that has been retained in a fireless cooker or insulated oven. It is accomplished by surrounding the thoroughly heated food with some insulating material to keep the heat from being lost rapidly.

FRICASSEE—To braise small pieces of fowl, game or meats, and then cook slowly in stock, gravy, or sauce.

FRY—(1) To cook in small amount of fat, also called sautéing or pan-frying. (2) To cook immersed in hot fat, also called deep-fat frying. (3) To cook in 1 to 2 inches of fat.

PAN-BROIL—To cook on a hot surface, greased only enough to prevent sticking, pouring off fat as it accumulates.

PAN-FRY—To cook in a small amount of fat. See FRY.

PARBOIL—To boil uncooked food until partially cooked.

PARCH—To brown by means of dry heat. Applied to grains.

PASTEURIZE—To preserve food by heating to 140° F. to 180° F. for 20 and 30 minutes or sufficiently to destroy microorganisms and arrest fermentation. Applied to milk and fruit juices.

POACH—To cook food by slipping into hot liquid to cover.

PRESSURE COOK—To cook in steam at a pressure of 5 to 30 pounds and at temperatures of 228° F. to 274° F.

ROAST—To cook by dry heat, usually in an oven or tightly covered kettle.

SAUTE—To cook in small amount of fat. See FRY.

SCALD—To heat liquid to temperature just below the boiling point. Scald milk over boiling water until foamy.

SCALLOP—To bake food, usually in small pieces, in a casserole with sauce, broken crackers, bread or cake; topped with crumbs.

SCRAMBLE—To cook while mixing.

SHIRR—To bake eggs in cream, vegetables or purée.

SIMMER—To cook in water at a temperature of 180° F. to 210° F., or below the boiling point of water.

STEAM—To cook in the steam generated by boiling water.

STEW—To cook slowly in a small amount of liquid.

COOKING PERIODS AND TEMPERATURES

Oven Temperatures for Baking	
	Degrees Fahrenheit
Slow oven	250 to 350
Moderate oven	350 to 400
Quick or hot oven	400 to 450
Very hot oven	450 to 550

When two degrees of temperature or two periods of time are given, separated by a dash, (e.g. 350—375 or 30—40) it means that the temperature of the cooking medium or the length of the cooking period may range between these two extremes.

When the temperature figures are separated by the word "to" (e.g. 400 to 350) it means that cooking is to be started at the temperature first given and that the heat is afterward to be reduced to the second figure.

TABLE I

BREAD, CAKES, COOKIES, MERINGUES AND PASTRY
Baking Times at Preheated Oven Temperatures

	Temperature Fahrenheit	Time in Minutes (Approximate)
Breads		
Baking powder biscuits . . . . 450°		12—15
Bread . . . . 400°		20
to 350°		40—50
Coffee bread . . . . 375°—400°		20—25
Coffee cake . . . . 400°		30
Corn bread . . . . 400°		30
Fruit or nut bread . . . . 350°		60
Muffins . . . . 425°		20—30
Popovers . . . . 450°		20
to 350°		15—20
Rolls . . . . 400°—425°		15—20
Spoon bread . . . . 350°		35—45
Cakes		
Angel Food . . . . 275°		30
Chocolate	to 300°	40—45
Layer . . . . 350°		25
Square . . . . 325°		60
Cup . . . . 375°		20—25

Cake (cont.)	Temperature Fahrenheit	Time in Minutes (Approximate)
Fruitcake		
Steamed 1 hour, then baked		
light . . . . 250°		1 hour
rich . . . . 250°		3 hours
Baked entirely . . . . . . 275°—300°		1½—4 hours
Gingerbread . . . . 350°		45—50
Jelly roll . . . . 350°		15—20
Layer . . . . 375°		25—30
Loaf (deep) . . . . 325°—350°		1—1¼ hours
Poundcake . . . . 275°—325°		1—2 hours
Spongecake . . . . 325°		1 hour
Square (shallow loaf) 350°		50
Tortes . . . . 350°		20—40
Upside-down cake . . . 350°		50
Cookies		
Fruit, molasses or choc-		
olate . . . . 325°—350°		12—15
Other drop and rolled . . 375°—400°		8—12
Other refrigerator (sliced) 400°		8
Ladyfingers . . . . 350°		10—12
Macaroons . . . . 300°		30
Meringues . . . . 275°		45—60
Pastry		
Pie shells . . . . 400°		15
Puff pastry . . . . 450°—500°		5—8
Puff shells		
Cream puffs and eclairs 450°		15
to 350°		20—25
Tarts . . . . 450°		10—15
Turnovers . . . . 450°		15
Pies		
Deep-dish pies . . . . 450°		10
to 350°		30—35
Meat pies		
Biscuit top . . . . 450°		15—20
Pastry . . . . 450°		15
to 350°		30
Meringues on cooked		
fillings . . . . 350°		15—20
One-crust (unbaked) . . . 450°		10
to 350°		25—30

TABLE II

CUSTARDS, PUDDINGS, SOUFFLÉS AND SCALLOPED DISHES
For table of oven temperatures, see page 5

	Temperature Fahrenheit	Time Minutes (Approximate)
Au Gratin Dishes		
(to brown crumbs)........400°		10
Custards ....300°		45—60
Puddings		
Batter, Cottage, etc........350°		35—45
Bread ....350°		45—60
Indian ....300°		3 hours
Rice....................325°		2 hours
Scalloped Dishes		
(not potatoes)...........350°		15—30
Soufflés...................300°		1¼ hours
Timbales		
(surrounded by water) ....250°—325°		35—45

MEAT, POULTRY AND FISH
ROASTED
For table of oven temperatures ,see page 5

The number of minutes per pound which a roast requires for cooking at a given temperature is only an approximation. The accurate way of determining doneness is by the internal temperature shown on the meat thermometer inserted into the roast.

All boned cuts require longer cooking time than those with the bones left in. Allow about 10 minutes per pound longer for cooking boned cuts.

Many hams now on the market require shorter cooking time. For these hams, follow directions given with them.

TABLE III

Meat	Oven Temperature Fahrenheit	Roasting Period Total, hrs.
Braised meats	350°	2—2½
Meat en casserole	350°	2—2½
		Total, mins.
Meat pie with crust (meat previously cooked)	450°	30

Beef	Oven Temperature	Internal Temperature	Minutes Per Pound
Rare	300°	140°	18—20
Medium	300°	160°	22—25
Well done.............	300°	170°	27—30
Pork			
Fresh (always well done)...	350°	185°	30—35
Smoked (precooked)	325°	170°	10—15
Lamb and Mutton			
Medium	300°	175°	25—30
Well done	300°	180°	30—35
Veal	325°	170°	25—35
Poultry			
Chicken................	325°		*
Duck, Goose	325°		*
Turkey	325°		*

*Poultry is done when drumstick joint yields easily.

Fish		Total, mins.
Large	350°	15—20
Small or fillets	350°—375°	20—25
Lobster, stuffed	350°	15—20

SIMMERED

Simmering temperatures range from 180° F. to 210° F.

Meat	Cooking Period
Fresh	
Pot roasts (3-4 pounds)...........	Total, hrs. 2—6
Swiss steak	Total, hrs. 2
Corned or smoked (4-5 pounds) ...	Mins. per lb. 30—40
Ham	Total, hrs. 4—5
Ox tongue	Total, hrs. 3—4
Poultry	
Chicken (3 pounds)	Total, hrs. 1—1½
Stewing Chicken (4 to 5 pounds)...	Total, hrs. 2½—4
Turkey	Total, hrs. 2—3½
Fish	
Small, thin	Mins. per lb. 5—10
Large, thick	Mins. per lb. 10—15

TABLE III *(Continued)*

BROILED

Meat	Temperature Fahrenheit	Cooking Period in minutes
Chops, lamb or mutton	550°	20—22
Ham patties or steaks............	550°	20—22
Liver, Calf or lamb	425°	20—22
Steak, 1 in. thick (rare to medium).	550°	10
1½ inch thick (rare to medium) .	550°	8—15
Poultry		
Chicken	350°	45—60
Quail	350°	35—45
Squab	350°	35—45
Fish		
Fillets	350°	15—20
Shad, whitefish, bluefish..........	350°	20—25
Lobster........................	350°	20
Oysters........................	350°	25—30
Crabs, soft-shelled..............	350°	8—10
Scallops	350°	3

TABLE IV

DEEP FAT FRYING

	Temperature of Fat Degrees Fahrenheit	Cooking Period in minutes
Croquettes		
(cooked food)	365°—382°	2—5
Doughnuts, Fritters		
(uncooked batter and dough)...	350°—365°	2—3
Fish and Sea Food.............	350°	5—10
Meat and Poultry	382°—390°	5—8
Timbale Cases.................	382°—390°	1—1½
Vegetables	382°—390°	4—6

TABLE V
Candy and Boiled Frosting Temperature Chart
(Sea Level)

Product	Stage of Concentration	Degrees Fahrenheit	Behavior at Stage Desired
Sirup	Thread	230°—234°	The sirup spins a two-inch thread when dropped from fork or spoon.
Fondant Fudge Panocha	Soft ball	234°—240°	When dropped into cold water forms a soft ball which flattens on removal.
Frosting 1 egg white to 1 cup sugar	Soft to medium ball	238°—242°	
Caramels Frosting 2 egg whites to 1 cup sugar	Firm ball	244°—248°	When dropped into cold water forms a firm ball which does not flatten.
Divinity Marshmallows Nougat Popcorn balls Salt-water taffy	Hard ball	250°—265°	When dropped into cold water forms a ball which is hard enough to hold its shape, yet plastic.
Frosting 3 egg whites to 1 cup sugar	Hard ball	254°—260°	
Butterscotch Taffies	Soft crack	270°—290°	When dropped into cold water separates into threads which are hard but not brittle.
Brittle Glacé	Hard crack	300°—310°	When dropped into cold water separates into threads which are hard and brittle.
Barley sugar	Clear liquid	320°	The sugar liquefies.
Caramel	Brown liquid	338°	Liquid becomes brown.

MEASUREMENTS

LEARN TO MEASURE ACCURATELY—All the measurements in this book are level. Do not heap or scant the measure.

HAVE ACCURATE EQUIPMENT FOR MEASURING, as follows:

A measuring cup holding ¼ quart and divided by ridges on one side into thirds and on the other side into fourths.

A quart measure divided by ridges into fourths. Each fourth is a cupful.

A standard tablespoon that holds 1/16 of a cup.

A standard nest of a teaspoon and its divisions.

A tested kitchen or sugar scale.

TO MEASURE DRY MATERIAL—Fill the cup, spoon or other measure to overflowing, then pass a spatula or the straight edge of a knife over the top, leveling the material. For an accurate half-tablespoon of dry material, fill spoon as above, then, owing to the difference in capacity of the tip and bowl of the spoon, divide the material lengthwise.

TO MEASURE FAT—An easy and accurate way to measure solid fat is by means of displacing water. For ½ cup of solid shortening, fill the cup half full of cold water, then drop in pieces of the shortening until the water reaches the top of the cup. Drain off water. The remaining shortening measures the correct amount. This method may be used for any fraction of a cup.

For spoonsful or divisions, pack the shortening into a standard measuring spoon and level off evenly with the straight edge of a knife as for dry material.

TO MEASURE LIQUIDS—Use measuring cup for liquids.

Equivalent Measures and Weights

3 teaspoons	1 tablespoon	4 cups	1 quart
4 tablespoons	¼ cup	2 pints	1 quart
16 tablespoons	1 Cup	4 quarts	1 gallon
½ cup	1 gill	8 quarts	1 peck
4 gills	1 pint	4 pecks	1 bushel
2 cups	1 pint	16 ounces	1 pound

Testing Fat for Frying

Fats should never be brought to the smoking point as a test of heat. Use a thermometer or drop into the fat a one-inch cube of bread from the soft part of the loaf. Judge the heat of the fat by the length of time it takes the bread to brown.

1. If the fat is the right temperature for large pieces of uncooked food—breaded chops, etc.,—(382°-390°F.) it will take 20 seconds for bread to brown.

2. If the fat is the right temperature for smaller pieces of uncooked food or uncooked batters and dough (350°-365° F.) it will take 60 seconds for bread to brown.

3. If the fat is the right temperature for most cooked foods —croquettes, fish balls, etc., (365°-382°F.) the bread will brown in 40 seconds.

HAVE THE RIGHT TEMPERATURE IN FRYING—If fat is too hot, it scorches the food or does not cook it thoroughly or spoils the fat. If it is too cool, the food becomes soaked with fat. Fats of low smoking temperature will naturally soak into food a little more than fats of high smoking temperature, because the food must remain longer in the fat.

Egging and Crumbing Foods for Frying

Except in the case of foods like doughnuts, fritters, potatoes and fried breads, foods are ordinarily either egged and crumbed or dipped in an egg batter before being fried. This is because the egg or egg batter hardens in the hot fat, making a case about the food which keeps it from becoming fat-soaked.

For crumbing, use dried crumbs rolled and sifted or soft crumbs forced through a strainer.

Break an egg into a shallow plate, add two tablespoons of water for each egg. Beat with a fork only enough to mix the yolk and white.

Place some crumbs on a board. Roll the food to be fried in crumbs, covering every part.

Dip the crumb-covered food into the beaten egg, being careful to cover completely.

Lift food from egg with broad-bladed knife and roll again in crumbs.

Let stand a few moments to dry. The food is then ready for frying. Foods may be egged and crumbed several hours or even a day before being fried.

Effects of Temperature on Eggs

The texture of eggs cooked alone or in custards is directly affected by the temperatures at which they are cooked.

Cooked at 180° to 200° F. (below the boiling point of water), the egg white is firm but delicate and very tender and easily broken apart. The egg yolk is tender and waxy.

Cooked at 212° F. (at the boiling point of water), the egg white is firm, but somewhat tough. The egg yolk is mealy.

Cooked at 350° to 400° F. (the temperature of fat hot enough for frying), the egg white and yolk are leathery where touched by the fat.

Eggs Thicken Liquids, Making Custards

The value of eggs in custard making is due to the fact that uncooked eggs are fluid and readily mix with water or milk. When the mixture containing the egg is heated, the particles of egg become solid and the liquid is thus thickened.

Proportion of Egg to Liquid in Custard Mixtures

1 cup liquid 1 whole egg or 2 egg yolks	Makes a mixture that has sufficient body to bake in small cups or for a medium-thick soft custard.
1 cup liquid 1½ whole egg or 3 egg yolks	Makes a mixture that has sufficient body to bake in a large baking dish and hold its form while in the dish; or, when baked in small cups, to retain the form of the cup when turned into another dish. Good foundation for ice cream if less than ¼ to ½ its bulk of cream is to be used.
1 cup liquid 2 whole eggs or 1 whole egg and 2 egg yolks	Makes a mixture that has sufficient body , when baked in a large baking dish, to hold the form of the dish when turned into another dish. Good foundation for frozen custard where no cream is used. Good foundation for salad dressings.

TO WHIP CREAM

To whip easily cream must be thick. This requires that it must contain not less than 20 per cent butter fat. Best results are obtained when it contains 25 to 40 per cent butter fat.

Fresh cream does not whip well even when it contains more than 20 per cent butter fat. This is because lactic acid is produced as cream ages, and the acid thickens the cream. The addition of ½ teaspoon commercial lactic acid to each pint of cream will do the same thing that is accomplished by twelve to twenty-four hours' standing.

Warm cream will not whip well because warmth thins cream. As cream is chilled, the fat congeals and the cream thickens. Cream referigerated for two hours will whip easily, if it is rich enough and old enough. The best temperature for whipping cream is 35°-50° F. Cream is doubled in bulk after whipping.

If variety in flavor is desired add to ½ cup of whipped cream 2 tablespoons maple sirup, 4 tablespoons Chocolate Sauce, or 4 tablespoons jam. This will make 1 cup of sauce.

TO WHIP EVAPORATED MILK

Milk, bowl and beater should be thoroughly chilled to about 40° F. If the milk fails to whip, it is not cold enough. Scalding the milk prior to chilling causes it to whip a little more readily and somewhat stiffer, but scalding is not absolutely necessary. To scald the milk, cover the unopened cans with cold water. Bring water to a boil and continue boiling for five minutes.

Lemon juice can be added for even greater and "permanent" stiffness, when the lemon flavor is suitable to the food with which the whipped milk is to be combined. When lemon juice is used, first whip the milk until stiff. Then add two tablespoons of lemon juice for every cup of milk. Continue whipping long enough to blend in the lemon juice.

Evaporated milk has only about one-fifth of the amount of fat contained in whipping cream. Instead, it has a much greater content of whole milk solids. For that reason it is an ideal ingredient for a dessert which completes an already rich meal.

APPETIZERS

STRICT convention in England and America at one time decreed that the formal dinner should begin with soup, but that custom is no longer binding even in the most formal household. Other dishes to introduce the meal have crept in and because of their savory qualities have found ready and general acceptance. Appetizers, they are usually called. Sometimes they are referred to as relishes or as *hors d'oeuvres,* because they are often a glorified edition of the old side dish now given a conspicuous place as a separate course by itself.

Characteristics of the Appetizer

The appetizer must have distinct, piquant flavor and appetite-whetting qualities. Pickled and salted foods, acids, pepper and paprika play a conspicuous part in their manufacture. Raw oysters and clams, grapefruit, melons and fruit cocktails, canapés and small sandwiches spread with pastes of sardines, anchovies and caviar, lobster and crabmeat, pâté dé foie gras, cheese, olives and other mixtures of high flavor, deviled eggs, small succulent salads, may all be included without prejudice in the list of appetizers. In parts of the United States, the dinner is always begun with the salad as the appetizer.

Serving the Appetizer

The appetizer should always be served in small portions because the purpose of this course is to whet but not to satisfy the appetite.

At formal dinners and luncheons, the same kind of appetizer is generally served to all the guests, but at more informal meals the hostess may give her guests an opportunity to choose their own appetizers. In that case a number of portions of various kinds are arranged on a regulation *hors d'oeuvre* tray or on a chop plate or small platter which is passed to each guest.

Each portion must be arranged so that it may be lifted from the tray by the guest and transferred to his plate without trouble. Suitable service silver—usually a tablespoon and large fork—must be laid on each tray.

The following combination will serve as a suggestion for the arrangement of an appetizer tray:

1. A crab salad
2. An onion and green pepper salad
3. Olives in lettuce cup
4. Water cress, brown bread and butter sandwiches
5. Aspic jelly with anchovies or sardines included
6. Deviled eggs in water cress nests
7. Cream cheese balls rolled in minced chipped beef
8. Large olives filled with cheese, wrapped in bacon; broiled
9. Celery stalks stuffed with cheese or anchovy paste
10. Small sweet pickles, rolled in cheese, then in smoked salmon and fastened with a toothpick
11. Rolled anchovies, caviar or tiny meat balls in broiled mushrooms
12. Chicken liver balls rolled in minced chipped beef

Shellfish

See pages 201, 202, 206, 217, 218 for shellfish used as appetizers.

Canapés

BREAD FOR CANAPÉS

Canapés are made from day-old white bread, cut into quarter-inch slices and then shaped with a cutter into circles two and one-half or three inches in diameter or cut into squares, strips, triangles or other fancy shapes. These portions of bread may then be fried in hot deep fat and drained on absorbent paper, or sautéed in just enough hot fat to keep them from burning, or toasted or set in the oven until they turn a delicate brown. When finished they should be nicely browned on both sides. They are then ready to be covered with the mixture preferred.

ANCHOVY CANAPÉS

6 portions prepared bread
3 tablespoons anchovy paste
3 teaspoons lemon juice
2 hard-cooked eggs
Whole anchovies for garnish (may be omitted)

Anchovy paste, which comes in tubes, jars or bottles, may be utilized, or whole anchovies may be reduced to a smooth paste with a wooden spoon. Season with lemon juice and spread the paste on the prepared pieces of bread. Split anchovy lengthwise and lay the halves diagonally across the canapé, marking the point where they cross by a little pyramid of riced yolk of hard-cooked eggs. Petal-shaped pieces of the hard-cooked white may radiate from this center pyramid. A large anchovy curved around a circle of hard-cooked egg in the center of a canapé is also effective. The anchovies may be omitted from the garnish.

SARDINE OR LOBSTER OR OTHER SEA FOOD CANAPÉS

6 portions prepared bread	Salt
6 large sardines or	Worcestershire sauce
6 tablespoons lobster or other sea food, chopped fine	Pickled beets
	6 large olives
Juice of 1 lemon	24 thin slices lemon

Remove skin and backbone and flake the sardines with a fork. Or chop cooked lobster meat very fine. Season with lemon juice, salt and a few drops of Worcestershire sauce. Spread the prepared bread with the mixture and decorate by placing in the center of each canapé a small circle of pickled beet. Cut a slice from the end of a large olive so that it will stand firmly and place this in the center of the beet. A narrow border of minced beet may be placed around the edge of the canapé with good effect. Garnish the plate with four thin slices of lemon placed symmetrically.

Crab meat, shrimps or any smoked or canned fish, highly seasoned and attractively garnished, may be utilized for canapés instead of the sardines or lobster meat.

CAVIAR CANAPÉS

6 portions prepared bread	3 tablespoons white onion,
3 tablespoons caviar	chopped fine
Garnish of green pepper or hard-cooked egg	

Cavair, which is the salted roe of the sturgeon, is highly esteemed by epicures as an appetizer. It is usually served with minced raw onion and decorated with hard-cooked egg and minced pickles. A favorite arrangement is to have an oblong canapé two by four inches, one half covered with the minced raw onion and the other half with the caviar. The striking difference in the colors is very effective. A sliver of green pepper may lie just where the two mixtures meet and little points of the green pepper extend out on each side, or a circle of the white of hard-cooked egg may decorate the center of the half covered with caviar and a little mound of the riced yolk ornament the section covered by the chopped onion.

CHEESE AND OLIVE CANAPÉS

6 portions prepared bread
3 tablespoons cream cheese
Olives stuffed with pimientos

Garnish of red pepper or pickled beet

Spread on the prepared bread a paste made by mixing equal proportions of cream cheese and chopped stuffed olives. Garnish with a quarter-inch border of the chopped olives and a star of red pepper or pickled beet in the center of each canapé.

PÂTÉ DE FOIE GRAS CANAPÉS

6 portions prepared bread
3 tablespoons pâté de foie gras or pâté de foie poulet

¼ cup cream
Cayenne pepper
Salt
Parsley

Add the cream and seasoning to the paste. Rub through a fine sieve and spread on portions of fried bread. Garnish with parsley.

PÂTĚ DE FOIE POULET

½ cup chicken livers
2 tablespoons chicken fat or butter

¼ onion, chopped
Salt and pepper
Mustard or celery salt

Carefully clean, cook and chop chicken livers and mash them to a paste with a wooden spoon. Chop the onion fine and fry in the fat until yellow. Place the livers, the fat and the onion in a cup, mix well and season with pepper and salt, and either mustard or celery salt, according to taste. Place at once on ice. This preparation makes excellent sandwiches.

Suggestions for Mixtures to Be Used in Making Canapés

1. Anchovy paste mixed with lemon juice.
2. Shredded tuna fish mixed with lemon juice and mayonnaise.
3. Chopped lobster meat mixed with cream and seasoned with salt, pepper and lemon juice.
4. Cream cheese and chopped stuffed olives.
5. Minced red and green peppers mixed with mayonnaise and seasoned with salt, pepper and lemon juice.
6. Sardine paste mixed with lemon juice, salt and Worcestershire sauce.
7. A layer of anchovy paste covered with a paste of shredded crab meat, cream cheese and butter, seasoned with salt and pepper.
8. Devilled ham mixed with chopped hard-cooked egg and horseradish.

Fruit Appetizers

Fruit cocktails may be made from mixtures of almost any fruits, canned or fresh. As a rule, combinations of a sweet and a sour fruit are most piquant in flavor. All fruit appetizers should be thoroughly chilled. Refrigerator trays are excellent for this purpose.

GRAPEFRUIT COCKTAIL

GRAPEFRUIT ON THE HALF SHELL.

Cut grapefruit in half, crosswise. With a pair of sharp shears or with a grapefruit corer, cut a circular piece from the center of each half, being careful not to cut through the skin. Then with a sharp knife loosen each section from the membrane and skin. Sprinkle with sugar and set in the refrigerator to chill. Pink the edges of the skin if you prefer, and remove the pieces of membrane between the sections of fruit if you have time. In this way the shell is left with only edible portions of the fruit. In any case each mouthful of fruit should be entirely detached from the shell. Serve a half grapefruit on a plate or in a special grapefruit glass, embedded in ice.

SOUPS

SOUPS may be roughly divided into two groups. In the first group belong the soups that are always made from meat stock. These are the various modifications of brown and white stocks, bouillons, consommés and broths. In the second group belong the soups that may be made either with or without meat stock. These are the various modifications of cream soups, purées and bisques, of chowders and stews and of vegetable soups.

The Value of Soup in the Dietary

The purpose of soup in the meal is two-fold; first, to improve digestion and stimulate appetite by introducing at the beginning of the meal a highly flavored liquid food which increases the flow of digestive juices; second, to increase the variety of nutrients in the meal, or even to furnish the main dish of the meal. Stock soups are chiefly valuable for the first purpose. Cream soups, purées, bisques, chowders and stews are more valuable for the second purpose.

A heavy meal should begin with an unthickened stock soup; a light meal may well begin with one of the cream variety.

Home Made and Ready to Use Soups

Not so long ago, all soups were made at home, and the stock pot was kept on the stove day in and day out; but with the gradual change from coal to gas and electricity as fuels, and with the perfecting of modern commercial canning and condensing methods, the long slow process of stock making has become less common in home kitchens.

However, in soup many valuable food materials that would otherwise be thrown out may be saved for the nourishment of the family, and some knowledge of the principles of soup making is worth while for every housekeeper. A home made soup which is lacking in strength or flavor may be easily improved by the addition of a can of soup or some of the various meat extracts obtainable.

For the small family, the canned soups are almost indispensable, and in the making of sauces and gravies, where only a small amount of stock is required, a can of soup supplies the required foundation at a minimum of trouble and expense.

Making Soup Stock

CUT MEAT IN SMALL PIECES and saw or crack bone. This is done to increase the surface exposed to the action of hot water.

BROWN FROM ONE-FOURTH TO ONE-HALF THE MEAT for brown stocks and consommés. This gives added color and improves flavor.

SOAK THE MEAT AND BONE IN COLD WATER for thirty minutes or more before cooking. This helps to extract the juices of the meat.

HEAT GRADUALLY TO THE SIMMERING POINT (180°-210° F.). If stock is to be used for bouillon or consommé or any clear soup, skim at this time. Continue to simmer for three or four hours to insure as complete extraction as possible of the juices and flavor of meat. If the mixture boils, it is not so fine in flavor.

ADD THE SPICES, HERBS, AND VEGETABLES, and continue simmering from one-half hour to one hour. The seasonings are added at this time rather than earlier to prevent the disagreeable flavor of over-cooked vegetables.

STRAIN THE SOUP INTO A LARGE BOWL or other container. If the stock is to be used for clear soups, place several thicknesses of cheesecloth over the strainer before pouring the mixture through it.

COOL THE STOCK QUICKLY, because quick cooling improves the keeping quality of the soup. Soup should, if possible, always be allowed to become thoroughly cold before being used, since the fat hardens and collects in a cake on top and can be removed easily. Do not remove fat from the top of soup stock until the stock is to be used. It protects the stock against spoilage.

KEEP STOCK IN A COLD PLACE, as it spoils quickly if it is not kept chilled. Spoiled stock, like spoiled meat, is dangerous food.

Using Soup Stock

When ready to use stock, loosen fat around the edges with the thin blade of a knife. Remove the cake of fat. If the stock is jellied, wipe off the remaining small pieces of fat and the edge of the bowl with a cloth wrung out of hot water. If the stock is very soft or liquid, pass small sheets of absorbent paper over the top of the stock.

WHEN STOCK MUST BE USED BEFORE COOLING, skim off all the fat possible. Most of the remainder of the fat may be removed in one of two ways. The first way is to pass over the top small sheets of absorbent paper or blotting paper. The second way is to cool the soup as much as possible beforehand, then to wrap a piece of ice in a cloth and let down into the stock. Move the ice around just below the surface so that the fat on the surface is suddenly chilled, and it will gather on the cloth around the ice. This must be done quickly to prevent unnecessary dilution of the stock.

FOR CLEAR SOUPS, take the stock from the top of the bowl, being careful to avoid any sediment which may have escaped through the sieve and settled to the bottom of the bowl. This sediment is valuable as a food and should be reserved for gravies or soups which are not necessarily clear. Clarify this stock if a translucent, sparkling soup is desired.

TO CLARIFY SOUP—Allow 1 egg white and shell to 1 quart of stock. Wash egg well. Separate yolk and white. Crush the shell into small pieces and mix with the slightly beaten egg white. Heat the stock just enough to liquefy it if it is jellied. Stir the egg white and shell thoroughly into the stock. Heat slowly to boiling, stirring constantly, then boil without stirring 2 to 5 minutes. Remove from heat. Add ½ cup of cold water and let settle. Strain through 2 thicknesses of cheesecloth. The coagulated egg gathers around itself the particles of solid substance in the soup which otherwise would be fine enough to pass through a strainer.

Serving Soup

Serve clear soups in bouillon cups for lunch or supper and in shallow-rimmed soup plates for the formal dinner. Cream soups are served in soup plates or cream soup cups at luncheon or supper. Soups should always be served very hot.

INGREDIENTS NEEDED TO MAKE ONE QUART OF STANDARD STOCK

BROWN STOCK OR BOUILLON.

2 pounds beef (¼ to ½ bone)
1¼ quarts cold water
4 to 6 peppercorns
2 cloves
1 bay leaf

1 blade mace
1 teaspoon sweet herbs
Sprig parsley
1 tablespoon, each, of carrot, onion, celery, turnip
1 teaspoon salt

A good stock can be made by using leftover meat scraps and bones instead of the beef specified, and by substituting any available vegetables, such as the outer leaves of lettuce, celery tops, etc., for those given above. After the stock is made, leftover vegetables, cereals, hard-cooked eggs, small pieces of meat, etc., may be diced or chopped and served in the soup.

CONSOMMÉ.

1 pound lean beef
1 pound veal
1¼ quarts cold water or
    1 pint cold water and
    1 pint chicken stock
2 peppercorns

1 clove
½ teaspoon sweet herbs
Sprig parsley
1 tablespoon each, celery, carrot, onion
1 teaspoon salt

MUTTON OR LAMB STOCK OR BROTH—Use the same ingredients as for brown stock or bouillon, using mutton or lamb instead of beef, and removing most of the fat from the meat.

WHITE STOCK.

2 pounds chicken or knuckle of veal
1¼ quarts cold water
2 peppercorns
1 clove

½ teaspoon sweet herbs
1 tablespoon, each, of onion and celery
1 teaspoon salt

The liquid in which a fowl or chicken is cooked is also a white stock or chicken broth.

FISH STOCK OR COURT BOUILLON.

2 pounds white fish or
  2 pounds head and
  trimmings
1¼ quarts cold water
2 peppercorns

1 clove
Sprig parsley
1 bay leaf
1 tablespoon, each, carrot,
  celery, onion

Fish stock needs to be cooked for only half the time required for other stock.

VARIATIONS OF BROWN OR WHITE SOUP STOCK

VEGETABLE SOUP—If a clear soup is desired, follow the directions for clarifying soup stock, and then add, to each quart of brown stock, one cup of diced vegetables, raw or cooked. If the vegetables are cooked, the soup needs to be boiled for only a few minutes. When raw vegetables are added, simmer until the vegetables are all tender, adding boiling water, if necessary, to replace any that may have evaporated. Season to taste and serve.

SAGO, RICE OR BARLEY SOUP—For each quart of brown or white stock, use two tablespoons sago, rice or barley. Soak sago or rice one-half hour in enough stock or water to cover it. Barley should be soaked over night. Bring remainder of stock to simmering point. Add soaked sago, barley, or rice and simmer in closed saucepan one-half hour.

MACARONI, VERMICELLI, SPAGHETTI, OR NOODLE SOUP—For each quart brown stock, use ¼ cup macaroni, spaghetti, vermicelli or noodles broken into small pieces. Simmer the pastes in the stock until tender, adding water if necessary.

VARIATIONS OF CONSOMMÉ

CONSOMMÉ PRINCESSE—Consommé served with shreds or small dice of cooked chicken and green peas.

CONSOMMÉ A LA ROYALE—Consommé served with tiny blocks of royal custard.

CONSOMMÉ JULIENNE OR JULIENNE SOUP—Consommé served with carrot, onions, turnips and celery cut into shreds about as thick as a match.

The vegetables should be boiled in clear water before being added to the consommé.

Unthickened Soups

Soups suitable for serving as the first course of a meal with a substantial main course are found in this group. Any of the variations of soup stock or consommé may be used for this purpose. The following recipes give directions for other soups of this variety.

CHICKEN OR TURKEY BONE SOUP

Never discard the bones of turkey or chicken as they always will make a delicious soup. Scrape the meat from the bones, break the bones, pack in a kettle, and cover with cold water, adding a small onion. Cover closely and simmer very gently for three hours. Strain and cool. One-half hour before it is to be served, return to the fire and for every quart of stock add one cup of the cold meat, season and keep hot till needed. This soup may be greatly improved by adding to it, three minutes before serving, ten oysters to each quart of soup.

CLAM BROTH

| 12 clams in the shell | 2 cups water | Paprika |

Purchase large clams in the shells. Scrub them thoroughly with a brush, place them in a kettle with cold water, closely covered, and bring water to the boiling point. As soon as the shells have opened, remove them from the broth. The clams may be served at once, in the half-shell, or taken from the shells and kept to be served in any form desired. Let the broth settle, strain, being careful not to pour out the sandy sediment, reheat, add a little red pepper or paprika, and serve hot. Twelve good-sized clams should make enough broth for six persons, but if there does not seem to be sufficient, add a little boiling water or milk. Clam broth seldom needs added salt. Water wafers heated in the oven, or divided crackers toasted on their broken surfaces buttered and heated for a few minutes in the oven, are generally served with this broth.

Clam broth may be served, hot or cold, in cups with a heaping teaspoon of whipped cream, into which has been beaten a little salt and pepper, placed upon the top of each cup. The cream adds richness to the flavor of the soup and increases its nourishing properties.

CLEAR TOMATO SOUP

1 quart brown soup stock	4 tablespoons butter
1 can tomatoes	2 sprigs parsley
½ teaspoon peppercorns	¼ cup each, onion, carrot,
1 small bay leaf	celery, raw ham, diced
3 cloves	Salt
3 sprigs thyme	Pepper

Cook onion, carrot, celery, and ham in butter five minutes. Add tomatoes, peppercorns, bay leaf, cloves, thyme and parsley, cover and cook slowly one hour. Strain carefully, add hot stock, and season with salt and pepper.

This recipe may be used for jellied soup or for salad.

JELLIED SOUP

1 quart clear brown, or	2 tablespoons gelatin
white stock, or tomato	½ cup cold water
or chicken soup	

Soften the gelatin in the cold water, add to the boiling hot soup, chill and serve in cups. Refrigerator trays are excellent for chilling soups.

Substantial Vegetable and Stock Soups

Soups in this group are suitable for serving as the first course of an otherwise light dinner or as the main course of an informal luncheon.

BEAN SOUP

3 slices bacon	1 tablespoon flour
2 cups baked or boiled beans	1 tablespoon butter
4 cups cold water	Salt, pepper, paprika

Cook bacon. Add to beans. Add cold water and cook until beans are soft, then rub through a strainer. Place on the heat and add a little more water, if needed, as the soup must not be too thick. Bind with the flour and butter. Cook two or three minutes. Season with salt, a dash of pepper, and paprika.

SOUPS, HOT AND THICK, OR
JELLIED CONSOMMÉ ARE
DOUBLY DELICIOUS WHEN
BEAUTIFULLY SERVED

WITH A LITTLE TIME YOU CAN
ROLL YOUR CHEESE STICKS OR
SANDWICHES

BLACK BEAN SOUP

1 cup black beans
1½ quarts water
1 onion
1 tablespoon fat for sautéing
2 stalks celery
1 lemon

2 tablespoons butter
2 tablespoons flour
2 hard-cooked eggs
½ teaspoon mustard
Pepper, salt, paprika

Soak the beans overnight. Next morning, drain them and cover with the cold water. Add sliced onion, which has been browned in the fat, also stalks of celery broken into inch pieces. Simmer until beans are soft, adding more water from time to time. Press through a sieve, again bring to the boiling point, and then add seasoning of mustard, pepper, salt, and paprika to taste. Thicken with roux of butter and flour to prevent soup from separating. Cut the eggs and lemon in thin slices, and add these to the strained soup just before serving.

BORSCHT
(A Famous Russian Soup)

1 bunch beets
1 cup tomatoes, fresh or
canned
4 cups water
1 small onion

½ pound breast of beef
1 tablespoon lemon juice
¼ cup sugar
¼ teaspoon salt
4 eggs

Pare the beets and cut them into long strips. Strain the tomatoes over the beets, not letting any seeds through. Add water. Put in the onion and meat, cut into small pieces, and simmer for thirty minutes. Add lemon juice, sugar, and salt. Boil one-half hour more. Beat the eggs with a pinch of salt. Add the hot borscht to this, a little at a time, stirring well to prevent the separating of the eggs. Serve at once.

BARLEY SOUP

½ cup barley
1 teaspoon salt
1 quart boiling water
2 quarts soup stock

½ cup diced celery
½ cup diced onions
½ cup diced carrots
1 green pepper, diced

Wash barley in cold water and cook in boiling salted water until tender, about 2 hours, adding stock when water has evaporated. Add vegetables ½ hour before soup is done.

BOUILLABAISSE

2 large onions, chopped
2 cloves garlic, chopped
2 tablespoons flour
2 tablespoons butter
2 cups tomato pulp
2 cups water
8 cloves
3 bay leaves
1½ teaspoons curry powder
½ cup sherry
Dash of Tabasco sauce
1 teaspoon salt
4 pounds fish fillets
1½ quarts boiling water
½ pound mushrooms, sliced
Hot buttered toast

Use red snapper and redfish in equal amounts. Sauté onions, garlic and flour in butter. Add tomato, 2 cups water, 4 cloves, bay leaves, curry powder, ¼ cup sherry and Tabasco; simmer 30 minutes; add salt. Add fish and remaining cloves and sherry to boiling water; simmer 15 minutes. Add mushrooms and sauce and simmer 5 minutes. Place toast on large platter, add fish and pour sauce over fish. Serves 12 to 15.

CHICKEN GUMBO

1 fowl (3 to 4 pounds)
½ cup salt pork fat
1 onion
1 quart okra, fresh
  or canned
5 tomatoes
1 cup cream
2 sprigs parsley
3 cups boiling water
½ teaspoon pepper
2 tablespoons salt
1 cup boiled rice

This is a noted Southern soup. Cut the chicken into convenient pieces and sauté until brown in salt pork fat, then place all the pieces in a saucepan. Cut a large onion into thin slices and sauté slowly for ten minutes in the fat. Add okra, cut fine, sliced tomatoes, and parsley sprigs. Sauté all of these ingredients one-half hour, quite slowly, and place them in the saucepan with the chicken. Add boiling water, pepper and salt. Simmer slowly two to four hours, or until the chicken is very tender, and then add boiled rice and cream. If more seasoning is needed, add it, and if necessary, thin with boiling water. Boil up once and serve. Cayenne pepper (one-fourth teaspoon) may be used instead of white or black pepper, if desired. Separate the bones from the chicken. Serve with pieces of chicken in the plate with the soup.

CHICKEN SOUP

This recipe provides a large bowl of substantial soup, as well as a cooked fowl, and when the soup is served the rest of the dinner should consist of light dishes. For more economical recipes see Index for chicken or turkey bone soup.

1 fowl (3 to 4 pounds)	1 cup milk
½ pound ham	1 tablespoon chopped parsley
1 onion	Salt and pepper
2 to 3 quarts water	1 tablespoon flour
¼ cup rice	1 tablespoon chicken fat

Cut up fowl into quarters, with the ham and onion, and add the water. Let this simmer until the meat is very tender, then strain, reserving the meat to be used in any way desired. Remove all possible fat, and to one and one-fourth quarts of this soup (the remainder can be used for sauce with the meat) add well washed rice, chopped parsley, salt and pepper. Simmer until the rice is tender, add milk, then add roux made of flour and chicken fat. Cook until the mixture is thickened (about five minutes), season and serve.

GREEN PEA SOUP

2 cups stock	2 sprigs mint
1 quart water	1 tablespoon flour
1 quart green peas	1 tablespoon butter
1 celery stalk	Salt and pepper
1 onion	Sugar
1 turnip	

Reserve one-half cup of peas, and to the stock, and water add the rest of the peas, the celery stalk, onion and turnip cut into pieces, and the mint. Stew until the mass is tender. Strain through a sieve or coarse cheesecloth. Thin with stock or water, if necessary; bind with a roux of flour and fat and season with salt, pepper, and a little sugar. Add the half cup of whole peas, stew for a few minutes, and serve.

SPLIT PEA SOUP

This recipe provides the main part of a dinner, since the ham end will serve as the meat dish. A ham bone, left over from a boiled or baked ham, will flavor pea soup quite as well as a piece bought especially for the purpose.

2 or 3 pounds ham end	3 quarts boiling water
1 carrot	1 cup split peas
1 onion	Salt and pepper
2 potatoes	2 tablespoons catchup

Put the end of a moderately lean smoked ham into a kettle with carrot and peeled onion, whole potatoes, and boiling water. Boil one hour and strain. Now rinse the ham thoroughly in hot water and return to the strained stock, together with split peas which have been soaking all night, and boil for one hour. Season with salt and white pepper and add catchup. Serve at once. Thin with boiling water if too thick.

ONION SOUP GRATINÉE

4 onions	1 quart chicken stock
½ cup butter, melted	Salt
2 tablespoons flour	8 slices French bread
½ cup Parmesan cheese	

Slice onions very thin, add to melted butter and cook slowly until tender but not brown. Add flour and blend well; then add hot chicken stock slowly, stirring constantly. Season. Toast bread, spread with melted butter, sprinkle with Parmesan cheese and heat under broiler until cheese is slightly melted. Place slice on each serving of soup. Serve extra cheese in separate bowl. Serves 8.

ONION STEW OR DUTCH BROTH

6 onions	3 tablespoons flour
5 tablespoons butter	2 cups scalded milk
3 cups cold water	Salt and cayenne
1 egg yolk	

Chop the onions and cook them in two tablespoons of the butter for five minutes, then add water and cook thirty minutes. Press through a sieve. Make a roux of the remaining butter and the flour, combine it with the scalded milk and add seasoning. Cook five minutes, stirring constantly. Add this milk mixture to the onion mixture. Mix thoroughly and add the egg yolk, slightly beaten. Serve individually in Dutch bowls and place one teaspoon of grated Edam cheese on the top. Set for a few minutes in a hot oven to melt the cheese.

Thick Soups, Chowders and Stews
Cream Soups

Cream soups are made by combining a very thin white sauce, see page 290, with a suitable quantity of cooked, mashed, strained vegetable, fish or meat pulp. Undiluted evaporated milk used instead of white sauce will greatly increase the food value and when used for making white sauce will increase the flavor. Flavor is improved, too, by the use of some highly flavored vegetables or the addition of a proportion of soup stock.

Purées

Purées are made in the same way as cream soups, but are somewhat thicker. They are often served under the name of "Cream Soup."

Bisques

The name bisque is usually given to a cream soup made from fish, and the fish is often diced or mashed through a coarse strainer. A familiar example of an exception in the use of the word is mock bisque soup, or tomato bisque, as it is often called.

Chowders

Chowders were probably the common ancestors of the more refined cream soups, purées, and bisques. The word chowder comes from the French *chaudière,* meaning caldron. The chowder originated as a community fish stew to which each neighbor contributed something; milk, fish, potatoes, crackers, pork or some seasoning. These contributions were all cooked together in the common caldron, from which chowder derives its name, and each contributor withdrew his share of soup when it was ready.

The chowder of today is much the same as the old chowder, and consists of pieces of different vegetables or of fish and potatoes and various seasonings cooked in milk with crackers added just before serving.

Fish Stews

Fish stews are made of milk and the juice of the fish which gives flavor to the soup. They differ from the cream soups in that they need not be thickened, though they often are, and from the chowders in being less complex in composition.

Binding Thick Soups

When a vegetable, meat or fish pulp is combined with milk or stock in making soups, they separate and the solid substance sinks to the bottom of the liquid. Some flour or cornstarch cooked into the mixture will overcome this. With many of these soups the reason for using the flour or cornstarch may not necessarily be to thicken a soup which the vegetable, meat or fish pulp has already made thick enough, but to blend the liquid with the solid so that all parts of the soup will have the same consistency.

Flour or cornstarch may be mixed with enough cold liquid —milk, water, or stock—to make a creamy thickness and added carefully to the soup; or it may be combined with the soup by means of a roux (page 289). When a colored roux is desired the fat is browned before the flour is added and the mixture is cooked to a reddish brown color. When a roux is made in this way, the liquid is usually added to it gradually.

Preventing Skin on Cream Soups

A cream or milk soup has a tendency to form a skin on the top as it cools. If it is beaten just before it is served, the froth protects it against skin formation.

A spoonful of whipped cream or beaten egg-white served on top of each portion of cream soup aids in preventing the skin formation and adds to the delicacy and attractiveness of the dish.

DIRECTIONS FOR MAKING A STANDARD CREAM SOUP

4 cups milk or part milk and part stock	2 cups vegetable pulp or meat or fish pulp
2 tablespoons flour	Salt, pepper, other seasonings
2 tablespoons fat	

1. Make a white sauce of the liquid, flour, and fat.
2. Cook the vegetables or meat or fish until tender, drain, and mash through a sieve.

3. Combine the vegetable, meat, or fish pulp with the white sauce.

4. Season, beat with rotary beater, and serve. A tiny portion of whipped cream or beaten egg white may be served on top of each portion.

The amount of flour may be increased for purées and bisques.

VARIATIONS OF CREAM SOUP

CREAM OF ASPARAGUS OR CREAM OF CELERY SOUP—Follow directions for making a standard cream soup.

CREAM OF CORN SOUP

5 cups corn, canned or fresh	2 tablespoons butter
5 cups milk or part milk and part white stock	Salt and pepper
	2 egg yolks
2 tablespoons flour	

Put the corn into a double boiler with one quart of the milk and cook for twenty minutes. Make a white sauce of the milk and corn, flour, and fat; add salt and pepper and cook five minutes. Press soup mixture through a strainer. Beat the yolks of the eggs well and add to them the remaining cup of cold milk; stir this mixture into the soup. Cook for a minute or two, stirring constantly. Beat and serve at once.

CREAM OF MUSHROOM SOUP

¼ pound mushrooms (or skin and stems of ½ pound)	2 tablespoons flour
	1 teaspoon salt
2 tablespoons butter	1 pint milk

Brush, wash and skin the mushrooms. Put the skins to simmer in a little water. Cut the mushroom caps and stems into very small pieces; add one pint of water and simmer until tender. Make a sauce of the fat, flour, salt, and milk and add the water in which the mushroom caps, stems, and skins were cooked.

CREAM OF ONION POTATO SOUP

3 cups scalded milk	4 medium potatoes
1 cup potato water	4 onions
2 tablespoons flour	1 tablespoon chopped parsley
2 tablespoons butter	Salt and pepper

Boil the potatoes and onions together until tender. Drain. Save the water, press the vegetables through a coarse strainer

Make a white sauce of the liquid, flour, and fat and combine with the potato and onion pulp. Season with chopped parsley. salt, and pepper. Beat with rotary beater and serve with croutons.

CREAM OF PEA SOUP—Follow directions for making a standard cream soup, but keep one cup of the cooked peas whole and add them to the soup just before serving.

CREAM OF SPINACH SOUP—Follow directions for making a standard cream soup.

CREAM OF TOMATO SOUP

1 quart milk or half milk and half white stock	1 pint tomatoes
	Salt and pepper
2 tablespoons flour	¼ teaspoon baking soda
2 tablespoons butter	

Make a white sauce of the liquid, flour, and butter. Cook the tomatoes until tender, and press through a coarse sieve. Just before serving, add the soda to the tomatoes and gradually add the tomatoes to the white sauce, stirring constantly. Season and serve at once. If soup begins to curdle, beat thoroughly with beater.

Purées
PURÉE OF ONION

3 large or 6 small onions	2 or 3 tablespoons butter or other fat
2 cups white stock	
2 cups milk	Salt and pepper
2 or 3 tablespoons flour	1 tablespoons chopped parsley

Make a white sauce with stock, milk, flour, and butter. Cook onions in water until very tender. Drain, and press through a sieve. Combine onion and sauce. Season with salt, pepper, and chopped parsley. Beat with rotary beater and serve.

FISH PURÉE

1 quart milk	4 tablespoons butter or other fat
1 small onion, minced	
4 tablespoons flour	2 cups cooked fish
	Salt and pepper

Scald the minced onion in milk. Make a white sauce of the milk, flour, and butter. Press the cooked fish through a sieve. Combine the fish and sauce. Season and serve.

PURÉE OF PEAS AND TOMATOES

½ pound dried yellow split peas
1 pint tomatoes
1 quart water
1 onion
1 or 2 celery tops
Salt and pepper
1 tablespoon flour
1 tablespoon butter

Soak peas overnight in water enough to cover them three or four inches. Drain, and put into a saucepan with the tomatoes, water, sliced onion, and celery tops. Cook until the peas are tender. Press through a sieve. Season with salt and pepper. Thicken with a roux made of flour and butter. Serve, garnished, with a thin slice of tomato or lemon and a few canned peas, if available. Serve with croutons.

SPLIT PEA OR LIMA BEAN PURÉE

1 cup split peas or dried lima beans
2 quarts
1 tablespoon flour
1 teaspoon onion juice
2 tablespoons butter
or other fat
Salt and pepper
Celery Salt

Soak peas or beans all night, then cover with water and place over the heat; bring to a boil. Cook slowly until soft. Press through a sieve, heat, and thicken with roux of flour and fat. Season with salt, pepper, celery salt, and onion juice. Stir or beat until smooth and serve with croutons.

Cold Fruit Purées

In hot weather, cold fruit purées are sometimes preferred to hot soups. They are always served in cups, usually of glass, and with a few pieces of the fruit floating on the surface. They should be thoroughly chilled. Refrigerator trays are excellent for this purpose. These fruit purees are really as closely related to the appetizers as to the soups.

CHERRY PURÉE

Juice from 1 quart of tart
cherries, freshly stewed or
canned

2 teaspoons arrowroot
Grated rind of 1 lemon

Heat the juice from the cherries. Add arrowroot moistened with cold water, stirring the mixture rapidly to prevent the forming of lumps. Flavor with the grated lemon rind. Serve very cold with a whole cherry floating on each portion.

ORANGE PURÉE

2 cups orange juice
1 teaspoon cornstarch
2 tablespoons cold water

½ cup sugar
1 teaspoon grated orange
rind

Place orange juice in saucepan and when it is thoroughly heated add the cornstarch mixed with the cold water. Cook slowly until clear. Add sugar and grated orange rind. Serve very cold in glass sherbet cups.

RASPBERRY PURÉE

½ cup granulated tapioca
6 cups water
½ cup currant juice

2 cups raspberries
Sugar

Boil tapioca in water and currant juice. When tapioca is transparent, add raspberries and sugar to taste. Set aside to cool. Serve very cold in sherbet glasses.

Bisques
BISQUE OF CLAMS

24 clams in the shell
2 cups rich milk or white
stock or part of each
1 tablespoon butter
1 tablespoon flour

2 cups water
1 tablespoon chopped celery
1 teaspoon chopped parsley
Salt and pepper

Make a white sauce of the milk, flour, and butter. Scrub the clams thoroughly, then pack into pot with a tight-fitting lid, using ½ cup water to steam. When all have popped open, remove, cool in their own liquor. Detach clams from shells, put through food chopper and add strained liquor. Add water, chopped celery and parsley a nd cook ten minutes. Press through a sieve and add to the white sauce. Season, beat with rotary beater, and serve.

BISQUE OF LOBSTER

1 medium-sized lobster	1 cup cold water
1 quart milk	Red pepper
4 tablespoons butter	Salt and pepper
4 tablespoons flour	

Make a white sauce of the milk, flour, and butter. Remove meat from freshly cooked lobster. Reserve the coral and the green fat. Put the cold water into a kettle and add the broken claws and shell and the finely chopped tail meat. Bring to the simmering point and simmer for twenty minutes. Drain, and stir into the white sauce. Add the remainder of the lobster meat, diced. Season with salt, pepper, and cayenne. Just before serving, add the coral mashed to a paste with the green fat. Mix thoroughly, reheat, and serve with croutons.

1 pint oysters	1 slice onion, chopped fine
2 cups milk	1 stalk celery, diced
1 cup dry bread crumbs	1 stalk parsley, chopped fine
1 tablespoon flour	1 bay leaf
1 tablespoons butter	Salt and pepper
2 cups water	

Scald the milk, add the bread crumbs and cook in a double boiler for twenty minutes. Press through a sieve. Make a white sauce of the milk and crumb mixture and the flour and butter. Chop the oysters, put them in a saucepan with their own liquor, the water, and the chopped vegetables and herbs. Simmer for twenty or thirty minutes. Press through a fine sieve and combine with the white sauce mixture. More milk or cream may be added if the bisque is very thick. Season and serve.

MOCK BISQUE OR TOMATO BISQUE SOUP

4 cups milk	2 cups cooked tomatoes
¾ cups dry bread crumbs	2 teaspoons sugar
½ onion stuck with 6 cloves	3 tablespoons butter
Sprig of parsley	1 teaspoon salt
½ bay leaf	⅛ teaspoon pepper

Scald milk with bread crumbs, onion, parsley, and bay leaf. Remove onion and bay leaf and press through sieve. Heat tomatoes with sugar to boiling; press through sieve. Reheat milk mixture with butter, salt, and pepper. Add tomatoes and serve at once with croutons or crisp crackers. If desired, garnish with whipped cream and a sprig of water cress. Serves 6.

VARIATIONS—Use cracker crumbs instead of bread crumbs, if desired.

Add ½ teaspoon sweet basil to tomatoes.

Chowders

CLAM CHOWDER

¼ pound salt pork, cubed	½ teaspoon pepper
2 small onions, minced	3½ cups milk
1 quart shucked clams	6 to 8 soda crackers,
6 to 8 medium potatoes	split
Water	Cold milk
Salt, if needed	

Brown salt pork in deep kettle. Add onion and cook 2 or 3 minutes. Remove stomach from clams, chop hard parts and leave soft parts whole or chop them, as preferred. Arrange potatoes and hard parts of clams in layers over onions, cover with cold water, heat to boiling and simmer until potatoes are tender. Add soft part of clams, seasonings, and milk. Heat to boiling and add crackers which have been soaked in cold milk. Heat thoroughly. Serves 6 to 8.

MANHATTAN CLAM CHOWDER—Add ½ green pepper, chopped, and ½ cup chopped celery when browning the onion. Add tomato juice instead of milk. Season with a dash of cayenne, sage and thyme. Add tomato juice last; heat only to boiling before serving.

RHODE ISLAND CLAM CHOWDER—Omit milk and add 1 cup tomatoes instead. Crackers may be omitted.

CLAM STEW

Make in same way as oyster stew, using clams.

CRAB STEW

6 hard-shell crabs	1 pint rich milk
1 tablespoon butter	1 quart water
1 tablespoon flour	Salt and pepper
1 onion	Parsley

Boil the crabs. Remove the meat and sauté it in butter with one small onion. Cook until the onion is quite brown. Add flour, salt, and pepper, cook a little longer, then add water and minced parsley. Simmer ten minutes, add milk and reheat.

OYSTER STEW

UNTHICKENED

1 pint oysters	Salt, pepper, paprika
4 tablespoons butter	1 quart rich milk

Put cleaned oysters, strained oyster liquor, butter, and seasoning into a saucepan and simmer gently until oysters begin to curl at the edges. At the same time, heat the milk, being careful not to scorch it. Add the hot milk to the oysters and oyster liquor and serve at once.

THICKENED—To the ingredients given above, add from four to eight tablespoons of flour, and, if desired, a little onion juice and mace. Scald the oysters in their own liquor. Make a white sauce of the milk, flour, and butter and season as desired. Combine the scalded oysters and oyster liquor with the white sauce. and serve at once.

YEAST BOUILLON

In recent years several varieties of autolyzed yeast have appeared on the market to be used as bouillon or in sandwich pastes. They have the flavor of strong meat extract but have the advantage of being of pure vegetable origin. If purchased in jars use according to direction. When in cubes use like any other bouillon cube. Of peculiar value for the high content of vitamins B and G, it is also called petite marmite.

SOUP ACCOMPANIMENTS

SOUP MAY BE SERVED with many accompaniments, such as crisped crackers, cheese sticks and pulled bread; and varieties of croutons, forcemeat balls, noodles, and vegetable pastes may be placed in the soup itself. Grated Parmesan cheese is passed with many kinds of soup to be sprinkled on each portion.

Recipes for some of the best-liked accompaniments for soup are given below.

CROUTONS

Cut stale bread into slices about one-third of an inch thick, and remove all crust. Spread with butter, cut in cubes and bake in the oven until delicately browned. If preferred, these cubes of bread may be fried in deep fat or sautéed in just enough fat to keep them from burning. Put into soup at time of serving, or pass in a separate dish, permitting each person to put as many croutons as he may wish in his portion of soup.

MOCK ALMONDS

These are merely croutons shaped to represent almonds.

CHEESE STICKS AND ROLLS

Cut bread in long, narrow strips, spread with butter, then with a thick coating of grated cheese. Brown in moderate oven (350° F.). Or cut crust from sliced bread, spread thickly with paste of grated cheese and butter, roll, fasten with wooden pick and brown as above.

HOT CRISPED CRACKERS

Toast thin wafers or crackers for three minutes in a hot oven (400°-425° F.). They are better if spread with a thin film of butter before being put into the oven. If Boston crackers are preferred, split them, arrange the halves, rough side up, on a plate, lay a bit of butter on each, and brown them in the oven.

VARIATIONS

Use the cookie cutters in any small design to cut sliced bread for toasting on a baking sheet or large pan. Or use the cutters on biscuit dough and bake or fry in deep fat.

NOODLES

1 egg   ½ teaspoon salt   Flour

Stir sufficient flour into a slightly beaten egg to make a very stiff dough. Add salt, knead, and roll as thin as possible. It should be of almost paperlike thinness. Cover with a towel and let remain untouched for half an hour. Then cut in small fancy shapes, and dry them. When needed, place in boiling water and cook rapidly for fifteen minutes. This dough may also be rolled into threads and used like macaroni in soup.

NOODLE BALLS—Roll the noodle paste as indicated above, fold it double and with a cutter make circles about one-fourth inch in diameter. Toss these balls into hot fat, (360°-370° F.) using a wire frying-basket. In about a minute they will turn a delicate brown and puff into balls. Drain on soft paper and serve with soup. As these soften quickly, it is better not to put them in the tureen, but to pass them after the soup has been served.

EGG BALLS

No. 1.

5 eggs   1 teaspoon salt
½ teaspoon pepper   Flour

Simmer four of the eggs in the shell twenty minutes and mash the yolks to a smooth paste in a bowl; then add the salt and pepper and the other egg, well beaten. Shape the mass into tiny balls, roll them in flour and sauté, tossing them about while frying to prevent their sticking to the pan. They may be made some time before needed. Use the hard-cooked egg whites for a sandwich or a salad.

No. 2.

Mash the four cooked egg yolks to a paste, season, and mix with the uncooked egg yolk. Form into small balls. Roll them in the uncooked egg white, then in flour, and poach in hot water. These are attractive in consommé.

MARROW AND LIVER BALLS

2 tablespoons melted marrow   Paprika
1 egg   ⅛ teaspoon onion juice
Salt and pepper   ½ cup soft bread crumbs

Strain melted marrow through cheesecloth, beat until creamy and then add beaten egg. Season with salt, pepper, paprika, and onion; add moist bread, and form into balls. Poach in boiling water. Use 1 cup chopped liver instead of marrow for liver balls.

PÂTÉ À CHOUX

1 teaspoon butter   1 egg
2½ teaspoons milk   Salt
¼ cup flour

Heat butter and milk together. When at the boiling point, add the flour and a pinch of salt, stirring constantly. Remove from the fire, beat in the unbeaten egg, and continue beating until the egg is well mixed with the other ingredients. When cool, drop small pieces from the tip of a teaspoon into deep, boiling fat. When brown and crisp, drain on absorbent paper. If desired, two tablespoons of grated Parmesan cheese may be added to this recipe.

CUSTARD FOR GARNISHING

Allow two tablespoons of milk, cream, or consommé to each egg. Mix well, season with salt and pepper, and pour into a buttered mold, making the custard one-half inch thick. Set the mold in a pan containing hot water and place in a slow oven (300°-350° F.). When the custard is set, remove from the oven and cool. Cut it into small pieces or fancy shapes. The egg white, the egg yolk or the whole egg may be used in making this custard.

CUSTARD ROYALE

2 egg yolks   Salt and pepper
1 egg   Cayenne
½ cup beef stock

Beat the yolks of the eggs slightly and then beat into them the one whole egg. Add beef stock, a little salt, pepper, and a few grains of cayenne. Pour the mixture into a shallow pan or dish, so that the custard will be about one-half inch deep. Set this pan into another holding water that is just below the boiling point and place both in a slow oven (300°-350° F.). The custard should set without bubbling and without forming a brown crust on top. When cold, cut in fancy shapes with vegetable cutter. Use care in placing these in the soup, so that they may not break. When used in consommé, they give the name "Consommé Royale" to the soup.

CHICKEN FORCEMEAT

WHITE—

2 breasts chicken (uncooked	1 cup milk
½ teaspoon salt	½ blade mace
1 cup dry bread crumbs	¼ teaspoon pepper
3 tablespoons butter	2 egg whites

Chop, pound and put through a food mill the uncooked breasts of chicken. There should be a full half-pint of meat. Add salt and pepper. Boil together the bread crumbs (no crusts), milk and mace for ten minutes, or until cooked to a smooth paste. Remove from the fire, put in butter and then add the seasoned meat and the well-beaten whites of eggs. Stir until all ingredients are thoroughly blended.

DARK—Use dark meat instead of light and the yolks of the eggs instead of whites. Chicken livers, also, may be used for forcemeat.

FISH FORCEMEAT

Free any kind of delicate fish from skin, fat and bone. Pound, strain, use one-half pint fish and proceed as for chicken forcemeat.

OYSTER FORCEMEAT

12 oysters	Cayenne
2 cups dry bread crumbs	1 teaspoon parsley
3 tablespoons butter	1 teaspoon lemon juice
2 egg yolks	3 tablespoons oyster juice
1 teaspoon salt	Nutmeg

Chop the oysters fine and add the bread crumbs, butter, salt, cayenne, minced parsley, lemon juice, oyster juice, the yolks of raw eggs and a grating of nutmeg. Pound to a smooth paste and rub through a food mill. Add more salt if necesssary. This is a fine forcemeat for timbales, or for stuffing poultry or fish. For use in soups, it may be made into balls, dipped in beaten egg yolks, then in bread crumbs and fried, or rolled into very small balls, dipped in egg yolks and browned in the oven.

QUENELLES—These are shapes made by forcing forcemeat through a pastry bag and tube into boiling water or stock. They are used to garnish entrées as well as soups.

COLORING FOR SOUPS AND SAUCES

To color brown, use browned flour or a little burnt sugar. (See Index for caramel recipe) or a few drops of commercial vegetable flavoring.

Spinach leaves give a fine green color. Pound the uncooked leaves, tie them in a cloth, squeeze out all the juice and add this to the soup five minutes before serving. The strained juice of tomatoes or the whole tomato if run through a sieve will color soup red. Grated carrots give an amber color. Okra imparts a pale green color as well as a delightful flavor.

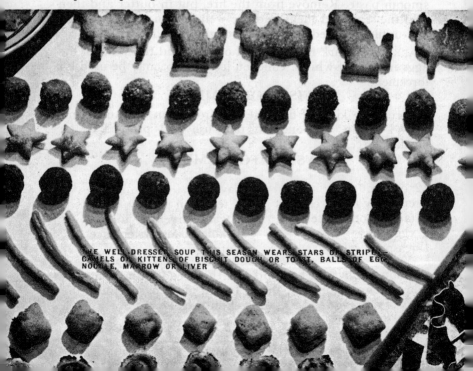

THE WELL-DRESSED SOUP THIS SEASON WEARS STARS OR STRIPES—CAMELS OR KITTENS OF BISCUIT DOUGH OR TOAST, BALLS OF EGG NOODLE, MARROW OR LIVER

YEAST BREADS

THE age-old dependence of man upon bread as food has not been disturbed by the most recent researches in nutrition. Indeed it is considerably strengthened. Bread is not only an inexpensive source of carbohydrates and vegetable protein but carries minerals and the B vitamins, especially when whole grains are used. The use of yeast increases these vitamins. Bread can be made of flour, salt, water and yeast; more valuable bread results if sugar, shortening and milk are added.

Flours and Meals Used in Breadmaking

While flours and meals made from oats, rye, corn, rice and other seeds are used to some extent with wheat flour in maing yeast breads, by far the larger amount of yeast bread is made from wheat flour only and most of it is made from white flour. This is because the gluten of wheat flour possesses properties which enable the dough containing it to stretch and hold the leavening gas produced by the action of yeast.

ALL-PURPOSE OR GENERAL-PURPOSE FLOUR is white flour containing the kind and quality of gluten which make it satisfactory for all types of household baking, for breads as well as pastries.

ENRICHED FLOUR is all-purpose flour which, according to government specifications, contains in each pound from 2.0 to 2.5 milligrams of thiamine, from 1.2 to 1.5 milligrams of riboflavin, from 16.0 to 20.0 milligrams of niacin and from 13.0 to 16.5 milligrams of iron.

WHOLE-WHEAT, ENTIRE-WHEAT AND GRAHAM FLOUR are ground from whole wheat and contain varying amounts of bran and germ. They do not make light-textured breads if used alone and are usually combined with an equal amount of white flour.

SELF-RISING FLOUR is all-purpose flour which contains salt and a leavening agent, usually bicarbonate of soda and calcium phosphate.

BUCKWHEAT, RYE AND SOYBEAN FLOUR may be used for yeast breads, but must be used in combination with wheat flour.

POTATO AND RICE FLOUR are often used to replace wheat flour in allergic diets.

CORN MEAL is a preparation of ground corn varying in degrees of fineness. It contains no gluten.

YEAST

YEAST grows in the presence of a given amount of moisture and sugar at a temperature of about 80° F., producing in the process tiny bubbles of carbon dioxide gas which leaven the bread dough. A dough must be leavened to rise and become light.

COMPRESSED YEAST (moist cake)—Grayish tan though may be slightly browned at edges; breaks with a clean edge and crumbles easily between the fingers when fresh; must be kept in refrigerator and used within a week for best results; soften in lukewarm water (80° F. to 85° F.).

ACTIVE DRY YEAST—May be kept without refrigeration; to obtain best results use before date on package expires; one package when softened has the leavening power of one cake compressed yeast; soften in warm water (110° F. to 115° F.).

Note: Compressed yeast cakes are available in several sizes. Yeast recipes included in this book refer to the small-size compressed yeast cake. (Active dry yeast may be substituted for compressed yeast.)

Amounts of Yeast

From one-sixth of a cake to two cakes of yeast may be used to one cup of liquid in making bread. With the minimum amount of yeast, the bread usually is allowed to rise overnight. With the maximum amount of yeast, the bread may be made and the baking finished three or four hours from the time it is started.

Liquids for Breadmaking

MILK is the best liquid to use because of its contribution to the food value as well as to the flavor and appearance of the loaf. It gives a creamy crumb and a rich golden brown crust. The loaf retains its moisture better than when no milk is used.

WATER is cheap but has no food value. It is used in making the crusty types of bread such as French and Italian breads.

POTATO WATER hastens the action of the yeast and produces a characteristic crust excellent in flavor. It yields a loaf which retains its moisture and does not get stale as quickly as when water alone is used.

Miscellaneous Materials Used in Bread

SUGAR is added to hasten the activity of the yeast, to improve flavor and to produce a better bloom on the crust. Too much sugar retards the action of the yeast. In making large quantities of bread, the liquid is decreased if a large quantity of sugar is used.

SALT is used to improve the flavor of bread. Too much salt retards the activity of the yeast.

SHORTENING is added to give slight tenderness to both crust and crumb and to improve the keeping qualities of the loaf. Any soft fat or oil of mild flavor may be used as shortening in bread.

Eggs give a yellow color to the crumb and a rich brown bloom to the crust and add flavor and food value. Because of their leavening power, eggs add to the lightness of the loaf.

DRIED FRUITS AND NUTS add flavor and food value and help give variety to breads.

Preparation of Materials for Making Bread

Scald milk (unless evaporated milk is used) to destroy bacteria and enzymes which might cause injury to the dough during the rising process at a warm temperature. Cool to lukewarm.

Add the yeast, softened in a small amount of lukewarm water with one teaspoon of sugar to start yeast activity. Or crumble compressed yeast into the lukewarm liquid and let stand five minutes to soften. Mix well. Another method is to mix compressed yeast with two tablespoons sugar until it liquefies.

Sift flour before measuring, except graham and whole-wheat flours, which are not sifted but stirred lightly before measuring.

Methods of Making Bread

SPONGE METHOD—Add sugar and softened yeast to lukewarm liquid, then stir in half the flour and beat well. Cover and set in a warm place (not warmer than a warm room) until batter is bubbly and light. Add salt, melted shortening, and enough more flour to make a dough of the desired stiffness. Turn onto a floured board and knead thoroughly until smooth and satiny.

STRAIGHT DOUGH METHOD—If scalded milk is used, add sugar, salt and shortening and cool to lukewarm, then add softened yeast. Otherwise, melt shortening and add to luke-warm liquid, then add sugar, salt and softened yeast. Add half the flour and beat well. Add enough more flour to make a dough of the desired stiffness, turn out onto a floured board and knead well until smooth and satiny. This method may be used with compressed or granular yeast.

KNEADING BREAD—Fold the dough over on itself and push it lightly away with the balls of the hands, exerting sufficient pressure to cause the part folded over to adhere to the part underneath. Turn dough one-quarter around and repeat motion. 'Continue turning, folding and kneading until dough is smooth and elastic and does not stick to an unfloured board.

FIRST RISING OF DOUGH—Put the dough into a greased receptacle large enough to hold at least twice the bulk of the dough. Grease the top of the dough, cover with a cloth and set in a warm place. Let it rise until it doubles its bulk or until it retains the imprint of the finger when pressed.

SECOND RISING OF DOUGH—When dough is light, punch down by folding in the edges and pressing down in the center of the dough. Turn the dough smooth side up, grease lightly, cover and let rise again. This second rising is not essential but improves the texture of the bread.

SHAPING INTO LOAVES—Divide dough into portions for loaves, shape into smooth balls, cover and let stand 10 minutes. This rest period may be omitted but it allows the dough to rise slightly and become less compact and therefore more easily shaped. Flatten the ball of dough and fold lengthwise, pressing the edges together. Stretch the dough lengthwise to about three times the length of the pan. Overlap the ends across the center and press the edges together. Fold again lengthwise and place seam down in greased bread pan. For a tender crust, brush top with oil or melted shortening; for a hard crust, brush with water; for a bright shine, bush with egg white. Cover and let rise in a warm place.

SHAPING INTO BRAIDS—Divide dough for each loaf into thirds and allow to rest 10 minutes. Shape each piece into a long roll, press the three ends together and braid rolls. Press ends together, place on greased baking sheet, cover and let rise.

BAKING BREAD—The temperature for baking bread depends upon the type of crust desired. Baking a 1-pound loaf (containing about 1 cup liquid and 3 cups flour) at 425°F. for 35 minutes produces a thin dark crust; starting the baking at 400° F.

and reducing the temperature to 375° F. after about 10 minutes produces a thicker, lighter crust. When the temperature is reduced, the total baking time should be 45 to 50 minutes. The latter method should always be used for breads containing eggs or extra sugar, since these rich breads tend to brown more rapidly.

When no oven regulator or thermometer is available, one may judge whether the baking is proceeding correctly by dividing the time into quarters and observing the bread at the end of each quarter.

First quarter: the dough rises quickly.

Second quarter: the dough sets and begins to brown.

Third quarter: the loaf continues to brown but does not become dark.

Fourth quarter: the loaf shrinks from the sides of the pan and is evenly browned over its entire surface.

Tests for Determining When Bread is Done

The color is a rich golden brown.

The loaf shrinks from the sides of the pan.

The loaf sounds hollow when tapped.

Characteristics of a Good Loaf of Bread

SIZE—A 1-pound loaf is a good household size. One cup of liquid and 3 cups of flour will make a loaf weighing about 1 pound.

SHAPE—A well-shaped loaf is symmetrical. The top is rounded but the middle is not appreciably higher than the ends. Its proportions are such that the slices cut from it will be approximately square. There is no bulge over edge of pan.

COLOR—Well-baked bread has an even golden brown color. The crumb is creamy in color with no streaks through it.

TEXTURE—A slice of bread with perfect texture feels silky smooth to the touch. The holes are small and uniform; there are no streaks or lumps. Perfect texture is the clearest indication of quality and depends upon a number of things: kneading the dough until it is smooth and elastic, allowing it to rise sufficiently and baking at the correct temperature.

CRUST—The crust of a good loaf is smooth and uniformly brown. It may be thick or thin, depending upon the preference.

FLAVOR AND AROMA—A good loaf of bread is fragrant and has a pleasing yet bland flavor.

Common Causes of Inferior Bread

POOR FLOUR—A cheap flour may be an expensive flour because it makes a loaf inferior in texture, color, flavor and volume.

OLD YEAST—Dead yeast plants cannot leaven bread. Old compressed yeast cakes or dry yeast which has been stored away until many of the yeast plants are dead will act very slowly if at all and will not give good results.

TOO MUCH OR TOO LITTLE KNEADING—Dough kneaded too much becomes sticky and will not rise well in the oven. Dough kneaded too little makes streaked bread, poor in texture, which sometimes contains lumps that might have been worked out in kneading.

TOO MUCH FLOUR—Too stiff a dough makes coarse-textured bread of small volume and dry crumb.

OVER-RISING—Too long rising gives a very porous loaf with little flavor, a pale crust and a porous crumb with broken, irregular texture. This bread crumbles badly. If the rising continues too long, the dough may become sour.

UNDER-RISING—Too little rising gives a loaf which is small and flat. It browns too quickly in the oven. The crumb is compact and dull.

TOO COOL AN OVEN—Bread will continue to rise too long if the oven temperature is too low. The result is bread that is very porous in the center and upper part of the loaf. The bread dries out before it begins to bake.

TOO HOT AN OVEN—The dough sets immediately and cannot continue to rise as it should the first ten or fifteen minutes it is the oven. The crust becomes very brown before the crumb is baked.

ROPE IN BREAD—Rope may appear at any time but is most likely during hot, damp weather. It gives bread a ropy, stringy quality and a very disagreeable odor and makes it unfit for use. It is due to a type of bacillus which may be in any one or more of the ingredients used in bread.

If rope develops, all utensils used in making bread and containers in which bread is stored should be sterilized with boiling water and rinsed with water to which vinegar has been added. Since acid inhibits the growth of the bacillus, 1 tablespoon vinegar for each quart of liquid should be added to each subsequent batch of dough until all the materials in stock at the time the rope appeared are used up.

KNEAD YOUR DOUGH
FIRMLY BUT QUICKLY
AND DEFTLY. FOLD IT
INTO LOAVES WITH THE
LEAST POSSIBLE FLOUR.
DIVIDE YOUR LOAF INTO
THREE AND BRAID IT
OCCASIONALLY

ROLL YOUR OWN INTO
CLOVER-LEAVES, CRESCENTS,
POCKETBOOKS AND PARKER
HOUSE

Care of Bread After Baking

Bread should be removed from the pans as soon as it is taken from the oven and placed on racks or crosswise of the pans so that air can circulate on all sides of it. Quick cooling prevents loss of moisture, but drafts of cold air on hot bread may crack the crust.

For a tender crust, brush with butter immediately upon removing from the pans and cover with a cloth.

As soon as the bread has cooled thoroughly, wrap carefully in waxed paper and store in a bread box which has air holes for proper ventilation. The breadbox should be washed, scalded and aired once a week, oftener during hot weather.

MOLD—Bread wrapped while hot molds quickly. If mold is found, the bread should be thrown away and the container scalded immediately.

STANDARD RECIPE FOR WHITE BREAD

1 cake yeast	2 tablespoons shortening
¼ cup lukewarm water	2 tablespoon sugar
1 teaspoon sugar	2 cups milk, scalded
1½ teaspoons salt	6 cups sifted flour, about

Add yeast to lukewarm water and 1 teaspoon sugar. Let stand 5 minutes. Add salt, shortening and remaining sugar to milk and cool to lukewarm. Add softened yeast and 3 cups flour. Beat well. Add enough more flour to make a soft dough. Place remaining flour on board, turn out dough on floured board and knead until smooth and elastic. Place in greased bowl, turn over, so that greased side is on top, cover with cloth and let rise until doubled in bulk. Punch down and let rise a second time if desired. Cut dough into halves, round into balls, cover and let stand 10 minutes. Shape into loaves and place in greased bread pans. Grease tops, cover with a cloth, and let rise until doubled in bulk. Bake in hot oven (400° F.) 10 minutes, reduce temperature to 375° F. and bake 35 to 40 minutes longer. Makes 2 (1-pound) loaves.

For detailed directions for kneading, shaping the loaves, and baking, see pages 50-51.

LIQUID STARTER OR POTATO YEAST

3 medium potatoes
4 cups boiling water
1 cake yeast
1 cup lukewarm water

1 cup sifted flour
1/3 cup sugar
1½ tablespoons salt

Pare and dice potatoes and cook in boiling water until very tender. Drain, saving liquid. Mash potatoes thoroughly and return to liquid. Cool to lukewarm. Soften yeast in lukewarm water and add to potatoes with remaining ingredients. Beat well. Cover and let stand at room temperature 24 hours. Pour into sterilized jar, cover and store in cool, dark place. Use 1 cup of the mixture to replace 1 yeast cake in recipes. Fresh starter should be prepared at least every 2 weeks, using 1 cup of the old or a fresh cake of yeast.

WHOLE-WHEAT OR GRAHAM BREAD

1 cake yeast
¼ cup lukewarm water
¼ cup brown sugar
1½ teaspoons salt
2 tablespoons shortening

2 cups milk, scalded
3 cups whole-wheat or
graham flour
3 cups sifted white flour

Mix and bake as for standard white bread. Makes 2 loaves.

RYE BREAD

6 tablespoons corn meal
½ cup cold water
1 cup boiling water
2 teaspoons salt
1 tablespoon shortening
1 cake yeast

¼ cup lukewarm water
1 cup mashed potatoes
2½ cups rye flour
1½ cups sifted white flour
½ tablespoon caraway seed

Mix corn meal with cold water, add boiling water and cook 2 minutes, stirring constantly. Add salt and shortening and cool to lukewarm. Soften yeast in lukewarm water. Add with remaining ingredients to corn mixture. Knead to a stiff dough. Dough will be sticky. Handle rapidly or too much flour is absorbed. Cover and let rise until doubled in bulk. Shape into 2 loaves, cover and let rise until doubled in bulk. Bake in 375° F. oven for 45 minutes.

COCKTAIL RYE—Shape into long loaves like French bread. Sprinkle with salt and seeds; let rise and bake as above.

CORN BREAD

½ cake yeast
¼ cup lukewarm water
½ cup corn meal
1¾ cups boiling water

1½ teaspoons salt
2 tablespoons sugar
1 tablespoon shortening
2¾ to 3 cups sifted flour

Soften yeast in lukewarm water. Cook corn meal in water 10 minutes; add salt, sugar, and shortening. Cool until lukewarm, stirring occasionally to prevent a film. When cool add softened yeast and beat well. All flour and mix well. Knead, using as little flour on board as possible. Put into a greased bowl and let rise until almost doubled in bulk. Knead down and let rise again. Shape into loaves, place in pan, and let rise until it has almost doubled in bulk. Bake as for standard white bread. Makes 2 loaves.

RAISIN BREAD

½ to 1 cake yeast
¼ cup lukewarm water
2 cups scalded milk
2 tablespoons shortening
¼ cup brown sugar

1½ teaspoons salt
¾ cup raisins, chopped
6 cups sifted white flour, about

Soften yeast in water. Follow general directions for making bread, either sponge method or straight dough method (page 49). Add raisins with the flour. Makes 2 loaves.

MONTE CARLO BREAD

2 cakes yeast
½ cup lukewarm water
2 cups milk, scalded
1½ teaspoons salt
1 cup sugar

1 cup shortening
9 cups sifted flour, about
6 eggs, slightly beaten
1½ cups currants

Soften yeast in lukewarm water. Add milk to salt, sugar, and shortening. When lukewarm add yeast. Add half the four and beat well. Let rise until very light. Add eggs, currants, and remaining flour. Knead lightly, let rise and when light place in greased bread pans. Let rise and when light bake as for white bread. When bread is 2 days old, cut into thick slices and toast. Makes 3 loaves.

GLUTEN BREAD

1 cake yeast
½ cup lukewarm water
2 cups scalded milk

1½ teaspoons salt
4 cups gluten flour
2 egg whites

Soften yeast in water. When milk is cool, add softened yeast, salt, gluten flour, a little at a time, and finally slightly beaten egg whites. The mixture should be of a consistency to drop from a spoon rather than to pour and should be baked in greased pans filled about half full. Follow general directions for rising (page 50). When light, bake in moderate oven (350° F.) 1 hour. If a less moist bread is desired, add enough white flour to make a dough, after beating in the gluten flour, and follow directions for straight dough method (page 49). Makes 2 loaves.

POTATO BREAD

1 cake yeast
½ cup lukewarm water
½ cup boiling water
1½ teaspoons salt
1 tablespoon sugar

1 tablespoon shortening
2 cups mashed potato
4 cups sifted flour (enough
   to make medium dough)

Combine in order given, following general directions for straight dough method (page 49). Makes 2 loaves.

ROLLED OAT BREAD

1 cup rolled oats
2 cups boiling water
½ to 1 cake yeast
½ cup lukewarm water
½ cup molasses

1½ teaspoons salt
1 tablespoon shortening,
   melted
4½ cups sifted flour

Combine rolled oats and boiling water, cover and let stand 1 hour. Soften yeast in lukewarm water. Add to cooled oats with molasses, salt, and melted shortening. Add flour and let rise. When light beat thoroughly, place in greased bread pans, let rise again and bake as for white bread. For a less moist bread, add enough flour to make a medium dough and follow directions for straight dough method (page 49). Makes 2 loaves.

ROLLED CINNAMON BREAD

1 recipe Standard White   6 tablespoons brown sugar
   Bread dough (page 55)   1 teaspoon cinnamon

When dough is light, divide into halves and roll each half into a sheet 9 inches square. Sprinkle with a mixture of brown sugar and cinnamon. Roll up like jelly roll and place, seam side down, in greased bread pans. Let rise until light. Bake in hot oven (425° F.) 15 minutes, then reduce temperature to moderate (375° F.) and bake 25 minutes longer. Remove from pans and cool. Makes 2 loaves.

SALT RISING BREAD

SPONGE—

   1 cup milk   1 teaspoon salt
   2 tablespoons corn meal   1 tablespoon sugar

SECOND SPONGE—

   1 cup lukewarm water   2 tablespoons shortening
   1 teaspoon salt   2 cups sifted flour
   1 tablespoon sugar

DOUGH—

   3¼ cups sifted flour
     (about)

Scald milk, cool to lukewarm, add corn meal, salt, and sugar, pour into fruit jar or pitcher, cover and place in pan of hot water (120° F.). Let stand 6 or 7 hours or until signs of fermentation (gas bubbles) appear. Add ingredients for second sponge, beat thoroughly and again cover and place in pan of hot water (120° F.). Let rise until very light; then add remaining flour gradually until dough is stiff enough to be kneaded. Knead 10 to 15 minutes, shape into 2 loaves, place in greased bread pans, brush top with melted shortening, cover and let rise until very light, more than doubled. Bake in moderate oven (375° F.) for 10 minutes, then lower to 350° F. and bake 25 to 30 minutes longer. If more than 2 loaves are to be made, for each additional loaf, add the amount of ingredients listed for "second sponge" except for the flour, at the time second sponge is made. Add 1 cup flour only for each additional loaf to be made and add 1⅝ cups more (about) when making the dough. Makes 2 loaves.

Rolls, Fancy Breads and Muffins

SOFT, LIGHT DOUGH—A softer dough is used for rolls than for loaves of bread, and rolls and fancy breads should be permitted to become lighter than loaves. This is because they are eaten fresh and should be very light and spongy in texture.

FOR PLAIN ROLLS, use the straight dough method. This saves time and they are just as good as when made by the sponge method.

FOR FANCY ROLLS when large quantities of fat, sugar and eggs are used, the best results are obtained by making a sponge of the yeast, liquid and one-half the flour, then adding the fat, sugar, and egg after the sponge is light. However, very good results can be secured by adding all ingredients before the first rising and such a change may be made in any of the following recipes.

BAKING ROLLS—Bake in hot oven (425° F.). Rolls are so small in size that slow baking dries them out. For crusty rolls, bake in individual gem pans or place ½ to 1 inch apart in baking pan. To obtain a soft, bright crust, grease the rolls before baking; for a crisp crust, do not grease either before or after baking.

STANDARD ROLL RECIPE

1 cake yeast	4 tablespoons sugar
¼ cup warm water	6 cups sifted flour (enough
2 cups scalded milk	to make a tender dough)
1½ teaspoons salt	4 tablespoons shortening

If a greater amount of sugar is used the rolls will be sweeter. If a greater amount of shortening is used, the rolls will be richer and more tender. Not less than 2 or more than 8 tablespoons of sugar or shortening should be used, however.

Follow general directions for making bread (page 49) kneading in a little less flour and permitting the dough to become lighter during each rising process, both after it is shaped and before the rolls are placed in the oven.

PLAIN ROLLS—When dough is light, cut it into pieces about the size of a small egg or a walnut. Fold sides under until top of roll is perfectly smooth. Brush top with fat. Place in greased bread pan, on baking sheet or in individual molds. When light, bake in hot oven (425° F.) 15 to 20 minutes. Makes about 30.

VARIATIONS OF STANDARD ROLL RECIPE

BOWKNOTS—See Brioche, page 64.

BRAIDS—Braid 3 narrow strips of dough; press ends to pan. Let rise and bake as for plain rolls.

BUTTERFLY—Roll out dough, brush with melted butter and roll up like jelly roll. Cut into 1½-inch slices and place on greased baking sheet 1 inch apart. Flatten across center with handle of spoon. Let rise and bake as for plain rolls.

BUTTER-LEAF ROLLS—Roll dough as thin as possible; brush with melted butter. Cut into strips 1½ inches wide and place strips in piles of 6. Cut into 1-inch slices and place in greased muffin pans with longer cut edge down. Let rise until light, then bake in hot oven (425° F.) about 20 minutes.

CINNAMON ROLLS—When dough is light, roll ¼ inch thick, brush with melted butter and sprinkle with sugar and cinnamon. Roll like a jelly roll and slice with very sharp knife. Place on greased baking sheet 1 inch apart. When light bake in hot oven (425° F.) about 20 minutes.

CLOVER-LEAF ROLLS—When dough is light, cut off pieces about the size of marbles, brush with melted butter and place 3 or 4 together in greased muffin pans. When very light, bake in hot oven (425° F.) about 15 minutes. The success of these rolls depends upon having the 3 or 4 balls together equal only as much dough as would be used in 1 ordinary roll and in letting them rise until very light before baking them.

CRESCENT ROLLS—When dough is light, roll out and cut into triangles. Brush with melted butter. Roll each triangle, beginning at the base. Place on greased baking sheet with point underneath, curving ends toward each other. Let rise and bake as for plain rolls. When nearly done, brush with egg yolk mixed with milk and return to oven to brown.

DINNER ROLLS—Add 2 egg whites after adding half the flour. Add remaining flour, knead and let rise. Shape into small balls the size of a walnut and place on greased baking sheet 1 inch apart. Let rise, glaze with egg white mixed with a little water and bake as for plain rolls.

ENGLISH MUFFINS—Make a very soft dough. Knead lightly, let rise, punch down and let rise again. Roll out ¼ inch thick on lightly floured board. Cut into large circles and let rise until light. Bake on hot ungreased griddle, turning when one side is brown. When second side is brown, reduce heat and bake more slowly. Baking may be finished in oven.

A variation of this recipe may be made by adding only enough flour to make a drop batter. Let rise until light. Drop batter into large, greased English muffin rings, arranged on greased baking sheet. Bake in hot oven (425° F.) until nearly done. Turn rings upside down and complete baking.

FINGER ROLLS—Follow standard roll recipe. When light cut and shape into long pieces about the size and shape of a finger. Place on well-greased pan and brush with melted fat or egg white. When light bake in hot oven (425° F.).

LUNCHEON ROLLS—Follow standard roll recipe using 6 to 8 tablespoons of shortening. Add 2 well-beaten eggs after half the flour has been added. Add remaining flour and knead. When light shape into small biscuits. Place 1 inch apart in well-greased pan. When doubled in bulk, brush with egg yolk diluted with milk and bake in hot oven (425° F.).

PARKER HOUSE ROLLS (POCKET-BOOK ROLLS)—Follow standard roll recipe. Four tablespoons each of sugar and shortening give excellent results. When light roll dough ¼ inch thick. Cut with biscuit cutter, brush each circle with melted fat and crease through center of each roll with dull edge of knife. Fold each roll over double. Place 1 inch apart on well-greased pan, brush with melted fat and when very light bake in hot oven (425° F.).

ROSETTE ROLLS—Shape dough into very small balls, brush with melted butter and place 6 together in greased muffin pans. Let rise until very light and bake as for plain rolls.

Or shape dough into long slender rolls, tie ends in a knot and bring 1 end up through the center. Place on greased baking sheet 1 inch apart. Let rise and bake as above.

TEA ROLLS—Follow standard roll recipe. When dough is light, roll and cut with biscuit cutter. Place on greased pans ½ inch apart. When light bake in hot oven (425° F.).

TWISTED ROLLS—Follow standard roll recipe. When light cut off dough into small pieces and roll out with palm of hand into rolls about 7 inches long and ½ inch thick. Taking an end of each strip between the thumb and forefinger of each hand, twist in opposite directions and bring the ends together. Shape the 2 ends alike, place ½ inch apart on well-greased pans and brush with melted fat or egg yolk diluted with milk. When light bake in hot oven (425° F.).

REFRIGERATOR ROLLS

¾ cup shortening
1 cup boiling water or
  scalded milk
2 eggs, beaten
¾ cup sugar

2 teaspoons salt
1 cup cold water
2 cakes yeast
½ cup lukewarm water
7½ cups sifted flour

Combine shortening and boiling water; stir until shortening is melted. Combine eggs, sugar, and salt and beat in cold water. Soften yeast in lukewarm water. Combine the 3 mixtures and add flour. Cover and chill overnight. Shape, let rise and bake as for standard rolls. Makes 36.

BREAD STICKS

1 cake yeast
¼ cup lukewarm water
1 cup milk
4 tablespoons shortening

1½ tablespoons sugar
½ teaspoon salt
1 egg white
3½ cups sifted flour

Follow standard bread recipe, adding egg white before the flour. When light shape into sticks the size of a pencil. Place far apart on greased baking sheet and let rise until light. Place in hot oven (400° F.) and reduce temperature to moderate (325° F.). Bake until dry and crisp. Makes 18.

If desired, brush rolls with egg white before baking and sprinkle with coarse salt or poppy seed.

RYE STICKS—Use rye bread dough (page 56) and shape as above. Place far apart on baking sheet sprinkled with corn meal. Before baking, brush with egg white mixed with water and sprinkle with coarse salt or caraway seed. Bake until dry and crisp, as above.

RUSKS

1 cup scalded milk
½ to 1 cake yeast
¼ cup warm water
3½ to 4 cups sifted flour
  (to make a soft dough)

¾ teaspoon salt
2 tablespoons sugar
½ cup shortening
1 egg

Prepare dough as for fancy rolls (page 60). When light roll out and cut with biscuit cutter. Place on greased baking sheet, let rise; bake in hot oven (400° F.). Makes 24.

BRIOCHE

2 cakes yeast
¼ cup lukewarm water
1 cup milk
2/3 cup butter
1 teaspoon salt

½ cup sugar
4 eggs, well beaten
4½ cups sifted flour
Melted butter

Soften yeast in water. Scald milk and add butter, salt, and sugar; stir until butter melts. Cool to lukewarm, then add yeast and eggs. Beat in flour. Allow to rise in warm place 6 hours. Chill overnight or until ready to use. Form quickly into small balls and place in greased muffin pans. Brush tops with melted butter and let rise until doubled in bulk. Bake in hot oven (400° F.) 20 minutes. Makes 2 dozen.

TWISTS—Roll dough lightly to a rectangular sheet ½ inch thick. Brush with softened butter and fold lengthwise into thirds. Cut into 1-inch slices, place on greased baking sheet and let rise until light. Lift each roll by the ends and twist one end. Replace on baking sheet and let rise again. Bake as above.

BOWKNOTS—Twist strips of brioche dough lightly and tie in a bowknot. Bring the ends down and press to the pan.

HOT CROSS BUNS

1 cake yeast
¼ cup warm water
1 cup scalded milk
¾ teaspoon salt
½ cup sugar

½ cup shortening
4½ cups sifted flour
(about)
3 egg yolks

Soften yeast in water. Add scalded milk to salt, sugar, and shortening. When lukewarm add yeast and 1½ cups flour. Beat well and let rise until very light. Add egg yolks and remaining flour. Knead lightly and let rise until doubled in bulk. Roll out dough to 1-inch thickness and cut into rounds. Place 2 inches apart on greased baking sheets and let rise. Glaze the surface of each bun with a little egg white diluted with water. With a sharp knife cut a cross on top of each bun. Bake in hot oven (400° F.) about 20 minutes. Just before removing from the oven, brush with sugar and water. Fill the cross with a plain frosting. A cup of raisins may be added to the dough if desired. Makes 2½ dozen.

RAISED MUFFINS

1 cake yeast	4 tablespoons sugar
¼ cup warm water	2 tablespoons shortening
1 cup scalded milk	3½ cups sifted flour
¾ teaspoon salt	1 egg, beaten

Soften yeast in lukewarm water. Add scalded milk to salt, sugar, and shortening. When lukewarm add yeast and 1½ cups flour. Beat thoroughly. When very light add beaten egg and remaining flour. Mix well and let rise until doubled in bulk. Shape into small balls and place in greased muffin pans. Brush tops with egg white, slightly beaten, and sprinkle with chopped nuts. Let rise and bake in hot oven (425° F.). Makes 2 dozen.

HONEY TWIST

1 cup milk, scalded	2 cakes yeast
¼ cup butter	¼ cup lukewarm water
½ cup sugar	2 eggs
1 teaspoon salt	5 to 6 cups sifted flour

Pour hot milk over butter, sugar, and salt. Crumble yeast into lukewarm water to soften. Cool milk to lukewarm, add yeast and well-beaten eggs. Beat in flour to make a soft dough, then turn out on floured board and knead until smooth. Form into a ball and place in greased bowl. Cover and let rise until doubled in bulk. When light, shape into long roll about 1 inch in diameter. Coil roll into greased cake pan, beginning at the outside edge and covering the bottom. Brush with honey topping. Let rise until doubled in bulk and bake in moderate oven (375° F.) 25 to 30 minutes.

If desired, sprinkle with chopped nuts and chopped candied cherries and pineapple before baking.

HONEY TOPPING—

¼ cup butter	1 egg white
2/3 cup confectioners' sugar	2 tablespoons honey, warmed

Cream all ingredients together and brush over Twist before setting to rise.

COFFEE CAKE

1 cake yeast	2/3 cup sugar
¼ cup lukewarm water	¾ teaspoon salt
1 cup scalded milk	4 tablespoons shortening
2 cups sifted flour (about)	Sugar
1 egg, beaten	Cinnamon

Soften yeast in water. Cool milk and add yeast and half the flour. Beat well and let rise until very light. Add egg, sugar, salt, and melted shortening, mix thoroughly and add remaining flour. Let rise until almost doubled in bulk. Pour into shallow greased pans. When light sprinkle thickly with sugar and cinnamon. Bake in hot oven (400° F.) 20 minutes. Serve hot. Makes 2 (9-inch) cakes.

SWEDISH TEA RING

1 cake yeast	6 tablespoons shortening
¼ cup lukewarm water	3½ cups sifted flour
1 cup scalded milk	1 egg, beaten
¾ teaspoon salt	Melted butter
¼ cup sugar	½ cup finely chopped nuts

Soften yeast in water. Combine scalded milk, salt, sugar, and shortening. When lukewarm add yeast and half the flour and beat well. Let rise until very light, then add egg and remaining flour and mix well. Let rise. Roll dough into a rectangular sheet on a lightly floured board. Brush with melted butter and sprinkle with nuts. Roll up like a jelly roll and form into a ring on greased baking sheet. Using a large pair of scissors, cut ring around edge at 2-inch intervals, leaving inner edge intact. Turn each slice to lie flat on pan. Let rise until light and bake in oven (400° F.) about 30 minutes. Frost while hot with confectioners' sugar frosting. Makes 1 large ring.

CARAMEL PECAN ROLLS

½ recipe Standard Roll dough (page 60)	½ cup brown sugar
3 tablespoons butter	¾ cup chopped pecans

When dough is light, roll out and spread with softened butter. Sprinkle with brown sugar and nuts and roll up. Slice and place cut side down on greased baking sheet. Let rise; bake at 400° F. about 25 minutes. Makes 12.

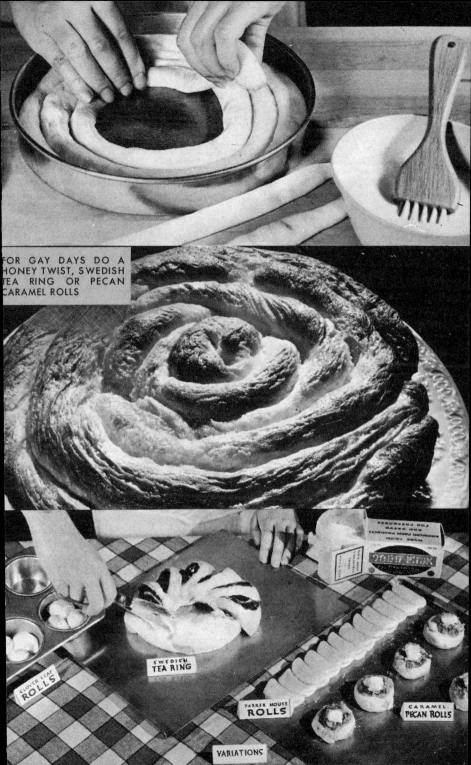

FOR GAY DAYS DO A
HONEY TWIST, SWEDISH
TEA RING OR PECAN
CARAMEL ROLLS

CLOVER LEAF
ROLLS

SWEDISH
TEA RING

PARKER HOUSE
ROLLS

CARAMEL
PECAN ROLLS

VARIATIONS

MAKE SEVERAL KINDS OF COFFEE CAKE AT THE SAME TIME, SUCH AS THESE STREUSEL, CHERRY AND FROSTED. POPOVER BATTER SHOULD HAVE A WARMHEARTED RECEPTION BY SIZZLING HOT BUTTERED PANS OR GLASS CUPS.

QUICK BREADS

QUICK BREADS are those breads or bread-like mixtures which are mixed and baked at once. The essentials of quick breads are a liquid and flour. When leavening agents are used, they are of the type which act quickly and make the mixture light without a long period of waiting.

Quick breads may be improved in flavor and texture by the addition of salt, sugar, eggs, shortening, etc. in various combinations and proportions.

READY-TO-USE FLOURS—Prepared flours which contain leavening and other ingredients require only liquid to make griddlecakes and biscuits. Follow directions on package. Added eggs, sugar, and shortening produce a batter suitable for muffins, waffles, shortcake biscuits, and similar quick breads.

Approximate Proportions of Liquid to Flour for Quick Breads

POUR OR THIN BATTER—Use 1 cup liquid with 1 to 1½ cups flour.

DROP OR THICK BATTER—Use 1 cup liquid with 1½ to 2 cups flour.

SOFT DOUGH—Use 1 cup liquid with 2 to 2½ cups flour.

STIFF DOUGH—Use 1 cup liquid with 3 to 5 cups flour.

Methods of Mixing Quick Breads

POUR OR THIN BATTER will pour easily from a spoon or a pitcher and varies in degree of thinness. Popover mixtures are examples of the thinnest batter, while the griddlecake and the waffle mixtures are examples of a thicker pour batter. Thin batter are best combined with a rotary beater. Beat eggs, add milk and melted shortening, add sifted dry ingredients and beat until smooth. For waffle mixtures, the eggs are often separated and the beaten egg white folded in last.

DROP OR THICK BATTER does not pour readily, but drops in a soft mass from a spoon or must be shaken or pushed free from it. Muffins and fritters are examples of the drop batter. They may be made with either solid or melted shortening. Solid shortening is added to the sifted dry ingredients and cut in thoroughly with a fork. Melted shortening or oil is added to the liquid mixture of milk and beaten eggs. In either case the dry and liquid mixtures are then combined with only enough stirring to dampen all the flour. The mixture will look lumpy. The cake method mixing may be used if a large amount of shortening is included in the recipe. Cream shortening and sugar until fluffy; add beaten egg, then sifted dry ingredients and milk alternately.

SOFT DOUGH can be handled more or less easily. Biscuits are made from soft dough and are mixed as quickly and deftly as possible. Have the shortening and liquid cold. Cut the shortening into the sifted dry ingredients with two knives or a pastry blender. Stir in the liquid quickly and knead on a lightly floured board a few seconds.

STIFF DOUGH can be handled without sticking and some energy must be used to roll it out. The Southern beaten biscuits and noodles are examples of the stiff dough.

POPOVERS

1 cup sifted flour	1 cup milk
¼ teaspoon salt	1 tablespoon melted
2 eggs	shortening

Sift flour and salt together. Beat eggs and add milk, shortening, and sifted dry ingredients. Beat until smooth with rotary beater. Fill greased muffin pans ½ full and bake in very hot oven (450° F.) 20 minutes. Reduce temperature to moderate (350° F.) and bake 15 minutes longer. Makes 8.

RYE—Use ¾ cup rye flour for ¾ cup white flour.

PLAIN MUFFINS

2 cups sifted flour	1 cup milk
½ teaspoon salt	1 egg
1 tablespoon sugar	2 tablespoons melted
4 teaspoons baking powder	shortening

Sift flour, salt, sugar, and baking powder. Combine remaining ingredients and add to dry ingredients. Stir just enough to dampen the flour. Pour into greased pans filling pans 2/3 full. Bake in hot oven (425° F.) 20 to 25 minutes. Makes 12.

PINEAPPLE MUFFINS—Add ½ cup flour, 3 tablespoons sugar, 2 tablespoons shortening and 1 No. 1 can crushed pineapple. Mix and bake as above.

RICE MUFFINS

¼ cup sugar
¾ cup cooked rice
1 egg
2 tablespoons shortening

1 cup milk
5 teaspoons baking powder
1 teaspoon salt
2¼ cups sifted flour

Mix sugar, rice, egg, melted shortening, and milk. Sift baking powder, salt, and flour together and add. Fill greased muffin pan 2/3 full; bake in hot oven (425° F.) 30 minutes. Makes 12. Use other cooked cereal instead of rice.

RAISIN BRAN MUFFINS

¾ cup sifted flour
3 teaspoons baking powder
½ teaspoon salt
1 cup bran
½ cup seeded raisins

1 egg
½ cup milk
1½ tablespoons molasses
1 tablespoon melted
    shortening

Sift flour, baking powder, and salt together; add bran and raisins. Beat egg and mix with remaining ingredients. Add dry ingredients, mixing only enough to dampen all the flour. Fill greased muffin pans 2/3 full and bake in hot oven (400° F.) 30 minutes. Makes 12.

BAKING POWDER BISCUITS

2 cups sifted flour
3 teaspoons baking powder
1 teaspoon salt

¼ cup cold shortening
2/3 cup cold milk

Sift flour, baking powder, and salt together and cut in shortening with 2 knives or a pastry blender. Add milk and mix quickly. Knead for a few seconds on lightly floured board. Pat out to ½-inch thickness and cut with biscuit cutter. Place in greased pan close together for crust on top and bottom only, far apart if crust is desired on sides also. Bake at once in very hot oven (450° F.) 12 minutes. Makes 12.

BISCUIT CRUST—Roll dough ¼ inch thick and cut to fit top of meat or chicken pie. Place on pie, pressing edges to dish. Cut opening in center to allow escape of steam.

DROP BISCUITS—Increase milk to 1 cup and drop mixture from spoon into greased muffin pans or onto greased baking sheet. Bake as above.

BUTTERMILK BISCUITS

2 cups sifted flour
½ teaspoon baking soda
2 teaspoons baking powder
1 teaspoon salt

¼ cup cold shortening
1 cup cold buttermilk or
  sour milk

Mix and bake as for baking powder biscuits.

Variations Using Baking Powder or Buttermilk Biscuit Dough

BUTTERSCOTCH—Roll dough to a rectangular sheet and brush with softened butter. Sprinkle with brown sugar and roll up like a jelly roll. Cut into 1-inch slices and place cut side down on greased baking sheet or in greased muffin pans.

CHEESE—Mix ½ cup grated cheese with dry ingredients.

CINNAMON—Follow directions for butterscotch biscuits, using granulated sugar and cinnamon instead of brown sugar.

GRAHAM—Use 1 cup graham flour and 1 cup white flour.

ORANGE—Dip cubes of sugar in orange juice and press 1 into the top of each biscuit.

Mix 1 tablespoon grated orange rind with milk and add 2 tablespoons sugar to flour.

PECAN CARAMEL—Follow directions for butterscotch biscuits, adding ½ cup chopped pecans to brown sugar. Mix butter and brown sugar and place a little of mixture in each muffin pan. Place slices of roll cut side down on top of mixture. Remove from pans as soon as baked.

SCONES—Roll dough into 2 circle ½ inch thick. Cut into wedges and bake on a hot griddle, turning to brown both sides. Split scones while hot, spread generously with softened butter and place in oven to melt butter.

BEATEN BISCUITS

3 cups sifted flour
1 teaspoon salt

1/3 cup cold shortening
½ cup cold milk

Sift flour with salt; cut in shortening. Add milk and mix to a very stiff dough. Place on floured board and beat with rolling pin or wooden potato masher 30 minutes, folding in edges after each stroke. Roll 1/3 inch thick and cut with biscuit cutter. Place on greased baking sheet and prick with a fork. Bake in hot oven (400° F.) 20 minutes. Makes 24.

SALLY LUNN

2 cups sifted flour
3 teaspoons baking powder
½ teaspoon salt
1 egg, beaten
1 cup milk
½ cup shortening
¼ cup sugar

Sift flour with baking powder and salt. Combine egg and milk. Cream shortening and sugar together and add flour alternately with liquid mixture. Place in greased loaf pan or muffin pans and bake in moderate oven (375° F.) 30 minutes. Makes 1 loaf or 12 muffins.

JOHNNYCAKE

2 cups corn meal
1½ teaspoons salt
1 teaspoon baking soda
2 tablespoons sugar
2 cups soured milk
2 eggs, beaten
2 tablespoons melted shortening

Sift dry ingredients together and add milk, eggs, and shortening. Mix well. Pour into greased pan and bake in hot oven (400° F.) 30 minutes. Makes 1 (8x10 inch) loaf.

SOUTHERN CORN BREAD

1½ cups scalded milk
1½ cups white corn meal
1 teaspoon salt
2 tablespoons shortening
2½ teaspoons baking powder
1 egg, beaten

Mix milk with corn meal and stir in salt and shortening. Cool. Add baking powder and egg yolk and mix well. Fold in stiffly beaten egg white. Pour into greased pan and bake in hot oven (400° F.) 20 minutes. Makes 1 (8x8 inch) loaf.

BACON—Sprinkle with diced bacon before baking.

SOUTHERN SPOON BREAD

2 cups boiling water
1 cup white corn meal
1 teaspoon salt
1 tablespoon shortening
1 cup milk
2 eggs, separated

Mix water, corn meal, salt, and shortening. Cool. Add milk and beaten egg yolks; mix well. Fold in stiffly beaten egg whites. Pour into greased baking dish and bake in hot oven (400° F.) 30 to 40 minutes. Serve from dish. Serves 6 to 8.

QUICK NUT BREAD

2 cups sifted flour	½ cup chopped nuts
½ cup sugar	1 egg
1 teaspoon salt	1 egg yolk
3 teaspoons baking powder	1 cup milk
¼ cup cold shortening	

Sift flour, sugar, salt, and baking powder together and cut in shortening with 2 knives or a pastry blender. Add nuts. Beat egg and egg yolk and add milk. Add to flour mixture and mix quickly, just enough to dampen all the flour. Pour into greased loaf pan and bake in hot oven (400° F.) 40 minutes. Makes 1 loaf.

HONEY SANDWICH BREAD

1 cup sifted flour	½ cup chopped nuts
3 teaspoons baking powder	1 egg
½ teaspoon salt	1 cup milk
1 cup graham flour	1/3 cup honey
½ cup bran	

Sift flour, baking powder, and salt together and mix well with graham flour, bran, and nuts. Beat egg and add milk and honey. Add to dry ingredients and mix only enough to dampen all the flour. Pour into greased loaf pan and bake in hot oven (400° F.) 30 minutes. Make 1 loaf.

WHOLE-WHEAT—Use 1½ cups whole-wheat flour instead of graham flour and bran. Use ¼ cup brown sugar for honey and add ¼ cup melted shortening.

PRUNE RYE BREAD

2 cups sifted rye flour	1 egg, slightly beaten
2 cups sifted wheat flour	1¾ cups milk
6 teaspoons baking powder	1 cup cooked prunes,
1½ teaspoons salt	chopped
¾ cup sugar	

Sift dry ingredients together. Combine egg and milk, and add to flour mixture, stirring only until well mixed; stir in prunes. Turn into greased loaf pans and bake in moderate oven (350° F.) about 1 hour. Makes 2 loaves, 6x3 inches, or 1 sandwich loaf, 11x3x3 inches.

QUICK COFFEE CAKE WITH CRUMB TOPPING

1½ cups sifted flour	1 egg
½ cup sugar	2/3 cup milk
2 teaspoons baking powder	3 tablespoons melted
½ teaspoon salt	shortening

Sift flour, sugar, baking powder, and salt together. Beat egg and add milk and shortening. Stir liquids into dry ingredients, mixing only enough to dampen all the flour. Pour into greased pan, sprinkle with crumb topping and bake in hot oven (425° F.) 25 minutes. Makes 1 (9x9 inch) coffee cake.

CRUMB TOPPING

2 tablespoons butter	¼ cup dry bread crumbs
2 tablespoons sugar	½ teaspoon cinnamon
¼ cup sifted flour	

Cream butter and sugar together. Add flour, crumbs, and cinnamon. Mix to consistency of coarse crumbs and sprinkle over coffee cake batter before baking.

SPICY APPLE COFFEE CAKE

2 cups sifted flour	2/3 to ¾ cup milk
1 tablespoon granulated sugar	2 or 3 apples
3 teaspoons baking powder	1/3 cup brown sugar
¾ teaspoon salt	½ teaspoon cinnamon
3 tablespoons shortening	1 tablespoon butter
½ cup grated nippy cheese	

Sift flour, sugar, baking powder, and salt together. Cut in shortening and cheese. Add milk to make a soft dough. Turn out on lightly floured board and knead ½ minute. Pat out dough in ungreased 9-inch layer-cake pan. Pare apples, core and slice thin. Arrange apples in petal design over top. Sprinkle with brown sugar and cinnamon and dot with butter. Bake in hot oven (425° F.) 25 minutes. Makes 1 (9-inch) coffee cake.

Omit cheese if preferred. Use an oblong pan and arrange apples in rows on top of dough.

BANANA BREAD

½ cup shortening
1 cup sugar
2 eggs
1 cup mashed ripe bananas
1 teaspoon lemon juice

2 cups sifted flour
3 teaspoons baking powder
½ teaspoon salt
1 cup nut meats, chopped

Cream shortening and sugar together. Beat eggs until light and add. Press bananas through sieve and add lemon juice. Blend with creamed mixture. Sift flour, baking powder, and salt together and mix quickly into banana mixture. Add nuts. Bake in greased loaf pan in moderate oven (375° F.) about 1¼ hours. Makes 1 (1-pound) loaf.

BOSTON BROWN BREAD

1 cup corn meal
1 cup rye flour
¾ teaspoon baking soda
1 teaspoon salt

1 cup graham flour
¾ cup molasses
2 cups sour milk or butter-
　milk

Sift corn meal, rye flour, soda, and salt together and mix well with graham flour. Add combined molasses and sour milk and mix well. Fill greased molds 2/3 full, cover closely and steam 3 hours. Remove covers and dry tops in moderate oven (375° F.). Makes 3 loaves.

RAISIN—Add 1 cup raisins.

DATE BRAN BREAD

2 cups sifted flour
1 teaspoon salt
3 tablespoons sugar
3 teaspoons baking powder
2 cups bran

2/3 cup sliced dates
1 egg
1½ cups milk
2 tablespoons melted
　shortening

Sift flour with salt, sugar, and baking powder. Stir in bran and dates. Beat egg and add milk and melted shortening. Add dry ingredients and mix only enough to dampen all the flour. Pour into greased molds, cover closely and steam 3 hours. Makes 3 loaves.

Griddlecakes, Waffles, Doughnuts and Fritters

GRIDDLECAKES

2 cups sifted flour	2 eggs
1 teaspoon salt	1½ cups milk
3 teaspoons baking powder	1 tablespoon melted
1 tablespoon corn meal	shortening
1 tablespoon sugar	

Sift flour with salt, baking powder, corn meal, and sugar. Beat eggs and add milk and shortening. Add sifted ingredients and beat until smooth.   Drop by spoonfuls on hot griddle. When full of bubbles turn to brown other side.   Makes 20. SOUR MILK OR BUTTERMILK—Use 2 cups sour milk or buttermilk instead of sweet milk. Add 1 teaspoon baking soda to flour and use only ¾ teaspoon baking powder.

FLANNEL CAKES

2 cups sifted flour	2 cups milk
1 teaspoon salt	1 tablespoon melted
3 teaspoons baking powder	shortening
2 eggs, separated	

Sift flour, salt and baking powder together. Beat egg yolks and add milk and shortening. Beat in flour mixture with rotary beater. Fold in stiffly beaten egg whites. Bake on hot griddle, turning to brown both sides. Makes 24.

CORN-MEAL GRIDDLECAKES

2 cups boiling water	1½ cups milk
1 cup corn meal	2 cups sifted flour
1 tablespoon sugar	3 teaspoons baking powder
1 teaspoon salt	2 eggs, beaten

Pour boiling water over corn meal, sugar, and salt and mix well. Let stand until meal swells. Add milk and let stand until cool. Sift flour and baking powder together and add. Fold in beaten eggs. Bake on hot griddle, turning to brown both sides. The cakes should be small and well cooked. They require longer cooking than wheat cakes. Makes 36.

RICE GRIDDLECAKES

1 cup cooked rice
2 cups milk
1½ cups sifted flour
½ teaspoon salt
1 tablespoon sugar

2 teaspoons baking powder
1 egg
1 tablespoon melted
   shortening

Mix rice with 1 cup milk and let stand overnight. Sift flour, salt, sugar, and baking powder together. Beat egg and add shortening and remaining 1 cup milk. Add to softened rice alternately with sifted dry ingredients. Drop from spoon onto hot greased griddle and bake, turning once to brown other side. Makes 24.

FRENCH OR JELLY PANCAKES

3 eggs, separated
1 teaspoon sugar
½ teaspoon salt
1 cup milk

½ cup sifted flour
1 tablespoon melted
   shortening
Tart fruit jelly

Beat egg yolks and add sugar, salt, and ½ cup milk. Add flour and shortening and mix until smooth, then add remaining milk. Fold in stiffly beaten egg whites. Bake on hot griddle, making cakes larger than usual and very thin. Spread with jelly and roll up while hot. Serve with overlapping edges of cakes on bottom to keep them from unrolling. Sprinkle with confectioners' sugar if desired. Makes 12.

APPLE FLAPJACKS

1 tablespoon shortening
1 tablespoon sugar
2 eggs
1½ cups sifted flour

1 teaspoon baking powder
½ teaspoon cinnamon
1 cup apples, chopped fine
1 cup milk

Cream shortening and sugar, add beaten eggs, flour sifted with baking powder and cinnamon, and the chopped apples. Then add milk gradually to make a medium batter. Bake on griddle as for ordinary pancakes and serve in an overlapping row around a platter of pork chops or serve separately with roast pork, either hot or cold. Cooked apples may be used with batter in the same way. Makes 16.

BREAD CRUMB GRIDDLECAKES

1½ cups dry bread crumbs   ½ cup sifted flour
1½ cups scalded milk   ½ teaspoon salt
2 tablespoons shortening   4 teaspoons baking powder
2 eggs

Soften crumbs in milk and melted shortening. Add eggs, well beaten, and dry ingredients, mixed and sifted. Bake on a hot greased griddle. The cakes are very tender and should be turned carefully. Makes 12.

BAKING POWDER BUCKWHEAT CAKES

1½ cups buckwheat flour   1 tablespoon shortening
½ cup sifted white flour   1½ cups milk
5 teaspoons baking powder   1 tablespoon molasses
½ teaspoon salt

Sift dry ingredients together. Combine melted shortening, milk and molasses, then add slowly to dry ingredients. Beat well and bake on a slightly greased, hot griddle. Makes 16.

RAISED BUCKWHEAT CAKES

2 cups boiling water   1 teaspoon salt
½ cup corn meal   2 cups buckwheat flour
½ cake yeast   ¼ teaspoon baking soda
¼ cup lukewarm water   1/3 cup hot milk
1 tablespoon molasses

Pour boiling water over corn meal and let stand until it swells. Soften yeast in the lukewarm water. After corn meal is cool, add molasses, salt, yeast, and flour. Beat thoroughly and set in warm place to rise overnight. It should rise and fall again by the morning. Add soda dissolved in hot milk, stir well and bake on a hot greased griddle. Makes 20.

When the cakes are desired frequently (say, three times a week), fresh yeast will not be required after the first making, if a little more than a pint of the batter is reserved each time and kept in a cool place to be used instead of the yeast. Molasses in buckwheat cakes helps to give them a good color. Without it, they may be gray and unattractive.

WAFFLES

1½ cups sifted flour
½ teaspoon salt
2 teaspoons baking powder
2 eggs, separated

1 cup milk
4 tablespoons melted
shortening

Sift flour, salt, and baking powder together. Beat egg yolks and add milk and shortening. Add flour and beat with rotary beater until smooth. Fold in stiffly beaten egg whites. Bake in hot waffle iron. Makes 4 waffles.

BUTTERMILK—Use 1¼ cups buttermilk instead of sweet milk. Reduce baking powder to 1¼ teaspoons and add ½ teaspoon baking soda.

RICE—Before folding in egg whites, add 1 cup cold cooked rice to either plain or buttermilk waffles.

CORN-MEAL WAFFLES

1½ cups boiling water
1 cup corn meal
1 teaspoon salt
4 tablespoons shortening
2 eggs, separated

1 cup sifted flour
½ teaspoon baking soda
2 teaspoons baking powder
½ cup sweet milk
2/3 cup buttermilk, about

Add boiling water to corn meal and stir in salt and short-ening. Cook in double boiler 10 minutes, stirring occasionally. Cool. Add beaten egg yolks. Sift flour with soda and baking powder and add alternately with sweet milk. Add enough buttermilk to make a pour batter. Fold in stiffly beaten egg whites. Bake in hot waffle iron. Makes 6.

CREAM WAFFLES

2 cups sifted flour
1 tablespoon corn meal
1 teaspoon baking soda

½ teaspoon salt
2 eggs, separated
2 cups sour cream

Sift flour, corn meal, soda, and salt together. Beat egg yolks and add cream. Add sifted dry ingredients and mix well. Fold in stiffly beaten egg whites. Bake in hot waffle iron. Makes 6.

DOUGHNUTS

Sweet Milk—

3 eggs
1 cup sugar
2 tablespoons shortening
3 teaspoons baking powder
1 teaspoon salt

½ teaspoon nutmeg
3½ cups sifted flour
1 cup milk
½ teaspoon lemon extract

Beat eggs until very light, beat in sugar, then add melted shortening. Sift baking powder, salt, and nutmeg with 1 cup flour and stir into first mixture alternately with milk. Add lemon extract and just enough flour to make a very soft dough. Chill. Roll out ¾ inch thick on lightly floured board. A soft dough makes light, tender doughnuts when cooked. Fry in deep fat (360°-370° F.) and drain on unglazed paper.

Sour Milk—

1 cup sugar
2 tablespoons sour cream or
  shortening
3 eggs
½ teaspoon lemon extract
1 cup soured milk

½ teaspoon baking soda
1 teaspoon baking powder
½ teaspoon salt
½ teaspoon nutmeg
4½ cups sifted flour
(more or less)

Mix sugar with cream and add beaten eggs, lemon extract, and sour milk. Sift remaining dry ingredients with 1 cup of flour and add to first mixture. Add additional flour to make a dough just stiff enough to handle. Toss on floured board, roll out, and cut. Fry in hot deep fat (365° F.). Makes 2 dozen.

CRULLERS

¼ cup shortening
1 cup sugar
2 eggs
3½ teaspoons baking
  powder

¼ teaspoon nutmeg
½ teaspoon salt
4 cups sifted flour
1 cup milk

Cream shortening. Add sugar, then well-beaten eggs. Sift baking powder, nutmeg, and salt with 1 cup of flour and add alternately with milk to the first mixture. Add additional flour to make a dough stiff enough to handle. Toss on floured board, roll ½ inch thick and cut into strips. Twist and fry in deep fat (365° F.). Drain on unglazed paper and when cold roll in confectioners' sugar. Makes 3 dozen.

RAISED DOUGHNUTS

1 cake yeast	2 tablespoons shortening
¼ cup lukewarm water	3½ to 4 cups sifted flour
1 cup scalded milk	1 egg
1 teaspoon salt	½ teaspoon nutmeg
¾ cup sugar	

Soften yeast in water. Add scalded milk to salt, sugar, and shortening. When lukewarm add softened yeast. Add 1½ cups flour. Allow the sponge to stand in a warm place until it is so light that it will fall at the slightest touch. Add egg, nutmeg, and remainder of the flour and knead. The dough should be softer than bread dough. Cover and set in a warm place to rise. Toss on a lightly floured board and roll ¾ inch thick. Cut with a doughnut cutter and let rise. Fry in hot deep fat (365° F.) 2 to 3 minutes. When frying put the raised side of the doughnut down in the fat. The heat will cause the top side to rise by the time the doughnut is ready to turn. Makes 2 dozen.

JELLY DOUGHNUTS—Cut doughnuts with cookie cutter and fry as above. Cut a hole in doughnut from side and fill with jelly. Replace cut-out section. Roll in sugar.

LONG JOHNS—Cut dough into strips and fry as above. Cut a slit in top and fill with jelly. Frost top with confectioners' frosting.

BANANA FRITTERS

1¼ cups sifted flour	1/3 cup milk
½ cup sugar	2 teaspoons melted
1¼ teaspoons salt	shortening
2 teaspoons baking powder	4 medium bananas
1 egg, beaten	

Sift 1 cup flour with sugar, salt, and baking powder. Mix egg and milk and add to flour mixture gradually, stirring until smooth. Add shortening. Peel bananas and cut crosswise into halves or quarters. Roll in remaining flour, then cover with batter. Fry in hot deep fat (375° F.) 4 to 6 minutes. The batter is stiffer than for most fritters and requires longer cooking. Serves 8.

FRUIT FRITTER BATTER

1-1/3 cups sifted flour	2 tablespoons sugar
¼ teaspoon salt	1 egg
2 teaspoons baking powder	2/3 cup milk

Sift dry ingredients and add well-beaten egg and milk. The batter should be just thick enough to coat the article it is intended to cover. If it is too thin, add more flour; if too thick, add more liquid. Makes 1½ cups.

PEACH FRITTERS

Peaches   Fritter batter
Sugar

Peel the peaches, split them in two, remove the stones, sprinkle sugar over them, dip each piece in fritter batter and fry in hot deep fat (365° F.) 2 to 3 minutes. Serve with confectioners' sugar or foamy sauce.

Apple Fritters

Pare, core, and slice tart apples; dip in fritter batter, covering each slice with batter. Fry in hot deep fat (365° F.) 2 to 3 minutes. Serve with confectioners' sugar.

RASPBERRY FRITTERS

1 cup sifted flour	2 eggs
1 teaspoon baking powder	2 to 3 tablespoons water
¼ teaspoon salt	1 cup raspberries
2 tablespoons sugar	

Sift flour, baking powder, and salt together. Add sugar, egg yolks, and water. Fold in stiffly beaten egg whites and the raspberries, leaving the fruit as nearly whole as possible. The amount of water may vary somewhat. The batter should be thin enough to fold in the fruit but thick enough to hold together well; otherwise, the fruit in cooking will soften it too much. Drop mixture from a tablespoon into hot deep fat (365° F.) and fry until brown, turning once. Serve with confectioners' sugar or foamy sauce. Makes 12.

SANDWICHES

AN ENCYCLOPEDIA published about 1900 defines a sandwich as "an article of food consisting of a slice of meat, fish, fowl or other food placed between two slices of bread, which may be plain or buttered." No such simple definition could be given today, for from these simple beginnings the sandwich has developed in all directions, and has adapted itself to such varied needs that it ranges from a fragile morsel served with afternoon tea to an elaborate combination of toast, meat, lettuce, tomato, sauce, and any number of other things which combine to make it a complete and satisfying meal.

Even the requirement of two slices of bread with something between them is no longer in force. "Open-faced" sandwiches offer almost unlimited opportunity for variety in both cold and hot meals. In these the slices of bread or toast are laid side by side. Sometimes, usually in hot meat sandwiches, both slices are covered with beef or chicken, or whatever gives the characteristic flavor, and the whole is covered with gravy. Often, especially in cold sandwiches, one slice holds its chicken or tomato or crab meat, while its companion is covered with cole slaw and dill pickles or a lettuce leaf holding a spoonful of mayonnaise. The possibilities are endless, and the suggestions given here can be combined and adapted to almost any requirement where a sandwich can be called into service.

Serving Sandwiches

Garnishes of fine parsley, cress, celery leaves, stuffed or ripe olives, or slices of lemon or pickle are effective on the serving-dish. Barberries and leaves, fresh nasturtium leaves and blossoms, or something to indicate the kind of sandwich may be used as a garnish.

Making and Keeping Sandwiches

The bread for flat sandwiches should be a day old because it can be cut more easily than fresh bread. For rolled sandwiches fresh bread should be used. Bread baked in special tins which provide slices that are perfect squares or circles is economical when the crusts are to be cut off, but any loaf of compartively fine grain may be used.

The Bread

ALL SORTS OF BREADS are made into sandwiches—white, brown, rye, whole-wheat, raisin, date, nut, etc. Sometimes two or more kinds are used together. Long narrow rolls are attractive when sliced lengthwise, buttered and filled. For picnics, where a substantial filling is desirable, the crumb of the roll may be removed and the hollow filled with sandwich filling. Thin salt wafers and crackers are often used instead of bread for paste sandwiches.

FOR FANCY SANDWICHES, to be used for tea or receptions, or as an appetizer at the beginning of the meal, or to be served with the salad, the bread should be cut into slices as thin as possible and the crusts should be removed. Use a sharp knife so that there will be no ragged edges.

PICNIC AND LUNCH-BOX SANDWICHES are cut somewhat thicker than fancy sandwiches, and the crusts are generally not removed.

Butter and Filling

The filling and butter for sandwiches should be increased in proportion to the thickness of the slice of bread.

PREPARING THE BUTTER—The butter should be thoroughly creamed before it is used or it will not spread evenly over the bread. To cream butter, place it in a warm bowl and beat it until it is soft. It will then spread well even on fresh bread. Sandwich butters are often made by creaming one cup of butter with one-half cup of cream. One-half cup of butter, creamed, will spread a two-pound sandwich loaf cutting forty to forty-five slices.

RELISHES such as mustard, salt, grated horseradish, chopped parsley, chives, and curry may be added to creamed butter for use in sandwiches of meat, tomato, game, chicken, fish, cheese, or eggs.

SPREADING BUTTER AND FILLING—A poorly buttered sandwich is very unpalatable. Spread the butter to the very edges of the slices, on the sides that are to be put together, being careful, however, not to let the butter spread over the edges so that it is untidy. If the slices need not be fitted together, it is often easier to spread the bread before cutting it from the loaf.   A pliable knife or small spatula is a help in spreading butter or filling.

Spread the filling on the buttered surface of one slice only of each sandwich. Have the filling come to the edge of the sandwich, if possible.

When mayonnaise is used, not combined with a filling, as in mayonnaise and lettuce sandwiches, it is more evenly distributed if it is spread on one of the slices of bread and the lettuce leaf placed upon it.

Shaping the Sandwiches

Sandwiches may be cut with a knife into triangles, oblongs, and similar outlines, or shaped with cutters into hearts, circles, crescents, or any preferred design. When sandwiches are shaped with these fancy cutters, the bread should be shaped before it is spread, to avoid waste of butter and filling. Care must be taken afterward, however, not to spoil the shape while spreading. Heart, club, spade, and diamond shapes are popular for card parties. Heart shapes are attractive for valentine and announcement parties and for showers. Strips, triangles, circles, crescents, and rolled and folded sandwiches are used for teas.

ROLLED SANDWICHES—Cut the crusts from a fresh loaf of bread. Spread a thin layer of butter on one end of the loaf and then cut from it as thin a slice as possible. If a filling is used, spread it on the buttered slice. Roll this slice with the spread side inward and lay it on a napkin, with the edge of the slice downward. When all the sandwiches have been prepared, draw the napkin firmly around the rolls and put them in a cold place until needed. The butter will harden and hold the rolls together.

Time Savers in Sandwich Making

In making sandwiches in quantity, route the work so that there will be no waste motions. Have a large enough space for (1) cutting the bread; (2) spreading the slices with butter and filling; (3) shaping and (4) wrapping the sandwiches.

Keeping Sandwiches

Sandwiches are best prepared just before serving, especially if the filling is of a kind that will become limp or soak into the bread. When it is necessary to make sandwiches several hours before they are to be used, they may be wrapped in paraffin paper or a slightly dampened cloth or placed in a stone jar.

Filling for Meat and Salad Sandwiches

When sliced meat is used, a sandwich is easier to eat and generally more palatable if the meat is cut as thin as a knife-blade with several tiny slices instead of one thick one in each sandwich. Fancy butters are excellent with sliced meat.

All kinds of potted and minced meats are used between slices of bread with or without mayonnaise. Salted meat and fish fillings are improved by lemon juice, chopped pickles, or capers. Pastes of fresh fish and meat require high seasoning.

All forms of meat may be used with lettuce or cress, between two slices of buttered bread, with or without salad dressing. The slices should be pressed together and the crust trimmed, if desired. Lettuce may be used in large, crisp leaves, or in "ribbons," to make the sandwich easier to eat. Where mayonnaise dressing is used, the sandwiches should be made at the last moment, and served promptly. Tomatoes and cucumbers with lettuce and mayonnaise make delicious salad sandwiches.

Filling for Tea Sandwiches

The tea sandwich is seldom made of meat, though such things as minced chicken, lobster, or crab meat, and sardines beaten to a paste, are sometimes used for it. The bread is cut very thin and the fillings may be a bit of lettuce spread with mayonnaise dressing, chopped olives, nasturtiums, water cress, and similar morsels. An attractive sandwich is made from diminutive Vienna rolls split not quite through and spread with vegetable filling. Another tea sandwich is made by spreading jelly or preserves between two salt crackers. If the crackers are spread with a thin film of butter and crisped quickly in a hot oven, this form of sandwich is really worth eating. Almond sandwiches of all varieties are delicious for the tea-table.

Filling for Sweet Sandwiches

Preserves of all kinds, drained from their sirup, marmalade, jam, jelly, crystallized and candied fruits are used for sweet sandwiches with graham or salt wafers, as well as with bread or sponge cake. The crystallized fruits may be sliced thin and dipped in cream, chopped fine, moistened in orange juice, and spread between bread or lady-fingers.

Scraped or grated maple sugar mixed with chopped nuts is used with brown bread.   Ice-cream is cut in slices and put between wafers or layers of sponge cake.

Tiny tea biscuits make an excellent foundation for sweet sandwiches. They are split and buttered while hot and filled with honey and almonds, cream cheese and jam, or chopped nuts and marmalade. They are best served warm.

Filling for Nut Sandwiches

Pignolias or pine nuts, butternuts, walnuts, hickory nuts, almonds, and pecans may all be put through a meat-chopper, mixed, a very little salt added, and spread over thin, buttered slices of brown or white bread. Or, to the ground nuts may be added a little sale and paprika, and either salad oil or creamed butter to make a smooth paste.

The salty taste of peanut butter is good with raisin bread. Peanuts may be rubbed to a paste with creamed butter and a layer of chopped preserved ginger added.

Butternuts, walnuts, hickory nuts, almonds, or pecans may be used in equal parts, ground fine, with cream cheese moistened with sweet thick cream and seasoned with salt. Grated American cheese may be used instead of cream cheese and melted butter instead of cream.

PETITE MARMITE

Yeast bouillon, on the market as cubes or paste, makes an excellent spread for sandwiches, hors d'oeuvres and appetizers. It may be used alone or mixed with butter or other pastes. Its strong flavor makes it especially desirable with milder flavored fillings.

PREPARED BUTTERS FOR SANDWICHES

ANCHOVY BUTTER

Yolks of 4 hard-cooked eggs   ½ cup butter
4 boned anchovies   Paprika

Rub the yolks of the eggs to a smooth paste with the anchovies and butter and add paprika to taste.

HAM BUTTER

½ cup cooked ham   Yolks of 2 hard-cooked eggs
½ cup butter   Pepper

Grind the ham and pound smooth with the butter and the yolks of the eggs and season with pepper.

SHRIMP BUTTER

1 cup cooked shrimps   1 cup butter
Salt   About ¼ cup tarragon vine-
⅛ teaspoon cayenne   gar or lemon juice

Pound the shrimps in a mortar with salt and cayenne. Add the butter and moisten the mixture with the tarragon vinegar or lemon juice.

Sandwiches with Nut Fillings
PEANUT BUTTER, FIG AND RAISIN SANDWICHES

¼ cup figs   ½ teaspoon salt
¼ cup raisins   ½ cup peanut butter
2 tablespoons light corn sirup   2 tablespoons lemon juice

Wash figs and raisins and put through a food-chopper. Add salt, peanut butter, lemon juice and corn sirup, and mix well. Use between thin, buttered slices of bread.

PEANUT BUTTER AND ORANGE MARMALADE SANDWICHES

½ cup peanut butter   ½ cup orange marmalade
¼ cup cream

Mix peanut butter with cream or milk until it is smooth and light in color. Spread generously on thin slices of bread, and add a layer of orange marmalade. The marmalade may be mixed with the peanut butter, if preferred.

PEANUT BUTTER AND BANANA SANDWICHES

½ cup peanut butter   ½ cup banana pulp or sliced
¼ cup cream or hot water   bananas
Lemon juice

Mix the peanut butter with the cream until it is smooth and light in color, then combine with the banana pulp and a little lemon juice and use between thin, buttered slices of bread. Or place slices of banana over layer of peanut butter on bread.

PEANUT BUTTER AND PICKLE SANDWICHES

½ cup peanut butter   ¼ cup cream or hot water
½ cup chopped pickle

Cream peanut butter and water together and add chopped pickle. Use between thin, buttered slices of bread.

PEANUT BUTTER AND ONION SANDWICHES

1 cup peanut butter   1 small Bermuda or
¼ cup mayonnaise   Spanish onion

Beat peanut butter, add mayonnaise and spread sandwiches. Slice onion in very thin slices and put a layer of these over mixture on bread.

ALMOND SANDWICHES

No. 1

1¼ cups almonds   3 tablespoons lemon juice
½ teaspoon salt

Chop the almonds fine, mix with the salt and lemon juice and use with thin slices of bread, buttered. Cut into small ovals, pressing a blanched almond in the center of each sandwich.

No. 2

Use the same quantities as for No. 1. Toast the almonds a light brown and grate them. Form into a paste with the lemon juice, add the salt and spread over the bread.

No. 3

1/3 cup almonds   2/3 cup shredded celery
¼ cup mayonnaise

Chop the almonds fine and mix them with the celery. Spread between thin, buttered slices of bread. Sandwiches filled with this mixture are an excellent accompaniment to salads or cold meats. When served with meats the celery and almonds may be moistened with a few spoonfuls of mayonnaise.

MARRON SANDWICHES

Grind marrons glacés (candied French chestnuts) fine, spread on rounds of buttered bread, and cover with rounds of bread from which the centers have been cut. Fill the centers with whipped cream, sweetened and flavored, and decorate with blanched and chopped pistachio nuts or tiny candied violets.

Sandwiches with Cheese or Egg Fillings
CHEESE SANDWICHES

No. 1

Place thin slices of American, Swiss, or any preferred mild or snappy cheese between two slices of buttered bread. Add a dash of mustard if desired.

No. 2

Grate sapsago and Parmesan cheese and sprinkle thickly over a slice of buttered bread. Then sprinkle with mild red pepper, and add another slice of buttered bread.

No. 3

Yolks of 3 hard-cooked eggs	Paprika Salt
2 tablespoons salad oil	1 tablespoon vingear
Mustard	1 cup grated cheese

Mash the yolks of the hard-cooked eggs. Add the oil, stirring it in very slowly with a fork, and mix thoroughly with a little mustard, paprika, salt, and the vinegar. Add the grated cheese and use between thin buttered slices of white or brown bread.

No. 4

½ pound American cheese, cheese, grated	¼ cup cream
	½ teaspoon dry mustard
2 tablespoons melted butter	Paprika Salt

Mix all the ingredients thoroughly and use between thin buttered slices of bread. This filling will keep indefinitely in closed jars in the refrigerator.

CHEESE AND ORANGE MARMALADE SANDWICHES

½ cup cream cheese   ½ cup orange marmalade
¼ cup cream

Spread half the slices of buttered bread with the cheese softened with the cream, and seasoned with salt, if desired. Spread the remaining slices with orange marmalade and press the slices together.

CHEESE COMBINATION SANDWICHES

1 cup cream cheese or cottage   ¼ cup chopped olives or
   cheese   ¼ cup chopped nuts or
¼ cup mayonnaise or   ¼ cup chopped pimientos

Mix the cheese with the mayonnaise, chopped olives, nuts, or pimientos, and use between very thin slices of brown or rye bread, lightly buttered.

CHEESE AND ONION SANDWICHES

1 cup cream cheese   Lettuce leaves
¼ cup chopped Bermuda   ¼ cup mayonnaise
   onion

Mix the cheese with the onion. Use with mayonnaise and a crisp lettuce leaf between slices of buttered bread.

ROQUEFORT CHEESE SANDWICHES

½ cup Roquefort cheese   2 tablespoons butter
Salad oil   Whole-wheat bread

To the cheese, add creamed butter and enough salad oil to make a paste. Use a thin layer between buttered slices of whoel-wheat bread.

CHEESE MAYONNAISE SANDWICHES

2 hard-cooked egg yolks   ½ teaspoon pepper
1 tablespoon melted butter   ½ teaspoon mustard
1/3 pound cheese   1 tablespoon vinegar
½ teaspoon salt

Blend the egg yolks and butter together until they make a smooth paste, then add the grated cheese, salt, pepper, and mustard, mixing thoroughly. Stir in the vinegar and spread filling between buttered slices of bread or crackers.

RUSSIAN SANDWICHES

½ cup cream cheese
¼ cup chopped olives
Lettuce leaves

¼ cup chopped pimiento
¼ cup mayonnaise
Boston brown bread

Spread the cream cheese on thin slices of Boston brown bread. Spread an equal number of buttered slices with chopped olives and pimientos mixed with mayonnaise dressing.

Press together in pairs with a crisp lettuce leaf between.

EGG SANDWICHES

No. 1

Hard-cooked eggs   Salt   Paprika
Pepper   Capers or pickles if desired

Slice the eggs and lay the slices between thin buttered slices of bread. Season to taste with salt, pepper, and paprika and add a layer of chopped capers or pickles, if desired. These are good for lunches for traveling or picnics.

No. 2

1 cup chopped, hard-cooked   Chopped capers or pickles
  egg   ¼ cup mayonnaise

Mix the chopped egg with the mayonnaise and add salt, pepper, and chopped pickles or capers to taste. Use between thin buttered slices of bread.

Sandwiches with Meat and Poultry Fillings
CHICKEN SANDWICHES

No. 1

1 cup cooked chicken meat,   ¼ cup mayonnaise
  white or dark

Chop the chicken meat very fine, mix with the mayonnaise, and spread thin slices of bread, buttered or unbuttered, with the paste.

No. 2

2 egg yolks	1 cup minced, cooked chicken
1 teaspoon melted butter	Salt Pepper
1 teaspoon lemon juice	1 teaspoon stock

Cook the eggs thirty to forty-five minutes in water just below boiling point, remove the yolks, and mash as fine as possible. Add to these the melted butter and lemon juice, the minced chicken, salt, pepper, and stock. Mix together well. This paste may be used as a filling for very delicate sandwiches.

No. 3

1 cup cooked white meat of chicken	6 tablespoons thick cream
1 tablespoon gelatin	½ teaspoon salt
1 tablespoon cold water	Dash of paprika

Chop the chicken very fine and pound to a paste, adding salt and a dash of red pepper. Soak the gelatin in the cold water for ten minutes, then add the thick cream. Dissolve the gelatin over boiling water, beat it slowly into the chicken, and add salt and paprika. Set aside to cool, spreading evenly. When cool, divide into squares, cut these squares into very thin slices and arrange on thin buttered slices of bread. If desired, bread may be cut into fancy shapes, removing the crusts.

No. 4

¾ cup cooked chicken meat	¼ cup chopped almonds
¼ cup chopped stuffed olives	¼ cup mayonnaise

Cut the chicken meat into small pieces and add the almonds and olives. Moisten with mayonnaise and spread on thin, buttered slices of bread.

CHICKEN, HAM AND CELERY SANDWICHES

1 cup cooked chicken meat	¼ cup mayonnaise
½ cup celery	¼ cup cooked ham
1 tablespoon green pepper	

Mince the chicken, ham, celery, and green pepper. Mix with the mayonnaise and spread on buttered bread.

CHICKEN AND DILL PICKLE SANDWICHES

Between buttered slices of white bread, use thin slices of white meat of roasted chicken and thin slices of dill pickle. Cut into triangles and serve on lettuce leaves.

CHICKEN LIVER SANDWICHES

1 cup cooked chicken livers
2 tablespoons chopped crisp bacon
Salt   Pepper
1 tablespoon lemon juice
2 tablespoons sliced truffles
4 drops tabasco sauce
2 stalks celery, minced

Mash the chicken livers, add the chopped bacon, salt, pepper, tabasco sauce, lemon juice, and sliced truffles. Use between slices of bread spread with creamed butter mixed with minced celery.

CHICKEN AND TONGUE SANDWICHES

2 cups minced cold boiled chicken and tongue, mixed
½ cup melted butter
1 egg yolk
Black pepper
1 teaspoon Worcestershire sauce

To cold boiled tongue and chicken add the melted butter, the yolk of the egg, beaten, a little black pepper, and the Worcestershire sauce. Spread this over buttered bread.

PÂTÉ DE FOIE GRAS SANDWICHES

No. 1

Moisten pâté de foie gras with cream to make a thin paste. Spread on lettuce leaves on buttered white bread and sprinkle with French dressing.

No. 2

1 tablespoon pâté de foie gras   2 tablespoons butter
¼ cup chopped boiled chestnuts

Mash the butter and chestnuts to a paste, add the pâté de foie gras and mix well. Spread very thin on slices of buttered bread.

CRAB OR LOBSTER SANDWICHES

1¼ cups cooked crab or   ¼ cup French dressing or
   lobster meat   mayonnaise

Butter thin slices of whole-wheat bread. Cover half of them thickly with flaked crab meat or finely diced lobster meat combined with French dressing or mayonnaise. Cover with the other buttered slices of bread and cut into fancy shapes.

OYSTER SANDWICHES

Large Oysters   Pepper
Salt   Tabasco sauce
Horseradish   Lemon juice
Worcestershire sauce   Cress

Fry the oysters and place two or three between two buttered slices of brown or white bread. Sprinkle with pepper, salt, horseradish, lemon juice, tabasco, Worcestershire, or water cress, according to taste.

SALMON SANDWICHES

1 cup cold cooked salmon   ¼ cup mayonnaise

Mix the salmon with the mayonnaise until a fine even mixture is obtained. Remove the soft crumb from French rolls and fill the space thus made with the salmon mixture.

SARDINE SANDWICHES

12 large sardines   ¼ cup mayonnaise or a little
1 hard-cooked egg   Worcestershire sauce, if
Pepper   desired
Lemon juice   Salt
Shrimp butter, if desired   Creamed butter, if desired

Drain the oil from the fish, remove the skins and pound the fish to a paste with a little salt, pepper, and lemon juice. Spread between thin buttered slices of bread. Shrimp butter may be mixed with the sardine paste and the flavor may be varied by the addition of Worcestershire sauce or mayonnaise or both.

The mashed yolk of the hard-cooked egg and three parts of creamed butter to one of the sardine mixture makes a delicious sandwich filling.

SHAD ROE SANDWICHES

1 shad roe
Yolks of 3 hard-cooked eggs
Butter
½ teaspoon paprika

3 drops tabasco sauce
1 teaspoon anchovy
paste
Salt

Cook the roe and mash it together with the yolks of the hard-cooked eggs. Add an equal amount of creamed butter, the paprika, tabasco sauce, anchovy paste, and salt to taste. Spread between thin buttered slices of bread. Slices of lemon, peeled and salted, may be put between rounds of buttered bread and passed with the shad roe sandwiches.

Sandwiches with Vegetable Fillings

CUCUMBER SANDWICHES

No. 1

Soak thin slices of cucumber for one hour in good white vinegar seasoned with salt and pepper. Add one teaspoon of chopped chives, if desired. Drain the slices and use them between thin, buttered slices of brown or white bread. Each sandwich may be the size of a cucumber slice, if daintiness is desired.

No. 2

Chop a peeled cucumber and mix with mayonnaise. Use between thin buttered slices of brown or white bread.

ONION SANDWICHES

Pour salted water over thin slices of onion (or chopped onion) and let stand for a time to extract the very strong flavor. Then drain the onion and use between buttered slices of bread, seasoning with pepper, salt, and a little mustard if desired.

PIMIENTO AND ANCHOVY SANDWICHES

¾ cup pimiento   1 tablespoon lemon juice
Butter   ¼ cup anchovy paste
½ teaspoon tabasco sauce   Salt

Crush pimientos to a paste with creamed butter, then season with tabasco sauce, lemon juice, anchovy paste, and salt. Spread between thin buttered slices of whole-wheat bread.

RADISH AND HAM SANDWICHES

½ cup potted ham   ½ cup sliced radishes
¼ to ½ cup mayonnaise

Spread thin slices of bread with potted ham. Arrange radish slices over ham and spread with mayonnaise.

TOMATO AND LETTUCE SANDWICHES

4 tomatoes   Lettuce leaves   ¼ to ½ cup mayonnaise

Spread thin slices of buttered bread with mayonnaise, cover with a crisp lettuce leaf and thin slices of peeled chilled tomatoes. Cover with a second slice of bread and cut into desired shape. Crisp bacon is a pleasing addition.

WATER CRESS SANDWICHES

1¼ cups water cress   2 tablespoons lemon juice
Paprika   or ¼ cup mayonnaise

Sprinkle water cress with salt, paprika, and lemon juice or mayonnaise. Use as a filling between brown bread slices.

THE PIE CANAPÉ

An attractive canapé plate may be made by cutting twice horizontally, through a round loaf of rye bread. The slice should be ¾ inch thick and free of crust. Spread with softened butter and mayonnaise dressing. Mark in circles as guides with increasingly larger articles—a small cookie cutter at center, a large cutter, a bowl, a small plate, and decorate in

AFTER A CHOICE OF FILLINGS AND BREADS ATTRACTIVE SAND-WICHES ARE A MATTER OF DESIGN

FILL CREVICES AND SPREAD SUR-FACE OF THIS LOAF WITH CHEESE AND BUTTER PASTE, THEN TOAST TO GOLDEN BROWN

FOR THE PIRATE'S TREASURE
CHEST RETURN THIN SAND-
WICHES TO THE LOAF FROM
WHICH THE CAME OR SLICE
YOUR LOAF LATERALLY, FILL
WITH VARIOUS PASTES AND
FROST WITH CREAM CHEESE
TO YOUR TASTE

concentric rings. Fill the center with caviar, piling chopped parsley or egg yolk at very center. Surround with circle of cream cheese tinted with vegetable coloring pressed from a pastry bag. Continue these rings of appetizer paste and colored cream cheese in accordance with your taste or color scheme. Use red salmon paste, sardellen paste, anchovy paste, shrimp paste, etc. When finished, use a very sharp knife to cut like a pie but do not separate. Serve cold within a few hours.

SANDWICH LOAF OR CAKE

Slice an uncut loaf of day-old white sandwich bread horizontally, making 3 or 4 long slices ¾ inch thick. Remove all crusts. Spread each slice with creamed butter and stiff mayonnaise, then each with a different chopped salad or sandwich mixture. Chicken, shrimp, salmon, or tongue salad; deviled egg, sardine, anchovy, liver, or cheese pastes may be used. Stack and cover the top and sides with soft cream cheese, garnish with flowers of colored cream cheese, paprika, or chopped parsley. Chill.

Miscellaneous Sandwiches and Sandwich Fillings

1. Raisins worked into cream cheese.
2. Chopped raisins, figs, dates, or prunes, mixed with chopped nut meats and moistened with mayonnaise dressing or lemon juice.
3. The well-whipped white of an egg mixed with a cup each of chopped raisins and nut meats, seasoned with a little salt.
4. Peanut butter moistened with salad dressing and mixed with raisins, dates, figs, or bananas.
5. Equal parts olives, peanut butter, celery, mixed with a little salad dressing.
6. Peanut butter mixed with chopped dill, sweet or sour pickles.
7. Cream cheese and chopped stuffed olives.
8. Chopped stuffed olives and chopped nuts moistened with salad dressing.
9. Cream cheese and crushed pineapple between very thin slices of bread.

10. Tunafish mixed with parsley, lemon juice seasoning and a bit of onion.

11. Cream cheese and chopped nuts.

12. Ground boiled ham and chopped pickles or chopped peanuts.

13. Cottage cheese and pickles, olives, nuts, or pimientos.

14. Currant jam with pounded walnut meats and creamed butter. Pass with cream cheese. Preserved currants may be substituted in this combination.

15. Boston brown bread with cream cheese or mayonnaise mixed with chopped nuts and raisins.

16. Rounds of brown bread spread with chopped olives, minced lettuce and water cress, tarragon, paprika, parsley, and chives mixed with mayonnaise.

17. Pimientos, cucumbers and onion or chives, minced, mixed with mayonnaise and spread on buttered entire-wheat bread.

18. Green pepper, pimiento, and olives with mayonnaise.

19. Boston brown bread with minced corned beef seasoned with mustard and mixed to a paste.

20. Cream cheese used with chopped parsley, pimientos and mayonnaise, chopped nuts, sliced sugared bananas, crushed pineapple, chopped or sliced olives, shredded sliced apples. The cheese may be mixed with butter or the creamed butter may be spread on the bread.

HOT SANDWICHES

The hot sandwich is now frequently used as a supper or luncheon dish with a salad. It is sometimes served as a breakfast dish and even a dessert may now be served in sandwich form, as, for instance, slices of ice cream between slices of sponge cake.

There are several types of hot sandwiches. Some are made from plain bread and served with hot sauce; in others the framework of the sandwich is toast, sautéed slices of bread, French-fried toast or fresh slices of bread baked with the sandwich-filling; and in still others hot baking-powder biscuit or crisp toasted crackers are used.

Then besides the regulation kind of sandwich—a filling between two slices of breadstuff—there is the open-faced kind, in which the top slice is left off and a garnish of cut parsley, pickle, olive, or grated cheese is used instead of the covering slice.

And, lastly, there is a third and novel type of sandwich in which the outer structure is of meat. This is cut in thin slices, dipped in fritter batter and fried in fat, and a filling of vegetables is placed between the slices.

GRILLED CHEESE SANDWICHES

Between two slices of medium thick bread, lay slices of cheese cut about one-eighth inch thick. Place in oven until cheese begins to melt. Then toast on both sides and serve hot. Or mash a soft cheddar cheese with cream. Spread this as a filling and toast the sandwich.

CHICKEN CLUB SANDWICHES
(For each sandwich)

3 slices toast
Mayonnaise
1/8 to 1/4 breast of chicken
Lettuce

Crisped bacon
Tomato slices or
  onion slices
Pickle or olives

For each sandwich remove the crust from three slices of toasted bread, buttered while hot. Spread the under slice with a thin layer of mayonnaise dressing. On this lay two small white lettuce leaves, allowing them to project beyond the edge of the toast. On the lettuce lay thin slices of breast of chicken spread with mayonnaise. Cover with a slice of toast, spread with mayonnaise and cover with slices of crisp bacon. A slice of tomato or onion may be placed over the bacon. Place the third slice of toast on this and garnish with pickles or olives. Serve while the toast and bacon are hot.

GRILLED TONGUE AND EGG SANDWICHES

1 cup chopped tongue
1 egg
1 teaspoon onion juice

1 cup milk
2 tablespoons mayonnaise

Mix the tongue with the onion juice and the mayonnaise and spread it on thin slices of unbuttered bread. Press the slices together and cut in two diagonally. Beat the egg, add the milk and dip the sandwiches in this mixture. Brown them in a small amount of butter, first on one side and then on the other. Garnish with parsley and serve at once on a hot platter.

EGG DISHES

To test an egg for freshness, place it in a glass of water. If the egg falls to the bottom of the glass and lies on its side, it is a fresh egg; if the large end rises slightly. the egg is somewhat stale; if it stands on end or floats, it is very stale. The shell of a fresh egg has a bloom; that of stale egg is usually shiny. If the contents of an egg rattle when it is shaken, it is not fresh.

EGGS COOKED IN THE SHELL

HARD-COOKED (CODDLED)—Place the eggs in a saucepan of cold water and heat slowly until the boiling point is reached. Set the container on the back of the range or reduce the heat so that the water will not boil again and let stand twenty to thirty minutes before removing the eggs. Another method of regulating the temperature is to cook them in the double boiler.

SOFT-COOKED (CODDLED)—Use one pint water for each egg up to six eggs, one-half pint for each additional egg, and use a small deep saucepan so that the water will cover the eggs. Bring the water to the boiling point in a vessel that can be covered closely. Put the eggs in at once, cover, set off heat and let stand in a warm place for four to six minutes, depending on consistency desired. In this way, the eggs will be cooked equally well in every part.

POACHED OR DROPPED EGGS

No. 1—Heat salted water to the boiling point in a frying-pan or other shallow pan. Break an egg into a saucer, then slip it gently into the water. Repeat until all the eggs are in. Remove the pan from the fire, cover and keep hot until the eggs are set to the desired degree. If the yolk is not entirely covered, dip the water over it carefully until it is coated with white. Remove with a skimmer or perforated ladle and slip on to a thin piece of buttered toast. Buttered muffin rings may be placed in the water and each egg slipped into a muffin ring for cooking, or an egg-poacher may be used.

PLAIN OMELET

PUFFY—

4 eggs   Salt and pepper
4 tablespoons hot water   Butter or other fat

Beat the egg whites until stiff. Beat the yolks until thick and lemon colored, beat into them the hot water and add salt and pepper. Cut and fold together the yolks and stiffly beaten whites. Melt enough fat in an omelet-pan to grease the bottom and sides of the pan. Turn the egg mixture into the pan and cook over a slow fire until it is puffy and a light brown underneath, then place in the oven until the top is dry. Touch the top of the omelet lightly with the finger and if the egg does not stick to the finger the omelet is done. Do not overcook it or it will shrink or be tough.

Loosen the edges of the omelet, cut through the center, slip a spatula or flexible knife under the side next to the handle of the pan, fold one-half over the other and press slightly to make it stay in place, slip on to a hot plate and serve at once.

FRENCH—

6 eggs   2 tablespoons fat
Salt and pepper

Beat the eggs just enough to mix the whites and yolks, and add salt and pepper. Heat the fat in an omelet-pan, pour a little of it into the beaten eggs and allow the remainder to get hot. Turn the eggs into the pan as the mixture cooks on the bottom and sides, prick it with a fork so that the egg on top will penetrate the cooked surface, and run under the sides. The work must be done quickly and carefully so that the eggs are not all stirred up like scrambled eggs. While the eggs are still soft, but slightly thickened, fold over, let stand a few minutes to brown, and turn on to a hot dish.

Individual omelets may be cooked in a small skillet.

VARIATIONS OF PLAIN OMELET

Variations of the plain puffy omelet or the plain French omelet may be made by adding any of the following ingredients to the omelet before it is put into the pan to cook, or by spreading one of them on top just before the omelet is folded. Allow one tablespoon of mixture to each two eggs used.

AUX FINES HERBS—This favorite French omelet is made by adding a mixture of parsley, thyme, and sweet marjoram to a plain omelet.

CHEESE—Scatter grated or ground cheese over the center of the omelet while it is cooking.

FISH—Use any cooked fish. Chop it fine, season with salt and pepper, and moisten with a little cream. Spread on the omelet before folding.

HAM OR OTHER MEAT—Scatter minced cooked meat over the center of the omelet while it is cooking. The meat may be browned in a small amount of fat before it is added.

JARDINIERE—Stir into the beaten eggs, before cooking, a mixture of chopped parsley, onion, chives, shallots, and a few leaves each of sorrel and chervil, minced.

JELLY—Spread any jelly or jam over the omelet just before folding.

ONION—Mix one tablespoon chopped onion and one teaspoon chopped parsley. Add to the omelet mixture before cooking.

PARSLEY—Scatter minced parsley over the center of the omelet while it is cooking.

VEGETABLE—Use cooked leftover vegetables, one vegetable alone or two in combination. Press the vegetable through a sieve, moisten with a little milk, cream or gravy, and season with salt and pepper. Lightly spread the mixture over the omelet before folding.

CHICKEN OR TONGUE OMELET

1 cup chicken or tongue	1 cup cream or milk
2 tablespoons fat	Salt and pepper
2 tablespoons flour	Plain omelet

Chop the meat until it is very fine. Make a sauce of the fat, flour, and milk or cream. Add salt and pepper and chopped meat. Make a plain omelet and spread the meat mixture on it just before folding.

MUSHROOM OMELET

1 cup mushrooms	½ teaspoon pepper
1 tablespoon fat	1 tablespoon flour
½ cup milk or cream	Plain omelet
1 teaspoon salt	

Use fresh or canned mushrooms, cut in pieces. Melt the fat in a saucepan, add the mushrooms, the milk or cream, salt, pepper and flour which has been mixed to a paste with a little cold milk. Cook for five minutes, then set aside until the omelet is made. Spread the mushroom mixture over the omelet just before folding.

MUSHROOM AND TOMATO OMELET

3 cups tomatoes	Salt and pepper
1 cup mushrooms	6 eggs
2 tablespoons chopped onion	½ cup milk
2 teaspoons sugar	

Strain the tomato, add the onion, sugar, salt and pepper and cook several minutes, then add the mushrooms, sliced very thin. Make a plain omelet of the eggs and milk. Pour part of the sauce over the omelet just before folding; fold; place on a hot plate; pour the remainder of the sauce around it and serve.

OYSTER OMELET

12 oysters	1 cup cream
½ tablespoon flour	6 eggs
2 tablespoons fat	Salt and pepper

Chop the oysters. Make a sauce of the flour, fat, and cream. Add the well-beaten eggs, season with salt and pepper, stir in the oysters and cook as a plain omelet.

POTATO OMELET

4 cold boiled potatoes	⅛ teaspoon pepper
3 tablespoons bacon fat	2 eggs
1½ teaspoons salt	2 tablespoons milk

Cut the potatoes into tiny cubes and cook in the bacon fat with the seasonings for five minutes. Beat the eggs slightly and add the milk, then pour over the potatoes. Cook slowly until set, fold, and turn onto a hot plate.

BAKED CREAMY OMELETS

2 slices bread	Salt and pepper
1 cup milk	Chopped onion
6 eggs	

Crumble the bread and allow it to soak in the milk while the eggs are being prepared. Beat the eggs until light, add seasonings and then the bread and milk mixture. Bake quickly (360° F.) in a well-greased shallow pan and when done roll as you would a jelly roll. Serves 6.

INDIVIDUAL OMELETS—Bake like pancakes on a griddle over low heat, turn and when lightly browned, remove to hot platter, fill and roll quickly. Makes 12-14.

CLAM OMELET

1 cup hard clams	Paprika
2 tablespoons butter	6 eggs, separated
1 teaspoon salt	⅔ cup cream

After clams have been steamed and removed from their shells, put them through a food chopper and sauté in butter. Add salt and paprika to egg yolks and beat until light. Add cream and chopped clams and mix thoroughly. Fold in stiffly beaten egg whites, pour mixture into buttered omelet pan or skillet and bake in moderate oven (350° F.) about 25 minutes, or until brown. Serves 6.

SPANISH OMELET

1 medium tomato	Olives
1 small green pepper	Mushrooms
½ onion	Salt and pepper
2 sprigs parsley	4 eggs
1 stalk celery	

Peel the tomato, add the pepper, onion, parsley, celery, olives, mushrooms, and chop all together in a chopping bowl. Place the mixture in a saucepan, add seasonings and cook for two to three minutes. Beat the eggs, put them in the omelet pan and as soon as they begin to cook, add the chopped vegetables. Finish as for plain omelet. Serves 4.

EGGS WITH TOMATOES

1 small onion	¼ teaspoon pepper
2 cups tomatoes	6 eggs
1 teaspoon salt	Toast

Cut the onion into small pieces and place with the tomato in a shallow pan. Stew very slowly for ten minutes. Add salt and pepper, then reduce the heat until the tomato stops bubbling. Break the eggs and slip them on top of the tomato, being careful not to break the yolks. Cook slowly until the whites of the eggs are set, then prick the yolks and let them mingle with the tomato and the whites. The mixture should be quite soft, but the red tomatoes should be quite distinct. Serve at once on buttered toast.

SPANISH EGGS

1 slice onion	6 eggs
1 tomato	1 teaspoon salt
1 tablespoon fat	¼ teaspoon pepper

Rub the onion over the inside of a skillet. Pare the tomato and cut it into small pieces. Melt the fat in the frying pan, add the tomato and cook for five minutes, stirring it now and then. Beat the eggs well and add to the tomato, then add salt and pepper and cook slowly, stirring constantly, until the eggs thicken like scrambled eggs. Pour into a hot dish and serve at once.

APPLE OMELET

5 tart apples	Cinnamon or other spice
½ tablespoon fat	2 eggs
½ cup sugar	

This is a very delicate dish to serve with broiled spareribs or roast pork. Cook the apples until very soft, then mash them and add fat, sugar, eggs and spice. Bake (250°-350° F.) in a shallow pudding-dish or pie-tin until brown.

DEVILED EGGS

COLD (PICNIC EGGS)—Cut hard-cooked eggs in half, either lengthwise or crosswise. Mash the yolks, season with salt, pepper, butter, a little mustard and vinegar. Minced potted ham may be added, or the yolks may be mixed with mayonnaise dressing. Refill the whites with the mixture; press two halves together, and wrap each egg in a square of waxed paper.

Hot—Omit vinegar, add nuts to the egg mixture, moisten with evaporated milk and refill whites. Cap with large sautéed mushrooms. Pack into greased baking dish, caps up, cover with rich white sauce, then buttered crumbs and brown in 350° oven.

EGG TIMBALES

1 tablespoon fat	3 eggs
1 tablespoon flour	Salt and pepper
⅔ cup scalded milk	Cayenne
1 tablespoon chopped parsley	Celery salt

Make a white sauce of the fat, flour, and milk, and add the egg yolks, slightly beaten. Add all the seasonings, then fold in the stiffly beaten egg whites. Fill greased baking dishes two-thirds full of the mixture. Set dishes in a pan of hot water and poach in a slow oven (250°-350° F.) until firm. Arrange on a platter and serve with tomato cream sauce.

SAVORY EGGS

6 hot hard-cooked eggs	Chopped parsley
Salt and pepper	Anchovy paste
¼ cup hot cream	6 slices hot buttered
1 cup hot thin white sauce	toast

Cut the eggs in two lengthwise and remove the yolks. Mash the yolks, add seasonings, cream, parsley, anchovy or any desired relish, and fill the whites. Place on slices of toast and pour the white sauce over them.

EGG FARCI

6 hot hard-cooked eggs	¼ teaspoon pepper
½ teaspoon salt	1 tablespoon butter
1½ cups white, Béchamel,	4 tablespoons milk
curry or tomato sauce	Onion juice

Remove the shells from the eggs and cut them in half crosswise, then cut an even slice from the end of each half so that it will stand up in a pan. Remove the yolks, mash, and add the salt, pepper, butter, milk and a few drops of onion juice. Mix thoroughly and heap into the hollow of the whites. Set in a shallow pan and bake in a slow oven (250°-350° F.) for about six minutes, then arrange on a hot dish, and pour over them any preferred sauce.

EGGS À LA GOLDENROD

6 hard-cooked eggs   Salt and pepper
2 cups thin white sauce   Paprika
8 slices toast

Separate the yolks from the whites of the eggs; chop the whites very fine, and add to the white sauce, with salt, pepper, paprika. Arrange six slices of toast on a platter and pour over them the white sauce mixture. Press the egg-yolks through a sieve and scatter over the top. Cut the two extra slices of toast into small triangles, or points, arrange on the platter and garnish with parsley.

CREAMED EGGS

6 hard-cooked eggs   2 tablespoons flour
2 tablespoons fat   2 cups milk
½ onion   1 teaspoon salt
6 slices hot buttered toast ¼ teaspoon pepper

Remove the shells from the eggs and cut each egg into six pieces. Heat the fat in a frying pan, and cook the chopped onion with it for a few minutes until yellow, but not brown. Remove the onion, make a sauce of the fat, flour, liquid and seasonings. When it thickens, add the eggs, and when they are well heated, turn the mixture out onto the buttered toast and serve at once.

SCALLOPED EGGS

Butter   Salt and pepper
6 hard-cooked eggs   Milk or cream
Crumbs

Grease a baking dish and place in it a layer of crumbs, then a layer of slices of hard-cooked eggs. Dot with bits of butter, sprinkle with salt and pepper, and add another layer of crumbs. Repeat in this order until the dish is full, having a layer of buttered crumbs on top. Pour cream or milk over the whole until it comes about halfway to the top of the dish, and brown in a moderate oven (350°-400° F.).

CHEESE

MANY of the well-known cheeses which originated in Europe are now reproduced in America with such success that they are considered as good as the European original. Moreover, the cheese manufactured in America is generally made on a much larger scale and under more carefully controlled conditions.

SEMIHARD CHEESE

Semihard cheese varies in flavor from very mild to sharp. Varieties also range in color from pale to deep yellow. In general they have a firm, rather elastic texture with or without holes. Most types may be used in sandwiches, for cooking or as dessert.

AMERICAN CHEDDAR CHEESE—Flavor ranges from mild to sharp, depending upon the time allowed for ripening. It may be made of whole milk (often called full cream), part skim or skim milk. This variety is sold in many shapes, such as daisies, longhorns and young Americas. IN RECIPES WHICH CALL FOR CHEESE WITHOUT SPECIFYING THE KIND, THIS CHEESE IS THE VARIETY USUALLY MEANT.

BRICK—An American Cheddar with a mild, sweetish taste, a rather elastic texture and many small round eyes or holes. It is a rennet cheese made from whole milk and molded into brick shape.

CHESHIRE—Hard rennet cheese somewhat like English Cheddar but with sharper flavor. Made from whole milk and colored with annatto. Made in England.

EDAM—Hard rennet cheese, round with red rind. Made from skim milk and from partly skimmed milk. Solid, dry, rather crumbly texture. Mild, slightly saline flavor. It was originally made in Holland, now some is made in the United States. Serve with salads, in rarebits or as dessert. To serve, cut off top and scoop out inside as needed.

EMMENTHALER—Hard rennet cheese with large holes and a mild, somewhat sweetish flavor. Holes should be uniform, very shiny and about the size of a quarter. It is made from whole milk. Use for cooking or with desserts or salads. Made in Switzerland.

ENGLISH CHEDDAR—Hard, sharp, white or yellow color. Made from sweet milk and sold as "full cream" (when whole milk is used), "part skim" or "skim," depending on the type of milk used.

GOUDA—Hard rennet cheese, round and flat. Made from whole milk. Similar to Edam cheese. Originally made in Holland but small quantities are now made in the United States.

GRUYÈRE—Originally the name applied to Emmenthaler cheese manufactured in France. Now made in the United States where the name is generally applied to packaged processed Swiss cheese.

HERKIMER—Aged Cheddar with sharp flavor. It is used in rarebits, cheese sauces and as dessert. Made in the United States.

PINEAPPLE—Hard, highly colored Cheddar made in pineapple shape, then hung and dried in a net, making diamond-shaped corrugations on surface. The outer coat is rubbed with oil, making it very hard and smooth. Made from whole milk. It is grated and used like other Cheddars. Made in the United States.

SAGE—A Cheddar cheese formerly made by adding sage leaves to the curd. Now sage extract is usually used. Made in United States.

SWISS—Similar to Swiss made Emmenthaler. Much is made in the United States. When processed the characteristic holes are lost.

UNCOOKED SOFT CHEESE

COTTAGE—Soft curds. Made commercially from pasteurized sour milk with or without rennet.

CREAM—A soft rich cheese with mild flavor. Genuine cream cheese is made from pasteurized rich cream thickened by souring or from sweet cream thickened with rennet. It is also made from thin cream thickened with rennet and from whole milk. When fresh it has a mild delicate flavor. It must be refrigerated at all times. Used as a basis for mixtures with pimiento, crushed pineapple, etc.

NEUFCHÂTEL—The French cheese is similar to cream cheese but has been ripened by mold. It is a very soft rennet cheese made from whole or skimmed milk. Domestic Neufchâtel is similar to cream cheese but is made from various grades of milk ranging from cream to skimmed milk. It is not ripened.

PROCESS CHEESE

Process cheese is produced by grinding various lots of cheese, blending and pasteurizing at 140° to 160° F. to produce a standardized product, uniform in flavor and texture, without rind and with good keeping qualities. Among the types of cheese sold in this form are mild or sharp American Cheddar, Swiss, brick and Limburger.

SOFT CHEESE

Soft, creamy cheese is usually served as a dessert.

BRIE—A soft rennet cheese with a definite odor, sharp flavor and red color on surface. It is made from whole or partly skimmed milk. It originated in France but is now made in the United States. To serve as a dessert, cut off top so cheese may be dipped out with a spoon.

CAMEMBERT—A soft rennet cheese covered with a firm rind of molds and dried cheese. The interior is almost fluid in consistency. It is made from whole milk or slightly skimmed milk. It originated in France but is now made in the United States also. Serve as Brie.

LIVEROT—Soft rennet cheese, somewhat like Brie. It is made from partially skimmed milk and has a strong piquant flavor. Made in France.

PONT L'ÉVÊQUE—Soft rennet cheese, somewhat like Brie. It is made from whole milk with or without added cream, a mixture of whole and skim milk or from skim milk. Mostly imported from France.

SEMISOFT CHEESE

Most semisoft cheese has been well ripened and consequently has a sharp pungent flavor. This cheese is rarely used for cooking but is excellent for sandwiches, with crackers as dessert or appetizer.

LIEDERKRANZ—An American cheese originated in Ohio. It has a strong odor and pungent flavor somewhat like Limburger but has a slightly softer texture. It should be kept under refrigeration, then warmed to room temperature before using.

LIMBURGER—Soft rennet cheese with strong odor and flavor. Made from whole milk, partly skimmed or entirely skimmed milk. Originated in Belgium but is now made in large quantities in the United States.

PORT DU SALUT—Similar to brick but a little stronger in flavor and a little softer in texture. May show tiny gas holes. Originated in France by Trappist monks. The Canadian version is called Oka or Trappist.

MARBLED CHEESE

Marbled cheese includes those varieties which are delicately streaked throughout with blue or green veins of penicillium mold. Such cheese has a strong, rather salty flavor which is highly prized by cheese-lovers. It is used for dessert or in salads or salad dressings.

BLUE OR BLEU—Similar to Roquefort but made with cows' milk. Originally made in Denmark and France but now widely made in the United States in various dairy sections where limestone caves are available for ripening the cheese.

GORGONZOLA—Marbled cheese made in Italy. Semisoft with sharp flavor. Made from whole milk.

ROQUEFORT—Originally made in France from sheep's milk. It is a semihard rennet cheese with streaks of blue and green mold. The mold is produced by adding a special wheat and barley bread which has been allowed to mold before grinding and combining with the curd. It is ripened in limestone caves. Holes are punched in the cheese during curing to allow air, essential to growth of mold, to enter.

STILTON—Hard rennet cheese with green or blue mold and wrinkled or ridged skin or rind. It is made from cows' milk with cream added and is usually allowed to ripen at least 2 years before being marketed.

GRATED HARD CHEESE

Some types of cheese are so hard that they cannot be sliced, but must be used grated. These are used for cooking or as an accessory to cooked dishes, especially Italian. Most grated cheese is too dry to melt without added moisture. A considerable quantity of the Italian type is made in the United States and also imported from South America.

CACIOCAVALLO—A hard, beet-shaped rennet cheese. Made of whole or partly skimmed milk. Is lightly smoked. Originated in Italy.

PARMESAN—Hard, rennet cheese made from partly skimmed milk. Has a sharp flavor and a green or black rind. Will keep indefinitely.

PROVOLE OR PROVOLLNA—Hard, round and held by a net. It is similar to Caciocavallo. made from cows' milk. Originated in Italy.

ROMANO—Hard, dry, salty with black coating. Originated in Italy.

SAP SAGO—Small, hard and green in color. It is made from skim milk and flavored with leaves from an aromatic species of clover. Use as appetizer or dessert. Made in Switzerland.

SCANDINAVIAN CHEESE

APPETITOST—Semihard, made from sour buttermilk.

GJEDOST—Hard, made from goats' milk, chocolate-colored, sweet taste.

MYSOST—Semisoft whey cheese of light brown color, mild sweetish flavor. Used as a snack or as a dessert.

NOKKELOST—Hard, made from skimmed milk with spices added.

MACARONI AND CHEESE

1 cup broken macaroni   Dash salt
½ cup milk   Dash pepper
½ pound cheese, grated   Buttered crumbs

Boil macaroni in salted water until tender. Drain and rinse with hot water. Place in casserole. Heat milk, add cheese and heat until cheese is melted. Add seasonings and pour over macaroni. Mix with fork, cover with crumbs and bake in moderate oven (350° F.) 15 minutes. Serves 6.

FROMAGE

2 egg yolks   ¼ teaspoon salt
1 cup milk   4½ cups grated cheese
Paprika   1 teaspoon butter, melted

Beat egg yolks light, add remaining ingredients, pour into buttered ramekins and bake in slow oven (300° F.) about 20 minutes or until set. Serves 6.

WELSH RAREBIT

No. 1.

2 tablespoons butter
1 teaspoon Worcester-
shire sauce
½ teaspoon salt
½ teaspoon paprika
¼ teaspoon prepared
mustard
½ pound sharp cheese,
grated
½ cup ginger ale
1 egg, slightly beaten

Melt butter and add seasonings and cheese. Stir in double boiler until cheese is soft. Add ginger ale, then add egg. Cook until thick. Serve on toast or crackers. Serves 3.

No. 2.

1 pound sharp cheese, grated
1 tablespoon butter, melted
1 teaspoon mustard
1 teaspoon cornstarch
¾ cup milk
1 egg, slightly beaten
½ teaspoon salt
1 tablespoon Worcester-
shire sauce

Melt cheese with butter in double boiler. Mix mustard and cornstarch, moisten with milk and add with remaining ingredients except toast. Cook until thickened. Serve on toast. Serves 4.

RINKTUM DITTY

1 small onion, chopped fine
1 tablespoon butter
2 cups cooked tomatoes
1 teaspoon salt
¼ teaspoon pepper
2 teaspoons sugar
½ pound cheese, grated
1 egg, beaten

Cook onion in butter until tender. Add tomatoes, salt, pepper and sugar and heat. Add cheese and cook until melted, stirring constantly. Add egg slowly, stirring constantly, and cook 1 minute longer. Serve on buttered toast. Serves 4.

GOLDENGLOW CASSEROLE

½ cup corn meal
½ teaspoon salt
2½ cups boiling water
½ pound cheddar cheese
½ cup milk

Add corn meal gradually to boiling salted water, stirring constantly; cook over boiling water 30 to 45 minutes. Pour into shallow pan. When cold cut into 1-inch squares. Melt cheese in top of double boiler. Add milk gradually, stirring constantly. Arrange layers of mush and cheese in casserole and bake in moderate oven (350° F.) 20 minutes. Serves 4.

CHEESE IN ANY FORM IS
THE GOURMET'S DELIGHT
WHETHER ON A SERVICE
TRAY WITH FRUIT OR IN
TANGY WELSH RAREBIT

TRY FILLING YOUR BISCUIT DOUGH WITH CHEESE AND CLIP IT INTO A SWEDISH TEA RING OR PILE UP STRIPS AND TUCK THEM, END UP, INTO BAKING CUPS

CHEESE CROQUETTES

3 tablespoons butter
⅓ cup flour
¼ teaspoon salt
¼ teaspoon paprika

1 cup milk
2 egg yolks, slightly beaten
1½ cups cubed cheese

Melt butter, blend in flour and add seasonings and milk. Cook until thickened, stirring constantly. Add to egg yolks; when well mixed add cheese. Cool. Shape into balls and fry in hot deep fat (380° F.) until browned. Makes 12.

CHEESE AND RICE CROQUETTES

¼ cup butter
⅓ cup flour
1 cup milk
1 cup grated cheese
¼ teaspoon salt

Dash pepper
Dash paprika
2 cups cooked rice
Fine dry crumbs
1 egg

Melt butter, blend in flour and add milk. Cook until thickened, stirring constantly. Add cheese and heat until melted. Add seasonings. Chill. Add rice and shape into croquettes. Roll in crumbs, in slightly beaten egg and again in crumbs. Brown in hot deep fat (380° F.). Makes 12.

HOMINY AND CHEESE TIMBALES

2 cups cooked hominy
⅔ cup grated cheese
2 eggs
¾ teaspoon salt
Dash pepper

2 teaspoons chopped pimiento
2 tablespoons chopped parsley
1 cup milk

Combine ingredients, pour into buttered individual baking dishes, place in pan of hot water and bake in slow oven (325° F.) 30 minutes. Serves 6.

CHEESE AND SPINACH SOUFFLÉ

1 teaspoon chopped onion
1 cup grated cheese
Salt and pepper

1 cup Thick White Sauce
1 cup chopped cooked spinach

3 eggs, separated

Add onion, cheese and seasonings to white sauce and heat until cheese is melted. Add spinach and well-beaten egg yolks. Mix well. Fold in stiffly beaten egg whites. Pour into buttered loaf pan, place in pan of hot water and bake in moderate oven (350° F.) 45 minutes or until firm. Serves 6.

CHEESE SOUFFLÉ

4 tablespoons butter
4 tablespoons flour
1½ cups hot milk
1 teaspoon salt

Dash cayenne
½ pound sharp cheese,
  grated
6 eggs, separated

Melt butter, add flour and blend. Add milk and cook until thickened, stirring constantly. Add seasonings and cheese; heat until cheese is melted. Add beaten egg yolks. Cool. Pour into stiffly beaten egg whites and mix well. Bake in 2-quart ungreased baking dish in 300° F. oven 1¼ hours. Serves 6.

CHEESE FONDUE

5 eggs, separated
1¼ cups milk
2 cups soft bread
  crumbs

¾ teaspoon salt
½ teaspoon dry mustard
½ pound American cheese,
  shredded

Beat egg yolks and add next 5 ingredients. Fold in stiffly beaten egg whites. Pour into buttered custard cups, place in pan of hot water and bake in slow oven (325° F.) until firm. Unmold and serve at once. Serves 8.

SPAGHETTI LOAF

2 cups broken spaghetti
1 clove garlic
½ pound sharp American
  cheese
1⅔ cups milk

2 eggs, beaten
¾ teaspoon salt
¼ cup minced parsley
1 tablespoon grated onion

Boil spaghetti with garlic in salted water until tender. Remove garlic, drain spaghetti and rinse. Melt cheese in milk over boiling water; add to eggs. Add salt, parsley, onion and spaghetti; mix thoroughly. Pour into buttered loaf pan. Bake in moderate oven (350° F.) 1 hour. Serves 6.

CHEESE RICE RING

2 tablespoons chopped onion
1 green pepper, chopped
2 tablespoons butter
1½ cups cooked tomatoes

3½ cups cooked rice
¼ teaspoon salt
Dash pepper
1½ cups grated sharp cheese

Cook onion and green pepper in butter until tender. Add tomatoes and rice. Cook slowly until rice has absorbed liquid. Add seasonings and cheese. Pack into buttered ring mold. Unmold onto serving plate and fill with scrambled eggs. Serves 6.

MEAT

THE name meat is given generally to all edible flesh of animals used for food. The name beef is used for the flesh of adult cattle; veal for the flesh of calves under one year of age; pork for the flesh of swine; mutton for the flesh of adult sheep and lamb for the flesh of sheep from six weeks to one year old.

SELECTION OF MEAT

Beef

Good beef has a fresh red color, a smooth covering of brittle creamy fat and small streaks of fat distributed through the lean. In other words it is well marbled with fat. The lean is firm, fine-grained and velvety. The bones in young beef are porous and red, in older animals they are white and flinty.

Lamb

Good quality lamb varies in color from a light to a dark pink, since the color darkens as the animal grows older, and in mutton deepens to red. The fat of young lambs is quite soft and slightly pink in color. As the animal grows older it becomes harder and whiter, so that mutton fat is white and rather brittle.

Veal

Veal is light grayish pink in color. The meat is very fine-grained, velvety and fairly firm, with little surface fat and no marbling. The fat is clear, firm and white and the bones are porous and red.

Pork

Good quality pork is grayish pink, changing to a delicate rose in older animals. The flesh is relatively firm, fine-grained, well marbled and covered with firm white fat. Fresh pork must be thoroughly cooked, so should not be broiled or fried.

FROZEN MEATS

Frozen meat may be thawed and then cooked as any other fresh meat. Cooking may also be started while the meat is still frozen with successful results. Additional time must be allowed for cooking, however, and the approximate times for cooking various cuts by either method are indicated below:

	MINUTES PER POUND	
CUT	Thawed	Unthawed
Standing Rib Roast (Roast at 300° F.)		
Rare	18	43
Medium	22	47
Well done	30	55
Rolled Rib Roast (Roast at 300° F.)		
Rare	32	53
Medium	38	57
Well done	48	65
Beef Rump (Braise)	30	50
Porterhouse Steak (Broil, rare to medium)		
1 inch	8—10	21—33
1½ inches	10—15	23—38
2 inches	20—30	33—43
Boneless Lamb Shoulder (Roast at 300° F.)	40	60
Leg of Lamb (Roast at 300° F.)...........	30—35	45—55
Pork Loin (Roast at 350° F.)		
Center cut	35—40	50—55
Rib or loin end	50—55	70—75
	Total Time Minutes	Total Time Minutes
Club Steak (Broil, rare to medium)		
¾ inch	16—20	24—28
1 inch	20	30
Round Steak (Pan-broil)		
½ inch	7	11
Beef Patties (Pan-broil)		
1 inch	8	10
Lamb Chops (Pan-broil)		
¾ inch	10	15
1½ inches	20	25
Shoulder Lamb Chops (Braise)		
½ inch	15	20
Pork Chops (Braise)		
¾ inch	45	55

Cuts of Meat

Animals dressed for market are divided lengthwise through the backbone into two parts, each of which is called a side. Each side is divided again into two parts, the forequarter and the hindquarter. Each quarter is then divided into smaller cuts which are sold in the retail market.

Comparative Cost of Various Cuts

As a general rule the price of the different cuts of meat is determined by considerations such as tenderness, grain, general appearance and convenience of cooking rather than by food values in terms of fat or protein, or the ease with which they are digested. The cheapest cuts for general use are the shanks, plates and chuck.

MEAT SPECIALTIES

LIVER—Calf and lamb liver are both very mild and tender. Beef and pork liver are somewhat stronger in flavor and coarser in texture, so are sometimes dipped into hot water for 5 minutes before using. All liver has a very high nutritive value, being particularly rich in iron and vitamins A and B. However, because of demand calf's liver is much higher in price.

KIDNEYS—Kidneys from veal, lamb, pork and beef may all be used for stews and pies. Lamb and veal kidneys should be selected for broiling.

SWEETBREADS—These are the thymus glands of calves and lambs. They are very delicate in flavor and texture. They should be cooked immediately since they are very perishable.

HEARTS—Calf, beef, lamb and pork hearts are all economical and nourishing foods with little or no waste. Beef heart is largest.

TONGUE—The tongues from various animals differ mainly in size. The beef tongue is largest and therefore slices best.

BRAINS—These are similar to sweetbreads in flavor and texture and may be obtained from calf, lamb, pork and beef. Brains are very perishable and should be used immediately.

TRIPE—Tripe is the muscular inner lining of the stomach of beef, sheep or pig. Veal tripe is most tender. Tripe may be honeycombed or smooth, the former being choicest.

Amount of Meat to Buy for Each Person

Meat shrinks from one-third to one-half in cooking. Therefore allow one-fourth pound of meat without bone for each serving, and one-half pound of meat consisting of lean, fat and bone as a minimum for each serving.

CARE OF MEAT IN THE HOME

As soon as meat comes from the market, the wrapping paper should be removed, and the meat should be put on a plate, covered lightly with waxed paper and placed in the refrigerator or other cool place.

Before cooking meat, wipe carefully with a damp cloth, remove outer membrane and inspection stamp. In hot weather, if meat is to be kept any length of time, store it in the freezer compartment of the refrigerator which has temperature of 25° F. or lower. Before storing, closely wrap meats in a freezer wrapping material. Even the most perishable meats and ground beef will keep several weeks under these conditions.

METHODS OF COOKING MEAT

Meat is cooked to soften connective tissue, to develop flavor, to improve appearance and to destroy bacteria or other organisms. The method of cooking depends on the kind and quality of the meat to be cooked. Only tender cuts of meat can be cooked successfully by dry heat. Less tender cuts of meat require moist heat and long, slow cooking.

BROILING—Broiling means to cook by direct heat and may be done over hot coals or under a flame or an electric unit. This method may be used for tender cuts of meat with adequate amounts of fat. Veal should not be broiled since it is too low in fat; pork should not be broiled. Preheat the broiler with the oven door closed, about 10 minutes. Slash the fat edge of meat in several places to prevent curling. If meat thermometer is used insert at the side and force bulb into center of cut. Place meat on broiler rack with surface of meat about 4 inches from the source of heat. Turn when surface is browned and about half the total cooking time has been used. Sprinkle browned side with salt, turn meat and cook until brown or to same internal temperature as for roast beef.

PAN-BROILING—Place meat in sizzling hot skillet and brown on both sides. Reduce temperature, pour off fat as it accumulates and cook until as well done as desired, turning from time to time. Pork is not cooked by this method.

ROASTING—Place meat on rack in roasting pan, fat side up and cook in slow oven, uncovered and without water until as well cooked as desired. Basting is not necessary. The large tender cuts of meat are cooked by this method.

COOKING IN WATER—Cover meat with boiling water, season with salt and pepper and cook slowly at simmering temperature, not boiling, until meat is tender.

STEWING—Cut meat into cubes. Brown if desired, on all sides in hot fat, cover with boiling water and cook at simmering temperature in a covered kettle until meat is tender. Less tender cuts containing much connective tissue are best cooked by this method which softens both tissue and fiber.

The best cuts for stews are those containing both fat and lean and some bone. The shank is the most economical of all cuts for this purpose. Other cuts used are the neck, plate, flank, heel of the round and short ribs. The brisket and the rump are sometimes used. Occasionally a cut like the round is used, as in beef a la mode.

BRAISING—This method of cooking by moist heat is used for the less tender cuts of meat which require long slow cooking in the presence of moisture to bring out the full flavor and make the meat tender. Many pork cuts are cooked by braising rather than broiling or pan-broiling since pork requires thorough cooking. Brown meat in a small amount of hot fat, then cover tightly and cook slowly in juices from the meat or in added liquid such as water, milk, cream, stock, diluted vinegar, fruit or vegetable juices. Add only a small amount of liquid at a time and do not let boil, but keep at a simmering temperature. Pork chops, pot roasts, fricassees, casserole meats, smothered steaks and similar favorites are all cooked by braising.

FRYING AND SAUTEING—Some meats, such as chops and cutlets, may be crumbed and fried in deep fat. Ham, liver, and some other meats are sometimes sauteed in a small amount of fat at low temperature, after the first searing.

PRESSURE COOKING—utilizes live steam in a special kettle.

BEEF

ROASTING

	WEIGHT POUNDS	OVEN TEMPERATURE	INTERIOR TEMPERATURE Rare	Med.	Well done	TIME PER POUND Minutes Rare	Med.	Well done
Standing ribs (3 ribs)	7–8	300°F	140°F	160°F	170°F	18–20	22–25	27–30
(1 rib)	2–6	350	140	160	170	33	45	50
Rolled ribs	6–8	300	140	160	170	32	38	48
Chuck ribs	5–8	300		150–170			25–30	
Rump	5–7	300		150–170			25–30	
Whole tenderloin	4–6	300	140	160		25	30–35	

BROILING

			TOTAL COOKING TIME Minutes	
Filet mignon—1 inch	⅓	550°F	5	6–7
1½ inches	½	550°F	9–10	12
2 inches	¾	550°F	15	18
Club steak—1 inch	1	550°F	9–10	12–14
1½ inches	1¼	550°F	14–16	18–20
2 inches	1½	550°F	18–22	24–30
Sirlon steak—1 inch	3	550°F	10–12	14–16
1½ inches	4¼	550°F	15–20	20–25
2 inches	5¾	550°F	20–25	25–30
Porterhouse steak—1 inch	2	550°F	9–10	12–15
1½ inches	2½	550°F	14–16	18–20
2 inches	3	550°F	18–22	25–30
Ground patties (1 x 3 inches)	¼	550°F	15	25

BRAISING

	AVERAGE WEIGHT OR THICKNESS	COOKING TIME
Pot roast	3–5 pounds	3–4 hours
Swiss steak	1½–2½ inches	2–3 hours
Fricassee	2-inch cubes	1½ hours
Beef birds	½x2x4 inches	1½ hours
Short ribs	Pieces 2x2x4 inches	1½ hours
Round steak	¾ inch	45–60 minutes
Stuffed steak	½–¾ inch	1½ hours

BEEF

BROWNED BEEF BRISKET

6 pounds beef brisket
Dash celery salt
Garlic

Salt and pepper
6 or more medium
boiled potatoes

If the brisket has much bone, part may be removed to use in making soup or stock. Cover meat with boiling water, add celery salt and garlic and simmer 3 hours or until tender, turning it once during the cooking. Remove meat, place in shallow pan with skin side up, score several times across the top and season. Drop potatoes into kettle to take up some of the fat; then place around meat and brown in hot oven (400° F.) about 20 minutes. Make a gravy with the remaining liquid and serve. Serves 6.

BRISKET OF BEEF

3 pounds beef brisket
½ cup sliced onions
½ cup sliced carrots

½ cup diced celery with leaves
1½ teaspoons salt

Cover beef with hot water, add vegetables and simmer, covered, until meat is tender, about 2½ to 3 hours. Do not boil. Add salt when half done and more water if necessary. Remove meat from broth, slice and serve with Horse-radish Sauce (page 305) or Onion Sauce (page 297). Allow ½ pound per serving.

TO CORN BEEF

Fresh-killed beef
1½ pounds fine salt

½ pound brown sugar
½ ounce saltpeter

Scrub a good oak barrel thoroughly. Put as much fresh-killed beef as desired to be corned in barrel and cover with cold water. Have the water 2 inches above meat. Let stand for 48 hours. Drain off the water and measure before discarding. Measure the same amount of cold water (spring water if possible) and to every gallon of water formerly used, add the above proportions of salt, sugar and saltpeter. Boil for 15 minutes and skim. When cold, pour over the beef. Place a heavy weight on meat to keep it under the brine. Store in cool cellar. The corned beef will be ready for use after 10 days.

BOILED CORNED BEEF

6 pounds corned beef   1 onion
1 carrot   Vinegar
                  Butter

Cover meat with cold water and let stand 1 hour. Drain and put into kettle with carrot and onion and enough cold water to cover. Add 1 teaspoon vinegar for each quart of water. Simmer until tender, 30 to 40 minutes for each pound. Let stand in the liquid 20 minutes, then drain and rub butter over the meat just before serving if desired. Serves 12.

BAKED CORN BEEF HASH

2 cups diced cold boiled   ⅜ cup cream
  potatoes   3 tablespoons butter
1½ cups chopped corned   Salt, pepper and paprika
  beef   6 eggs
1 small onion, minced

Combine potatoes, corned beef and onion. Add ¼ cup cream and 1 tablespoon melted butter. Season and mix well. Place mixture in buttered oblong baking dish. With the bottom of a custard cup, make 6 indentations in the hash and dot each with bits of butter, using 1 tablespoon in all. Bake in very hot oven (450°F.) 15 minutes. Remove from oven and into each indentation break one egg. Season and cover with 1 teaspoon of cream to each egg and dot with remaining butter. Bake in moderate oven (350° F.) until the eggs are set, 15 to 20 minutes. Serves 6.

RED FLANNEL HASH

9 cooked beets, chopped   ½ cup fat, melted
6 cooked potatoes, chopped   2 teaspoons salt
1½ cups chopped cooked   ⅛ teaspoon pepper
  corned beef   6 tablespoons water

Combine beets, potatoes, corned beef, fat, salt, pepper and water. Place in greased baking dish and bake in moderate oven (350° F.) about ¾ hour. Serves 6.

OLD-FASHIONED BOILED DINNER

6 pounds corned beef
  brisket
3 white turnips
1 cabbage

6 beets
6 onions
4 carrots
6 potatoes

Cover meat with cold water, heat rapidly to boiling, then remove scum, reduce heat and simmer until tender, 3 to 4 hours. Prepare vegetables, cutting turnips into quarters and cabbage into eighths. Cook beets in boiling water until tender. About 45 minutes before serving, skim fat from liquid. Add vegetables except beets and cook until vegetables are tender. Drain and add beets. Serves 10.

SCALLOPED CORNED BEEF

1 stalk celery, chopped
2 slices onion, chopped
1 cup Medium White Sauce

2 cups chopped cooked
  corned beef
Buttered bread crumbs

Cook chopped celery and onion in the sauce. Place corned beef in shallow baking dish and add the sauce. Sprinkle with buttered bread crumbs. Cook in moderate oven (350° F.) 20 to 25 minutes. Serves 5.

Variation—Heat corned beef mixture over direct heat instead of baking in oven. Serve on buttered toast. Omit bread crumbs.

BRAISED OXTAIL

1 oxtail (cut into 2-inch
  pieces)
2 tablespoons fat
2 small onions, sliced
1 carrot, chopped
1 tablespoon chopped celery

2 tablespoons flour
1 cup hot water
1 cup tomatoes
3 bay leaves
3 whole cloves
Salt and pepper

Brown pieces of oxtail in fat. Add onion, carrot and celery and cook until brown. Sprinkle with browned flour. Add hot water, tomatoes, bay leaves, cloves, salt and pepper. Place in casserole and cook in moderate oven (350° F.) until very tender. Serves 5 or 6.

Variation—Use beef stock instead of tomatoes and water, and omit cloves and garlic. Serve with noodles.

BEEF STEW WITH DUMPLINGS

1½ pounds shank, neck, plate, flank, rump or brisket
¼ cup flour
1½ teaspoons salt
¼ teaspoon pepper

1 small onion
⅓ cup cubed carrots
⅓ cup cubed turnips
4 cups potatoes, cut into quarters

Wipe meat, remove from bone, and cut into 1½-inch cubes. Mix flour with salt and pepper and dredge meat with it. Cut some of fat from meat and heat. When part of fat has fried out, brown meat in it, stirring constantly. Add enough boiling water to cover the meat or add a pint of tomatoes, stewed and strained and simmer until meat is tender, about 3 hours. Add onion, carrots and turnips during the last hour of cooking and the potatoes 20 minutes before serving. Add dumplings to stew, 15 minutes before serving. Cover kettle closely and do not remove cover for at least 12 minutes. Serves 6.

SAUERBRATEN

4 pounds beef (chuck, rump or round)
Salt and pepper
1 pint vinegar
4 bay leaves
12 peppercorns

4 cloves
1 bunch carrots, cut into strips
6 onions, sliced
1 tablespoon sugar
12 gingersnaps

Wipe meat with damp cloth and sprinkle thoroughly with salt and pepper. Place in an earthen dish and add vinegar and enough water to cover. Add bay leaves, peppercorns and cloves and let stand tightly covered in a cool place for 5 days. Drain meat, place in a Dutch oven and brown well on all sides. Add carrots, onions and 1 cup of spiced vinegar mixture. Cover tightly and cook over low heat about 3 hours or until meat is tender. When meat is cooked, add the sugar and crumbled gingersnaps and cook for 10 minutes. This makes delicious gravy. If necessary, more of the spiced vinegar may be added for cooking meat or making gravy. Serves 8.

VARIATION—Omit gingersnaps and thicken gravy with flour moistened with water.

HOT MARINADE—Combine salt, pepper, vinegar, peppercorns, cloves, 1 carrot, 1 onion and sugar. Add 2 cups water. Cook until vegetables are tender. Strain.

BRAISED SHORT RIBS

3 pounds short ribs of beef	Salt, pepper
Flour	1 cup water

Cut meat into serving portions. Dredge with flour and brown in a hot kettle or oven. Season with salt and pepper, add water, cover and cook in kettle at simmering temperature or in a slow oven (300° F.) until tender, 1½ to 2 hours. Allow ½ pound per serving.

VARIATIONS—Use Barbecue Sauce (page 159) for water.

2. Spread prepared mustard over ribs and use tomatoes or tomato juice in place of water.

3. Add sauerkraut during the last 45 minutes of cooking.

4. Add uncooked pared potatoes, carrots and onions to the ribs about 45 minutes before ribs are done.

BEEF GOULASH

8 onions	Vinegar
⅓ cup fat	Summer savory
3 pounds beef chuck	1 teaspoon salt
½ teaspoon paprika	

Cook onions slowly in fat. Cut beef into cubes or slices and sprinkle with vinegar and savory. Add salt, paprika and cooked onions. Cover tightly and simmer about 2 hours. The liquid may be increased just before serving by the addition of beef stock or cream, either sweet or sour. Serves 6.

SAVORY BEEF

3 large onions, sliced	¼ teaspoon black pepper
3 tablespoons fat	¼ teaspoon ground cloves and
2 pounds beef, shank, plate	thyme or summer savory
rump or round	1 pint brown stock or boiling
3 tablespoons flour	water and meat extract
1 teaspoon salt	2 tablespoons vinegar
1 tablespoon catchup	

Brown onions slowly in fat. Cut meat into serving pieces, add to onions and brown. Mix flour and dry seasonings. Sprinkle over meat. Add stock, vinegar and catchup. Cover closely. Simmer until meat is tender, allowing 2 hours for shank or plate and 1½ hours for rump or round. Serves 6.

POT ROAST OF BEEF

4 pounds chuck, round 　　　3 tablespoons fat
　　or rump of beef 　　　　Salt and pepper
¼ cup flour 　　　　　　　　½ cup water

Dredge meat with flour and brown on all sides in hot fat. Season with salt and pepper. Add water, cover and cook slowly until tender, 3 to 4 hours. As the liquid cooks away add more, as needed. Serve with gravy and vegetables. Serves 8.

VARIATIONS—1. Add uncooked pared potatoes, carrots, green beans, celery and onions just long enough before serving to cook them. They may be whole, quartered or sliced.

2. Use tomatoes or tomato juice in place of water.

3. After browning, pour ¼ cup horseradish over meat.

4. Before cooking, cut slits in the meat and insert stuffed olives, pushing them into the meat.

SMOTHERED BEEF

3 pounds rump 　　　　　　2 tablespoons mild pre-
Flour mixed with salt and 　　pared mustard
　　pepper 　　　　　　　　1 teaspoon celery seed
3 large onions, sliced 　　　1 cup strained tomatoes or
3 tablespoons fat 　　　　　½ can tomato soup

Dredge the meat with flour and brown it in a heavy pan. Brown the onions in the fat; add the mustard, celery seed and tomatoes. Pour over meat and simmer 3 hours. Serves 6.

SWISS STEAK

½ cup flour 　　　　　　　2 tablespoons fat
Salt and pepper 　　　　　Few slices onion
2 pounds steak cut 2½ 　　½ green pepper, chopped fine
　　inches thick from shoul- 　1 cup boiling water
　　der, rump or round 　　　1 cup strained tomatoes

Season flour with salt and pepper and pound it into the meat with a wooden potato masher or the edge of a heavy meat mallet. Brown the meat in fat. Add onions, green pepper, boiling water and tomatoes. Cover closely. Simmer for 2 hours. This may be cooked in casserole in moderate oven (350° F.) about 1 to 1½ hours. Vegetables may be added as desired. Serves 6.

BEEF LOAF

1½ pounds chopped beef
1 egg
1½ cups bread crumbs
2 tablespoons chopped parsley
½ teaspoon pepper

2 teaspoons salt
2 tablespoons chopped onions
2 tablespoons chopped celery
leaves
Dash thyme or savory

Mix meat thoroughly with egg, crumbs, chopped parsley and seasonings. Place in bread pan. Bake in hot oven (350° F.) about 1½ hours, basting frequently with stock or butter melted in hot water. Garnish with parsley or watercress and serve with Mushroom Sauce or Onion Sauce. Serves 6.

MEAT CROQUETTES

1 tablespoon fat
4 tablespoons flour
1 cup milk
2 cups finely ground
cooked meat
1 tablespoon chopped onion

½ teaspoon salt
⅛ teaspoon pepper
1 teaspoon minced parsley
Fine dry bread crumbs
1 egg

Melt fat, add flour and blend. Add milk and cook until very thick, stirring constantly. Add meat, onion, seasonings and parsley. Chill thoroughly. Form into cylinders, pyramids or patties. Dip into crumbs, then into slightly beaten egg mixed with 2 tablespoons water and into crumbs again. Chill. Fry in hot deep fat (380° F.) until brown. Serves 4.

BEEFSTEAK PIE

2 pounds rump, flank
or chuck steak
1 recipe plain pastry
½ cup chopped onion

Salt and pepper
2 cups sliced cooked potatoes
Butter or other fat
Flour, egg

Cut meat into 2x1 inch strips. Cover meat and bones with water and simmer about 1 hour. Line sides of baking dish with pastry; put in a layer of meat and onion and sprinkle with salt and pepper; add a layer of sliced potatoes and dot with butter. Alternate steak and potato layers until dish is full. Thicken gravy with browned flour and pour into dish; cover with a top crust, brush with beaten egg and bake in hot oven (400° F.) about 30 minutes. Serves 6.

ROAST BEEF WITH YORKSHIRE PUDDING

Wipe roast with damp cloth but do not wash. Rub with salt in proportion of 1 teaspoon per pound of meat. Rub with pepper, onion or garlic if desired. Place meat, fat side up, on rack of pan. If meat has little or no fat, place strips of bacon, salt pork or suet over it. This will baste the roast and no other basting is needed. Do not add water and do not cover pan. If meat thermometer is to be used, insert into center of thickest part of cut, being sure bulb of thermometer does not touch bone or fat. Roast at temperature given on page 126 for required length of time or until the thermometer registers the desired internal temperature. If a roast is not cut immediately upon removal from oven, it will continue to cook and the temperature at the center will continue to rise. This may continue 30 to 45 minutes. Allow about ½ pound per serving.

YORKSHIRE PUDDING

1 cup sifted flour   1 cup milk
½ teaspoon salt   2 eggs
          Drippings from roast beef

Mix flour and salt. Combine milk and eggs, add to flour and beat well with rotary egg beater until smooth. Pour hot drippings into hot shallow pan to depth of 1 inch. Pour in mixture quickly and bake in hot oven (400° F.) ½ hour. The pudding may then be placed under the rack holding the roast beef and left for 15 minutes to catch the juices from the roast. If a rack is not used, cut pudding into squares and arrange in pan around roast. Serve with the meat.

FILET MIGNON

3 pounds beef fillet   Butter or other fat
Salt pork   Salt and pepper
                Flour

The fillet is the under side of the loin of beef, the tenderloin. Remove skin, fat and ligament with a sharp knife. Lard the upper surface with strips of fat salt pork and rub the entire surface with soft butter or other fat. Dredge well with salt, pepper and flour, and place the fillet, without water, in a small pan. Bake in slow oven (300° F.), see page 126. Or cut tenderloin into steaks and broil. Serves 8.

START WITH YOUR THERMOM-
ETER AT THE HEART OF THE
ROAST AND YOU NEED NEVER
WORRY ABOUT THE PERFECT
FINISH

THE ROLLED ROAST A
THE PLANKED STEAK
EASY TO DO AND V
FESTIVE

BROILED STEAK

1 porterhouse or   Salt and pepper
  sirloin steak   2 tablespoons butter

Select a steak at least 1½ inches thick. Heat broiler for 10 minutes with regulator set at 550° F. Arrange steak on a rack. Place rack 4 inches under heat. For rare steak broil 7 to 8 minutes, season with salt and pepper, turn and broil on other side for same length of time. Remove to a hot platter. Place butter on top of steak, sprinkle with salt and pepper and serve at once. Allow ½ pound of meat per person.

Other steaks may be broiled in the same way. See page 126 for broiling time.

PAN BROILED STEAK

1 porterhouse or   Butter
  club steak   Salt and pepper

Heat a heavy skillet until sizzling hot. Place meat in hot pan and brown well on both sides. Reduce temperature and cook until the desired degree of doneness, turning from time to time, being careful not to pierce meat. Pour off fat as it accumulates in the pan. Place meat on a hot platter, spread with butter and season with salt and pepper. Allow ½ pound per person.

WITH MUSHROOMS

Use mushroom caps, whole or sliced. Sauté slowly in hot butter 5 to 10 minutes, stirring frequently. Allow 2 tablespoons butter for ½ pound mushrooms.

WITH ONIONS

Slice onions into water and drain. Place in shallow pan, cover closely, and cook over a slow heat 15 to 20 minutes, or until tender. Pan-broil the steak. Brown onions in pan in which the steak was cooked and serve with steak.

WITH OYSTERS

1 tablespoon flour   3 tablespoons butter
           1 quart oysters

Rub flour and fat together. Heat oysters to boiling in a little of their own liquid. Remove any foam and stir in flour mixture. Boil 1 minute, pour over steak and serve at once.

PLANKED STEAK

1 steak, 2 inches thick
Duchess potatoes
Cooked vegetables

Butter
Minced parsley
Salt

Paprika

Trim the fat and make outline of the steak even. Broil (see page 126). Oil a heated plank (see directions for planked fish), place steak on plank, and arrange border of Duchess potatoes around it. Arrange other cooked vegetables, such as stuffed tomatoes or green peppers, small boiled onions, peas, string beans and cubes of carrot or turnip, around the steak, also, so that the board is entirely concealed. Place the plank in the oven until the potato border is browned and all the vegetables are heated through. After removing it from the oven, spread steak with butter and sprinkle with minced parsley, salt and paprika. Serve on plank. Serves 4 to 6.

STUFFED STEAK

2 pounds flank or
   round steak
1 cup crumbs
½ cup stock or water
1 teaspoon salt

¼ teaspoon pepper
1 tablespoon chopped onion
¾ cup chopped celery
1 small turnip, diced
1 small carrot, diced

The meat should be cut from ½ to 1 inch thick. Wipe steak, remove skin and place meat flat on a board. Combine crumbs, stock or water, salt, pepper, chopped onion and ¼ cup celery. Spread on meat. Roll steak with the grain, so meat will slice across the grain when it is cut. Place remaining vegetables in roasting pan and place meat on top. Add 2 or 3 cups of water, depending upon size of pan. Cover and bake in moderate oven (350° F.) 3 hours, or until tender.

To cook on top of stove, melt ½ cup suet in flat-bottomed heavy kettle, flour roll thickly and place in kettle. Turn from side to side until it is well browned, then add hot water to nearly cover and simmer for 3 hours. When meat is cooked, remove from kettle and thicken broth, using 1 to 2 tablespoons flour to each cup of broth.

VARIATION—Omit stuffing suggested above. Stuff steak with Bread Stuffing No. 2, Sausage Stuffing, Potato Stuffing or Oyster Stuffing.

LIVER LOAF WITH PAN GRAVY

1½ pounds beef liver
1½ cups boiling water
2 slices salt pork,
    ¼ inch thick
1 medium-sized onion
¼ cup chopped parsley

2 cups soft bread crumbs
2 eggs, slightly beaten
1 teaspoon salt
¼ teaspoon pepper
1½ cups cold water
2 tablespoons flour

Wash liver quickly under running water, cover with boiling water and let stand 10 minutes; drain. Grind with salt pork and onion; add parsley, crumbs, eggs, salt and pepper; mix thoroughly. Press into (8x4x3 inch) baking pan and bake in moderate oven (350° F.) about 1 hour, or until browned. Remove loaf to hot platter. Stir flour into drippings and brown; add water gradually and cook five minutes, stirring until thickened; season and pour over loaf. Serves 6.

SAVORY LIVER

¼ cup chopped onion
2 tablespoons chopped parsley
2 tablespoons butter
2 tablespoons flour
¾ teaspoon salt

Dash pepper
3 tablespoons vinegar
2½ cups bouillon
1½ pounds beef liver,
    sliced thin

Brown onion and parsley in butter; stir in flour, seasonings and vinegar, and add bouillon gradually, stirring constantly. Cook until thickened. Place liver in gravy and cook, covered, 15 minutes, turning once. Serves 6.

LIVER PIQUANTE WITH VEGETABLES

2 pounds liver
Fat salt pork
½ pound lean salt pork
2 cups boiling water
1 cup sliced carrots

½ cup sliced onion
1 tablespoon chopped
    parsley
Bit of bay leaf
Small sprig of thyme

Buy liver in solid piece, wash thoroughly, dry and lard with strips of fat pork or bacon. Cut lean salt pork into pieces and try out slightly; add liver and brown on all sides. Add hot water, vegetables and seasonings, cover and bake in moderate oven (350° F.) until liver is tender, or about 1 hour for veal liver and 2 hours for beef liver. Serve on hot platter surrounded by vegetables. Serves 8.

LIVER CASSEROLE

1 pound calf's liver
¾ cup tomato sauce
Dash salt and pepper

1 teaspoon Worcestershire
sauce

Wash liver, cut into 1½-inch cubes and place in casserole. Add sauce and seasoning, cover and bake at 350° F. ½ hour. Just before serving, add Worcestershire sauce. Serves 4.

BRAISED LIVER WITH STUFFING

1 calf's liver (about 2 pounds)
Bread Stuffing No. 2
  (page 220)
Salt and pepper

Flour to dredge
3 strips salt pork
½ cup water

Wipe liver with a damp cloth and dry. Make an incision in the thickest part using a sharp knife. Fill with stuffing, sew edges together, season with salt and pepper and dredge with flour. Place in a baking pan and place strips of salt pork on top. Add water, cover pan and cook in a moderate oven (350° F.) until tender, 1½ to 2 hours. About 10 minutes before serving remove cover so that salt pork may brown. Thicken gravy in pan and serve with meat. Serves 8.

VARIATION—Bacon may be used in place of salt pork.

LIVER AND BACON

½ pound sliced bacon
1½ pounds calf's liver,
  cut ½ inch thick

Flour
1 teaspoon salt
⅛ teaspoon pepper

Place a single layer of bacon in a cool frying pan and place over low heat. Turn bacon frequently and drain off excess fat so that the bottom of the pan is well greased. Cook slowly until bacon is light golden brown and crisped. Drain on absorbent paper. Keep in a hot place. Wipe liver with a damp cloth and dry thoroughly. Roll in flour to which salt and pepper have been added. Sauté in drippings at reduced heat 5 to 8 minutes, until browned on both sides and center is just done. Overcooking ruins liver. Serves 4.

Serve liver with slices of broiled corned beef instead of bacon.

SWEETBREADS

PREPARING SWEETBREADS—Plunge sweetbreads into cold water and let stand 30 minutes. Parboil 20 minutes in acidulated, salted water (add 1 teaspoon salt and 1 tablespoon vinegar to 1 quart of water). Drain and plunge into cold water again. Remove any little strings and membranes.

BROILED—

2 pairs sweetbreads	Butter
Salt and pepper	Lemon juice

Prepare sweetbreads as above, cut into thin slices, sprinkle with salt and pepper, dot with butter and broil under moderate heat about 10 minutes. Serve with melted butter combined with a little lemon juice. Serves 4.

FRIED—

2 pairs sweetbreads	Bread or cracker crumbs
Salt and pepper	2 tablespoons flour
1 egg, beaten	1 cup milk

Prepare sweetbreads as directed above and cut into slices. Sprinkle with salt and pepper, dip into egg, then into crumbs and brown in hot fat. Place on platter. Add flour to 2 tablespoons of fat in which sweetbreads were fried, mix until smooth, add milk and season with salt and pepper. Serves 4.

CREAMED—

2 pairs sweetbreads	2 cups Medium White Sauce
1 teaspoon minced parsley	

Prepare sweetbreads as directed above, dice and heat in the white sauce, while stirring constantly. Add minced parsley. Serves 4.

LARDED—

2 pairs sweetbreads	2 cups seasoned stock
Salt pork for larding	6 slices toast

Prepare sweetbreads as directed above. Lard with salt pork, letting ends of strips curl over the edges of the sweetbreads. Place in roasting pan, pour stock over them, cover pan and cook in moderate oven (350° F.) 1 hour. Serve on toast. Thicken liquid in pan and serve with sweetbreads. Serves 4.

SWEETBREADS SUPREME

1 pound sweetbreads	¼ cup flour
1 quart fresh mushrooms, sliced	3 cups milk
	½ pound dried beef
¼ cup butter	Toast

Precook sweetbreads and dice. Add sliced mushrooms to butter, cover and cook slowly 5 minutes. Sprinkle flour over mushrooms, blend and add milk, dried beef and sweetbreads and cook slowly until thickened, stirring occasionally. Serve on toast. Serves 8 to 10.

MIXED GRILL

Mixed grills consist of two or more kinds of meat broiled with vegetables or fruits. Combinations should be planned so that they will broil in about the same length of time. The meat may be liver, steaks, chops, kidneys, bacon, ground meat patties, precooked sweetbreads or sausages. Halves of tomatoes, mushroom caps, halves of boiled sweetpotatoes or white potatoes are suitable. The fruits may be sliced apples, whole or halved bananas, canned peach or apricot halves or sliced pineapple. The food should be basted with melted butter or margarine while cooking to keep it moist.

STEWED CALF'S HEART

2 calves' hearts	2 tablespoons flour
1 bay leaf	2 tablespoons butter
Salt and pepper	½ lemon

Wash hearts carefully and remove veins, arteries and clotted blood. Cover hearts with boiling water and simmer 1½ hours. Remove all fat and set aside to cool. Cut hearts into small pieces, remove cords and artery cases and use only lean portions. Place chopped heart in saucepan, add water, bay leaf, salt and pepper and simmer for 10 minutes. Rub flour and butter together, add with sliced lemon, and cook 5 minutes stirring constantly. Serves 4.

WITH VEGETABLES—Dredge hearts with salt and pepper, brown in fat, then add water as above with ½ cup chopped celery, 2 tablespoons chopped onions, ¼ cup sliced carrots, 2 slices turnips, 1 bay leaf and ¼ teaspoon peppercorns. Cover and simmer 1½ hours or until tender.

STUFFED HEART

1 beef or 2 veal hearts	2 tablespoons flour
½ recipe Sausage Stuffing	2 tablespoons fat
1½ cups water	

Wash heart, trim and fill with stuffing. Tie firmly with string. Dredge with flour, brown in fat and season with salt and pepper. Add water, cover closely and simmer about 2 hours or until tender. Thicken liquid with additional flour. Serves 6.

1. BRAISED HEART—Reduce water to ½ cup. Prepare as above but cook, covered, in moderate oven (350° F.) instead of simmering. Allow 1½ to 2½ hours for lamb, pork or veal hearts, 2½ to 3½ hours for beef hearts.

2. Use bread Stuffing No. 2 with braised heart. Cook vegetables in pan with heart.

SWEET-SOUR HEARTS

2 veal hearts	6 tablespoons vinegar
2 tablespoons flour	2 teaspoons sugar
2 tablespoons fat	¼ teaspoon pepper
1 teaspoon salt	3 cups water
1 small onion, chopped	

Clean hearts, remove membrane and large veins, and cut hearts into ½-inch cubes. Brown flour in fat and add meat and remaining ingredients. Cover and simmer for 1½ hours or until tender. Serve with noodles. Serves 4.

STEAK AND KIDNEY PIE

1½ pounds steak (beef or veal	1 tablespoon chopped onion
½ pound kidney	1 tablespoon minced parsley
Salt and pepper	½ pound mushrooms, sliced
	Pastry

Cut steak and kidney into ½-inch cubes and dredge with flour. Season with salt and pepper. Arrange meat in greased casserole and add onion, parsley, mushrooms and sufficient water to cover meat. Cover casserole and cook in a moderate oven (350° F.) 1 hour or until meat is almost tender. Remove cover and replace it with pastry, pricking crust to allow steam to escape. Return to very hot oven (450° F.) and bake for 15 minutes or until crust is browned. Serves 4.

SAUTÉED KIDNEYS

Remove skin from kidneys. Cut into thin round slices, cover with cold salted water and let stand 30 minutes. Drain and dry. Sauté until tender in butter or other fat. Serve with Brown Sauce or Tomato Sauce.

If preferred, cut kidneys into halves after skinning, remove white tubes and fat and slice kidneys lengthwise.

SPANISH KIDNEY

1 beef kidney or 3 pairs lamb or pork kidneys	6 slices tomato Bacon

Cut beef kidney into 6 pieces or split open lamb or pork kidneys. Remove tubes and fat. Soak in cold water 30 minutes. Arrange tomato slices and a pieces of bacon on each kidney. Broil under moderate broiler heat, 10 to 15 minutes or until kidney is tender. Cover and simmer over direct heat 4 or 5 minutes. Serve with parsley butter. Serves 6.

SMOKED BEEF TONGUE

1 smoked beef tongue	1 cup Spanish Sauce
10 chopped cooked mushrooms	

Scrub tongue and let stand overnight in cold water. Cover with fresh cold water and simmer for 4 hours or until tender. Drain, place in cold water 2 or 3 minutes, remove skin and roots, and place in hot water for a few minutes. Drain. Place on serving dish. Add mushrooms to Spanish sauce and pour over tongue. Serves 6.

VIRGINIA BEEF TONGUE

1 fresh beef tongue	¼ cup butter
1 cup brown sugar	1 tablespoon whole cloves
1 cup stewed cranberries	½ lemon, sliced

Scrub tongue and simmer in water to cover until tender, 3 to 4 hours. Remove skin and trim root end. To 1 cup of liquid in which tongue was cooked, add remaining ingredients. Simmer tongue in mixture 15 minutes. Serves 6.

CALF'S BRAINS AND OYSTERS

1 set calf's brains	½ cup cream
1 dozen oysters	Salt and pepper
1 cup water	½ teaspoon soy sauce
1 tablespoon flour	1 teaspoon lemon juice

Place the brains in cold water for 30 minutes. Remove membrane and veins. Cook oysters in water 2 minutes. Remove oysters and cook brains in oyster broth 15 minutes. Place the brains on serving dish. Combine flour with cream, add to broth and heat until slightly thickened. Add salt, pepper, soy sauce, lemon juice and oysters. Pour over brains. Serves 4.

BRAISED BRAINS

1 set calf's brains	Flour or cracker crumbs
Salt and pepper	Fat

Soak brains in cold water for 30 minutes. Remove veins and membrane. Season, roll in flour or crumbs, brown in fat and cover skillet tightly. Cook slowly about 20 minutes. Serves 2.

VARIATION—Cook sweetbreads in the same manner.

TRIPE PATTIES

1 pound boiled tripe	½ teaspoon onion juice
1 egg	1 teaspoon salt
½ cup bread crumbs	Dash pepper

Grind tripe and combine with remaining ingredients. Shape into patties and fry in greased skillet until browned. Serves 4.

VARIATIONS—Make patties ½ inch thick and brown under low broiler heat.

BAKED TRIPE WITH BACON—Wrap each patty with slice of bacon and bake in hot oven (425° F.) 8 to 10 minutes, or until bacon is crisp.

TRIPE FRITTERS—Sift 1 cup sifted flour with ½ teaspoon salt. Combine 1 cup milk, 1 tablespoon melted shortening and 1 egg, slightly beaten. Add to flour and mix until smooth. Dip tripe patties into the batter and fry in hot deep fat (380° F.) until browned.

VEAL
Time and Temperature Charts
ROASTING

	Weight Pounds	Oven Temperature Constant	Interior Temperature When Done	Time Per Pound In Minutes
Leg roast	7-8	300° F.	170° F.	25
Loin	4½-5	300° F.	170° F.	30-35
Rack (4-6 ribs)	2½-3	300° F.	170° F.	30-35
Shoulder	7	300° F.	170° F.	25
Shoulder-Rolled	5	300° F.	170° F.	40-45

BRAISING

	Average Weight or Thickness	Cooking Time
Breast—Stuffed	3-4 pounds	1½-2 hours
Breast—Rolled	2-3 pounds	1½-2 hours
Birds	½x2x4 inches	45-60 minutes
Chops	½-¾ inch	45-60 minutes
Chops—Breaded	½-¾ inch	45-60 minutes
Steaks or Cutlets	½-¾ inch	45-60 minutes
Shoulder chops	½-¾ inch	45-60 minutes

STUFFED VEAL SHOULDER

5-pound veal shoulder   1 recipe Celery or Bread
Salt and pepper   Stuffing
Melted fat or salt pork

Have bones removed from veal shoulder, season cavity and fill with stuffing. Sew or skewer edges together and place on rack of roaster. Brush with fat or cover with strips of salt pork. Bake uncovered in moderate oven (325° F.) allowing 40 minutes to the pound, or until meat thermometer registers 175° F. Serves 10.

VEAL COLLOPS

2 pounds veal   1 cup cracker crumbs
1 egg   Salt and pepper

Cut the veal in pieces the size of an oyster, dip in beaten egg, roll in cracker crumbs and season with salt and pepper. Fry in deep fat (375° F.). Serves 6.

STUFFED BREAST OF VEAL

4 pounds breast of veal   ¼ teaspoon pepper
2 cups bread crumbs   ¼ cup minced onion
¼ cup salt pork drippings   ½ cup diced celery
1 teaspoon salt   ½ cup hot water

Have a pocket cut in veal breast. Make a stuffing by combining remaining ingredients and tossing together lightly. Pack stuffing into pocket and sew or skewer edges together. Brown the meat in hot fat, then add ⅔ cup water, cover and cook in a moderate oven (350° F.) 1½ to 2 hours or until tender.

VARIATIONS—Add ½ cup cooked pitted prunes, apricots or seedless raisins to the stuffing.

Stuff breast with cooked and seasoned rice or noodles.

VEAL BIRDS

2 pounds veal steak (cut   Salt
  ¼ inch thick)   Flour, fat
1 cup Bread Stuffing No. 2   1 cup milk or water

Cut veal into 2x4 inch pieces. Place a mound of stuffing on each piece, fold veal over stuffing and fasten with toothpick. Season, roll in flour, brown in fat and add milk. Cover and simmer or bake in moderate oven (350° F.) 1 hour. Serves 6.

VARIATIONS—1. Wrap veal around sausages, cooked whole carrots, pickles or olives instead of stuffing.

2. Pour mushroom soup over browned meat instead of milk.

VEAL OR BEEF FRICASSEE, JARDINIÈRE

2 pounds veal or beef rump   2 carrots, sliced
2 tablespoons flour   1 cup water or stock
Fat   ½ cup sliced celery
Salt and pepper   2 onions, sliced
1 teaspoon minced parsley   1 cup cooked peas or
2 bay leaves, minced   mushrooms

Cut veal into 1-inch cubes, dredge in flour and brown in fat; season and add parsley, bay leaves, carrots, water, celery and onions. Cover tightly and cook in moderate oven (350° F.) 45 to 60 minutes, or until meat is tender. Remove veal. Add peas and thicken liquid with flour mixed with a little cold water. Cook until thickened. Pour over veal. Serves 4 to 6.

CURRIED VEAL

2 tablespoons butter
2 tablespoons minced onion
¼ cup flour
1 tablespoon curry powder

2 cups stock
1 teaspoon salt
Dash cayenne
1½ pounds veal shoulder

Melt butter, add onion and cook 2 to 3 minutes without browning. Combine flour and curry powder, add to butter and mix until smooth. Add stock, salt and cayenne and cook until thickened. Cut veal into 1-inch cubes, add to sauce, cover closely and simmer 1½ hours or until meat is tender. Add more liquid if necessary. Serves 5.

ROAST VEAL

4 pounds veal
Salt and pepper

Flour
Fat salt pork or bacon

A roast may be cut from the leg, the rump or the shoulder. Wipe the meat, dredge with salt, pepper and flour and place on rack of roasting pan with fat side up. If meat thermometer is used insert it into center of thickest part of meat. If cut has no fat or if layer is thin, place strips of salt pork or bacon over top. Place in slow oven (300° F.) and cook, uncovered and without water, until tender. See page 146 for time allowances for various cuts. Allow about ⅓ pound per serving.

VARIATION—Have bone removed from roast cut from leg and fill roast with Bread or Sausage Stuffing. Use bone for making soup or stock.

BRAISED VEAL STEAK WITH MUSHROOMS

2 pounds veal steak
1 egg, slightly beaten
2 tablespoons milk

2 cups crushed cereal flakes
4 tablespoons fat
1 small can mushrooms

Have veal steak cut 1 inch thick. Cut into pieces for serving. Dip into mixture of egg and milk. Roll in finely crushed cereal flakes. Brown in hot fat and cover with mushrooms and mushroom liquid. Cover tightly and cook very slowly until tender, about 45 minutes. Thicken liquid for gravy and serve with veal steaks. Serves 6.

VEAL STEW WITH DUMPLINGS

⅛ pound salt pork
2 tablespoons flour
2 pounds veal breast
or shoulder

2 cups water
2 teaspoons salt
½ green pepper, chopped
1 cup peas

1 recipe Dumplings

Cut salt pork into cubes and fry until brown; add floured veal cut into pieces and brown well. Add 2 cups cold water, salt and green pepper and cover closely. Simmer 1½ hours. Add peas and drop in dumplings. Cover closely and steam 15 minutes. Do not remove cover until dumplings are done. Serves 5 to 6. For old-fashioned potpie, omit salt pork and use ¼ teaspoon ground pepper instead of green.

PAPRIKA CREAM SCHNITZEL

4 slices bacon cut fine
1½ pounds veal steak
2 tablespoons chopped
onion

1 teaspoon paprika
Salt
1 cup sour cream
½ cup tomato sauce

Fry bacon until crisp, add veal (cut into serving portions) and brown in hot bacon fat. Add onion and brown. Season with paprika and salt. Stir in sour cream and tomato sauce. Cover pan and cook about 30 minutes. Serve cutlets with the sauce and cover with boiled or fried noodles. Serves 6.

WIENER SCHNITZEL

6 veal chops or steaks
Salt and pepper
2 eggs, slightly beaten
Flour

3 tablespoons bacon drippings
Juice of 1 lemon
1 tablespoon flour
1 cup thick sour cream

Sprinkle veal with salt and pepper. Dip into eggs, then into flour. Brown on both sides in hot bacon drippings. Cover and cook slowly until chops are tender, about 1 hour. Sprinkle with lemon juice and arrange on hot platter. Blend flour with fat in pan, add sour cream and cook 3 minutes, stirring constantly. Season with salt and pepper and serve with chops. Garnish with lemon slices. Serves 6.

Melt currant jelly in liquid in which chops were cooked, instead of adding flour and cream.

LAMB

Very little mutton appears in the retail market for household use, since the majority of the sheep are sold for slaughtering while they are still young enough to be classified as lambs.

Time and Temperature Tables

ROASTING

	Weight Pounds	Oven Temperature Constant	Interior Temperature When Done	Time Per Pound In Minutes
Leg	6½-7½	300° F.	175-180° F.	30-35
Shoulder—Rolled .	3-4	300° F.	175-180° F.	40-45
Shoulder	4½-5½	300° F.	175-180° F.	30-35
Cushion	3-4	300° F.	175-180° F.	30-35
Rack of ribs (6-7 ribs)	2	300° F.	175-180° F.	45-50
Crown (12-15 ribs)	4	300° F.	175-180° F.	30-35

BROILING

			Cooking Time	
	Weight		Rare Minutes	Medium Minutes
Shoulder chops—1 inch	3	ounces	10	12
1½ inches	6	ounces	15	18
2 inches	10	ounces	18	22
Rib chops—1 inch	2	ounces	10	12
1½ inches	4	ounces	15	18
2 inches	5	ounces	18	22
Loin chops—1 inch	3	ounces	10	12
1½ inches	5	ounces	15	18
2 inches	6	ounces	18	22
Ground patties (1x3 inches) ..	4	ounces	15	18

BRAISING

	Average Weight or Thickness	Cooking Time
Breast—Stuffed	2-3 pounds	1½-2 hours
Breast—Rolled	1½-2 pounds	1½-2 hours
Neck slices	¾ inch	1 hour
Shanks	½ pound each	1-1½ hours

STUFFED LAMB BREAST

Lamb breast and foreshank
Salt and pepper
1 cup cooked rice or barley
1 tablespoon grated onion

Have foreshank removed from breast and the meat ground. Have bones of breast cracked so that the meat may be carved between the ribs. Make a pocket lengthwise in the breast by cutting the meat close to the ribs. Sprinkle pocket with salt and pepper. Combine ground meat from the foreshank with cooked rice or barley. Season with onion, salt and pepper. Fill pocket with stuffing and sew or skewer edges together. Sprinkle outside with salt and pepper. Place uncovered in pan and bake in a slow oven (300° F.) for 1 hour, then cover and continue cooking until tender, about 1 hour longer. Serves 6.

ROAST LEG OF LAMB

1 leg lamb (5 to 6 pounds)
1½ tablespoons salt
¼ teaspoon pepper

Have shank bone removed at the market, if desired. Do not remove the fell. Rub meat with salt and pepper. Place, fat side up, on rack in an uncovered roasting pan. Roast in a moderately slow oven (300°-325° F.) 30 to 35 minutes to the pound, or until a meat thermometer registers 175° to 180° F. Serve with sliced pineapple and garnish with sprigs of watercress.

1. Rub meat with the cut edge of a clove of garlic or place slivers of garlic into deep narrow gashes cut in meat, or insert clove of garlic into joint of leg and remove before serving.

2. Rub 1 teaspoon ginger over surface of meat.

3. Baste lamb with vinegar which has been seasoned with finely cut mint leaves.

4. Baste lamb with a mixture of ½ cup tomato catchup and 2 tablespoons Worcestershire sauce.

5. Rub meat with ½ cup finely chopped mint leaves. Baste meat frequently the last hour of roasting with ½ cup grape jelly melted in ½ cup hot water.

6. Rub 2 cups cooked apricots and juice through a sieve, add ¾ cup sugar and cook until thickened. Baste roast with this during last hour of roasting.

7. Cover meat with pineapple slices 1 hour before meat is done. Brush with butter so that pineapple will brown.

ROAST STUFFED SHOULDER OF LAMB

3-4 pound shoulder lamb 2 recipes Bread Stuffing
Salt and pepper No. 2 (page 220)

Have shoulder bone removed from shoulder and sew on 2 sides, leaving 1 side open for stuffing. Season with salt and pepper. Fill cavity in meat with stuffing and sew or skewer edges together. Place fat side up on rack in an open roasting pan and roast in slow oven (300° F.) until tender, allowing 35 to 40 minutes per pound. Serves 6.

VARIATIONS—1. Add ½ cup chopped mint to stuffing.

2. Add ½ cup finely chopped dried apricots to stuffing.

3. Omit milk in stuffing and add 1 cup tomato pulp.

4. Saute ½ pound sliced mushrooms in melted fat with onion and proceed with stuffing as directed.

5. Use Sausage Stuffing (page 222) in place of Bread Stuffing.

STUFFED PORK SHOULDER—Use boned pork shoulder. Prepare as above and roast in moderate oven (370° F.) 45 to 50 minutes per pound.

LAMB STEW

2 pounds lamb cubes, shank, 6 carrots
breast, neck or shoulder 3 onions
2 tablespoons flour 4 white turnips
2 tablespoons fat 1 cup fresh peas
Salt and pepper 3 tomatoes
Hot water Flour
6 potatoes

Dredge lamb with flour and brown well in hot fat. Season with salt and pepper, cover with water and simmer until nearly tender, 1 to 1½ hours. Add peeled vegetables, except tomatoes, whole or cut in cubes and simmer 30 minutes longer or until tender. Add tomatoes and simmer 10 minutes longer. Mix a little flour with water to a smooth paste and add enough to the liquid to thicken slightly. Serves 6.

SHEPHERD'S PIE—Use leftover stew. Line baking dish with hot mashed potatoes. Fill center with hot stew, cover with additional mashed potatoes and place in hot oven (425° F.) 15 minutes or until potatoes are browned.

THE CANDLE ROAST OF PORK IS AN INTERESTING VARIATION

WHEN THE BONE IS A NUISANCE, REMOVE IT AND STUFF THE HAM BEFORE BAKING

A CROWN ROAST OR LEG O'LAMB
HELPS CELEBRATE THE SPRING

ROAST CROWN OF LAMB

1 crown of lamb or mutton   1 recipe Mushroom
Salt and pepper   Stuffing   (page 222)
Sliced salt pork

A crown is usually prepared at the market and is made by shaping the ribs (12-15) into a crown and frenching or scraping the rib ends. Season with salt and pepper. Fill center of crown with stuffing. Wrap rib ends with salt pork or bacon slices. Place crown on a rack in an open roasting pan and roast in a slow oven (300°F.) allowing 30 to 35 minutes per pound. To serve, remove salt pork from rib ends and slip paper frills over them. Allow 2 ribs to each serving.

VARIATIONS—Do not stuff. Roast cown upside down without wrapping ribs. To serve, turn right side up and fill center with vegetables: mashed potatoes, potato balls, peas, diced carrots or cooked whole cauliflower.

BRAISED LEG OF LAMB OR MUTTON

½ cup each finely chopped   6 whole cloves
    celery, carrot and onion   1 clove garlic
2 tablespoons drippings or   2 tablespoons chopped
    other fat   parsley
3 cups vinegar   12 peppercorns
3 cups water   ½ bay leaf
1 leg lamb or mutton   1 tablespoon salt
½ teaspoon each of powdered 1 pint sour cream
    thyme and marjoran   ½ pint stock

Saute celery, carrot, and onion in drippings until light brown, add vinegar and water and cook until vegetables are tender. Cool. Place meat in deep dish, pour first mixture over meat, being careful to have meat entirely covered. Add seasonings. Marinate meat in this mixture for 24 hours. Drain and dry thoroughly. Place in roasting pan, bake in slow oven (300° F.) for 30 minutes. Add sour cream and stock, cover and cook until tender, allowing 30 to 35 minutes per pound. Baste frequently. Boil liquor in which meat was marinated until only a small amount remains, strain and pour over meat when serving.

BARBECUED LAMB

6-pound leg lamb
2 teaspoons salt
Flour
1 onion, sliced
1 cup water

½ cup catchup
2 tablespoons A-1 sauce
2 tablespoons Worcester-
shire sauce
¼ teaspoon cayenne

Wipe leg of lamb with damp cloth, rub with salt and dredge with flour. Place in a roasting pan and surround with onion. Combine remaining ingredients, mix well and pour over meat. Roast in a 350° F. oven 30 minutes for each pound. Baste every 20 minutes with the sauce. Serves 8.

LAMB CURRY PIE

2 pounds lamb shoulder
1 onion, diced
1 tablespoon fat
3 cups hot water
¼ teaspoon thyme

2½ teaspoons salt
2 tablespoons flour
1 teaspoon curry powder
¼ cup water
3 cups cooked rice

Cut lamb into 1-inch cubes. Brown lamb and onion in fat; add water, thyme and salt; simmer 1½ hours or until meat is tender. Combine flour and curry powder; add cold water and mix to a smooth paste; add to lamb. Line greased baking dish on sides and bottom with rice, pressing rice firmly into place. Fill center with lamb mixture and bake in moderate oven (350° F.) 20 minutes. Serves 6.

SPICY LAMB SHANKS

4 lamb shanks
Salt and pepper
Flour
1 cup water
1 cup cooked prunes, pitted
1 cup cooked dried apricots

½ cup sugar
½ teaspoon cinnamon
½ teaspoon allspice
¼ teaspoon cloves
3 tablespoons vinegar
¼ teaspoon salt

Season meat with salt and pepper, dredge with flour and place in greased baking dish. Cover and bake in moderate oven (350° F.) until meat is tender, 1¾ to 2 hours. Combine remaining ingredients, heat to boiling and simmer about 5 minutes. Drain most of fat from cooked shanks, add fruit mixture to meat, cover dish and bake at 400° F. 30 minutes. Serves 4.

PORK (Always cooked well done)
Time and Temperature Charts
ROASTING

FRESH	Weight Pounds	Oven Temperature Constant	Interior Temperature When Done	Time Per Pound In Minutes
Loin—Center	3-4	350° F.	185° F.	35-40
Whole	8-15	350° F.	185° F.	15-20
Ends	3-4	350° F.	185° F.	50-55
Shoulder—Whole .	12-14	350° F.	185° F.	30-35
Boned and rolled	4-6	350° F.	185° F.	40-45
Cushion	4-6	350° F.	185° F.	35-40
Spareribs	1½-1¾	350° F.	185° F.	40-45
Pork Butt	4-6	350° F.	185° F.	45-50
Ham	10-18	350° F.	185° F.	30-35
SMOKED				
Ham—Whole	10-12	300° F.	170° F.	25
Tenderized ..	10-12	300° F.	145-150° F.	15
Half	6	300° F.	170° F.	30
Tenderized ..	6	300° F.	145-150° F.	20
Shank end	3	300° F.	170° F.	40
Butt end	3	300° F.	170° F.	45
Cottage Butt	2-4	300° F.	170° F.	35
Picnic	3-10	300° F.	170° F.	35

BROILING

	Weight Pounds	Total Cooking Time
Ham slice—½ inch	¾-1	20
1 inch	1½-2	25-30
Ham slice—tenderized		
½ inch	¾-1	10-12
1 inch	1½-2	16-20

BRAISING

	Average Weight or Thickness	Cooking Time Minutes
Chops	¾-1½ inches	45-60
Spareribs	2-3 pounds	90
Tenderloin		
Whole	¾-1 pound	45-60
Fillets	½ inch	30
Shoulder steak	¾ inch	30-45

BRAISED PORK STEAK WITH GRAPE APPLES

2 pounds pork shoulder steaks
2 tablespoons flour
2 tablespoons fat
Salt and pepper
3 large apples
½ glass grape jelly
¾ cup boiling water

Dredge pork shoulder steaks in flour and brown in hot fat. Season with salt and pepper. Add ¼ cup water, cover tightly, and cook very slowly until tender, about 45 minutes. Pare apples, core and cut into halves. Dissolve grape jelly in boiling water, add apples and cook until tender. Serve around pork steaks. Serves 4.

BRAISED PORK CHOPS

Heat heavy frying pan until very hot. Add 1 tablespoon fat, or if the chops have a good covering of fat, place in the pan with fat edge down and cook out enough fat to grease frying pan. Brown chops on both sides. Do not add water. Reduce temperature, cover pan closely and cook slowly until chops are thoroughly done, about 45 minutes. Turn chops occasionally to cook uniformly.

STUFFED PORK CHOPS

6 double pork chops
2 cups bread crumbs
¾ teaspoon salt
¼ teaspoon pepper
1½ tablespoons minced parsley
1 teaspoon sage
1 tablespoon grated onion
3 tablespoons milk
Fat

Cut a pocket on the bone side of each chop. Combine next 7 ingredients and mix well. Stuff each chop with mixture. Brown chops in fat, season, add a little water and bake in moderate oven (350° F.) about 1 hour or until tender. Serves 6.

FRESH PORK WITH VEGETABLES

1 pound pork butt
4 large carrots
4 large parsnips
1 small red cabbage, quartered
1 teaspoon salt

Simmer pork 45 minutes. Add vegetables and salt and cook 45 minutes longer or until tender. Cut pork into thin slices and vegetables except cabbage into strips. Serves 3 or 4.

PORK CHOPS WITH BARBECUE SAUCE

6 pork chops   Flour   Barbecue sauce

Wipe the pork chops with a damp cloth and dust with flour. Sear on both sides until browned, then place 1 tablespoon sauce on each chop. Reduce heat, cover and cook slowly 5 to 8 minutes. Turn chops and place 1 tablespoon of sauce on other side. Cover and cook slowly until tender, about 40 minutes. Serve with sauce.

BARBECUE SAUCE

4 tablespoons minced onion
1 cup tomato purée
¾ cup water
3 tablespoons vinegar
2 tablespoons Worcester-
  shire sauce

1 teaspoon salt
1 teaspoon paprika
1 teaspoon chili powder
½ teaspoon pepper
¼ teaspoon cinnamon
Dash ground cloves

Combine all ingredients in order listed. Heat to boiling and use as directed above.

PORK PIE

2 pounds pork shoulder
2¼ cups boiling water
  or stock
1 teaspoon salt

1 bay leaf
2 cups cooked carrots
6 small cooked onions
1 recipe Plain Pastry

Cut pork into cubes, brown in fat and add water, salt and bay leaf. Cover and cook slowly until meat is tender, about 1 hour. Thicken gravy with flour mixed to a smooth paste with cold water. Add carrots and onions, pour into baking dish, cover with pastry and bake in very hot oven (450° F.) 20 minutes or until browned. Serves 6.

PORK TENDERLOIN

1 pound tenderloin
Flour

3 tablespoons bacon drippings
Salt and pepper

¾ cup sour cream

Cut tenderloin crosswise into 2-inch slices. Flatten out and dredge with flour. Place in hot skillet containing drippings. Brown on both sides; season with salt and pepper. Reduce heat, add cream, cover and simmer 30 minutes. Serves 6.

VARIATIONS—Place unflattened slices on a baking sheet. Spread with a thick layer of catchup and bake in a moderate oven (350° F.) until tender, about 45 minutes.

CROWN AND CANDLE ROAST OF PORK

Crown of pork   Pepper
1½ tablespoons salt   Cubes of salt pork

Have crown prepared at the market. Rub salt and pepper into meat. Cover tip of each bone with salt pork. Roast in a moderate oven (350° F.) allowing 30 minutes per pound. To serve, replace salt pork with paper frills. If desired, center of roast may be filled with stuffing and baked. See Roast Lamb (page 155). For candle roast, do not roll ribs but leave loin in one straight piece. Roast with fat side up.

ROAST SPARERIBS

2 pounds of spareribs   Salt and pepper

Place spareribs in a shallow baking dish and sprinkle with salt and pepper. Roast in a moderate oven (350° F.) allowing 40 to 45 minutes per pound. Allow 1 pound per serving.

Cover spareribs with greased paper and roast for ¾ hour, then roast, uncovered, for remaining time. Just before taking meat from oven, sprinkle with 1 cup bread crumbs seasoned with ¼ teapoon each of sage and minced onion. Baste with drippings in pan and return to oven 5 minutes longer.

STUFFED SPARERIBS—Use 2 matching sections of spareribs. Sew the edges together, except at 1 end. Fill with Bread stuffing, Celery Stuffing (page 221) or apple stuffing, and sew or skewer the edges together. Bake in slow oven (325° F.) for 1½ hours.

BARBECUED SPARERIBS—Brown spareribs under broiler. Pour Barbecue Sauce (page 260) over ribs, cover pan and bake.

WITH SAUERKRAUT—Brown spareribs. Place sauerkraut in a greased baking dish. Sprinkle with brown sugar. Add ½ cup water and arrange spareribs on top. Cover dish and cook in moderate oven (350° F.) for 1 hour.

BRAISED SPARERIBS—Place spareribs in a baking dish and brown in very hot oven (450° F.). Season with salt and pepper, add ½ cup water, cover pan and return to oven. Reduce temperature to slow (325° F.) and continue cooking until tender, about 50 minutes longer. If desired, place cored apples around the ribs. Fill centers of apples with brown sugar and nut meats or raisins.

BAKED HAM

1 smoked ham   Glaze
Whole cloves

Have ham warmed to room temperature and bake according to directions given by packer, or as follows: Wipe ham with clean cloth and place fat side up on rack of shallow pan. Do not cover pan or add water. For baking allow 15 minutes per pound for hams, 12 pounds or over; allow 18 minutes per pound for hams, under 12 pounds; allow 22 minutes per pound for half hams; or bake to an internal temperature of 150° F., being sure bulb of thermometer is inserted into center of thickest part of meat and does not touch bone. Bake in slow oven (300° F.) until within 45 minutes of total baking time. Remove rind from ham, make a series of shallow cuts across fat to cut into squares or diamonds, spread with desired glaze and insert 1 clove into each square of fat. Bake uncovered in 325° F. oven for remaining 45 minutes.

GLAZES—

One cup brown sugar, juice and grated rind of 1 orange.

One cup brown or white sugar and ½ cup maraschino cherry juice, cider or sweet pickle juice from pickled fruit.

One cup honey.

One cup brown sugar, 1 tablespoon mustard.

One cup puréed apricots, rhubarb or applesauce.

One glass currant jelly, melted.

Use maraschino cherries and mint cherries fastened with pieces of toothpicks instead of cloves.

Three-fourths cup pineapple juice, ¾ cup strained honey and ½ teaspoon mustard cooked until thick.

One-half cup maple sirup, ½ cup cider or apple juice and 2 tablespoons mustard.

One-half cup orange marmalade.

Cook ½ pound fresh cranberries with 1 cup maple sirup until skins pop open. Press mixture through sieve and spread over ham.

Instead of using cloves, make a flower on top of glaze, using pineapple rings and apricot halves.

BOILED HAM

Wash ham thoroughly, cover with boiling water and simmer, partially covered, for 25 to 30 minutes per pound or to an internal temperature of 160° F. If ham is to be served cold, let stand in water to cool, peel off rind and slice. If it is to be served hot, peel off rind and glaze as for Baked Ham. Whenever possible follow packers' cooking directions.

BROILED HAM

Remove rind from slice of smoked ham and slash edges of fat. Arrange on broiling rack and place 4 inches from heat in the broiler preheated to 550° F. Broil half required time *(see page 157)*. Turn meat and broil remaining time.

HAM BAKED IN MILK

1 teaspoon dry mustard   1 slice ham (2 inches thick)
4 tablespoons brown sugar   Milk

Mix mustard and brown sugar together and spread over ham. place in casserole, add enough milk to barely cover ham. Bake in slow oven (300° F.) 1 hour. Center slice of ham will serve 6.

FRIED HAM WITH CREAM GRAVY

1 pound ham in ½ inch slices   1 tablespoon flour
1 cup milk   Pepper

Place meat in hot pan and cook without additional fat, unless ham is very lean, in which case a spoonful of drippings should be used. When ham is brown, place on platter and add milk to fat in pan. Add 1 to 2 tablespoons flour mixed smoothly with a little milk and cook until thickened. Season and pour over ham. Serves 4.

SPICED HAM LOAF

1 cup bread or cereal   ½ pound ground fresh pork
  crumbs   1 tablespoon brown sugar
½ cup milk   ¼ teaspoon cloves
2 cups ground cured ham   1 egg

Soften crumbs in milk. Combine meat, seasonings, crumbs and egg. Mix and pack into loaf pan. Bake in moderate oven (350° F.) 50 minutes. Serves 6.

POULTRY AND GAME

POULTRY includes all the domesticated birds that are used for food—chicken, turkeys, squabs, geese, ducklings and guinea hen. Game includes wild birds (such as ducks, geese, pheasant, partridge, quail and grouse) and animals (such as deer, rabbit and squirrel) that are hunted and taken in field or forest and are suitable for food.

The flesh of game is less tender than other meat, especially when it is freshly killed. Properly stored, it "ripens," becomes more tender, and acquires the fine and distinctive flavor that makes it prized by connoisseurs.

Styles of Poultry

There are two principal styles of poultry available on the market today: Dressed and Ready-to-Cook. Dressed poultry refers to birds that have been bled and stripped but still have head, feet and viscera intact. This type of poultry requires a considerable amount of attention even after the meatman has drawn it. Ready-to-cook poultry is fully cleaned—inside and out—tagged, graded, and ready for cooking. It is marketed in three different ways: fresh, ice-chilled, and quick-frozen. Since 1953 only ready-to-cook poultry is permitted to carry United States Department of Agriculture grades on individual birds. Because of its high quality and convenience, ready-to-cook poultry, both fresh and quick frozen, has far outstripped dressed poultry in sales.

Quick-frozen poultry should be kept frozen until it is to be used and then thawed according to directings on the package or label. In whole birds, the separately wrapped giblets and neck are packed in the body cavity.

In many markets, chicken and turkey pieces and chicken giblets are sold separately, fresh or quick-frozen in packages. These separately available pieces—especially the breast, thighs, wings and drumsticks—greatly simplify the cooking and serving of poultry and facilitate meal-planning.

Selection of Poultry

The consumer's safest guide in the selection of dressed poultry is in the labeling information (government grading and brand names) attached to the bird on band, tag or label, or printed on the wrapper. When grading is not present, or in the absence of a brand name, certain general characteristics of poultry may be used as guides.

A broiling or frying chicken is relatively small, has smooth soft skin, a flexible breastbone and very little fat. Roasting chickens compare with broilers and fryers in appearance but they are somewhat larger and have slightly more fat. Stewing chickens are usually large and rounded, have firm flesh and thick skin. They are fully matured chickens, usually hens, and have a high fat content and a rigid breastbone.

Size in turkeys is not an indication of age or tenderness. Fully matured turkeys have coarse skin and are less tender than young birds. They are seldom found in consumer markets.

Age is not readily discernible in geese, and label or retailer information is the only completely reliable guide.

The consumer is always certain of obtaining a tender bird when buying duckling since growers market only the young birds.

Generally speaking, there is more meat in proportion to the amount of bone in chickens weighing five to six pounds than there is in smaller birds. Broilers usually weigh 1½ to 2 pounds; fryers up to 3 pounds.

Ready-to-cook poultry costs slightly more per pound than dressed style, but since the price applies only to the usable portions of a bird the difference in cost is more apparent than real.

To Clean Dressed Poultry

Cut off the head and remove the pin-feathers with a sharp pointed knife or a strawberry huller. Singe by holding the bird over a flame (candle flame may be used), turning quickly on all sides until all down and hair have been burnt off. Wash birds carefully, but do not soak in water. Soaking dissipates flavor.

Dressed poultry should always be drawn without delay. Whole birds may be refrigerated, loosely wrapped in paper, for two or three days.

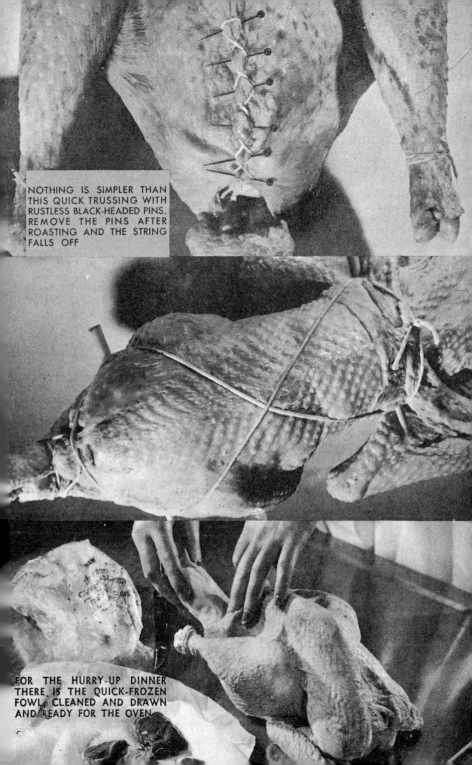

NOTHING IS SIMPLER THAN THIS QUICK TRUSSING WITH RUSTLESS BLACK-HEADED PINS. REMOVE THE PINS AFTER ROASTING AND THE STRING FALLS OFF

FOR THE HURRY-UP DINNER THERE IS THE QUICK-FROZEN FOWL, CLEANED AND DRAWN AND READY FOR THE OVEN

Full-O-Flavor Chicken Thigh

Parmesan Fried Chicken

Special Barbecued Chicken

To Prepare Poultry for Roasting

To Draw Poultry—If meatman has not drawn bird, make a lengthwise incision below breastbone. Cut out vent; remove entrails, gizzard, heart and liver. Last three are giblets. Care should be taken not to break the gall bladder attached to the liver. Cut away and discard quickly. Slit gizzard carefully just to the inside sac and remove the latter whole and discard. Remove the blood vessels from the heart.

Remove the lung tissue and discard. Slit the neck skin down the back; remove crop, windpipe and gullet from the neck opening. This leaves the skin over the breast unbroken. Cut off the neck close to body, but leave enough of the neck skin intact to fold down under the back while roasting. Save the neck for soup stock. Cut out the oil sac above the tail and discard.

Wash the bird inside and out in cold water; do not soak in water. Stand bird upright to drain thoroughly; pat dry. Rub body cavity with a mixture of salt and monosodium glutamate.

To Stuff and Truss Poultry—Lightly fill body and neck cavities with stuffing. To close body cavity, sew or skewer and lace with cord. Fasten neck skin to back with skewer. Tie the drumsticks of chicken and turkey to the tail of the bird. Bring wings onto back. Or tuck drumsticks under the band of skin which may be cut above the tail, and which is usually a feature of ready-to-cook poultry, both fresh and quick-frozen. If roasting a half or quarter turkey, tie the leg and tail together. The short legs of duckling make tying unnecessary. Before stuffing goose, remove any layers of fat from body cavity. Proceed as with other poultry. Loop cord around the legs and tighten only slightly.

When a roast-meat thermometer is used, place it in the center of the inside thigh muscle. When chicken or turkey is done the thermometer will register 190° F.

All poultry should be roasted in an open pan. Brush turkey and chicken with melted fat and cover them loosely with a cloth that has been dipped in fat. Keep the cloth moist during roasting by brushing occasionally with fat from the bottom of the pan. Roast goose and duckling breast side up. Chicken and turkey may be roasted breast side up or down, but must be turned before done for even browning. The roasting time for turkey may be appreciably shortened by wrapping the unstuffed bird in medium-weight aluminum foil and closing foil with a drugstore fold. A 10-pound, ready-to-cook turkey roasts in about three hours. Fold foil back from bird the last twenty minutes.

Chickens
ROAST CHICKEN

Clean and singe or thaw chicken; rinse and pat dry. Rub inside with salt. Stuff lightly. Place chicken on rack in shallow, open roasting pan, breast side up or down. Cover with thin cloth dipped in melted fat. Roast in moderate oven (325° F.) until tender. If cloth dries during roasting period, moisten again with fat from pan. Chickens weighing 4¾ to 6 pounds roast in 3½ to 4 hours; those weighing 2½ to 3½ pounds in 2 to 3 hours; small chickens (1½ to 2½ pounds) require 1¼ to 2 hours. Deduct 5 minutes per pound for unstuffed chickens.

ROAST HALF-CHICKEN—Arrange stuffing in outline of chicken in bottom of greased shallow pan. Press chicken, cut side down, on stuffing. Brush with melted fat. Roast uncovered at 325° F. 40 to 45 minutes per pound.

BROILED CHICKEN

Cut small chicken into halves and remove breastbone, neck and backbone. Secure wing under shoulder. Brush both sides with melted fat, place in pan, skin side down, and season. Set pan in broiler with top of chicken 7 to 9 inches from heat. Broil slowly 45 to 60 minutes, or until chicken is tender and browned on both sides. Turn every 15 minutes.

PANNED CHICKEN

Prepare the chicken as for broiling. Place in a pan, cover with bits of fat and roast uncovered in a moderate oven (350° F.), allowing 15 to 20 minutes per pound. Baste with drippings every half hour. When nearly done, remove from the oven, season with salt and pepper, cover with additional fat, dredge with flour and return to oven to brown slightly on both sides.

When done, place on platter, skin side uppermost. Make gravy by pouring 1 cup of hot milk into roasting pan and adding cracker or bread crumbs. Season with salt and pepper; add onion juice, if desired. Boil 1 minute and pour over chicken. Serves 3 to 5.

FRIED CHICKEN

No. 1—SOUTHERN STYLE

2 broilers   Flour
Salt and pepper   ¼ cup fat

Cut each chicken into four or six pieces, dip each piece quickly into cold water, drain, season with salt and pepper, and roll in flour to make a thick coating. Sauté the chicken in a little fat until each piece is tender and brown on both sides. Drain the pieces well and arrange on a warm platter, setting dish in a hot place to keep the meat from cooling while the gravy is being made. Serves 4.

No. 2—FRENCH FRIED

Cut the chickens into pieces and dip each piece into a fritter batter made of 1 cup milk, 1 cup flour, 1 tablespoon melted fat and 1 slightly beaten egg. Fry in deep fat (375°-390° F.) until brown. Transfer to a casserole or baking dish and bake in a moderate oven (350° F.) for 30 to 40 minutes.

For an interesting variation, roll the pieces of chicken in whole cereal flakes instead of flour before frying.

SMOTHERED CHICKEN

1 5-pound chicken   2 or more tablespoons fat
Salt and pepper   Flour

Remove neck and split chicken down the back. Season inside and out with salt and pepper and dredge thoroughly with flour. Lay the chicken, inside down, in a small roasting pan and add a small amount of water. The pan should be only slightly larger than the chicken so the gravy will not be too quickly evaporated. Cover and roast in a moderate oven (325°-350° F.) 2½ to 3 hours. If roasted without a cover, baste every 10 minutes after the first 20 minutes.

Add more fat, if necessary. When done, place the chicken on a hot platter, add 2 tablespoons of flour to the pan, stir until smooth, then add enough water to make 2 cups of gravy. Should chicken be too fat, remove all but 2 tablespoons of fat from pan before making the gravy. Season gravy with salt and pepper, pour over the chicken and serve at once. Serves 8.

FULL-O-FLAVOR CHICKEN THIGHS

Thaw as directed on package 1 pound frozen chicken thighs. Roll in ½ cup flour; brown in 2 tablespoons butter or margarine in hot skillet. Remove chicken to a greased casserole. Heat 1 tablespoon butter in skillet; blend in 1½ tablespoons flour. Add gradually 1¼ cups milk, 1 teaspoon salt, ⅛ teaspoon paprika, ½ teaspoon thyme, ½ teaspoon marjoram. Cook until slightly thickened; pour over chicken. Bake uncovered at 325° F. 50 minutes.

PARMESAN FRIED CHICKEN

½ cup flour
1 teaspoon salt
⅛ teaspoon pepper
1 egg, beaten slightly
2 tablespoons grated Parmesan cheese
½ cup fine dry bread crumbs
1 pound package quick-frozen chicken breasts, drumsticks or thighs

Thaw chicken according to package directions. Coat with flour seasoned with salt and pepper. Dip floured chicken in beaten egg; roll in combined cheese and bread crumbs. Heat fat (half hydrogenated vegetable shortening and half butter or margarine) to ½-inch depth in skillet until hot. Fry chicken, turning to brown evenly. Use tongs or pair of spoons to turn chicken. After browning, lower heat; continue to cook, covered, for 45 minutes or until chicken is tender.

SPECIAL BARBECUED CHICKEN

½ cup butter or margarine, melted
1½ teaspoons salt
1 large clove garlic, minced
2 tablespoons lemon juice
½ cup ketchup
⅓ cup diced onion
1 tablespoon Worcestershire
4 drops tabasco

Quick-frozen split broilers or cut-up fryers

Prepare barbecue sauce by melting butter or margarine and mixing with other ingredients. Store covered in refrigerator. Thaw chicken according to package directions. Place chicken on grill and set grill no higher than 2 to 3 inches above bed of glowing coals. Brush chicken with barbecue sauce. Turn chicken every 5 minutes with long-handled fork or tongs (avoid piercing meat) and brush with barbecue sauce. Watch closely. Reserve some of sauce for sprinkling over chicken before serving. Grill chicken 45 minutes to 1 hour, or until knife cuts easily into thickest part of drumstick and no pink color shows at bone.

FRICASSEE OF CHICKEN

WHITE

1 3-pound chicken
2 tablespoons fat
Salt and pepper
1 tablespoon dry herbs
3 slices salt pork

2 cups chicken stock
2 tablespoons flour
1 cup milk or cream
1 egg yolk
Cooked rice or dumplings

Singe, clean and cut up chicken. Brown in pan with fat. Cover with boiling water, add salt, pepper, herbs and salt pork. Simmer 1 hour, or until tender, strain and thicken 2 cups of liquid with flour mixed to a smooth paste with a little cold water; add milk or cream beaten with yolk of egg. Heat again until slightly thickened, pour over chicken and serve with rice or dumplings, page 236. Serves 4.

BROWN

1 3-pound chicken
2 or 3 small slices salt pork
2 tablespoons flour

2 cups boiling water
1 teaspoon onion juice, if desired

Salt and pepper

Cut into pieces as for white fricassee. Place salt pork in a frying pan; when hot, brown chicken, turning frequently. Add flour to fat, stir well and cook 2 minutes. Add boiling water. When gravy is smooth and boiling replace chicken, season with salt and pepper, cover and simmer gently until chicken is tender. Add a teaspoon of onion juice, if desired, and serve at once. Serves 4. Fat from any smoked meat may be used instead of salt pork. If desired, top with biscuits cut into 1-inch squares, strips or diamonds. Bake at 450° F. for 12 minutes.

BROWN WITH MUSHROOM SAUCE

Cut the chicken into serving portions. Add cold water, 1 slice onion, 2 slices carrot, 1 stalk celery, salt and pepper. Bring to a boil and simmer until tender, about 2 or 3 hours. Drain off chicken stock. Roll pieces of chicken in flour seasoned with salt and pepper. Sauté in butter until brown. Arrange chicken for serving and cover with hot Mushroom Sauce, page 297. Serves 4.

Capons

Capons are large, plump, tender young castrated roosters weighing 6-7 pounds and especially fattened for the table. They are prepared for cooking in the same way as chickens. For stuffing, choose a mild dressing such as oyster, chestnut, mushroom, celery or nut, as the meat is very delicately flavored.

Turkeys
ROAST TURKEY

Dress as directed for roast chicken, stuff and truss. Place the turkey breast up, on rack of a shallow pan. Brush with melted unsalted fat and cover with a cloth dipped into melted unsalted fat, being sure breast, wings and legs are well covered. Roast uncovered in a slow oven (325° F.) until tender. Allow 25 minutes per pound for birds under 12 pounds, or 20 minutes per pound for larger birds. Baste several times with melted fat, fruit juice, white wine, sugar in water, or drippings in pan. Season when half done. The cloth may be removed during last half-hour for additional browning. Serve with Giblet Gravy page 295. Allow ¾ to 1 pound per serving.

BRAISED TURKEY

1 8-pound turkey	½ cup chopped carrots
Stuffing	½ cup onion
½ pound salt pork	½ cup turnip
½ cup chopped celery	Salt and pepper
4 cups water or stock	

Stuff the body and breast of the turkey with a desired dressing and truss. Spread thin slices of salt pork over breast and legs and cover turkey with a sheet of heavy oiled paper, fastening paper on by passing string around body. In a large double roasting pan, spread sliced salt pork and chopped vegetables. Lay the turkey in the pan, breast up, sprinkle with salt and pepper, cover pan tightly and roast in a moderate oven (350° F.) allowing 25 minutes per pound.

At the end of 30 minutes, add water or stock. Uncover pan for last half hour and remove paper and pork from the turkey.

At the end of 30 minutes, add water or stock. Uncover pan for last half hour and remove paper and pork from the turkey. This permits the meat to brown lightly. Serve with gravy for 10.

TURKEY CURRY

1 cup mushrooms	½ teaspoon salt
⅓ cup minced onion	3 tablespoons flour
1 large apple, peeled and diced	1 to 1½ teaspoons curry
3 cups cooked turkey, cut in	powder
pieces	1½ cups turkey stock and
6 tablespoons fat	top milk or cream

Sauté mushrooms, onion, apple and turkey fat until the onion and apple are tender, 10 to 15 minutes. If fresh mushrooms are used, sauté several minutes before adding other ingredients. Remove from heat, add salt, flour and curry powder, and stir thoroughly. Add liquid and cook until thickened. Set over hot water, cover and cook 15 minutes longer to blend the flavors. Add more seasoning, if desired. Serve with hot boiled rice cooked with little or no salt.

Goose
ROAST GOOSE

1 8-pound goose	Salt and pepper
Potato Stuffing, page 221	Flour

Select a young goose, clean, singe, wash and pat dry. Fill body cavity lightly with Potato Stuffing, skewer the opening or truss. Roast in a slow oven (325° F.) for 45 minutes, on rack in uncovered roasting pan. Remove from oven, pour off fat, season with salt and pepper, dredge with flour and return to oven.

When the flour is browned, pour 1 cup hot water into pan and baste goose often, dredging each time with a slight sifting of flour to absorb fat. Allow 20 minutes per pound for a young goose, and 25 minutes for older goose. Remove from pan, add 1 cup hot water to gravy and thicken, if necessary, with browned flour. Garnish goose with parsley and serve with Giblet Gravy. Serves 5. Serve with applesauce, hot or cold spiced fruit, cranberry-orange relish, or coddled minted apples.

SALMIS OF GOOSE—Use leftover roast goose. To 4 cups sliced goose, add 2 tablespoons each of lemon juice and Worcestershire sauce, and 2 cups goose gravy; simmer 20 minutes. Add ½ cup sherry and 12 ripe, sliced olives, and reheat. Garnish with parsley and serve on hot buttered toast.

ROAST GOOSE WITH BAKED APPLE

1 8-pound goose
2 quarts bread crumbs
2 onions, chopped
2 tablespoons fat
1 teaspoon sage
2 teaspoons salt, dash pepper
6 to 8 apples
¼ cup brown sugar
3 cooked, mashed sweet-potatoes

Cook giblets until tender, chop and mix with bread crumbs, onion, fat, sage, salt and pepper. Clean and wash the goose thoroughly. Rub inside of goose with salt, stuff with bread mixture and truss. Place in a roaster on rack and roast uncovered in a slow oven (325° F.) until tender allowing about 25 minutes per pound. Every hour, skim off fat from broth in pan. Wash and core apples; sprinkle with brown sugar, stuff with seasoned sweetpotatoes and place in the pan with goose 1 hour before goose is done. Serves 6.

ROAST GOOSE STUFFED WITH SAUERKRAUT—Stuff goose with 2 quarts of drained sauerkraut instead of bread stuffing. Add 1 peeled whole apple to sauerkraut.

ROAST GOOSE AND CABBAGE—Clean and prepare goose for roasting. Cut into serving pieces, place in a roasting pan and roast in a slow oven (325° F.) until almost tender, about 2½ hours. Pour off most of the fat into large saucepan; sauté 3 sliced onions in fat and when brown, add 1 head of red cabbage, chopped. Cook for several minutes; season. Place pieces of goose on top of cabbage. Sprinkle with salt and pepper. Cover tightly and simmer for 1 hour or until goose is tender and cabbage cooked. Serves 6.

DEVILED GOOSE

1 8-pound goose
Potato Stuffing, page 221
¼ cup vinegar
1 teaspoon pepper
2 tablespoons prepared mustard
1 teaspoon salt

Singe and clean goose. Cover with boiling water and simmer for 1 hour. Remove, drain and dry. Fill body and neck lightly with Potato Stuffing, skewer or truss. Roast in moderately hot oven (350°-400° F.), allowing 15 to 20 minutes per pound. Mix vinegar, pepper, salt and mustard and use to baste goose. Serve with Giblet Gravy.

An old, less-tender goose may be prepared this way, allowing 2 hours for simmering instead of 1. Serves 6.

Ducks
ROAST DUCK

Epicures prefer young ducks rare, and without stuffing. Some people consider that ducks have too strong a flavor, and to absorb this flavor lay cored and quartered apples inside the body. These apples are removed before the duck is sent to the table. Celery and onions also may be placed inside the duck to season it and improve the flavor, two tablespoons of chopped onion being used to every cup of chopped celery, which may consist of the green stalks that are not desired for the table. This stuffing is also removed from the bird before it is sent to the table. Most people prefer ducks that are stuffed for roasting.

Wash, singe, and clean a 5-pound duck; season with salt and pepper, rub with garlic and fill with apples mixed with raisins. Place in pan and roast uncovered in a slow oven (325° F.), allowing 20 to 30 minutes per pound. Baste every 10 minutes using 1 cup of orange juice, if the flavor is desired. Serve with currant or cranberry jelly. Green peas are usually served with roast duck. Serves 5.

Duck may be stuffed with Potato Stuffing, if desired, filling it while very hot.

BRAISED DUCK

1 4-pound duck	Salt and pepper
4 slices bacon	4 cups boiling water
1 onion, minced	1 small turnip, diced
1 carrot, diced	2 tablespoons melted fat
½ teaspoon powdered thyme	4 tablespoons flour
2 tablespoons minced parsley	¼ cup cold water

Prepare duck as for roasting and sauté in bacon fat until brown. Add onion, carrot, thyme, parsley, salt and pepper and cover with water. Simmer until the duck is tender, then remove from stock. Sauté turnip in fat until brown, then drain and cook in stock until tender. Strain stock. Blend flour and cold water together until smooth and add gradually to stock, stirring constantly. Pour gravy over the duck. Garnish with pieces of turnip. Serves 4.

BRAISED DUCK WITH MUSHROOMS—Omit bacon and carrot. Use ½ pound of mushrooms, sliced, and sauté in fat in place of turnips.

DUCK A LA CREOLE

2 tablespoons fat	½ cup chopped celery
1 tablespoon flour	1 tablespoon chopped parsley
2 tablespoons chopped ham	1½ cups consommé
Salt, pepper, and paprika	1 whole clove
2 tablespoons minced onion	¼ teaspoon mace
2 tablespoons chopped sweet pepper	2 cups diced cooked duck

Melt fat, add flour and stir in ham. Season with paprika, salt, pepper, onion, sweet pepper, celery and parsley. Stir for 2 minutes, add the consommé, clove and mace. Simmer 1 hour. Strain the broth and stir in diced, cooked duck. Heat thoroughly and serve with fried hominy or mush. Serves 2.

Wild Ducks

Nearly all Spring wild ducks are likely to have a fishy flavor, and when dressed by an inexperienced cook are often unfit to eat. This flavor may be much reduced by placing in each duck a small peeled carrot, plunging the fowls into boiling water and simmering them for ten minutes before roasting. The carrot will absorb some of the unpleasant taste. An onion will have somewhat the same effect, but unless a stuffing with onions is used, the carrot is to be preferred. When there is an objection to par-boiling (as when the ducks are young) rub them lightly with an onion cut in two and put three or four uncooked cranberries in each before cooking.

To pluck wild duck, remove large feathers dry. Melt ⅜ pound of paraffin in 7 quarts of boiling water. Dip the duck into the mixture several times and let the paraffin harden. Strip off the paraffin and feathers at the same time. Singe and remove any remaining pin feathers.

CANVASBACK DUCK, DELMONICO STYLE

This bird is in season from the last of November until March. As it feeds mainly on wild celery, it requires no spices in cooking. Dress in the usual way and wipe with a wet towel. Truss the neck under the wing, place in a dripping pan and roast in a moderate oven (350° F.), allowing 20 to 25 minutes per pound. Baste frequently. Season with salt and pepper and serve with gravy remaining in pan. Allow 1 pound per person.

ROAST WILD DUCKS

Clean, wiping inside and outside with a damp towel. Tuck back the wings and truss. Dust with salt, pepper and flour. If not fat, cover breast with 2 thin slices of salt pork. Place duck in a pan and add 1 cup of water and 2 tablespoons of fat. Roast uncovered and breast down in a moderate oven (350° F.), allowing 20 to 25 minutes per pound, according to rareness desired. Baste frequently. Turn breast up when half done. Serve with slices of lemon or orange and a brown gravy or with Olive Sauce, p. 298. Wild ducks are served rare and are seldom stuffed when roasted. Allow 1 pound per person.

MALLARD WILD DUCK

These ducks, in season during the Fall and Winter, are very dry when roasted, since they feed on grain. Braising is the best method of preparing them. Dress birds and stuff with a bread dressing. Truss and place in a covered roaster. Add water to the depth of 1 inch, a slice of onion and a small amount of thyme. Cover the roaster and cook in a slow oven, (325° F.) about 1 hour. Remove cover so the bird will brown and cook another 30 minutes. Use only enough water to prevent burning. Add water to pan and make a gravy to pour over ducks. Allow 1 pound per person.

Guinea Fowls
ROAST GUINEA FOWLS

1 guinea fowl	2 strips fat bacon
Salt	Stuffing, if desired

Clean and draw fowl. Rub inside with salt. Fowl may be roasted with or without stuffing. Cover breast with fat bacon which may be removed 5 minutes before serving. Roast, uncovered, in a slow oven (300°-325° F.) until tender, allowing 18 to 20 minutes per pound. Baste frequently. Season with additional salt when half done. Serve with currant jelly and Giblet Sauce. Serves 2 or 3.

FRICASSEE OF GUINEA FOWL

1 guinea fowl	2 tablespoons flour
4 slices bacon	Salt and pepper

Clean fowl and cut into serving pieces. Fry bacon to extract fat and sauté pieces of fowl in fat until brown. Add the flour, stir until thoroughly mixed; add 2 cups hot water, salt and pepper, and stir until gravy boils. Cover and simmer until tender, about 1½ hours. Serve with gravy for 2 or 3.

Peafowl

These fowls are cooked in the same way as wild turkeys. They should be larded with shreds of bacon, trussed and roasted about 30 minutes per pound at 325°-350° F. They are apt to be tough.

Pheasant, Partridges, Quail and Grouse

Game should not hang too long after being killed. In cold weather, birds may hang 10 days without becoming tainted, but during the warm season, they should be refrigerated at once. Hang in cool, dry room where air circulates freely. If birds are to be kept for several days, draw, but do not pick. Game is considered "high" when tail feathers are easily plucked. Game that is just slightly under the "high" stage has the best flavor. The inside of the bird is more susceptible to mold growth than the outside, because there is little fat covering. Placing a piece of charcoal in the body and sifting powdered charcoal into the feathers will delay tainting. Partridge taints first in crop, other birds around vent. At the first signs of tainting, dry-pick and cook bird.

A distinction must be made between white meat and dark meat in cooking game. Quail and partridges are white meat and, like chicken, must be thoroughly cooked, but not dry. Ducks, pigeons or squabs, grouse (prairie chicken), snipe and woodcock are dark meat and are cooked rare and served very hot.

All these birds are cooked by the same methods, varying only as to the degree of rareness desired. Pick out shot from birds with a sharp pointed knife. Wash quickly under running water. Small birds may be skinned when they are clean. The woodcock may or may not be drawn, as desired, the entrails being considered edible by some.

BROILED BIRDS

Clean the birds and split down the back. Season with salt and pepper and dust with flour to keep in juices. Broil in a wire broiler, placing inside of the bird near the fire first. Brown on both sides, allowing 8 to 12 minutes for quail, 25 to 40 minutes for partridges and pheasants. A strip of bacon, smoked ham butt, or salt pork may be placed over the top of each bird. When done, brush with melted butter. During broiling, if the breasts are quite thick, cover broiler with a pan and lengthen the cooking time, using lower temperature. Serve on toast with currant jelly.

PLANKED BIRDS—Prepare as for Broiled Birds; place on greased hot plank and brush with melted butter. Arrange a border around edge of plank of fluffy mashed potatoes, brushed with beaten egg. Bake in hot oven (450° F.) 10 minutes, or until potatoes are browned. Garnish with parsley and buttered green peas.

PANNED BIRDS

Clean and draw birds and split down back. Dip quickly into hot water and season with salt, pepper and dredge with flour. Water causes the seasoning to adhere more thickly to the meat. Place the birds in a small baking dish inside up; place a teaspoon of fat in each bird, add 1 cup of water, and roast in a moderate oven (350° F.), allowing 15 to 20 minutes for quail, and proportionately longer for larger birds. Baste every 5 minutes after the first 15. Thicken gravy, add more salt and pepper, if necessary, and pour over the birds. Allow ½ to 1 bird per person.

WITH MUSHROOMS—Add 1 cup chopped cooked mushrooms to gravy.

ROASTED BIRDS

Clean, stuff and truss the birds. Brush with unsalted melted fat. If the birds are dry, lard by laying strips of salt pork across breasts. Roast uncovered in a moderate oven (350° F.) until meat is tender and bird is well browned. Baste every half hour with fat and water. Season bird with salt when about half done. Place on a warmed platter and cover with gravy made from pan drippings. Garnish platter with parsley and serve with Bread Sauce, p. 295. Allow ½ to 1 bird per person.

LARDED GROUSE

Grouse are rather dry birds and need to be larded to be palatable. Clean and wash quickly under running water. Cover bird entirely with thin slices of bacon, tying them in place with crossing of soft string. Place in a roasting pan and pour over enough boiling water to use for basting the birds. Roast in a moderate oven (350° F.) bout 45 minutes. Baste frequently. When done, remove bacon strips, brush birds with oil and melted fat, dredge with flour and place in oven again until brown. The liquid in the pan may be thickened, seasoned, and used as gravy. Arrange the birds on a platter and garnish with rings of sautéed green pepper, and strips of bacon. Allow 1 grouse per person.

ROAST QUAIL

6 quail	Salt and pepper
6 large oysters	Flour
Strips of bacon	Butter or other fat

Dress, clean and stuff each bird with one large oyster. Truss, season and dredge with flour. Lard breast and legs with strips of bacon. Bake as directed for larded grouse, allowing 15 to 20 minutes for cooking. Serves 6. Serve with hot spiced crabapples.

GAME PIE

6 birds	2 whole cloves
4 cups water	¼ pound diced salt pork
Salt and pepper	2 tablespoons, flour, browned
¼ cup minced parsley	2 tablespoons fat
½ chopped onion	1 recipe Plain Pastry, p. 387

2 cups diced cooked potatoes

Clean the birds thoroughly and split into halves. Cover with water and heat to boiling. Skim top and add salt, pepper, parsley, onion, cloves and salt pork. Simmer until tender, keeping birds covered with water. When done, thicken the liquid with browned flour and let the gravy come to boiling. Add fat, remove from fire and cool. Line the sides of a greased baking dish with pastry. Fill dish with alternate layers of bird and potatoes. Pour in gravy and cover with top crust, slashed in center. Bake in a hot oven (450° F.) for 10 minutes, then in a moderate oven (350° F.) for 30 minutes. Serves 6.

Pigeons and Squabs

Domestic pigeons are the most desirable. Wild pigeons are likely to be tough. Squabs are the nestlings of pigeons, usually marketed at about 4 weeks of age. They are tender and delicately flavored. Both are prepared by the same methods as chicken, with pigeons taking a long, slow cooking time.

BROILED SQUAB

6 squabs
Salt and pepper

Butter
Toast

Wash birds quickly under running water, split the birds down back, flatten breast, season and broil. When browned, brush with melted butter and serve on toast for 6.

PIGEON AND MUSHROOM STEW

3 pigeons
1 tablespoon fat
2 cups stock or gravy
Salt, pepper, cayenne

2 tablespoons mushroom catchup
½ cup mushrooms
2 tablespoons cream

Clean and cut pigeons into serving portions. Sauté in fat, but do not brown. Add stock or gravy, salt, pepper, cayenne, and mushroom catchup. Simmer 1 hour, or until tender, add mushrooms, simmer 10 minutes more, and stir in cream. Serve on a hot platter with mushrooms arranged around pigeons. Serves 3.

POTTED PIGEONS

6 pigeons
Stuffing
3 slices bacon
1 diced carrot
1 diced onion

1 teaspoon minced parsley
4 cups hot water or stock
¼ cup melted fat
¼ cup flour
Buttered toast

Clean and dress pigeons; stuff, truss and place upright in pan upon slices of bacon. Add carrot, onion, and parsley, and cover with boiling water or stock. Cover pot closely and simmer from 2 to 3 hours, or until tender, adding boiling water or stock when necessary. Combine fat and flour and add to 2 cups of stock remaining in pan. Serve on toast with gravy for 6.

PIGEON PIE

6 pigeons

Bread Stuffing, p. 220

Salt and pepper

3 tablespoons fat

3 tablespoons flour

1 recipe Plain Pastry, p. 387

3 hard-cooked eggs

Stuff each pigeon with bread stuffing. Loosen joints with a knife, but do not cut them through. Simmer, with water to cover, until nearly tender; then season with salt and pepper.

Combine fat and flour with the liquid in which the pigeons have been cooked to make a gravy, and let cool. Line the sides of a greased baking dish with pastry. Cut eggs into slices and fill baking dish with alternate layers of egg, pigeon and gravy. Cover with a layer of pastry and bake at 450° F. for 10 minutes, then lower temperature to 350° F. and bake 30 minutes. Serves 6.

Venison

Venison differs little from beef or veal except that it is less fat. The flavor is gamy, but not strong, and the texture of the meat is fine. The most desirable cut is the round, which may be used for steaks, but which is most satisfactory for roasting. Other roasting pieces are the saddle and the leg.

Venison is shipped frozen and must be handled with the same care as any other frozen meat. It should be allowed to thaw slowly at a low temperature, and cooked at once, or cooked frozen, allowing the same additional time as for frozen beef. Most people prefer venison served rare, with a tart jelly.

Leg of venison

¼ cup fat salt pork

Salt and pepper

Flour

ROAST LEG OF VENISON

Wipe carefully and remove dry skin. Lard the lean side of the leg with strips of pork. Soften fat, rub it over the meat and dredge with salt, pepper and flour. Lay the leg on rack of roaster, sprinkling bottom of pan with flour. Roast uncovered in slow oven (300° F.), allowing 20 to 22 minutes per pound. When flour in the bottom of pan is browned, add boiling water to cover bottom. Baste venison frequently, renewing water in pan as often as necessary. Serve with a gravy made from the juices in the bottom of the pan. Always serve a tart jelly like currant, wild grape or plum with venison. Allow ½ pound per person.

BROILED VENISON STEAK

2-pound venison steak   Cooking oil
Salad oil and lemon juice   Salt and paprika

If venison is strong, marinate in salad oil and lemon juice for 2 hours before cooking. Brush generously with oil. Place on preheated broiler rack and broil 7 to 10 minutes on each side at 550° F. Season with salt and paprika and serve on a very hot platter. Garnish with mushrooms, parsley and watercress. Serves 4.

Serve with slices of lemon, or spread with a mixture of butter and currant jelly, allowing half as much jelly as butter.

FRIED VENISON STEAK

2-pound venison steak   Cracker crumbs
Salt and pepper   ½ cup fat
Flour   1 tablespoon currant jelly

Rub the steak with a mixture of salt and pepper, dip in flour or cracker crumbs and sauté in hot fat until browned on both sides. Place on a hot dish and cover to keep warm. Dredge 2 teaspoons of flour into fat in bottom of pan and stir until brown. Dissolve 1 tablespoon of currant jelly in 1 cup boiling water; add to gravy and stir a few minutes. Strain, pour over the meat and serve. Serves 4.

Rabbits and Hares

Avoid wild rabbits. Buy ONLY domestic rabbits, cleaned and dressed. Domestic rabbit meat is white and delicately flavored throughout. Most domestic rabbits are marketed at 8 to 10 weeks of age, and are then called "fryers." Since these rabbits are grown quickly, the bones are very brittle and in preparing for cooking, care should be taken to break them in such a way that they do not sliver. Because of their tenderness, young rabbits can be cooked by the quick methods of frying or broiling. Older rabbits need longer, slower cooking.

Choose rabbits with soft ears and paws—stiffness is a sign of age. Neither hares nor rabbits should be drawn before hanging, as they may become musty. In Winter, select a dry place for hanging, and they may remain for some time.

Dressing and Trussing

To skin and dress a rabbit, hare or squirrel, cut off the fore feet at the first joint, cut the skin around the first joint of the hind leg, loosen it and then with a sharp knife slit the skin on the under side of the leg at the tail. Loosen the skin and turn it back until it is removed from the hind legs. Tie the hind legs together and hang the rabbit to a hook by this fastening. Draw the skin over the head, slipping out the fore legs when they are reached. Cut off the head and thus remove the entire skin. Wipe with a damp cloth. Slit down the front and remove the entrails, saving heart and liver, and wipe carefully inside. Wash inside and out with acidulated water, using 1 tablespoon vinegar to each cup of water. Rinse and wipe thoroughly.

If blood has settled in any part, cut with the point of a knife where it is black and soak in warm water. Skewer firmly between the shoulders, draw the legs close to the body and fasten with skewers.

ROAST HARE OR RABBIT

1 hare or rabbit	Currant jelly
Salt and pepper	Poultry fat or oil
Sausage Stuffing, p. 222	

Wash dressed hare or rabbit under running water and dry. Season with salt and pepper, stuff and sew up. Roast uncovered in moderate oven (325° F.) 1½ to 1¾ hours or until tender. Baste with fat. A thin piece of cheese cloth dipped in oil may be placed over the back for the first 45 minutes. Serve on hot platter with brown gravy and currant jelly. Garnish with parsley or watercress. Serves 4 to 6.

BROILED HARE OR RABBIT

1 hare or rabbit	Butter
Salt and pepper	

Skin and clean the rabbit or hare, wipe dry, split down the back and pound flat. Wrap in heavy oiled paper. Broil at 350° F. until browned and tender, turning frequently. Remove the paper and serve on a hot platter, seasoned with salt, pepper and butter, turning over and over so it will take up the fat. Hare or rabbit may be broiled without the oiled paper, but it will not be so juicy. Serves 4.

FRIED HARE OR RABBIT

1 hare or rabbit	Salt and pepper
1 egg, beaten	1 cup milk or cream
Bread crumbs	2 tablespoons flour

Clean and dress as directed. Simmer 15 minutes and drain. When cold, cut into serving pieces, dip into beaten egg, then into bread crumbs, and season with salt and pepper. Sauté in hot fat until brown on all sides. Remove to warm platter. Brown flour in fat and add milk or cream. Bring to boiling and pour over rabbit. Garnish with sliced lemon and parsley. Serves 4.

HARE OR RABBIT SALMI

1 hare or rabbit	2 cups hot water
1 slice onion	1 teaspoon salt
1 stalk celery, minced	1 tablespoon Worcestershire
1 bay leaf	sauce
2 tablespoons oil	1 tablespoon capers
2 tablespoons fat	12 pitted olives
2 tablespoons flour	Chopped parsley

Clean and dress as directed. Place in baking pan and add onion, celery and bay leaf; brush with oil and roast at 350° F. for 45 minutes. Remove meat from pan, add the fat and flour and stir until a rich brown. Add hot water, stir well, and when smooth, add salt, Worcestershire sauce, capers and olives. Replace meat, cover closely and roast in moderate oven (350° F.) for an additional 30 minutes or until tender. Arrange rabbit on platter, cover with strained sauce, arrange olives as a garnish and sprinkle with finely chopped parsley. Serves 6.

HARE OR RABBIT PIE

1 hare or rabbit	Salt and pepper
Lemon juice	1 recipe Southern Pastry, p. 388

Clean and dress as directed and cut into serving pieces. Back may be cut into three pieces. Cover with salted water and let stand for ½ hour. Dry and rub with lemon juice, salt and pepper. If the rabbit is plump, cut gashes in thickest parts to allow the seasoning to penetrate. Follow directions given for game pie. Serves 6.

FISH

THE main difference between fish from fresh water and those from salt water, as food, is that the salt-water fish are an important source of bromine and iodine in the diet, and are considered desirable because of the value of iodine in preventing goiter. Some of the most common salt-water fish are cod, haddock, halibut, smelt, mackerel, salmon, shad, herring, oysters, clams, scallops, lobsters, crabs, shrimp and prawns, and some terrapins. Fish as food may be divided into:

WHITE FISH—Fish that have less than two per cent fat, examples of which are smelt, flounder, yellow perch, pike, pickerel, sea bass, cod and haddock.

MEDIUM FAT FISH—Fish that have two to five per cent fat, examples of which are weakfish, brook trout, mullet, and white perch.

FAT OR OILY FISH—Fish that contain five per cent or more of fat, examples of which are salmon, shad, herring, lake trout, bluefish, Spanish mackerel, butterfish, and eels.

SHELLFISH—Oysters, clams, scallops and mussels; lobsters, crabs, shrimp, prawns and crayfish or crawfish. Frogs, terrapins and turtles are usually included in this group.

Amount of Fish to Buy

If the fish bought is solid flesh, one-third of a pound should be allowed for each person. If fish is bought in the round (with bones, head, tail, etc.) at least one-half pound must be bought for each person.

Selecting and Caring for Fish

FRESH AND FROZEN FISH—Fresh fish, or fish that was frozen while fresh, has full or bulging bright eyes, bright red gills, firm and elastic flesh and fresh odor. Be sure that the flesh along the backbone smells fresh; it spoils there first. Fresh fish sink in fresh water. If it floats, it should not be used. As soon as fish comes from the market, clean it and put it into the refrigerator or other cool place until it is needed.

Fish that is frozen immediately after it is caught, and is kept frozen until the time for cooking does not lose its flavor. It is preferable to clean and draw it without thawing, but if it is too hard to handle soak in cold water or allow to thaw in the refrigerator overnight until just flexible. Skinning is sometimes easier than scaling. Then it should be cooked at once without further thawing. Quick frozen fish on the market today is cleaned and ready for use. Cook at once without thawing, allowing only slightly more than the usual cooking time allotted to broiling or baking as the case may be.

Cleaning and Dressing Fish

Although fish may have been cleaned and dressed at the market, they are likely to need additional cleaning before they are cooked. If any scales have been left on a fish that is to be cooked with the skin on, remove them with the back of a knife. Draw the knife over the fish, from tail to head, slanting it toward the body of the fish at an angle of about 45°. If the fish is to be split, remove the head and tail. Wash quickly under cold running water and wipe the fish thoroughly, inside as well as outside, with a wet cloth. Then wipe dry, sprinkle with salt and keep on a plate in a cold place until ready to use. When roe is found in the fish it should be saved and cooked separately.

To Skin a Fish

Remove the fins, cut off a strip of skin along the backbone, and cut the skin around the gills. Pull the skin off with the fingers. If the flesh is soft, work slowly and follow the skin closely with the knife, to avoid tearing the flesh.

To Bone and Fillet a Fish

Clean and skin the fish. Insert a sharp knife close to the backbone at the tail end, and cut the flesh from the bone, working toward the head and keeping the knife as close as possible to the bone. Small bones that adhere to the flesh or are embedded in it must be removed with the fingers.

Flounders are often boned, to form fillets, and are served as fillets of sole. The English sole is seldom imported, and most of the fillet of sole that is served in America is made from the flounder, which has a white, delicate flesh similar to sole.

A fillet is merely a piece of fish without skin and bones. Fillets look better on the serving platter if they are approximately the same size. Rolled fillets are called turbans. They are fastened with wooden toothpicks to keep in shape during cooking, but the picks are removed before serving.

Salted, Smoked, Frozen and Canned Fish

The following varieties are likely to be in any market the year around:

DRIED SALT FISH—Cod, haddock, hake, pollack, whiting.

BRINE-SALTED FISH—Herring, mackerel, mullet, salmon, shad.

SMOKED FISH—Carp, catfish, eel, finnan haddie, hake, halibut, lake trout, pollack, salmon, sturgeon, whitefish.

CANNED FISH—Cod, haddock, herring, mackerel, salmon, sardines, tuna, oysters, shrimp, lobsters, clams.

PICKLED FISH—Sardines, eels, sturgeon, oysters, clams, scallops, lobsters and mussels.

FRESH FROZEN—Many dried, smoke or salted fish are now frozen. They are prepared like fresh fish.

To Simmer or Steam Fish

To simmer a large fish whole, place it in a wire frying basket or in the strainer of a fish kettle and lower it into water or Court Bouillon which is almost boiling. Add one teaspoon salt and one tablespoon vinegar or lemon juice for every two quarts of water. The acid whitens the flesh and helps to keep it firm. Heat to simmering and cook until flesh may be easily separated into flakes, 8 minutes per pound for the first 4 pounds and 5 minutes for each additional pound.

Fillets or slices of fish should be placed on a plate, tied in a piece of cheesecloth and lowered into the water or Court Bouillon (page 489). Cook about 10 minutes per pound.

To steam fish, oil upper part of steamer, place fish in it and set over boiling water. Sprinkle fish with salt and a few drops of lemon juice, cover and allow water to boil vigorously. Cook 10 to 15 minutes per pound.

Use cooking stock as a basis for sauce or chowder.

FISH COOKED IN PARCHMENT

2 pounds boneless fillets　1 tablespoon minced parsley
2 tablespoons butter　1 tablespoon lemon juice
2 tablespoons minced onion　Salt and pepper

Dampen 2 sheets of parchment paper and spread out flat. Brush with oil. Cut fish into serving pieces and place half the pieces on each sheet of paper. Place 1 teaspoon each of butter and onion on each serving and sprinkle with parsley, lemon juice, salt and pepper. Gather edges of papers and tie securely. Place in boiling water and cook 15 minutes. Remove fish to hot platter, taking care not to lose any of the juices. Serves 6.

Fish That Are Good Boiled, Steamed or Poached

FISH	SUGGESTED SAUCES	GARNISHES
Codfish	Butter, caper, oyster, shrimp	Parsley or cress
Flounder	Béchamel	Chopped parsley
Haddock	Egg	Parsley or cress
Halibut	Béchamel, creamy egg, hollandaise	Parsley or cress
Mackerel	Caper, parsley	Cucumber, lemon
Red snapper	Mushroom, tomato	Parsley
Salmon	Egg, hollandaise, tartare	Cress, lemon
Sheepshead	Drawn butter	Parsley and lemon
Sole (flounder)	Béchamel	Parsley
Trout	Horse-radish	Lemon

BONED HERRING

6 large herring　Parsley
Pepper　Vinegar
Salt　6 slices buttered toast

Select fish with roes. Split, wash, scrape and remove heads, roe and backbone. Sprinkle generously with pepper, salt and minced parsley, then roll each piece tightly, beginning with the wide end, and tie with a string. Place in boiling water seasoned with pepper, salt and vinegar and simmer 10 to 15 minutes. Cut roe into pieces and fry. Place the fish and roe on buttered toast, garnish and serve. Serves 6.

PICKLED SALMON

4 to 5 pounds salmon
2 quarts vinegar
1 ounce peppercorns

1½ teaspoons nutmeg
6 blades mace
1 tablespoon salad oil

Wrap salmon in cheesecloth and simmer in salted water about 45 minutes. Drain, wrap in dry cloth and chill until ready to use. Combine 1 quart of the cooking water with vinegar and spices. Cover and cook 5 minutes. Cool. When quite cold, pour over salmon, then add oil. Cover closely and store in a cool dry place. This pickle will keep for several months. Serves 8 to 10.

POACHED FISH

Small fish and fish fillets are poached by simmering in a small amount of seasoned liquid. The liquid is then strained and used in making a sauce suited to the type of fish.

1 teaspoon salt
1 slice onion
1 slice lemon

½ teaspoon peppercorns
1 bay leaf
2 pounds fish fillets

Fill skillet half full of water and add salt, onion, lemon, peppercorns and bay leaf. Heat to boiling. Add fish and simmer 5 to 15 minutes, depending on thickness of fish. Remove carefully to serving plate. Strain stock and use in preparing sauce. Serves 6.

FISH POACHED IN TOMATO SAUCE

2 cups tomatoes
½ teaspoon salt
1 bay leaf
1 tablespoon minced onion

½ teaspoon peppercorns
2 pounds fish fillets
1 tablespoon butter

Cook tomatoes, salt, bay leaf, onion and peppercorns in greased skillet until reduced about half. Add fish and simmer 5 minutes. Turn fish carefully and simmer 5 minutes longer. Remove fish to hot platter. Strain tomato sauce, add butter and pour over fish. Serves 6.

IN MILK—Use 1½ cups milk instead of tomatoes and do not cook down. Add 2 stalks celery, chopped, to seasonings. When fish is done, strain milk and use in preparing sauce.

Broiled Fish

To broil a whole fish, continue the slit made in cleaning the fish so that it can be opened flat. Dry and season with salt, pepper and lemon juice. Place skin side up on greased shallow pan and brown skin quickly under broiler. Turn carefully and cook flesh side 6 to 12 minutes, depending on thickness. Fillets are cooked 4 to 6 minutes on each side. Do not overcook. Fat fish need no basting but lean fish should be basted well with butter during broiling.

Fish That Are Good Broiled

FISH	SUGGESTED SAUCES	GARNISHES
Black Bass (split)	Melted butter	Lemon and parsley
Bluefish	Melted butter	Chopped almonds
Butterfish	Lemon	Watercress
Cod (sliced)	Melted butter	Lemon
Flounder (split or filleted)	Tomato, lemon	Parsley
Halibut (sliced)	Butter, hollandaise	Parsley, lemon
Mackerel (split)	Maître d'hôtel, lemon	Lemon, cucumber, parsley
Perch	Caper, anchovy	Parsley
Pompano (split)	Maître d'hôtel,	Cucumber, cress
Red Snapper	Lemon butter	Cucumbers
Salmon (sliced)	Anchovy, caper	Chopped parsley
Shad (split)	Maître d'hôtel, butter	Parsley, radishes
Smelt (whole)	Remoulade, bechamel	Parsley
Swordfish (sliced)	Melted butter	Parsley
Trout	Melted butter	Lemon wedges
Whitefish	Mushroom	Watercress

BROILED SMELT

¼ cup butter, melted
1 tablespoon lemon juice
1 teaspoon salt
¼ teaspoon pepper
1 pound smelt
½ cup flour

Mix butter, lemon juice, salt and pepper. Clean smelt, splitting them open if they are large. Dip each in butter mixture, then roll in flour. Place in double broiler rack and broil 6 minutes, turning once. Serves 4.

Baked Fish

Fish weighing from 3 to 5 pounds may be baked whole, either with or without stuffing. The head and tail may be removed or left on. Clean fish, dry and rub inside with salt. Stuff if desired and sew or skewer. Place a sheet of greased heavy or parchment paper in baking pan, having it large enough so that it can be used to lift fish from pan when done. Place a bay leaf and a few slices of onion and bacon or salt pork on the paper and lay the fish on top. If fish is lean, cut a few slashes down its back and place a strip of salt pork in each. Bake in quick or hot oven (425° F.) 10 minutes, then reduce heat to 350° F. and bake 15 to 20 minutes longer. Allow ten minutes per pound for the first 4 pounds and 5 minutes for each additional pound.

Small fish, steaks or fillets may be dipped in milk and rolled in bread crumbs. Sprinkle with melted butter or oil and bake in moderate oven (350°-375° F.) 20 to 25 minutes. Fillets are often rolled to form turbans and baked in muffin pans.

Fish To Bake Whole

Fish	Stuffings	Suggested Sauces	Garnishes
Bass (sea)	Bread stuffing	Tomato sauce	Tomato
Bluefish	Bread stuffing	Catchup	Parsley
Cod	Oyster stuffing	Egg sauce	Lemon
Haddock	Pickle-caper	Drawn butter	Lemon
Mackerel	Parsley		Lemon
Pickerel	Pickle-caper		Cucumber
Shad	Bread stuffing		Tomato
Tilefish	Bread stuffing	Maître d'hôtel	Parsley
Weakfish	Bread stuffing	Lemon juice	Watercress
Whitefish	Bread stuffing	Egg sauce	Egg

Fish to Bake in Steaks, Cutlets or Fillets

Fish	Suggested Sauces	Garnishes
Cusk	Creole	Lemon
Flounder	Egg	Egg
Haddock	Oyster	Lemon
Halibut	Brown, hollandaise	Tomato, parsley
Mackerel (horse)		Lemon
Salmon	Lemon	Parsley and lemon
Tilefish	Tomato	Parsley

Planked Fish

Select any fish suitable for baking. Large fish may be cleaned, split, boned, seasoned and planked flat; small fish may be cleaned, seasoned and planked whole. Oil plank and preheat thoroughly in hot oven. Place fish in center of plank; brush lean fish with melted butter or French dressing. Bake in very hot oven (425° F.) 10 to 15 minutes, reduce temperature to moderate (350° F.) and finish baking, allowing about 10 minutes per pound. About 15 minutes before fish is done, remove from oven and garnish with mashed potatoes pressed through a pastry tube and other vegetables as desired. Return to oven to finish baking and brown potatoes. Garnish.

FILLET OF FLOUNDER AU GRATIN

2½ pounds flounder fillets
1½ tablespoons butter
1 tablespoon flour
1 tablespoon chopped onion
½ bay leaf

1 cup chicken stock
Salt and pepper
½ tablespoon lemon juice
½ cup bread crumbs

Cut fillets into serving pieces and place in greased baking dish. Melt butter, add flour and onion and blend well. Add bay leaf and chicken stock and simmer 15 minutes, stirring until thickened. Remove bay leaf. Season with salt and pepper and add lemon juice. Pour over fish and sprinkle crumbs over top. Bake in hot oven (425° F.) 20 minutes. Serve at once. Serves 6.

HALIBUT CREOLE

2 tablespoons butter
1 tablespoon flour
1 tablespoon minced green
   pepper

1 tablespoon minced onion
2 cups cooked tomatoes
Salt and pepper
2 pounds halibut steaks

Melt butter and blend in flour. Add minced green pepper and onion and cook 3 minutes. Add tomatoes and cook until thickened, stirring constantly. Simmer 10 minutes longer, then rub through strainer and season with salt and pepper. Season halibut steaks with salt and pepper and arrange in greased baking dish. Pour Creole sauce over fish. Bake in hot oven (400° F.) 30 minutes. Serves 4.

SCALLOPED FISH

2 hard-cooked eggs
2 cups medium white sauce
2 cups flaked cooked fish

Salt and pepper
1 cup buttered bread
crumbs

Rub egg yolks through sieve and chop egg whites. Mix well with white sauce. Arrange alternate layers of fish and sauce in greased baking dish. Season fish with salt and pepper. Cover with buttered crumbs. Bake in moderate oven (350° F.) 20 minutes or until crumbs are browned. Serves 4.

FISH TIMBALES

1 cup cooked fish
½ cup cooked mushrooms
1 cup bread crumbs
2 cups milk

⅓ cup butter
Salt and pepper
Few grains nutmeg
4 eggs, beaten

Remove skin and bones from fish, add mushrooms and chop very fine. Rub through sieve. Cook crumbs and milk in double boiler 10 minutes. Add butter and season with salt, pepper and nutmeg. Add fish and beaten eggs. Pour into greased molds or custard cups. Bake in moderate oven (350° F.) until firm, about 30 minutes. Unmold and serve with hollandaise sauce or tomato sauce. Serves 4.

This mixture may be baked in a large mold, about 60 minutes.

FISH SOUFFLÉ

1 teaspoon onion juice
½ teaspoon salt
⅛ teaspoon pepper

1 cup medium white sauce
2 eggs, separated
1 cup flaked cooked fish

Add onion juice, salt and pepper to white sauce. Stir in beaten egg yolks and flaked fish. Beat egg whites until stiff and fold into mixture. Pour into greased baking dish and place in pan of hot water. Bake in moderate oven (350° F.) 60 minutes. Serve from the same dish. Serves 4.

KEDGEREE

2 cups flaked cooked fish
1 cup cooked rice
2 hard-cooked eggs

4 tablespoons butter
Salt and pepper

Heat fish, rice and chopped egg whites in butter. Season and sprinkle with sieved egg yolks. Serves 6.

SCALLOPED SALMON

2 cups cooked salmon	½ cup dry bread crumbs
2 tablespoons lemon juice	1 cup thin white sauce
Salt and pepper	

Flake salmon and place half of it in greased baking dish. Season with lemon juice, salt and pepper. Cover with half the crumbs. Repeat layers of salmon, seasoning and crumbs. Pour white sauce over the top and bake in moderate oven (350° F.) 20 minutes or until thoroughly heated and slightly browned on top. Serves 4.

AU GRATIN—Season salmon, mix with white sauce and place in greased small molds. Cover with buttered crumbs. Add grated cheese if desired. Bake as above.

SALMON WIGGLE

2 cups flaked cooked salmon	2 dozen crisp crackers
2 cups cooked peas	Paprika
2 cups white sauce	

Heat salmon and peas in white sauce. Serve on crackers and sprinkle with paprika. Serves 6.

SALMON LOAF

2 cups cooked salmon	¼ cup butter, melted
2 eggs, beaten	Salt and pepper
⅓ cup soft bread crumbs	1 tablespoon minced parsley

Flake salmon and add beaten eggs. Add remaining ingredients and place in greased loaf pan. Bake in moderate oven (350° F.) 40 minutes. Serve with egg sauce. Serves 4.

SALMON PUFFS

2 cups cooked salmon	½ cup soft bread crumbs
½ teaspoon salt	1 tablespoon lemon juice
⅛ teaspoon pepper	3 eggs, separated

Chop salmon fine and add salt, pepper, crumbs and lemon juice. Add beaten egg yolks, mixing thoroughly, then fold in stiffly beaten egg whites. Place in greased custard cups. Set in pan of hot water and bake in moderate oven (375° F.) 30 minutes. Unmold on a hot platter, garnish each with a sprig of parsley and serve with a sauce. Serves 6.

FISH STICKS WITH CHEESE AND PIMIENTO

2 packages fish sticks 3 canned pimientos
Parmesan cheese

Heat oven to 425° F. Separate fish sticks. Cut pimientos into strips. Wrap fish sticks with pimiento strips. Place on a lightly greased baking sheet and sprinkle with Parmesan cheese. Bake for 15 minutes. Serves 6.

FISH STICKS IN TOMATO SAUCE ON RICE (CREOLE)

1 package fish sticks
½ cup of chili sauce
¼ cup minced onions
¼ cup vinegar or lemon juice
salt and pepper

1 tablespoon Worcestershire sauce

Prepare rice for serving of four. Place fish sticks on baking sheet. Heat in hot oven (425° F.) for about 15 minutes. Mix remaining ingredients in a sauce pan and heat. Remove fish sticks; place on servings of rice. Pour heated sauce over fish.

TUNA EN CASSEROLE

1 medium onion
4 tablespoon fat
4 tablespoons flour
2 cups tomato juice
1 teaspoon sugar
1 teaspoon paprika
¾ teaspoon salt
Few grains cayenne
Juice 1 lemon
1 cup flaked cooked tuna
2 cups seasoned mashed potatoes

Chop onion, add to fat and cook until tender. Blend in flour and add tomato juice, sugar paprika, salt, cayenne and lemon juice. Cook, stirring constantly, until thickened. Add tuna and pour into casserole. Cover with potatoes. Bake in moderate oven (350° F.) about 20 minutes or until potatoes are browned. Serves 4.

SCALLOPED TUNA AND PEAS

2 cups cooked peas
2 cups flaked cooked tuna
½ teaspoon salt
½ cup cream
½ cup buttered crumbs

Place peas and tuna in layers in greased baking dish. Add salt to cream and pour over fish. Cover with crumbs and brown in moderate oven (350° F.). Serves 6.

CREAMED CODFISH

1 cup salt codfish	2 tablespoons flour
1 cup milk	1/8 teaspoon pepper
2 tablespoons butter	1 egg

Separate the fish into very small pieces and leave in cold water for 3 hours, changing the water 3 times. Heat milk in double boiler. Add well-drained codfish and cook for 10 minutes. Blend butter, flour and pepper and stir into milk. Cook 10 minutes, stirring constantly until thickened. Remove from heat, add beaten egg, stir well and serve at once. If the sauce is cooked after the egg is added, it is likely to curdle. The egg may be omitted. Serves 4.

NEW ENGLAND SALT FISH DINNER—Serve over opened baked potatoes and top with browned cubes of salt pork.

CODFISH BALLS

1 cup flaked salt codfish	2 tablespoons butter
3 cups sliced potatoes	1/8 teaspoon pepper
2 tablespoons milk	1 egg, beaten

Simmer fish and potatoes together in a large amount of water until potatoes are tender. Drain well and mash. Add remaining ingredients and beat until light. Shape into balls and fry in hot deep fat (380° F.) until brown. Serves 4.

FILLETS WITH ONION RINGS

1 package frozen fillets	1/2 teaspoon garlic salt
1 tablespoon butter	1/4 teaspoon thyme
1 teaspoon salt	3/4 cup light cream

1/2 cup thinly sliced onion separated into rings

Place fish in baking dish after following directions for defrosting. Dot with butter and add seasonings. Arrange onion rings over fish, and pour on light cream and bake at 350° F. about 25 minutes, until fish is flaky. Garnish.

FILLETS IN MUSTARD SAUCE

One package frozen fillets.

Thaw fish according to directions on package. Place fillets in one layer in shallow baking dish.

Mix together:

6 tablespoons melted butter	2 teaspoons salt
1 tablespoon lemon juice	2 teaspoons dry mustard

2 teaspoons prepared horseradish

Pour over fish and bake at 350° F. 25 to 30 minutes, or until fish is tender.

SALT FISH WITH EGG GARNISH

2 cups salt fish   2 cups white sauce
2 hard-cooked eggs

Soak fish overnight, drain and cover with fresh water. Simmer 10 minutes. Add to hot white sauce and pour onto hot platter. Slice eggs and arrange around edge. Serves 4.

BROILED FINNAN HADDIE

2 pounds finnan haddie   2 tablespoons butter
1 teaspoon lemon juice   Pepper

If dried, cover finnan haddie with boiling water for 10 minutes. Drain and place on greased broiler rack. Sprinkle with lemon juice and brush with softened butter. If fresh frozen, sprinkle with lemon juice and proceed to brown under moderate heat, turn and brush the other side with lemon juice and butter. Brown. Sprinkle lightly with pepper and serve with egg or pickle sauce. Serves 6.

CREAMED FINNAN HADDIE

2 pounds finnan haddie   2 cups medium white sauce
Paprika

If dried, cover finnan haddie with cold water for 20 minutes. Heat to boiling and simmer 30 minutes. If fresh frozen, just cover with boiling water and simmer 15 minutes. Drain, separate into flakes and add to hot seasoned white sauce. Sprinkle liberally with paprika. Serves 6.

FINNAN HADDIE CHEESE TOAST

2 tablespoons minced onion   1 cup grated American
½ cup butter   cheese
4 tablespoons flour   6 slices bread
½ teaspoon salt   1 cup flaked cooked finnan
Few grains cayenne   haddie
½ teaspoon paprika   Parsley
2 cups milk   3 hard-cooked eggs

Cook onion in ¼ cup butter, blend in flour and seasonings, add milk and cook until thickened, stirring constantly. Add cheese, remove from heat and stir until melted. Toast bread on 1 side, butter untoasted side and cover with fish. Heat in broiler. Cover with cheese sauce and garnish with parsley and quartered hard-cooked eggs. Serves 6.

Salt Mackerel

To FRESHEN—Soak mackerel in running or in frequently changed water for 2 to 3 hours. Place fish on a rack, cover with water in a heavy skillet and heat to boiling. Drain. Cover again with fresh water and simmer until tender. Fish is then ready for use in any recipe. Allow ¼ pound per person.

BREAKFAST SALT MACKEREL—Simmer mackerel in milk for 5 to 7 minutes, brown in butter and serve very hot.

BAKED SALT MACKEREL—Place mackerel, skin side down, in a baking pan, cover with thin cream and bake in a moderate oven (350° F.) for 15 minutes.

BROILED SALT MACKEREL—Place well-drained fish on broiler rack and brush with butter. Broil in preheated broiler 3 inches from source of heat until fish is browned.

OTHER WHOLE SALT FISH may be prepared in the same ways.

Oysters

Oysters in the shell are sold by the dozen; shucked oysters by the quart or pint. Oysters in the shell should be alive when purchased as indicated by tightly closed shell. Shucked oysters should be plump with no sunken areas or evidence of shrinkage. The liquor should be clear and should smell fresh.

Opening and Cleaning Oysters

Scrub shells thoroughly with water and a brush. To open an oyster, hold it firmly with the thick part of the shell toward the palm of the hand. Push a strong, thin knife between the shells near the back and run it along until it cuts the strong muscle which holds the shells together. Drop the oysters into a strainer, set over a bowl. and save the liquor that drains through to be used in cooking the oysters or making soup or sauce. Then examine each oyster with the fingers and remove all particles of shell. They are then ready to be used in any way desired.

OYSTERS ON THE HALF SHELL

Open oysters and serve in the deep half of the shell. Arrange 5 or 6 oysters on a plate of cracked ice and place a small glass of cocktail sauce in the center. Place a wedge of lemon on one side and serve very cold.

OYSTER COCKTAIL

30 large oysters	3 tablespoons tomato catchup
COCKTAIL SAUCE	1 teaspoon salt
2 teaspoons prepared	2 tablespoons vinegar
horseradish	4 tablespoons lemon juice

¼ teaspoon Tabasco sauce

Chill oysters. Mix remaining ingredients well and chill. Place oysters in chilled glasses and cover with sauce. Serves 6.

OYSTERS BAKED IN SHELLS

Scrub unopened oysters well and place, deep shell down, in pan. Bake in hot oven (450° F.) until shells open, about 10 minutes. Season with butter, salt and pepper; serve in shells.

PANNED OYSTERS

1 pint large oysters	¼ cup oyster juice

6 slices buttered toast

Place oysters in a shallow baking pan and pour over them a small quantity of oyster juice, but not sufficient to raise or float them. Place dish carefully in hot oven (425° F.) and just heat the oysters through. Be careful not to bake them. Moisten hot buttered toast with hot juice from oysters and serve oysters on toast. Serves 6.

OYSTER CASINO

30 oysters in the shell	Buttered crumbs
Lemon juice	30 (1-inch) squares sliced
Pepper and salt	bacon

Wash and open the oysters. Into each shell put a half teaspoon of strained oyster liquor, a few drops of lemon juice, then the oyster. Sprinkle with pepper and salt and cover with buttered crumbs. On each place a square of bacon and bake in hot oven (425° F.) 10 to 12 minutes. Shallow ovenware dishes, with the half shells embedded in coarse salt, are excellent for this purpose. The salt keeps the shells from tipping during baking. Where shells are not available, arrange the oysters for each portion in a shallow ramekin or in mushroom or tomato cups.

SCALLOPED OYSTERS

6 tablespoons butter   Salt and pepper
2 cups fine cracker crumbs   ½ cup milk
1 pint oysters   Parsley

Melt butter, add crumbs and mix well. Spread ⅓ of the mixture in a greased baking dish. Arrange half the oysters in one layer on top and cover with half the remaining crumbs. Season with salt and pepper and add a second layer of oysters and crumbs. Season. No more than 2 layers of oysters should be used, otherwise the top and bottom layers will be over-cooked and tough before those in the middle are well heated through. Pour the milk over the top. Bake in moderate oven (350° F.) about 30 minutes or until top is brown. Garnish with parsley. Serves 6.

DEVILED OYSTERS

1 pint oysters   1 tablespoon chopped
3 tablespoons butter   parsley
2 tablespoons flour   1 tablespoon lemon juice
1 cup milk or cream   Salt and pepper
2 egg yolks   ½ cup cracker crumbs

Drain oysters and chop slightly. Drain again. Melt 2 table-spoons butter and blend in flour. Add milk and cook until thickened, stirring constantly. Beat egg yolks slightly and add to sauce, mixing well. Add oyster liquor, parsley, lemon juice and oysters. Season with salt and pepper. Place in greased ramekins or scallop shells. Melt remaining butter and mix with crumbs. Sprinkle over creamed mixture. Brown in hot oven (425° F.) about 7 minutes. Serves 6.

OYSTERS EN BROCHETTE

30 large oysters   6 slices buttered toast
            30 squares bacon

String oysters and bacon squares alternately on 6 skewers, taking care to put skewers through firm part of oysters. Place across deep baking pan so that oysters hang down but do not touch bottom of pan. Bake in very hot oven (475° F.) until bacon is crisp, about 5 minutes. Place a skewer on each slice of toast and pour juice over. Serves 6.

PIGS IN BLANKETS

24 large oysters 24 thin slices bacon
Salt and pepper 6 slices buttered toast

Season oysters with salt and pepper; wrap each in bacon and fasten with a pick. Fry quickly in a hot skillet until bacon is brown. Remove crusts from toast, cut into quarters and serve an oyster on each square. Serves 6.

OYSTERS ROCKEFELLER

4 dozen oysters in half shell ¼ teaspoon pepper
8 slices crisp bacon ¼ teaspoon paprika
2 cups chopped spinach ⅓ cup lemon juice
3 tablespoons minced parsley 4 drops absinthe
½ cup chopped celery leaves 1 tablespoon white wine
2 green onion tops ½ cup butter, melted
½ teaspoon salt ½ cup buttered crumbs

Heat a 1-inch layer of rock salt in pans until very hot. Arrange oysters in shells on salt and heat in very hot oven (475° F.) until edges curl, about 5 minutes. While oysters heat, chop bacon, spinach, parsley, celery and onion tops very fine and add seasonings, lemon juice, wines and butter. Place a little of the mixture on each oyster, sprinkle with crumbs and return to oven to brown, about 2 minutes. Serve at once in the pans of salt. Serves 8.

Clams

There are two general types of clams, the soft clam and the hard or quahog clams. Hard clams include three classes: the littlenecks (small), the cherry stone (medium) and the large chowder clams. The littleneck and cherry stone clams may be used uncooked. Clams are purchased in the shell by the dozen, shucked by the quart or pint or canned.

If clams are purchased in the shell, discard any which are not tightly closed or which do not close when lightly tapped. They are unsafe for use. Cover with cold water and sprinkle corn meal over the top, using 1 cup for each peck of clams. Let stand 3 hours or overnight to allow the clams to take in the meal and work out any sand which might be in them, then scrub the shells well and open with a strong knife as for oysters. The larger clams are usually steamed open.

CLAMS COOKED IN THE SHELL

STEAMED—

30 clams in the shell   Juice of ½ lemon
  6 tablespoons butter   Salt and pepper

The hard-shelled clam is used for steaming. Scrub the shell with a brush and wash free of sand in several waters. Steam the clams in a steamer for 10 minutes, or until opened. While the clams are steaming, melt the butter and mix with the lemon juice, salt and pepper. Lay a napkin on a hot platter and place the clams in their shells on this. Cover with a second napkin and serve. In eating, remove the clam from the shell and dip it in the sauce. The thin, tough part known as the neck or siphon is not eaten.

ROASTED IN THE OVEN—Prepare the clams as for steaming, place in a pan, set the pan in a hot oven (425° F.) and bake until the shells open. Remove the top shell, being careful not to spill the liquid. Arrange the clams in the half shell on plates and on each place a piece of butter and a little pepper and salt. Add lemon juice if desired. Serve immediately.

CLAMBAKE—The seashore is the natural place for a clambake, but it is possible to have one at any place where there is a flat open space. Preparations should begin several hours before the time set for the meal.

Make a circle of flat stones—from 2 to 4 feet in diameter, according to the size of the party—and on this circle build a hot fire of wood. Let this burn for 2 to 3 hours. Then rake off the fire and cover the hot stones with fresh seaweed. On this lay fresh clams in their shells; also, if desired, oysters, potatoes in the skins, corn in the husk, and any other food that may be steamed. Cover with a thick layer of seaweed, and over all spread a large piece of sailcloth, fastening down the edges with stones. Leave for 2 to 3 hours; remove the cloth and the top layer of seaweed, and rake out the clams and other foods as needed.

The same materials may be cooked in a large kettle with the bottom covered with water and wet cheesecloth between the layers, but will lack the fine flavor of the real clambake.

CLAMS ON THE HALF SHELL

Small clams are served raw on the half shell, just as raw oysters are served. (See Index.)

CLAM COCKTAIL

Follow recipe for oyster cocktail. (Page 200.)

CREAMED CLAMS

4 quarts clams	1 to 1½ cups milk
1 tablespoon minced onion	Salt and pepper
4 tablespoons butter	6 slices buttered toast
4 tablespoons flour	Parsley

6 strips pimiento

Steam clams and remove from shells, saving liquor. Cook onion in butter until yellow; blend in flour. Add milk to clam liquor to make 2 cups and add to flour and butter. Cook until thickened, stirring constantly. Add clams and season with salt and pepper. Serve on toast, garnished with parsley and pimiento. Serves 6.

DEVILED CLAMS

2 cups clams	4 tablespoons butter
½ cup clam liquor	1 teaspoon salt
2 tablespoons minced onion	⅛ teaspoon pepper
2 tablespoons minced green pepper	3 drops Tabasco sauce
¼ cup chopped celery	½ teaspoon prepared mustard

¾ cup cracker crumbs

Chop clams fine and simmer in their liquor 5 minutes. Cook onion, green pepper and celery in butter until tender. Mix with clams and remaining ingredients. Fill greased ramekins or scallop shells and bake in moderate oven (350° F.) 20 minutes. Serves 6.

CLAM CAKES

1 cup shucked clams	¼ teaspoon salt
1 cup cracker crumbs	2 eggs, beaten

Chop hard parts of clams; mix with soft parts, clam liquor, crumbs and salt. Let stand 5 minutes. Add eggs, shape into cakes and fry in hot deep fat (375° F.). Serves 4.

CLAM PIE

2 quarts clams
1 cup hot water
2 onions, sliced
2 potatoes, sliced
3 tablespoons butter
3 tablespoons flour

1 teaspoon salt
⅛ teaspoon pepper
2 cups milk
Plain pastry, using 2 cups flour
1 tablespoon minced parsley

Scrub clams well and place in kettle with hot water. Cover closely and steam until clams open. Remove clams from shells and chop fine. Strain liquid through fine cheesecloth and cook onions and potatoes in it until just tender. Melt butter, blend in flour, salt and pepper, add milk and cook until thickened, stirring constantly. Add clams, vegetables and liquor and pour into deep baking dish lined with pastry. Sprinkle with parsley. Cover with top crust; cut hole in center to allow for escape of steam. Bake in very hot oven (425° F.) 15 minutes, reduce heat to moderate (350° F.) and bake 25 minutes longer. Serves 6.

SCALLOPED CLAMS

6 clams in shells
18 opened clams
Pepper
2 tablespoons minced celery

48 tiny cubes bacon
3 tablespoons fine cracker crumbs
2 tablespoons butter

Open the 6 clams carefully so as not to break the shells. Scrub shells with water and a brush. Place 2 clams in each shell and sprinkle lightly with pepper. Add ½ teaspoon celery and 4 bacon cubes to each. Dust with cracker crumbs and dot with butter. Bake in moderate oven (375° F.). Serve 2 or 3 shells to each person. Serves 4 to 6.

FRIED SOFT CLAMS

1 pint soft clams
2 cups fine bread crumbs

1 egg, beaten
Salt

Wash soft clams and dry between towels. Dip in crumbs, in beaten egg and again in crumbs. Fry in hot deep fat (375° F.) until browned. Drain on absorbent paper and sprinkle with salt. Clams may be dipped in batter as for fried oysters instead of in egg and crumbs. Serve with tartare sauce. Serves 6.

Scallops

The scallop is a bivalve having a large round fluted shell. Scallop shells are frequently used as individual baking dishes. Of the meat, only the adductor muscle, a firm cube of white meat, is used. The bay scallops, ¾ inch in diameter, are the tenderest and most delicate in flavor; the sea scallops, 2 inches in diameter, are best halved across the grain before cooking.

SAUTÉED SCALLOPS

1 pint scallops	1 cup dry bread crumbs
Salt and pepper	1 egg, beaten

Drain scallops and remove any bits of shell. Season with salt and pepper. Dip in fine crumbs, in beaten egg and again in crumbs. Saute quickly in shallow fat, turning to brown all sides. Do not cook longer than 5 minutes. Drain on absorbent paper. Serve with tartare sauce. Serves 4.

FRIED SCALLOPS

Prepare as for sauteed scallops; fry in hot deep fat (380° F.).

BROILED SCALLOPS

Dip scallops in melted butter or French dressing and roll in seasoned crumbs. Place on greased baking sheet and brown quickly on all sides, not more than 5 minutes.

SCALLOPS EN BROCHETTE

1 pint scallops	6 to 8 slices bacon
3 tablespoons butter	Salt and pepper

Cook scallops in butter 5 minutes. Cut bacon into 2-inch pieces. Arrange scallops and bacon alternately on skewers. Season with salt and pepper. Stand skewers upright in large uncooked potato and bake in moderate oven (350°-400° F.) until bacon is crisp, about 15 minutes. Or place on broiler rack and brown on all sides under broiler. Serve on skewers or lay each brochette across a slice of toast and remove skewer. Serves 4.

SCALLOPS À LA FRANCAISE

1 pint scallops
¾ cup water
¼ cup white wine
½ teaspoon salt
Few grains cayenne
1 small onion, chopped
2 tablespoons butter

2 tablespoons flour
½ clove garlic, minced
1 teaspoon minced parsley
1 egg yolk
¾ cup buttered crumbs
2 tablespoons grated Parmesan cheese

Simmer scallops 5 minutes in mixture of water, wine, salt and cayenne. Drain, reserving liquid. Cook onion in butter until tender, blend in flour, add liquid drained from scallops and cook until thickened, stirring constantly. Add garlic and parsley and cook 5 minutes longer. Add gradually to beaten egg yolk, mixing well. Chop scallops and add to mixture. Place in buttered scallop shells, top with buttered crumbs and Parmesan cheese and brown in hot oven (400° F.). Serves 6.

SCALLOPS À LA NEWBURG

1 pint scallops
2 tablespoons butter
1½ teaspoons flour
¼ cup cream, about

2 tablespoons sherry
2 egg yolks
½ teaspoon salt
2 drops Tabasco sauce

Simmer scallops in their own liquor 3 minutes. Drain, saving liquor. Cook scallops slowly in butter 5 minutes, blend in flour and add ½ cup combined cream and scallop liquor. Cook until thickened, stirring constantly. Add sherry, slightly beaten egg yolks, salt and Tabasco sauce. Heat 2 minutes longer, stirring constantly, but do not allow sauce to boil. Serve in patty shells or on toast. Serves 6.

BROILED SCALLOPS HAWAIIAN

24 small scallops
24 pineapple wedges

24 (4-inch) strips bacon
6 slices buttered toast

Place a scallop and a pineapple wedge at opposite ends of each bacon strip. Roll strips toward the center so that scallops and pineapple are wrapped in bacon. Place 2 together on skewers. Broil until bacon is crisp, about 10 minutes, turning to brown all sides. Place 2 on each slice of toast and remove skewers carefully. Serves 6.

Sea Mussels

Sea mussels are as agreeable to the taste as oysters, and may be eaten when oysters are out of season. Canned mussels are obtainable nearly everywhere. When fresh mussels are used, the shells may be opened by steaming, or with a knife. The horny "beard" must be removed and discarded.

Mussels may be used instead of oysters in any oyster recipe.

Lobster

Lobsters are in season from June to September and it is possible to obtain them at any time of the year. The shell of a live lobster is usually a mottled dark green. Boiling makes the shells of all lobsters turn bright red.

Uncooked lobsters should be alive when purchased. In buying a boiled lobster, straighten its tail; if it springs back into place, the lobster was alive, as it should have been, when boiled.

To Boil and Dress a Lobster

Pick up live lobster back of claws and plunge it into boiling water, head downward. Add one tablespoon salt, cover the kettle and keep water boiling. A medium-sized lobster will cook in about 20 minutes. Plunge it into cold water and when cool enough to handle, take the meat from the shell in the following order: Chop off the claws. Split the body lengthwise and remove and discard the stomach, a small sac just back of the head. Running from the stomach to the base of the tail is the intestinal canal. If this does not pull out with the stomach, it must be lifted out with a fork, in pieces, if necessary, and removed entirely.

Crack the claws and remove the meat. If the lobster is not to be served whole, take out the meat from the body, the creamy green fat which constitutes the liver, and the coral or spawn found in female lobsters. The spongy particles between the meat and shell are not used.

In cutting up the meat of cooked lobster, always use a silver knife or one of stainless steel, if possible, as an ordinary steel knife discolors or darkens the meat.

Save the body shell of the lobster to use in serving.

WHETHER BAKED OR PLANKED, ONLY
CAREFUL HANDLING
WILL BRING FISH
TO THE TABLE
LOOKING
ITS BEST

THE LORDLY LOBSTER IS STILL THE ARISTO-
CRAT OF THE FESTIVE OCCASION

ASSORTED FROZEN FISH STICKS AND SHRIMPS.

COLD LOBSTER EN COQUILLES WITH MAYONNAISE

Serve cold boiled lobster in the shell on a bed of lettuce. Color mayonnaise red with lobster coral and place on lobster. Canned lobster meat may be chilled thoroughly and served on lettuce with anchovy mayonnaise.

BROILED LIVE LOBSTER

1 large lobster   Salt and pepper
Melted butter

Kill lobster by inserting a sharp knife in its back between the body and tail shells, severing the spinal cord. Split lengthwise, remove the stomach and intestinal canal, crack the large claws and lay the lobster flat. Brush the meat with butter, season with salt and pepper, place in broiler with the shell side down, and broil slowly until browned. Serves 2.

A small lobster will cook in 15 minutes; larger ones may require 20 to 25 minutes. The lobster may be turned once, if desired, but this is not necessary and results in loss of juices. Serve a small dish of drawn butter with each lobster. A nutcracker may be used at the table for further cracking of the claws. Serves 2.

BAKED LIVE LOBSTER

Prepare as for broiling. Place lobster in a baking pan, shell side down, and season with salt, pepper and butter. Bake in hot oven (400° F.) about 40 minutes, basting it twice with melted butter.

BAKED STUFFED LOBSTER

1 large live lobster   3 tablespoons butter, melted
1 cup soft bread crumbs   Salt and pepper

Prepare lobster as for broiling. Toast bread crumbs in the oven and mix with butter and green fat and mashed coral from the lobster. Season with salt and pepper. Fill cavities in lobster with mixture and cover exposed meat with a thin layer. Bake as above. Serves 2.

LOBSTER FARCI

2 lobsters	1 tablespoon minced parsley
1 tablespoon butter	Salt and pepper
1 tablespoon flour	Few grains nutmeg
1 cup milk	3 egg yolks, hard cooked
2 tablespoons bread crumbs	¼ cup buttered crumbs

Boil lobsters and cut meat into small pieces. In opening the lobsters be careful not to break the body or tail shells. Melt butter, blend in flour, add milk and cook until thickened. Add crumbs, parsley, lobster, salt, pepper, nutmeg and egg yolks mashed very fine. Mix all together well. Wash shells, wipe dry and cut off the under part of the tail shells with a pair of scissors. Join the large ends of both tail shells to one body shell to form a boat-shaped receptacle. Place lobster mixture in this boat, sprinkle with buttered crumbs and bake in moderate oven (350° F.) 15 to 20 minutes. Serves 2 or 3.

LOBSTER THERMIDOR

1 boiled lobster	½ cup sherry
3 mushrooms, sliced	2 tablespoons flour
5 tablespoons butter	1 cup cream
Dash paprika	½ teaspoon salt
⅛ teaspoon mustard	2 tablespoons grated Par-
1 tablespoon minced parsley	mesan cheese

Cut lobster into halves, remove meat and break it into small pieces. Cook mushrooms in 3 tablespoons butter and add paprika, mustard, parsley and sherry. Heat to boiling. Melt remaining butter, blend in flour, add cream and cook until thickened, stirring constantly. Season with salt and add mushroom mixture and lobster. Fill shell with mixture. Sprinkle with cheese. Bake in very hot oven (425° F.) 15 to 20 minutes. Serves 2.

CREAMED LOBSTER, SALMON OR TUNA

2 cups diced cooked lobster, salmon or tuna	2 teaspoons lemon juice
2 cups medium white sauce	2 drops Tabasco sauce

Heat lobster in white sauce; add lemon juice and Tabasco sauce. Serve on toast or crackers. Serves 6.

LOBSTER BÉCHAMEL

1 boiled lobster
3 tablespoons butter
3 tablespoons flour
¾ cup chicken stock
¾ cup cream
½ bay leaf

½ teaspoon salt
⅛ teaspoon pepper
1 teaspoon minced parsley
1 teaspoon lemon juice
2 egg yolks
6 patty shells

Remove meat from lobster and cut into dice. Melt butter, blend in flour, add chicken stock, cream and bay leaf and cook until thickened, stirring constantly. Add salt, pepper, parsley and lemon juice and cook 5 minutes longer. Remove bay leaf. Add lobster and heat thoroughly. Add slightly beaten egg yolks and cook 1 minute longer, stirring constantly. Serve in patty shells. Serves 6.

DEVILED LOBSTER

2 cups diced cooked lobster
1 cup soft bread crumbs
1 hard-cooked egg
2 teaspoons lemon juice
1 tablespoon butter

1 tablespoon flour
1 cup milk
½ teaspoon salt
Few grains cayenne
½ teaspoon anchovy paste

Mix lobster with half the crumbs. Chop egg very fine and add to lobster with lemon juice. Melt butter, blend in flour, add milk and cook until thickened, stirring constantly. Season with salt, cayenne and anchovy paste. Mix well with lobster mixture and fill greased scallop shells or ramekins. Top with remaining crumbs. Brown in moderate oven (375° F.) about 15 minutes. Serves 6.

LOBSTER WITH CORAL SAUCE

1 boiled lobster
3 tablespoons butter
2 tablespoons flour

½ teaspoon salt
2 cups boiling water
2 tablespoons lemon juice

Dice lobster meat and mash coral with 1 tablespoon butter. Melt remaining butter, blend in flour and salt, add water and cook until thickened, stirring constantly. Add coral and cook 4 minutes. Strain, add lobster meat and lemon juice and heat to boiling. Serves 4.

Fresh Water Crawfish

Crawfish, or crayfish, look like lobsters, but are much smaller. They may be prepared and served in the same way as lobsters.

Add bay leaf, celery leaves, peppercorns and caraway seeds to boiling salted water, then drop crawfish into the water and cook 5 minutes. Drain, cool and remove shell. Take out the intestines by pinching the extreme end of the center fin and jerking it suddenly. This removes the gall cyst which is very bitter. Two pounds crawfish will serve 6.

Crabs

The blue crab, found on the Atlantic coast and in the Gulf of Mexico, is about 2½ inches long by 5 inches wide. The Dungeness crab of the Pacific coast is much larger. Crabs go through a molting season, in the spring and summer. During the few days between the shedding of the old shell and the hardening of the new one, they are called soft-shelled crabs. At other times, they are called hard-shelled crabs.

Oyster crabs are tiny, almost transparent, grayish-white crabs found in the shells with oysters. They are often served in oyster stews.

Dressing Crabs

All uncooked crabs should be vigorously alive when purchased, or the meat is not good.

SOFT-SHELLED CRABS—Place live crabs face down on a board; slice across just back of the eyes. Lift apron at opposite end of crab, scrape off spongy portion beneath and cut off apron. Remove sand bag. Lift each point at the sides and remove all the gills. Wash and dry.

HARD-SHELLED CRABS—Drop the live crabs head first into rapidly boiling salted water and boil 20 minutes. Drain and cool. Take the crab in both hands, with the thumbs at the tail end, and pull the upper and lower shells apart. Discard the material that sticks to the upper shell and pull off all the orange waxy material and white spongy substance between the halves of the body and at the sides. The edible part of the crab lies in the two compact masses remaining and in the small flakes that may be extracted from the large claws.

BROILED SOFT-SHELLED CRABS

6 soft-shelled crabs   ¼ teaspoon salt
¼ cup butter, melted   ⅛ teaspoon cayenne
2 tablespoons lemon juice   Flour

Clean crabs as directed. Mix butter, lemon juice, salt and cayenne and roll each crab first in this mixture, then in flour. Place on broiler rack and broil 4 minutes on each side. Serve garnished with toast triangles. Serves 6.

FRIED SOFT-SHELLED CRABS

6 soft-shelled crabs   2 eggs, slightly beaten
Salt and pepper   1½ cups fine bread crumbs

Clean crabs and sprinkle with salt and pepper. Dip in egg, then in crumbs. Fry in hot deep fat (375° F.) 3 to 4 minutes. Serves 3 or 6.

DEVILED CRABS

8 hard-shelled crabs   ½ teaspoon prepared
1 cup medium white sauce   mustard
1 egg, beaten   2 hard-cooked eggs
2 tablespoons tomato catchup   ½ cup buttered crumbs
     2 tablespoons minced parsley

Boil crabs as directed; remove and flake meat, saving claws for garnish. Add hot white sauce to beaten egg, then add catchup, mustard, crab meat and finely chopped hard-cooked eggs. Fill 4 crab shells with mixture and sprinkle with crumbs and parsley. Bake in hot oven (400° F.) until crumbs are browned, about 10 minutes. Serves 4.

CREAMED CRAB MEAT

2 cups cooked crab meat   ½ teaspoon prepared
2 tablespoons butter   mustard
2 tablespoons flour   ¼ teaspoon paprika
Few grains pepper   1 cup milk
½ teaspoon salt

Remove spines from crab meat. Melt butter, blend in flour and seasonings, add milk and cook until thickened, stirring constantly. Add crab meat and heat thoroughly. Serve very hot in patty shells or on toast. Serves 6.

SCALLOPED—Add ½ cup crumbs, place in shells, top with buttered crumbs and bake in moderate oven (350° F.) 15 minutes.

CRAB MEAT IN SHELLS

½ cup butter
½ cup flour
Few grains cayenne
1 teaspoon salt
¼ teaspoon pepper

3 cups milk
½-pound can crab meat
½ cup minced parsley
4 hard-cooked eggs, chopped
½ cup buttered crumbs

Melt butter; blend in flour and seasonings. Add milk and cook until thickened, stirring constantly. Flake crab meat and remove spines. Add to sauce with parsley and eggs. Place in buttered shells and top with buttered crumbs. Brown in moderate oven (375° F.) about 10 minutes. Serves 8.

CRAB NEWBURG

½ pound cooked crab meat
¼ cup butter
¼ teaspoon salt
Dash cayenne

1 cup cream
2 egg yolks, beaten
1 tablespoon sherry
4 patty shells

Heat crab meat in butter; add salt and cayenne. Mix 1 tablespoon cream with egg yolks and add remainder to crab meat. Add egg yolks and sherry and heat until it begins to thicken, stirring constantly. Do not boil. Serve in patty shells or on hot buttered toast. Serves 4.

AVOCADO CRAB CUTLETS

2 cups cooked crab meat
3 tablespoons butter
4 tablespoons flour
½ teaspoon salt
⅛ teaspoon pepper

1½ cups milk
2 cups diced avocado
Fine bread crumbs
3 eggs, beaten

Remove spines from crab meat. Melt butter and blend in flour. Add salt, pepper and milk and cook until thickened, stirring constantly. Add avocado and crab meat and mix well. Shape into cutlets and roll in crumbs, then in egg and again in crumbs. Fry in hot deep fat (360° F.) until browned, 2 to 4 minutes. Serves 6.

Or add ½ cup cream, place mixture in casserole and cover with buttered crumbs. Brown in moderate oven (350° F.).

CRAB COCKTAIL

Follow recipe for oyster cocktail. (See Index.)

SHRIMP AND PRAWNS

Shrimp and prawns are very similar, but the prawn is larger than the shrimp. The shrimp is seldom more than 2 inches long, while the prawn is often 6 to 7 inches.

To PREPARE FRESH SHRIMP—Add bay leaf, celery leaves, peppercorns and caraway seeds (tied in cheesecloth if desired) to boiling salted water. Simmer a few minutes. Wash shrimp under running water, then drop into boiling seasoned water and simmer 10 to 15 minutes. Paprika is sometimes added to intensify the red color. Allow to cool in this liquor. When cold, remove shells carefully and remove the black line which runs the length of the back. Use in recipes as desired. If canned shrimp are used, they too must be cleaned by removing the black line, which is the intestinal tract. Strained liquor may be used in Court Bouillon or jellied fish salads.

SHRIMP COCKTAIL

Follow recipe for oyster cocktail, using cleaned cooked shrimp. (Page 200.)

CREAMED SHRIMP

2 cups cooked shrimp	¼ teaspoon celery salt
1 teaspoon lemon juice	1½ cups white sauce

Add shrimp, lemon juice and celery salt to hot white sauce and heat thoroughly. Serve on toast or on crisp crackers. Garnish with paprika and parsley. Serves 4.

SHRIMP WIGGLE

4 tablespoons butter	2 cups milk
4 tablespoons flour	Few drops onion juice
½ teaspoon salt	2 cups cooked shrimp
⅛ teaspoon pepper	1 cup cooked peas
½ teaspoon celery salt	Crackers

Melt butter and blend in flour, salt, pepper and celery salt. Add milk and onion juice and cook until thickened, stirring constantly. Add shrimp and peas and heat thoroughly. Serve on crisp crackers. Serves 6.

If desired, omit celery salt and cook ½ cup diced celery in butter before adding flour and seasonings. Add 1 tablespoon diced pimiento or sprinkle freely with paprika.

SCALLOPED SHRIMP

4 tablespoons butter	¼ teaspoon dry mustard
2 tablespoons minced onion	2 cups milk
1 tablespoon minced green pepper	2 cups cooked shrimp
4 tablespoons flour	1 cup buttered crumbs

Melt butter and cook onion and green pepper in it until tender. Blend in flour and mustard. Add milk and cook until thickened, stirring constantly. Add shrimp. Pour into greased casserole, cover with buttered crumbs and bake in moderate oven (350° F.) about 20 minutes. Serves 6.

CHARLESTON SHRIMP PILAU

1 cup diced bacon	1 cup uncooked rice
2 tablespoons chopped onion	1 pound shrimp, cooked
2½ cups cooked tomatoes	

Fry bacon until crisp, remove and cook onion in bacon fat until a light yellow. Add tomatoes and rice, mix well, cover and heat to boiling point. Lower heat and simmer 20 minutes, occasionally stirring lightly with fork. Set in warm place where there is no danger of scorching for another 20 minutes, to allow rice to become fluffy. Add shrimp and bacon, place in casserole and bake in a 350° F. oven 15 minutes. Serves 6.

SHRIMP CREOLE

½ medium-sized onion, chopped	Dash of cayenne
½ cup chopped mushrooms	¼ teaspoon thyme
2 tablespoons butter	1 bay leaf
2 tablespoons flour	2 pimientos, chopped
1 cup mushroom broth	2 cups cooked shrimp
1 cup water	4 wheat biscuits
½ teaspoon salt	Butter
⅛ teaspoon pepper	3 sprigs parsley

Sauté onion and mushrooms in butter 3 minutes; stir in flour and cook 1 minute, then add liquid gradually and cook until thickened, stirring constantly. Add seasonings, pimientos and shrimp and cook 5 minutes. Remove bay leaf. Serve on wheat biscuits, which have been cut lengthwise into halves, toasted and buttered. Garnish with parsley.

SHRIMP PASTE

2 cups cooked shrimp   Salt, celery salt, cayenne
½ cup butter

Grind shrimp very fine; mix with softened butter. Season with salt, celery salt and cayenne, place in small pan and bake at 350° F. 30 minutes. Chill and slice. Serves 8.

SHRIMP GUMBO

6 green onions   1 green pepper
2 cups chopped okra   ½ teaspoon thyme
1 tablespoon bacon fat   1 bay leaf
1 cup chopped tomatoes   1 teaspoon salt
6 cups stock   1 pound shrimp, cooked
1 pod red pepper

Clean onions, reserving green tops. Chop and sauté with okra in bacon fat. Add tomatoes and cook 5 minutes. Add stock, peppers, green onion tops cut into strips, thyme, bay leaf and salt. Heat to boiling and cook 10 minutes. Add shrimp, cut into halves, cover closely and simmer 1½ hours. Serve with rice. Serves 8.

JAMBALAYA SHRIMP

1 tablespoon fat   1 green pepper, chopped
1 tablespoon flour   1 tablespoon minced parsley
1 pound ham, cooked   Salt, pepper and paprika
  and chopped   1 teaspoon Worcestershire
1 cup cooked shrimp   sauce
1½ cups cooked tomatoes   1 red pepper, chopped
1 onion, sliced   4 cups water
¼ teaspoon thyme   1 cup uncooked rice
1 clove garlic, crushed

Melt fat and add flour, stirring until smooth and slightly brown. Add chopped ham, shrimp and tomatoes and cook for 3 minutes. Add onion, seasonings and water. Simmer for 10 minutes. Add rice and boil until tender, 30 minutes. The mixture should not be stirred, although it may be necessary to lift it from the bottom of the kettle from time to time in order to keep rice from burning. Keep covered during cooking. Serves 6.

STUFFINGS FOR MEAT, FISH, POULTRY AND GAME

STUFFING does not necessarily have to be baked in the fowl or meat. If the bird is small or if there is some stuffing left over, it may be baked or steamed in a well-greased ring mold, loaf pan or individual molds. Fill center of ring with vegetables. Croquettes of stuffing, made by the usual method, are served in a circle around the bird.

BREAD STUFFING

No. 1

1½ cups soft bread crumbs
1 egg, slightly beaten
¼ cup butter

¼ teaspoon salt
Dash pepper

Moisten bread crumbs with egg and the melted butter. Season and mix well. This makes a rich, moist dressing. Makes 1½ cups.

No. 2

2 to 3 tablespoons melted fat
1 tablespoon chopped onion
1 cup dry bread crumbs
¼ teaspoon salt
Dash pepper

½ teaspoon each sage,
chopped celery, parsley
1 to 2 tablespoons milk
or stock

Melt fat in frying pan; add onion and sauté until tender. Add bread crumbs and seasonings and mix well. Then add milk or stock. This makes a loose, light stuffing much preferred by many to the soft moist or compact type. It can be varied by omitting onion or sage, by adding chopped celery or by adding 2 tablespoons seeded raisins. Makes 1 cup.

No. 3

½ cup milk
2 cups grated bread crumbs
1½ tablespoons melted fat
1 egg, slightly beaten
½ teaspoon salt

¼ teaspoon pepper
¼ teaspoon thyme
½ teaspoon powdered sage
½ teaspoon chopped onion
¼ teaspoon summer savory

Pour milk on crumbs and let stand about 1 hour. Add remaining ingredients. Makes 2 cups.

CRACKER CRUMB STUFFING

2 tablespoons butter
1 cup cracker crumbs
¼ cup boiling water

⅛ teaspoon pepper
¼ teaspoon salt
¼ teaspoon poultry seasoning

Melt butter and mix with crumbs. Add water and seasonings. When this stuffing is used, a greater allowance than usual must be made for swelling. Makes 1 cup.

POTATO STUFFING

2 cups hot mashed potato
1 cup bread crumbs
½ teaspoon pepper
½ teaspoon salt

1 teaspoon sage
4 tablespoons melted
butter or other fat
2 tablespoons onion juice

Mix the ingredients in order given. Makes 3 cups.

CELERY STUFFING

2 tablespoons butter
2 cups dry bread crumbs
2 cups finely chopped celery

1 teaspoon salt
½ teaspoon pepper

Melt butter, add crumbs and mix well. Add celery, salt and pepper. Makes 4 cups.

OYSTER STUFFING

2 cups oysters
2 cups dry bread crumbs
1 teaspoon salt

¼ teaspoon pepper
¼ cup melted fat

Mix oysters well with bread crumbs and seasoning and add the melted fat. Makes 4 cups.

PINEAPPLE NUT STUFFING

4 cups dry bread, ½ inch
  cubes
¾ cup finely chopped celery
½ cup chopped walnuts
¾ cup diced pineapple
1 pimiento, diced
1 teaspoon paprika
Dash cayenne
1½ teaspoon salt
¼ cup butter
2 eggs

Combine bread, celery, walnuts, pineapple, pimiento and seasoning. Melt butter, remove from heat, stir in unbeaten eggs and add to bread mixture. Toss lightly. Use as stuffing for turkey, chicken, duck, veal roll, lamb chops or pork chops. Use crisp bacon cut into small pieces instead of nuts, reduce salt one-third and add grated onion, or use red or green bell pepper instead of pimiento. Makes 6 cups.

SAUSAGE STUFFING

½ pound sausage meat
2 cups dried bread crumbs
Salt and pepper
1 tablespoon onion juice
1 tablespoon minced parsley

Mix sausage and crumbs, then add seasonings. Makes 3 cups.

MUSHROOM STUFFING

3 cups dry bread crumbs
6 tablespoons melted butter
½ cup chopped mushrooms
½ teaspoon salt
½ teaspoon powdered
  thyme
1 teaspoon minced parsley

Mix ingredients in the order given. Makes 3½ cups.

RICE STUFFING

1 cup milk
1 cup soft bread crumbs
1 onion, chopped
1 tablespoon fat
4 cups cold boiled rice
½ pound sausage meat
½ teaspoon sage
1 tablespoon minced parsley
½ teaspoon thyme
1 teaspoon salt
⅛ teaspoon pepper

Pour milk over crumbs. Cook onion in fat until brown, then add rice, soaked crumbs, sausage and seasonings. Makes 6 cups.

CORN-BREAD STUFFING

1 (1½-pound) loaf bread
3 cups crumbled corn bread
½ pound sausage meat
2 eggs

⅛ teaspoon pepper
1 large onion, minced
2 stalks celery, minced
1 teaspoon poultry seasoning

Slice bread and brown lightly in slow oven. Shred finely and mix well with remaining ingredients. Moisten with warm water until it will just hold together. Will fill a 16-pound turkey.

CHESTNUT STUFFING

1 quart chestnuts
¼ cup bread crumbs
2 tablespoons butter

2 tablespoons cream
Salt and pepper
½ teaspoon onion juice

Shell and blanch chestnuts and cook in boiling water until tender. While hot, rub through coarse sieve. Mix with remaining ingredients. Makes 2½ cups.

RAISIN-NUT STUFFING

2 cups dry bread crumbs
⅓ cup butter, melted
½ cup chopped seeded raisins
½ cup broken walnut meats

½ teaspoon salt
⅛ teaspoon pepper
½ teaspoon sage

Mix ingredients together lightly with fork. Makes 2½ cups.

WILD RICE AND MUSHROOM STUFFING

⅓ cup chopped onion
¼ cup butter
1 cup chopped mushrooms

¼ pound sausage meat
3 cups boiled wild rice
1 teaspoon salt

Sauté onion in 2 tablespoons butter 5 minutes, or until lightly browned, and remove from pan; add remaining 2 tablespoons butter and mushrooms, and cook 5 minutes, then remove from pan. Fry sausage meat until lightly browned, stirring constantly; remove from heat and stir in onion and mushrooms; add wild rice and salt, mixing lightly. This makes a light goose stuffing. Makes 5 cups stuffing or enough for 1 (10-lb.) goose.

ADDITIONAL ENTRÉES

A N entrée is a dish that is served as an independent course between two main courses of a meal. In an informal meal, an entrée of protein food may be served as the main course.

An entrée is usually a "light" dish, small in bulk, and is often accompanied by a sauce which may or may not be an integral part of the dish. It may be served either hot or cold. Hot entrées are often accompanied by a hot sauce, such as Hollandaise or maître d'hôtel; and cold entrées by cold sauces,—vinaigrette, tartar, etc. Ordinarily the hot entree precedes the roast and the cold entrée follows it.

Entrees may be made of a great number of foods—eggs in many attractive forms; fish of all kinds; meat, such as lamb, veal and tender cuts of fowl and beef, cooked by some method other than roasting; macaroni and spaghetti; some fruits; and many kinds of vegetables.

Increasingly in America today vegetables are served as entrées. This is undoubtedly due to the fact that the eating habits of the nation have changed, because we have a growing knowledge of and interest in the food-values of vegetables and fruits. For luncheon and dinner now one vegetable is often raised to the dignity of becoming a course by itself.

Hot Entrées

CREAMED MIXTURES—These are the most simple and easily prepared of the hot entrées. Any well-seasoned creamed mixture may be used. It must be kept hot and transferred at the last possible moment to the container in which it is to be served. This may be merely a slice of toast, an individual case such as a ramekin, patty shell or timbale case, or a border formed of bread, rice or potato.

FORCEMEATS—These should have a smooth, velvety texture. They call for more effort in preparation than any other type of entrée. They are made of cooked or uncooked meat or fish in finely divided form, those made of the uncooked material being considered the more choice. Such foods as chicken and ham, shell fish and any fine white fish make typical force-meats. Forcemeats may be used in combination with other materials or cooked alone to form cutlets and timbales. The cutlets are cooked in shallow, chop-shaped molds and the timbales in deep, straight sided molds.

CROQUETTES—Croquettes are made of cooked and chopped ingredients held together, usually, by means of a thick sauce. When the mixture is cold, it is made into shapes of uniform size, which are coated with flour or sifted crumbs, then rolled in an egg mixture so that the egg forms a continuous film, then rolled in crumbs again. The egg mixture is made by adding two tablespoons of water or milk to each egg required, and beating just enough to break up the white of the egg. The croquettes may be allowed to stand until dry or may be fried at once in deep hot fat. This is a good way to use left-over cooked foods.

Croquettes are made in the form of balls, rolls, cones, nests or cups, cutlets or flat cakes. Whatever shape is desired, it is usually easier to attain it by making the mixture into a ball first, thus insuring a compact mass from which the chosen form may be readily molded.

CUTLETS—This word, as used in this chapter refers to the form in which the food is cooked rather than a distinct type of food. Sometimes cutlets are made by packing forcemeat into shallow, chop-shaped molds, but more often they are croquettes, cut or shaped to look like breaded chops or cutlets. The term may be extended to include boiled cereal, such as rice or cornmeal, which has been packed into a shallow dish, left until cold, and then cut into pieces, rolled in egg and crumbs and fried or sautéd.

FRITTERS—These may be composed of a piece of fruit enclosed in a batter, then fried in deep hot fat and served with an appropriate sauce; or chopped fruit, chopped vegetable, or other chopped food, such as clams or lobster, stirred into the batter and fried by spoonfuls.

TIMBALES—This term is sometimes used to describe forcemeat cooked in straight-sided deep molds. More frequently perhaps it refers to sugarless custards cooked in timbale molds. In timbales of this types, where egg is the thickening agent, savory seasonings are used, and the milk which ordinarily forms an important component of custard is replaced in part or entirely by meat stock or vegetable purée.

All timbales are cooked in molds of some sort; they are cooked by oven-poaching and are not browned. They are turned out of the molds before they are served. A circle of buttered paper laid in the bottom of the mold before it is filled insures perfect unmolding.

HOT SOUFFLÉS—These are the lightest of the entrées, being made so by well-beaten egg white folded into the seasoned foundation mixture. This may be simply a fruit purée or pulp; it may be a white sauce combined with egg yolks and the characterizing ingredient; or it may be a panada made by cooking either cracker or bread crumbs with milk and adding the prepared ingredient, this method being best for meat soufflés. Soufflés need the same careful baking given to egg timbales and are served in or from the baking dish. The top should be browned.

FILLETS—This type of entrée is composed of a solid piece of meat or fish, and may comprise breasts or joints of poultry, chops, large oysters, scallops, crabs, fillets of fish and the first three cuts of beef tenderloin. These when used as entrées, may be cooked by broiling, sautéing, frying or oven-poaching, but never by roasting because the flavor and effect would be too much like that of the main course.

Vegetable Entrées—Hot or Cold

The following vegetables are suggested for service as entrées: asparagus, cauliflower and broccoli, hot with Hollandaise or butter sauce, or cold with vinaigrette; tomato surprise, stuffed, for instance, with mushrooms; corn on the cob; mushrooms; baked Lima beans; long, thin string beans, not cut or split; large beets hollowed out and filled with bread crumbs and tiny peas or chopped carrots or both; stuffed peppers; eggplant; baked Hubbard squash, Brussels sprouts; braised celery or endive; cucumbers; and artichoke bottoms stuffed with forcemeat and baked.

Cold Entrées

ASPICS—Aspic is a spiced tart jelly made from brown or white meat stock alone or in combination with gelatin. It is used to enclose a variety of foods in a mold or to give a transparent coating of shining, sparkling finish. Various foods may be molded in aspic—for instance, stuffed olives, plain or stuffed tomatoes, eggs, birds, beef tongue, chicken salad or a mousse.

Aspics give ample opportunity to show inventiveness in design, for they are usually elaborately decorated. Decorative shapes may be cut from pimiento, green or red pepper, olives, pickles, hard-cooked egg-white, yellow custard, parsley, truffles or cooked vegetables. Green peas and capers, also, are frequently used.

CHAUD FROIDS—For these dishes, the sauce is made up hot but the finished product is served cold. The sauce, which may be white, yellow or brown, and stiffened with gelatin, is used to give a smooth, glossy surface to eggs, cutlets, breast or other choice pieces of chicken, fish fillets, etc., all of which must be plainly cooked and well seasoned. A decoration is usual, also a final coating of aspic.

MOUSSES—This term, used in connection with entrées, refers to a dish made of a meat, fish or vegetable purée stiffened with gelatin and made light by means of beaten cream. It is molded to give it shape, chilled, then unmolded for serving.

COLD SOUFFLÉS—It is difficult to differentiate these from the mousses. About the only difference is the manner of serving. The mixture may be put into individual dishes of china, or paper cases, having paper bands pinned about the top to give greater height. When the mixture is chilled, the bands are removed. The mixture, extending above the edge of the container, gives the effect of great lightness, thus simulating a soufflé.

SALADS—Salads are not usually thought of as entrées, but in a formal menu are so considered.

Borders and Cases
BREAD CROUSTADES

Cut slices of bread from one to two inches thick. Remove the brown part of the crust. Cut each trimmed slice into two oblongs or two triangles, for large croustades, or into four squares or four triangles, for small croustades. Or shape the bread with cookie cutters into circles, diamonds, etc. Insert the point of a sharp knife into the top of the shaped piece, one-half inch from the edge, and cut around the outline running the knife down to within one-half inch of the bottom. Insert the knife point horizontally through one side of the slice, one-half inch from the bottom, and cut out and remove the center, leaving a box with half-inch walls and bottom. Fry these cases in deep fat, (375°-390° F.) or, if you prefer, brush them over with melted fat and set them in a moderate oven (350°-400° F.) to brown.

RICE CROUSTADES

Cook one cup of washed rice in white stock instead of in water. Drain well, mix with a thick white sauce, and spread in a greased pan to the depth of about two inches. Cover with oiled paper and place weights on top, so that the mixture may become very compact when cold. When it is perfectly firm, cut it in circles, make a cavity in the center of each, dip the case thus made in fine bread-crumbs, then in egg, and again in crumbs, and fry in deep fat (375°-390° F.).

POTATO BORDER

9 medium-sized potatoes	1 tablespoon salt
2 tablespoons butter	2 eggs
½ cup hot milk	

Boil and rice the potatoes. Add remaining ingredients except ¼ teaspoon salt and the egg whites. Beat the mixture until very light. Pack into a border mold, well greased, and set in warm place eight minutes. Unmold onto an oven-proof platter. Beat egg whites, with remaining salt, to a froth, spread over the border and brown in a slow oven (300°-350° F.).

POTATO TIMBALES—Peel potatoes and cut into tiny strips lengthwise. Heat in a small amount of fat until slightly soft—don't brown. Remove, sprinkle with salt and arrange nests inside large deep muffin tins, pressing firmly against sides and bottom. Bake in hot oven (450° F.) for 15 minutes. Use carrots, parsnips, macaroni, spaghetti or fine noodles instead of potatoes.

RICE BORDER

1 cup rice	2 tablespoons butter or
3 cups white stock	other fat
1 tablespoon salt	3 tablespoons milk or cream
2 egg-yolks	

Cook washed rice in white stock for one-half hour, then add salt and butter or other fat and cook slowly twenty minutes more. Beat the yolks of the eggs with the cream or milk and stir in. Grease a border mold, pack the rice firmly into it, let it stand eight to ten minutes in a warm (not hot) place and turn out on a hot platter. Fill the center with any meat preparation warmed in sauce.

TIMBALE ROSETTES

1 egg	½ cup flour
10 tablespoons evapo-	⅛ teaspoon salt
rated milk	1½ teaspoons sugar

Beat egg slightly. Add milk. Sift flour, then measure. Resift with salt and sugar into the egg and milk mixture. Stir until batter is smooth. It should be about the consistency of heavy cream. Use a deep, heart-shaped timbale iron. Dip in the hot fat to heat, then in the batter, being careful that the batter does not come up over the top of the iron.

Have ready a small, deep kettle of fat, place the iron in it and heat until the fat is hot enough to brown a piece of bread while counting sixty (370° F.). The fat should be deep enough to cover the mold end of the iron. Take out the heated iron, remove surplus fat with a piece of absorbent paper and lower the iron into the batter until it is covered not more than three-fourths its height. This is necessary to allow for the rising of the batter during cooking. If only a thin layer of batter adheres to the iron, plunge it in again, and repeat if necessary until there is a smooth layer of partly cooked batter. Plunge it quickly into the hot fat and cook from two to three minutes. Remove from the fat, slip the case from the iron on to absorbent paper and continue until you have the required number of cases.

A fluted iron is easier to work with than a plain one, because the case does not slip off until thoroughly cooked. A properly cooked case, however, should slip easily from the mold. If the cases are not crisp, the batter is too thick and should be diluted with milk.

These cases may be filled with a creamed vegetable, creamed oysters, chicken or sweetbreads, or with fresh or cooked fruit topped with whipped cream or powdered sugar. When sweet fillings are used, they are served as a dessert. This recipe makes about 20 cases with an iron of average size.

RISSOLES

These are practically little turnovers, filled with a highly seasoned mixture of chopped chicken and ham or other delicate meat moistened with white sauce. Roll puff-paste very thin and cut in circles. Place a teaspoon of the mixture in the center of each circle, moisten half the circumference with cold water, and fold the other half over, pressing the edges closely together. Dip in slightly beaten egg mixed with a tablespoon of water. Fry in deep fat (360°-370° F.) and drain thoroughly.

BOUCHÉES

Small pastry shells or cases filled with creamed meat or game are called bouchées, and are much in vogue for entrées. They provide an excellent way of utilizing left-overs of chicken, sweetbreads, fish, etc. Paper cases, bought at the confectioner's, may be used instead of the pastry shells.

PATTY CASES

Roll puff-paste to the thickness of one-half inch and with a cookie cutter shape circles two and one-half to three inches in diameter. With a tiny cutter, remove the centers from half of the circles. Brush the edges of the complete circles with water and lay the rings on top. Chill thoroughly, then bake in a hot oven (400°-450° F.) from fifteen to twenty minutes. At the same time, bake the small centers removed from the upper layers of the cases, and use them as lids for the filled patties.

VOL-AU-VENT

A vol-au-vent is a large patty. The French name signifies something that will fly away in the wind. Roll out puff-paste one and one-half inches in thickness, and cut a circle about six inches in diameter, using a cutter or, with a sharp knife, cutting around the edge of a plate laid on the paste. Place the circle on a baking-tin and, with a sharp pointed knife or a smaller cutter, cut a circle around the top about one and one-half inches from the edge and about an inch deep. Do not remove the center but bake the entire circle in a large, flat pan in a hot oven (450°-500° F.) from thirty to fifty minutes.

REMOVE ALL BUT BOTTOM CRUST.
CUT AND SCOOP OUT CENTER.
TOAST, FILL WITH CREAMED SAL-
MON MIXTURE. CRUMB AND BROWN
TO SERVE.

THE CLEVER HOSTESS WILL MAKE TIMBALES OF SHREDDED POTATOES, SPAGHETTI OR FINE NOODLES AND FILL THEM WITH SALMON A LA KING — FOR INSTANCE

When the outer crust is cooked, lift out the center, remove the uncooked paste from below, and the shell is ready to be filled. It may be filled with lobster meat, oysters, chicken, or any kind of delicate meat or fish chopped and seasoned, and heated in Béchamel, white, brown or mushroom sauce, or with sweetmeats of any kind or fresh berries, sweetened. In using fish, always add one teaspoon of lemon juice to the mixture after it is taken from the fire.

HOT ENTRÉES

Creamed Mixtures

PATTIES

Patty cases are usually made ahead of time and must be thoroughly heated before they are filled. To heat them, place them in a moderate oven (350°-400° F.) fifteen or twenty minutes before they are to be filled.

Chicken—Fill hot patty cases with creamed chicken.

Clam—Fill hot patty cases with creamed clams (See Index.)

Lobster—Fill hot patty cases with creamed lobster.

Sweetbread—Fill hot patty cases with creamed sweetbreads.

CHICKEN OR SALMON À LA KING

2 tablespoons butter
1 green pepper, minced
1 cup sliced mushrooms
2 tablespoons flour
1 cup chicken stock
2 cups diced cooked chicken or boned canned red salmon

1 cup sour cream or evaporated milk
2 egg yolks
1 pimiento, diced
Salt and pepper
4 teaspoons sherry

Melt butter, add green pepper and mushrooms and sauté until tender. Lift out. Add flour to butter; add stock and cook until thickened. Add chicken or salmon, cooked pepper and mushrooms and heat thoroughly. Remove from heat and add cream mixed with beaten egg yolks and remaining ingredients. Serve at once or place over hot, not boiling, water to keep hot. Do not boil after adding egg yolks.

CHOP SUEY

2 pounds uncooked chicken-breast cut into pieces one-sixteenth inch by one inch by one-half inch

Bean sprouts equal in measure to the chicken

2 cups onions cut into threads

2 cups bamboo shoots cut into pieces the same size as the chicken

2 cups mushrooms sliced thin

Fat or oil

Put the chicken meat, bean sprouts, onions, bamboo shoots and mushrooms into a frying pan with a little fat or oil to prevent sticking and sauté for ten minutes. Add hot water to cover and cook for fifteen minutes longer. Add Chinese gravy; season to taste; remove from fire and serve at once.

CHINESE GRAVY—

1 cup primary soup or chicken stock

1 teaspoon cornstarch

Sesamum seed oil

Sugar   Salt

1 teaspoon Chinese sauce (can be bought ready prepared)

Mix the cornstarch in a little cold water, stir in the primary soup or chicken stock and let it boil until it thickens. Add the Chinese sauce, a few drops of sesamum seed oil and sugar and salt to taste. Stir well.

PRIMARY SOUP—

½ pound lean pork

½ pound chicken

1 pint water

Chop the meat into small pieces and simmer in water 2½ hours, then strain through several folds of cheesecloth.

SWEETBREAD AND OYSTER PIE

1 pair sweetbreads

2 dozen oysters

1 tablespoon fat

1 tablespoon flour

1 cup cream or milk

2 egg yolks, hard cooked

Pepper and salt

Puff or plain pie paste

Prepare sweetbreads (see Index). Make a white sauce with fat, flour and cream or milk, and add the egg yolks, chopped very fine. Add sweetbreads and prepared oysters to the sauce. Season, put into a deep baking dish, cover with a layer of paste, and bake.

SHIRRED CLAMS OR OYSTERS WITH MUSHROOMS

12 toast rounds	1½ cups milk
12 large mushroom caps	1½ tablespoons butter
12 clams or oysters	1½ tablespoons flour
Melted butter	¼ teaspoon onion juice
Salt, lemon juice	1 or 2 tablespoons an-
Paprika	chovy paste

Arrange toast in baking dish; place large peeled mushroom caps on the toast. Dip clams or oysters in melted butter seasoned with salt, lemon juice and paprika and lay on mushrooms, using enough butter to season mushrooms also. Bake in a moderate oven (375° F.), until mushrooms are tender and clams are cooked. Make a thin white sauce of milk, butter and flour, season with onion and anchovy and color with vegetable bouquet. Pour around the toast and serve.

SCOTCH WOODCOCK

2 tablespoons fat	1 tablespoon anchovy paste
1 tablespoon flour	½ teaspoon salt
1 cup milk	6 slices of bread
5 hard-cooked eggs	

Prepare a white sauce with fat, flour and milk, add eggs chopped fine, anchovy paste and salt. Have the bread toasted and lay it on a hot dish. Pour the hot mixture over it and serve immediately.

Dumplings

IRISH STEW DUMPLINGS

1 cup sifted flour	1 teaspoon bacon
½ teaspoon salt	drippings
2 teaspoons baking powder	⅓ to ½ cup milk

Sift dry ingredients together, cut in fat and add enough milk to make a drop batter. Drop by spoonfuls over top of stew. Cover kettle and let dumplings steam 15 minutes without lifting cover. The stew should be kept boiling. Serves 6.

BISCUIT DUMPLINGS

2 cups sifted flour   ¼ cup shortening
2 teaspoons baking powder   ¾ cup milk
1 teaspoon salt

Sift flour, baking powder and salt together. Cut in shortening with 2 knives or pastry blender. Add milk, using more if necessary to make a soft dough. Pat out ½ inch thick and cut into 1-inch squares, strips or diamonds. Drop into boiling chicken stock. Cover and simmer 15 minutes. Serves 6.

WHOLE-WHEAT—Use 1 cup whole-wheat for 1 cup white flour.

FEATHER DUMPLINGS

2 cups sifted flour   1 egg, well beaten
1 teaspoon salt   3 tablespoons melted
4 teaspoons baking powder   butter
¼ teaspoon pepper   Milk (about ⅔ cup)

Sift dry ingredients together. Add egg, melted butter and enough milk to make a moist, stiff batter. Drop by teaspoons into boiling liquid. Cover very closely and cook for 18 minutes. Makes 2 dozen dumplings.

EGG DUMPLINGS

1 teaspoon salt   1 egg, beaten
½ cup milk   1½ cups sifted flour

Add salt and milk to beaten egg and stir into flour to form a smooth batter. Drop by teaspoons into boiling salted water or soup, cover tightly and cook 15 minutes, being careful not to lift the lid during this time. Drain in colander. These may be served with hot fat poured over them or with meat gravy or stew. Makes 8 dumplings.

DUMPLINGS FOR PEPPER POT

1 cup finely chopped suet   ¼ teaspoon salt
2 cups sifted flour   Water

Combine suet, flour, salt and enough water to make a stiff dough. Roll into dumplings about the size of marbles. Drop into hot soup and cook about 10 minutes. Sprinkle with parsley and serve at once. Makes about 24 dumplings.

DUMPLINGS FOR STEW

2 cups sifted flour
1¼ teaspoons baking
  powder

¾ teaspoon salt
1 tablespoon butter
Milk (about ⅔ cup)

Sift flour, baking powder and salt together. Cut in butter with pastry blender or 2 knives. Add sufficient milk to make a soft dough. Turn out on a well-floured board and roll about ½ inch thick. Cut into small squares, drop in hot liquid, cover closely and cook for 20 to 25 minutes. Cooking utensils must always have a tight-fitting cover or dumplings will be heavy. Makes 12 dumplings.

POTATO DUMPLINGS

9 medium potatoes
1 teaspoon salt
3 eggs, well beaten
1 cup sifted flour

⅔ cup bread crumbs or
  farina
½ teaspoon nutmeg

Boil potatoes in their jackets until soft, remove skins and press potatoes through a ricer. Add salt, eggs, flour, ⅔ cup bread crumbs and nutmeg. Mix thoroughly. Form mixture into dry balls about the size of walnuts (if mixture is too moist, add more bread crumbs). Drop balls into boiling salted water. When balls come to the surface, boil uncovered for 3 minutes. Remove one from liquid and cut open; if center is dry, they are sufficiently cooked. Remove balls from liquid. Serve with Mushroom or Onion Sauce (page 297). Serves 12.

LIVER DUMPLINGS

½ pound liver
½ onion
1 tablespoon minced parsley
½ teaspoon salt
Dash pepper

2 slices bread
1 egg
¼ cup flour
3 cups meat broth

Wash liver and force through food chopper with onion. Add parsley, salt and pepper. Crumble bread into mixture and add unbeaten egg and flour. Beat until thoroughly mixed. Drop by teaspoons into boiling broth, cover and cook 25 minutes. Serve in broth. Serves 2 or 3.

CROQUETTES

Croquettes are an excellent means of utilizing leftovers of meat, fish, poultry or vegetables. They are made by combining one of these cooked foods with thick smooth white sauce, mashed potatoes or eggs to bind it together. Cool and shape into balls, cones, cylinders, cutlets or as desired. Roll each croquette in sifted fine dry crumbs of bread, crackers or cereal flakes. Dip in slightly beaten egg diluted with 1 tablespoon water and again in the crumbs; fry in hot deep fat.

The cooked meat or poultry should be chopped fine enough that it can be held together but should not be pasty. Usually 1 cup white sauce is used to 2 cups cooked food though this proportion varies according to moistness of cooked food. Chicken or meat stock may be used instead of half the milk in making the white sauce. The mixture must be well seasoned. It should be as soft as possible, yet stiff enough to hold together when chilled. The coating of egg and crumbs must cover croquettes completely. If there are any small uncovered spots, the croquettes may break open in frying. Place in frying basket or drop into hot fat. Do not allow croquettes to touch one another. Fry until browned. Drain on absorbent paper. Serve very hot.

Croquettes are frequently served with some sort of sauce selected to blend with or enhance the flavor of the material used in making the croquettes. Tomato or Mushroom Sauce is good with meat croquettes. Fish croquettes are good with a Medium White Sauce, to which cooked peas have been added, or with Tomato Sauce. Medium White Sauce or Cheese Sauce may be used with vegetable croquettes.

PEA AND CARROT CROQUETTES

1 cup mashed cooked carrots	1 cup Thick White Sauce
	1 tablespoon melted butter
1 cup cooked peas	Salt and pepper
1 teaspoon minced parsley	Crumbs and egg

Combine carrots, peas, parsley, white sauce and butter, being careful not to mash peas. Season, cool and shape into croquettes. Roll in crumbs, then in egg and again in crumbs. Fry in hot deep fat (380° F.) 3 to 5 minutes. Drain. Makes 6.

CHICKEN CROQUETTES

No. 1

1 cup Thick White Sauce	1 teaspoon lemon juice
1¾ cups minced cooked chicken	¼ teaspoon minced onion
Salt and pepper	1 teaspoon chopped parsley
¼ teaspoon celery salt	Crumbs and egg

Combine white sauce, chicken and seasonings. Cool, shape and roll in fine crumbs, then in egg and again in crumbs. Fry in hot deep fat (380° F.) 3 to 5 minutes. Drain. Makes 6 croquettes.

No. 2

2 cups minced cooked chicken	½ teaspoon minced onion
¼ cup chopped cooked mushrooms	1 tablespoon lemon juice
	2 tablespoons fat
1 teaspoon salt	1 tablespoon flour
½ teaspoon pepper	1 cup milk or cream
1 teaspoon minced parsley	4 eggs
	Crumbs

Mix chicken, mushrooms, salt, pepper, parsley, onion and lemon juice. Melt fat, add flour and blend. Add milk and cook until thickened. Add chicken and cook 3 minutes. Stir in 2 of the eggs beaten until light. Pour into a greased flat dish and chill. Shape and roll in fine crumbs. Beat remaining 2 eggs in a deep plate. Dip croquettes in egg, then in crumbs and fry in hot deep fat (380° F.) 3 to 5 minutes. Drain. Serve with Béchamel Sauce (page 292) or Mushroom Sauce (page 297). Makes 8 croquettes.

SURPRISE HAM CROQUETTES

2 cups mashed potatoes	Cayenne
1 tablespoon fat, melted	1 cup chopped cooked ham
3 egg yolks	Crumbs and egg

Mix potatoes, fat, 2 egg yolks and cayenne. Beat until smooth, then cool. Mix ham with remaining yolk and cook until mixture thickens. Chill. Take a large tablespoon of the potato mixture, make a hole in center, put a large teaspoon of the chopped ham inside, close the hole and form a ball. Roll in crumbs, then in egg, again in crumbs and fry in hot deep fat (380° F.) about 5 minutes. Drain. Makes 8.

EGG CROQUETTES

2 cups chopped hard-
  cooked eggs
1 cup Thick White Sauce
½ teaspoon salt

⅛ teaspoon pepper
Dash cayenne
Crumbs and egg

Chop eggs fine and moisten with sauce until as soft as can be handled. Season and chill thoroughly. Shape, roll in crumbs, then in egg, again in crumbs and fry in hot deep fat (380° F.) 3 to 5 minutes. Drain. Makes 6 croquettes.

SWEETPOTATO CROQUETTES

2½ cups mashed sweet-
  potatoes
1½ tablespoons butter

Salt and pepper
2 tablespoons brown sugar
Crumbs and egg

Combine sweetpotatoes, butter, salt, pepper and brown sugar. Beat until fluffy. Chill. Shape, roll in crumbs, then in egg and again in crumbs. Fry in hot deep fat (380° F.) 3 to 5 minutes. Drain. Makes 6 croquettes.

SALMON CROQUETTES

No. 1

1¾ cups flaked cooked
  salmon
1 cup Thick White Sauce
Salt and pepper

Cayenne
1 teaspoon lemon juice
Crumbs and egg

Combine salmon, white sauce, seasoning and lemon juice. Chill and shape. Roll in fine crumbs, then in egg and again in crumbs and fry in hot deep fat (380° F.) 3 to 5 minutes. Drain. Makes 6 croquettes.

No. 2

1 cup hot mashed potatoes
1 cup flaked salmon
Salt and pepper

1 teaspoon lemon juice
Crumbs and egg

Combine potatoes and salmon. Season with salt, pepper and lemon juice. Shape, roll in crumbs, then in egg and again in crumbs and fry in hot deep fat (380° F.) 3 to 5 minutes. Drain. Makes 4 croquettes.

Any fish desired may be used instead of salmon.

THE TRADITIONAL CROQUETTE MAY BE VARIED TO SUIT TIME AND OCCASION, AS IN THESE MEAT BALLS ON HOT PEACH HALVES

MAKE QUICK TIM-
BALES OF TOAST
OR FORMAL ONES
WITH THE FLUTED
IRON

POTATO CROQUETTES

4 cups mashed potatoes	Few drops onion juice
2 tablespoons milk or cream	Dash cayenne
3 tablespoons melted butter	2 egg yolks
½ teaspoon salt	Fine dry crumbs
2 teaspoons minced parsley	1 egg, slightly beaten

Combine potatoes, milk, butter, seasonings and egg yolks. Beat until light. Shape into cones, roll in crumbs, egg and again in crumbs and brown in hot deep fat (385° F.). Serves 6.

HOMINY—Use cooked fine hominy instead of potatoes. Press through sieve, if desired, before shaping.

ALMOND—Shape croquettes into balls, roll in flour, then in egg and finally in shredded, blanched almonds.

SPINACH—Add ½ cup chopped cooked spinach to potatoes.

CHILE CON CARNE

¼ cup olive oil	2 cloves garlic
2 pounds lean beef (cut into 10 ¾-inch cubes)	2 tablespoons chili powder
	1 tablespoon paprika
¼ pound beef suet (cut into 10 ¾-inch cubes)	2 teaspoons oregano
	Salt and pepper
1 cup minced onions	1 to 2 cups hot water

Heat the olive oil, add the meat and suet and cook until meat is brown. Add onions and garlic and cook about 5 minutes, stirring constantly; then stir in the chili powder, paprika, oregano, salt and pepper. Add 1 cup water and simmer until meat is tender. Add more water if necessary.

WITH BEANS—Add 2 cups red kidney beans to meat just before serving. Use 2½ cups cooked tomatoes instead of water.

CHILI KIDNEY BEANS

2 medium onions, chopped	2 tablespoons chili powder
1 pound ground beef	1 No. 2 can tomatoes
2 tablespoons fat	1 No. 2 can red kidney beans
2 teaspoons salt	
⅛ teaspoon pepper	

Cook onions and beef in fat until lightly browned, stirring often. Add seasonings and tomatoes and simmer gently for 1 hour. Add kidney beans and simmer 5 minutes. Serves 6.

FRIED OR SAUTÉED MUSH

No. 1

Make mush according to directions given (Index). Turn it into a shallow greased pan, smoothing the surface. When it is cold, turn it from the pan, cut in slices or cubes, dip in fine bread or cracker crumbs, then in beaten egg, adding three tablespoons of milk to each egg, and then again in the crumbs. Fry in deep fat (375°-390° F.). Drain on soft paper. Serve hot with jelly sauce or sirup.

No. 2—Cut cold mush into slices about one-fourth of an inch thick, and sauté until brown and crisp in a very little fat; if preferred, the slices may be sprinkled with flour, or dipped first in salted beaten egg and then in bread or cracker crumbs, before sautéing. Hominy and other cereals may be fried in the same way.

Fritters
(For sweet fritters and fritter batter, see Index)

CLAM FRITTERS

24 soft clams	1 cup milk
2 cups flour	½ cup clam liquor
2 teaspoons baking powder	2 eggs
½ teaspoon salt	Salt and pepper

Make a batter of flour, baking powder, salt, milk, clam liquor and well-beaten eggs. Chop the clams, season with salt and pepper and add to the batter. Drop by tablespoonfuls into deep fat (360°-370° F.) and fry two or three minutes.

CORN FRITTERS

2 cups corn, fresh or canned	1 teaspoon melted fat
1 teaspoon salt	½ cup milk
⅛ teaspoon pepper	2 cups flour
1 egg	2 teaspoons baking powder

Chop the corn very fine and add salt, pepper, well-beaten egg, melted fat, milk, flour and baking powder. Fry two to three minutes in deep fat (360°-370° F.).

OYSTER FRITTERS

1½ cups oysters	2 cups flour
2 eggs	2 teaspoons baking powder
1 cup milk	½ teaspoon salt

Chop the oysters. Make a batter of the eggs, milk, flour, baking powder and salt. Stir the oysters into the batter and drop by spoonfuls into deep hot fat (350°-365° F.).

PARSNIP FRITTERS

3 parsnips	1 cup milk
2 eggs	1 teaspoon salt
1 tablespoon fat	3 tablespoons flour

Boil the parsnips until tender, grate fine or mash and remove the fibrous parts. Beat the eggs light, and stir into the parsnips, beating hard. Add the fat, milk, salt and flour. Drop by spoonfuls into deep fat (350°-365° F.) and fry 2 to 3 minutes.

BREADED CALVES' BRAINS

Soak 2 pair of calves' brains in cold water ½ hour; then remove the thick membrane covering them and see that they are perfectly white and bloodless. Divide into servings for 4. Put into enough boiling water to cover and simmer for 15 minutes. Then take them up and plunge them into cold water. When they are cool, drain and season generously with salt and pepper. Dip into flour, then into beaten egg, seasoned with salt and pepper, then into fine bread crumbs; place in a frying basket and cook in deep fat (375°-380° F.) 5 to 8 minutes. Serve with Ravigote or Spanish Sauce.

FLANK STEAK FILLETS

1 flank steak, unscored	1 cup tomatoes, strained
½ pound kidney suet or salt pork	½ onion, chopped
	2½ teaspoons salt
½ green pepper	¼ teaspoon pepper

Cut suet or salt pork into 1-inch strips. Place on steak and roll meat tightly around the fat, skewering it through the roll

1½ inches apart. Cut roll between skewers forming individual fillets of steak with small squares of fat in center. Flour; brown fillets on both sides, place in casserole or covered pan; add tomatoes, onion, pepper and seasoning. Other vegetables, fine cut, may also be added. Simmer 1 hour or until tender or finish in 300° F. oven.

RING MOLDS

The ring mold is one of the most satisfactory ways of serving entrées since it is decorative, permits endless variety in appearance but involves no additional labor. Any recipe baked in a loaf may be used in the ring mold. Grease the mold as any pan for baking and unmold on the plate to be used for serving. The center may be filled with another cooked vegetable, a stew, creamed fish or poultry, or a china, glass or silver bowl of the exact size may be slipped into the center and filled with the sauce or dressing to be served with the ring.

NOODLE RING WITH CREAMED CHICKEN

1 pound noodles
3 eggs
1 cup milk
Dash of salt and pepper

2 tablespoons catchup
1 cup grated Cheddar cheese
½ tablespoon Worcestershire sauce

Cook noodles and drain. Beat eggs well. Combine with other ingredients. Add to noodles and pour into buttered ring mold. Set in pan of hot water and bake in a moderate oven (350° F.) 45 minutes. Unmold carefully onto a large platter and fill the center with creamed chicken. Spaghetti, macaroni or rice can be used instead of noodles.

BROWN RICE RING

1 quart boiling water
1 cup brown rice

4 tablespoons butter
2 teaspoons salt

Pick over rice and wash well. Cook as for Boiled Rice, page 282. Melt butter, add salt and mix carefully with the rice. Turn rice into a greased ring mold, place in pan of boiling water and bake in a moderate oven (350° F.) about 30 minutes. When ready to serve, unmold and fill center with creamed sea food, pp. 212 and 217 or vegetables, pp. 266-288.

KIDNEY À LA FRANCAISE

1 beef kidney	1 bay leaf
Flour	Salt and pepper
Fat	¼ inch slice of lemon

Wash and remove skin from kidneys, simmer in water to cover for ten minutes. Cut out the cords and most of the center fat. Cool, slice thin, dip each piece in flour and sauté in fat until brown. Remove the meat from the pan, add flour to fat, stirring well, until thoroughly brown. Add boiling water, stirring until smooth. Return meat to the pan, add bay leaf, salt, pepper and slice of lemon from which the peel has been removed. Simmer for one hour with the pan covered, adding more water if needed. Remove bay leaf, and serve on a heated platter.

KIDNEYS EN BROCHETTE

Split the kidneys, put over the fire in cold water and bring to the boiling point rapidly. Drain, wipe and slice each half. Arrange these slices on small metal skewers, alternating with slices of fat bacon the same size. Broil quickly and serve on toast, leaving the skewer in.

SWEETBREADS EN BROCHETTE

Prepare the sweetbreads (p. 141), cut into pieces about one inch square and one-half inch thick, season, dip into melted fat and then into flour and string on small skewers alternately with thin squares of bacon. Broil, or lay the skewers across a narrow pan and cook in a hot oven (400°-450° F.).

BRAISED SWEETBREADS À LA PARLOA

3 pairs sweetbreads	1 teaspoon beef extract
1 teaspoon minced carrot	1 bay leaf
2 teaspoons minced onion	1 sprig parsley
2 tablespoons fat	1 teaspoon lemon juice
1 tablespoon flour	Salt and pepper
1 cup water	

Prepare sweetbreads according to directions (p. 141) and arrange in deep baking dish. Cook vegetables in fat for fifteen minutes. Add flour and stir until the mixture becomes frothy. Add the water gradually, stirring all the time. When

this liquid boils, stir in the meat extract and seasonings. Cook
for five minutes and strain over the sweetbreads. Cover the
pan and cook in a moderate oven (350° F.) for one hour, basting every fifteen minutes with the gravy in the pan. Arrange
the sweetbreads on pieces of toast on a warm dish, and pour
mushroom sauce around them.

Vegetable Entrées
STUFFED PEPPERS

Cut tops off 6 peppers or cut them lengthwise into halves.
Remove inner fibers and seeds. Cook in boiling water 2 to 3
minutes. Drain, sprinkle with salt and fill with corned beef
hash, creamed cooked corn or one of the following stuffings.
Cover with buttered crumbs and bake in moderate oven (375°
F.) about 25 minutes. Serves 6.

CHEESE STUFFING

2 cups crumbs, cooked rice   1 teaspoon minced onion
  or cooked macaroni   1 tablespoon melted butter
1¾ cups grated cheese   Salt
  Combine ingredients.

MEAT STUFFING

2 cups minced cooked meat   Salt and pepper
  (veal, chicken or ham)   1 tablespoon fat, melted
1¼ cups crumbs or cooked   ½ onion, minced
  rice   1 cup water or stock (about)

Mix meat with crumbs and add salt, pepper, melted fat and
onion. Moisten with water.

VARIATION—Increase meat to 3 cups, reduce crumbs to ½
cup and add 1 egg. Omit water.

SWEETBREAD STUFFING

2 cups cooked sweetbreads   Dash Worcestershire sauce
1 cup Medium White Sauce   Salt, pepper and paprika
¾ cup cooked mushrooms

Prepare sweetbreads (see Index); break into pieces and
combine with white sauce, mushrooms and seasonings.

STUFFED ACORN SQUASH

1 acorn squash
1 teaspoon chopped onion
1 teaspoon finely chopped
   green pepper
2 tablespoons butter
½ cup grated cheese
1 cup soft bread crumbs
Salt and pepper

Bake squash in hot oven (400° F.) about 35 minutes or until tender. Cut lengthwise into halves, discard seeds and scoop out center, leaving shells about ¼ inch thick. Mash pulp and add remaining ingredients. Pile in squash shells and place in moderate oven (350° F.) to brown tops. Serves 2.

EGGPLANT STUFFED WITH HAM

1 large eggplant
Salted water
1 onion, minced
1 green pepper, chopped
   fine
2 tomatoes, quartered
2 tablespoons butter
½ teaspoon salt
⅛ teaspoon pepper
1 cup diced boiled ham
Bread crumbs

Wash and dry eggplant and cut off a slice from top. Scoop out inside to within ½ inch of skin. Cover shell with salted water and set aside. Chop eggplant pulp and combine with onion, pepper and tomatoes. Cook in a small amount of boiling salted water until tender. Drain and mash. Add butter, salt, pepper and ham. Drain shell well and fill with mixture. Sprinkle top with bread crumbs and bake in moderate oven (350° F.) about 25 minutes. Serves 4 to 6.

STUFFED CUCUMBERS

3 medium cucumbers
1 cup chopped tomato
1 onion, minced
1½ cups minced cooked
   chicken
1 tablespoon tomato catchup
1 teaspoon salt
¼ teaspoon pepper
½ teaspoon sugar
Paprika
1 cup Thin White Sauce
Buttered crumbs, browned

Cut cucumbers lengthwise into halves, pare and scoop out inside, saving pulp. Salt shells lightly and place close together in buttered pan. Mix pulp with tomato, onion, chicken, seasonings and white sauce and fill cucumber shells. Bake in moderate oven (350° F.) 20 to 25 minutes. Cover with crumbs. Serves 6.

ASPARAGUS TIMBALES

1 bunch asparagus
1 cup bread crumbs
¼ cup hot milk
2 eggs
¼ teaspoon salt

Few grains of cayenne
1½ tablespoons melted fat
½ tablespoon onion juice
1 tablespoon minced parsley

Wash the asparagus thoroughly; cut the tender parts into bits one-half inch long, and put into boiling salted water. Boil rapidly for ten minutes and drain thoroughly. In the meantime, cover the bread crumbs with the hot milk. When the crumbs are soft, add the eggs, and mix well together. Stir in salt, cayenne, melted fat and onion juice; then stir in asparagus tips, carefully. Grease small timbale molds, sprinkle them with minced parsley and fill two-thirds full. Set in a baking pan that contains boiling water, but do not allow the water to reach the top of the molds. Cover with a sheet of greased paper and cook in a slow oven (250°-325° F.) for thirty-five to forty-five minutes. Invert on a heated platter, garnish with parsley and serve with a white sauce.

Cold Entrées
ASPIC JELLY

1 quart Brown Stock
Consommé or White
Stock (page 23)

1 to 2 tablespoons
unflavored gelatin
½ cup cold water

Remove fat, strain stock and clarify if this has not been done already. Soften gelatin in cold water 5 minutes. Heat half of stock to boiling, add gelatin and stir until dissolved. Add remaining stock and chill until firm.

The amount of gelatin to use depends on the consistency of the chilled stock. If considerable bone was used for making it the stock may form a fairly firm jelly without gelatin. Such stock will require only one tablespoon gelatin. If the chilled stock jellies only slightly or not at all, use 2 tablespoons gelatin for 1 quart stock.

TOMATO—Use 2 cups strained tomato juice instead of 2 cups of the stock and use 2 tablespoons gelatin.

MINCED HAM IN CIDER CUPS

1 cup boiled ham	½ cup celery
3 hard-cooked eggs	2 tablespoons gelatin
½ teaspoon salt	2 cups cider
Pepper	½ cup sugar
¼ teaspoon cayenne pepper	½ cup cold water
3 tablespoons lemon juice	1 cup whipped cream

Soak gelatin in cold water, and pour over it boiling cider to which the sugar and lemon have been added. Strain into border molds. When firm, remove from the molds and fill with the mixture made of the other ingredients and serve immediately.

BRAISED TONGUE WITH ASPIC JELLY

1 beef tongue	1 blade of mace
2 onions	1 bunch thyme
1 stalk celery	1 bunch parsley
4 cloves	1 box gelatin
Salt and pepper	1 cup cold water
1 teaspoon sugar	

Wash and scrub the tongue well in salt water and simmer (180°-210° F.) it until tender. Remove the skin, and place the tongue in a stew-pan with onion, celery, cloves, salt and pepper. Cover it with the liquor in which it was boiled and add sugar, mace, thyme and parsley. Simmer for two hours. Take out the tongue. Add to the liquor gelatin, soaked in the cold water, boil for two minutes stirring constantly, strain and pour over the tongue. Serve cold.

CHAUD FROID OF EGGS

6 hard-cooked eggs	Paprika
2 tablespoons butter	2 Tablespoons chopped
Chaud-froid sauce	olives or pickles
Salt and pepper	

Cook eggs hard and cut in halves lengthwise. Remove yolks and mash to a paste with the melted butter, pepper, salt, paprika, and chopped olives or pickles. Refill whites and mask with chaud-froid sauce. Garnish each with a star cut from a truffle or from a green or red pepper. Let stand in a cold place till firm. These may be served at luncheon or supper.

CHICKEN MOUSSE

2 cups ground cooked chicken
½ cup salad dressing
2 tablespoons lemon juice
¾ teaspoon ground celery seed

¾ cup heavy cream whipped
Salt, pepper
1½ tablespoons gelatin
½ cup cold chicken stock
Lettuce, Brussels sprouts

Carrots and parsley

Blend the chicken, salad dressing, lemon juice and celery seed. Fold in the whipped cream. Season to taste. Fold in the gelatin which has been softened in the cold chicken stock, dissolved over hot water, then cooled. Pour into a ring mold and chill until firm. Unmold, on lettuce, fill the center with Brussels sprouts and garnish the platter with carrots and parsley.

HAM MOUSSE

Follow the directions for chicken mousse, substituting cooked ham for the cooked chicken. Chopped mushrooms are a delicious addition to this dish, and mushrooms may be mixed with the sauce when ready to serve, and also may be used as decorations.

SALMON MOLD PIQUANTE

1 tablespoon gelatin
¼ cup cold water
1½ teaspoons salt
1½ teaspoons mustard
Dash cayenne
2 egg yolks, slightly beaten

¾ cup milk
1½ tablespoons melted butter
4 tablespoons lemon juice
1 cup flaked salmon
Lettuce

Soften gelatin in cold water 5 minutes. Combine seasonings, egg yolks and milk in top of double boiler, and cook over hot water 6 to 8 minutes or until thickened, stirring constantly. Add butter, lemon juice and gelatin, stirring until gelatin is dissolved. Remove from fire and fold in salmon. Turn into fish mold; chill until firm. Unmold on bed of crisp lettuce and serve with cucumber cream dressing.

VEGETABLES

Roots, stems, leaves, buds, seeds and fruits of plants used as food are called vegetables. They classify as follows:

Roots—Beets, carrots, parsnips, turnips, salsify, radishes, horseradish, rutabagas, celeriac, sweet potatoes, yams, cassava.

Stems—Enlarged underground stems called tubers: Irish potatoes and Jerusalem artichokes, dasheen or taro, yautia, kohlrabi, fennel.

Stem and Bud—Asparagus.

Bulbs—Onions (green, called scallions), leek, garlic, shallot.

Leaf Stalks—Celery, rhubarb.

Leaves—Lettuce, endive, spinach, romaine, watercress, chard, chives, chicory, tops of beets, turnips, dandelion, fennel, mustard, dill, and parsley, escarole, Chinese cabbage, collards, kale.

Buds—Cabbage (terminal), Brussels sprouts (axillary).

Flowering Heads—Cauliflower, French artichoke, broccoli.

Fruit—Cucumbers, squash, eggplant, peppers, okra, pumpkin, tomatoes, string beans, green peas, green corn, vegetable marrow, zucchini, chayote, Lima beans.

Seeds—Peas, beans, lentils, corn, rice, Lima beans, soybeans, grains, cereals.

Fungi—Mushrooms, truffles.

Selection of Vegetables

Buy vegetables in their season. Many vegetables are in the market the year round, and modern agriculture has greatly extended the season for many others but some, when out of season, lack flavor and freshness.

Vegetables should be fresh, firm (not hard), and ripe. Do not buy vegetables that are old, withered, moldy or bruised, underripe or overripe; there is no saving in cost from purchasing such vegetables. Head vegetables should be solid, with few waste leaves. Cauliflower should be white and firm, with no blemishes. Leafy vegetables should not be wilted. Peas and beans should have crisp pods. Buy vegetables of medium size and regular shape.

Buy only the amount of summer vegetables you can use immediately, because they deteriorate in quality very quickly and are best when cooked soon after gathering.

Winter vegetables may be bought in larger amounts if there is a suitable dry, cool place for storage.

Get acquainted with vegetables that you or your family have never eaten. For the first time buy only enough for your own lunch and cook them after your favorite method. If that is successful, try them on the family. If not, try again with another recipe, until you find one you think they will like.

Care of Vegetables

SUMMER VEGETABLES—If these are not to be cooked at once, they should be put in the refrigerator or some other cool dry place. Peas and corn, especially, should be cooked soon after they are gathered, because they lose their sweetness on standing. Lettuce should be sprinkled and wrapped in a heavy cloth or paper, and put into the refrigerator until it is used. Salad greens keep a week or more in mechanically cooled refrigerators if they are washed and placed in closely covered enamel or porcelain containers after being well drained. Cloths or paper wrappings dry out too quickly in mechanically cooled refrigerators.

Cut the stems of wilted vegetables and plunge into cold water to freshen.

WINTER VEGETABLES—These should be in good condition, firm and uninjured and stored in a dry, cool, well ventilated place. Most of them keep better if they are piled up so that the air is excluded. Squash, however, keep better if they are spread out so that they do not touch one another. Squash and sweet potatoes require a warmer place than other vegetables. Vegetables cannot be kept successfully in an unpartitioned cellar containing a furnace. Vegetables should not be overripe when stored, but should be nearly mature. Parsnips improve in flavor if they are allowed to freeze before they are stored. They should be watched carefully and if they show signs of spoiling, should be used at once or removed from the other vegetables.

Preparation of Vegetables for Cooking

Wash all vegetables before cooking, even though they look clean. A vegetable brush is almost a necessity. Soak wilted vegetables before peeling them. Vegetables that are soaked after they are peeled lose some soluble food materials. Dry winter vegetables may be improved by soaking them for several hours. Scrape thin-skinned vegetables; pare thick-skinned vegetables or remove the skin after cooking. Make thin parings except in the case of turnips, from which a thick layer of corky material should be removed. Discard decayed vegetables.

Many vegetables, particularly of the bud, head and fruit groups, need to be immersed for a period in cold salt water. This freshens the fiber and drives out any insects that have taken refuge in crevices. Leaf vegetables need to be washed in several waters, the first of which should be salted for the same reason. The leaves should be lifted out of the water rather than the water poured off. This permits any sand to sink to the bottom of the pan. A tablespoon of liquid ammonia added to the last gallon of wash water will remove the last film that carries an earthy flavor.

What Vegetables Provide

The appreciation of vegetables as food has greatly increased in recent years with an extended understanding of their peculiar values. The modern woman realizes that these values, having been paid for at the market, must be retained in the preparation, if her family is to benefit by her intelligent purchases. Vegetables are one of the three groups of food that protect growth and vitality and preserve the characteristics of youth, the others being milk and fruits. The importance of these protective foods may be realized by the fact that scientists have found an astonishing relation between the early onset of old age and the food habits of persons involved. The modern woman knows that vegetables provide not only starches and sugars for energy, as well as several forms of protein, but what is most important they provide impressive amounts of Vitamins A, B, C, E, and G, in addition to mineral salts. These mineral salts are especially Calcium, Phosphorus, Iron, Copper, Manganese, and Sulphur, as well as Iodine, in vegetables grown along the seashore. Besides all this, she knows that the generous use of many vegetables helps to keep up the body's normal alkaline balance which contributes so very largely to sound health and vitality.

Cooking to Retain These Values

Many vegetables can be and are eaten uncooked with all their values intact. But many more need to be cooked before they can be served. Preparation by cooking should result in the least possible loss while it enhances values not otherwise available. For this reason cooking should:

1. Swell and burst the starch cell so that the center is softened and made digestible.
2. Sterilize the vegetable thoroughly.
3. Break up tough fiber so it is edible and digestible.
4. Release food proteins and minerals from their fiber cells.
5. Provide hot food.
6. Increase many flavors and some colors.

BAKING is the best method to secure all these results and still preserve Vitamins and minerals. Dry baking in their skins, generally used for potatoes, sweet potatoes, squash, turnips, carrots, onions, and parsnips, is a simple method whereby the vegetable is packed in a pan or laid on the rack of a hot oven to remain until just tender when pierced with a sharp fork. Baking, however, also includes the roasting of whole vegetables with meat, gravy, or fat, especially when potatoes or sweet potatoes are scraped, thus preserving mineral values just under the skin.

AU GRATIN AND SCALLOPING are other forms of baking, especially when fresh vegetables are used. In the latter method, layers of the vegetables are alternated in a baking dish or ring mold with white sauce, cream or milk, and seasonings, and in the former method a covering of buttered bread crumbs or buttered crumbs and cheese is added. Leftover cooked vegetables may be prepared by these methods also, but the Vitamin and mineral value will be determined by the first cooking Only baking in the jacket will insure the preservation of the Vitamins.

BROILING is the exposure to direct heat and can be used for some vegetables. The minerals will be less injured than the Vitamins, for the high heat destroys most of the latter.

DEEP FAT FRYING, next to baking, is another satisfactory way to retain most of the food values. The vegetable is sliced or cut into convenient form, dipped in egg and crumbs or batter, and immersed in enough very hot fat to cover well. This permits quick cooking with little loss.

IN SAUTÉING, the shredded or broken vegetable is turned into a shallow pan or skillet in which a small amount of fat has been heated. Cooking takes longer and more fat is absorbed by the food, hence, the process is not always advisable.

BOILING does the most damage to fresh vegetables, yet it is used most frequently by the largest number of homemakers. Although there are methods that reduce the losses to a minimum, the modern woman will remember that boiling is to be used least often, and always to be overbalanced by the better methods. Most of the mineral salts occurring in vegetables are easily dissolved in water and the loss of Vitamins during boiling takes place in several ways. They may be destroyed by overheating, by prolonged exposure to the air, and by dissolving out in the cooking water. When this is drained off and discarded, the principal food values gained by the intelligent buying of vegetables has been thrown away. In every case only the smallest possible amount of water should be used and it should be boiling rapidly when the vegetables are dropped in. They should be cooked only until just tender, and by this time most of the water has been evaporated. Greens such as spinach, chard and dandelions need only the water that clings to the leaves. They go into a cold pot with the heat turned on after the vegetable is in the kettle.

TO BOIL VEGETABLES THE PROPER WAY, four methods must be taken into account:

1. The green vegetables are best cooked in water that is slightly alkaline. In many sections of the country, drinking water may be decidedly acid. If there is any doubt, add a bit of baking soda the size of a pinhead. No drinking water would be acid enough to need more. Use an uncovered kettle and cook only until tender to the fork. If overcooked, green vegetables turn brownish because of chemical changes in the coloring matter, the fine flavor is ruined, while food values are lost.

2. White fresh vegetables such as cabbage, cauliflower, and onion are

strong flavored, due to their special oils. Hard water changes these oils so that the white color turns to yellow or brown. To prevent this, add 1 teaspoon of lemon juice or white vinegar. Drop the vegetable into enough rapidly boiling water to cover and cook with the kettle uncovered until just tender to the fork. Add the drained water, if any, to your soup stock.

3. The red color in vegetables is produced by acid and needs to be kept that way. Tomatoes usually have enough acid of their own to keep the color, but beets and red cabbage need a teaspoon of lemon juice or white vinegar. Cook in a small amount of water in a covered kettle.

4. Yellow vegetables are among the most valuable and stable. That rich yellow color is not only beauty but actually the foundation of Vitamin A. Not much damage can be done to it although the minerals and other Vitamins can still be destroyed if the vegetable is carelessly handled.

In general, the destruction of Vitamins is reduced when vegetables are boiled at high temperatures for the shortest possible time, in the smallest possible amount of water. Then the minerals, too, will be saved.

STEAMING as a method of cooking vegetables is valuable for those that can stand a high temperature for a long period, or those that are cooked in the meat pot so that the extracted minerals and Vitamins are used in the gravy. It is particularly good for dried and starchy ones. The long, slow process gives the starch cell time to swell and gelatinize. It is most valuable at high altitudes, because the extra pressure keeps the steam at 212° F. or more, while in the open-air cooking the high altitude reduces the boiling point below 212° F.

WATERLESS COOKING of fresh vegetables is any process in which no water is added. The water in the vegetable itself does the cooking. A thick-walled kettle with a tight-fitting lid is the necessary equipment. Very low heat is used, and the vegetable is tender in a very short time because neither heat nor steam escapes. No minerals are lost and the loss of Vitamins is almost as low as in baking.

All cooking of vegetables reduces the Vitamin C content, although tomatoes and the baked potato manage to retain most of theirs. To insure an adequate daily supply of Vitamin C, the modern woman never loses sight of the fact that some fresh fruits and vegetables must be served every day.

ARTICHOKES

The FRENCH artichoke is boiled in salted water, served hot with brown butter or Hollandaise sauce, or cold with mayonnaise. The spiny choke below the leaves and above the heart must be discarded. The JERUSALEM artichoke is washed, pared, boiled like a potato and dressed with seasoning, melted butter and minced parsley.

ASPARAGUS

Trim off hard stalks and scales to the head. Tie in bunches, stand upright in boiling salted water. After 10 minutes turn into loaf pan and continue with heat under the stems. Serve with browned butter or Hollandaise.

GOLDENROD ASPARAGUS

1 No. 1 can asparagus tips   2 cups Medium White
3 hard-cooked eggs   Sauce
12 stuffed olives   Buttered toast

Heat asparagus in juice. Chop egg whites and olives and add to sauce. Arrange hot asparagus on toast, cover with sauce and garnish with sieved egg yolks. Serves 6.

BOSTON BAKED BEANS

2 cups pea beans   ½ teaspoon salt
1 small onion   ½ teaspoon dry mustard
⅛ pound salt pork, scored   2 tablespoons molasses

Soak beans in cold water overnight. Simmer until skins begin to burst, turn into the bean pot over onion. Bury pork in beans, leaving only the rind exposed. Mix salt, mustard and molasses in a cup, fill with hot water, stir until well mixed and pour over beans. Add water to cover and bake in a slow oven (300° F.) 6 to 8 hours, adding more water to cover until the last hour. Remove cover and raise pork to the surface to brown.

QUICK METHOD—Use same ingredients as above but do not soak beans overnight. Cover with cold water and heat slowly to boiling. Simmer for 15 minutes, drain and cover with boiling water. Add onion and pork and simmer until beans are tender. Turn into bean pot and bake as above.

SOYBEANS

Of the many varieties of soybeans grown in this country, the yellow variety is the most popular for cooking purposes, though the black and green beans are used, and are particularly good in soup. Soybeans require longer cooking than white beans, but the length of time required is lessened if the beans are soaked for twelve hours before cooking.

BAKED SOYBEANS

2 cups yellow soybeans	2 tablespoons molasses
1 tablespoon salt	1 teaspoon mustard
1 small onion	¼ pound fat salt pork

Soak the beans for twelve hours, then heat to boiling and simmer until tender. Unless the beans are tender before they are baked, they will not be good. Prepare as directed for "Baked Beans." Eight to ten hours will be required to bake them.

BOILED LIMA BEANS

1 quart green lima beans or	1 tablespoon fat
2 cups dried lima beans	1 cup milk or cream if
Salt and pepper	desired

If the green beans are used, put them into just enough boiling water to cover, and boil slowly until tender. Salt the water just before cooking is completed. Add fat and salt and pepper to taste. If desired, a cup of milk or cream may be added and the beans allowed to simmer in it for a moment.

If dried beans are used they may be soaked twelve hours in plenty of cold water, and boiled in the same water with one-eighth teaspoon of soda added for each quart of water; or the process may be hastened by soaking them for one hour and simmering them for two hours. If they are not soaked at all, they can be made tender by simmering for two and one-half hours. The water should be drained off before the milk or cream is added.

STRING BEANS

1 quart string beans	Butter
Salt and pepper	

Wash beans, string and snap or cut into short pieces. Cover with least possible amount of boiling water and cook gently

TICHOKES WITH
LLANDAISE SAUCE
E WORKS OF ART

TENDER GREEN
ASPARAGUS WITH
CHEESE FONDUE AND
A STRIP OF PIMIENTO
FOR COLOR CON-
TRAST

COOKED CARROTS ROLLED IN BREAD CRUMBS AND BAKED ARE EASY TO MAKE AND SERVE

A NEW PRESENTATION OF PEAS IN A CARROT RING, WITH SLICED CARROTS AND PARSLEY GARNISH

until tender. Salt the water just before cooking is completed. When done, drain and season with butter, salt and pepper.

If the flavor of salt pork is liked cut slice of salt pork into small pieces and fry until brown, then add one tablespoon flour, one cup hot water, and the beans. Simmer for a few minutes and serve hot.

BOILED BEETS

Wash the beets thoroughly and remove the leaves, being very careful not to break off the little fibers and rootlets which retain the juices and coloring matter. Use plenty of water in cooking. If the beets are tough and withered, soak them for twenty-four hours in plenty of cold water before beginning to cook them.

Try with a fork, and when they are tender drop them into a pan of cold water and slip off the skins with the hands. If small, serve whole. If large, slice those to be used immediately, place in a dish and season with salt, pepper, and butter or savory fat. A teaspoon of sugar may be added also if the beets are not naturally sweet enough. Set them over boiling water to heat thoroughly and serve hot, with or without vinegar. Cold beets left over may be covered with vinegar and used as pickles.

BEET GREENS

Carefully wash and clean young beets, leaving roots and tops together. Put them into a kettle with very little boiling water and allow them to cook until just tender. Salt the water just before cooking is completed. Drain as dry as possible, in a colander. Chop, if desired. Serve hot with vinegar or with butter, salt and pepper.

BROCCOLI

Broccoli is a variety of cauliflower that is green instead of white. It was very popular in Colonial gardens and continued to be grown and sold along the east coast but gained popularity very slowly among native Americans. Within the last ten years growers on the west coast have promoted it and it is now as popular and often more abundant and lower priced than cauliflower. Shipped in ice from early cuttings, even the largest stalks are often tender. Choose heads and leaves that are bright green and crisp. Cut off only such portions of the stalk as are too hard and tough to admit the knife. Wash under running water and refrigerate, if not to be used at once.When ready to cook, use a deep kettle just large enough for the head or heads and bring salted water to a rapid boil. Insert carefully, stem end down, leave uncovered and when the water stops boiling add soda the size of a small pea to the water around the stems. The heads should not be submerged. When water boils up again they will cook more slowly than the stems and both will be tender in 15-25 minutes. If the heads are under water, they cook so much more rapidly that they will be mushy before the stems are tender. Broccoli heads, stems and leaves are valuable sources of vitamins A and G, as well as iron and calcium.

Serve with brown butter sauce, brown butter and crumbs, Hollandaise sauce or au gratin. Broccoli can be used instead of spinach for cream soup, especially when the green color is wanted.

BRUSSELS SPROUTS

Pick off the dead leaves from the sprouts, soak the sprouts in cold salted water for one-half hour, wash them and put them on the heat in plenty of boiling water. Boil in an uncovered saucepan until tender. Just before they are done, salt the water. Drain in a colander. Reheat; season with salt and pepper, and serve with cream sauce or melted butter.

BOILED CABBAGE

Cut the cabbage into desired shapes. Place it in a kettle with a generous amount of water. Cook uncovered until just tender. Add salt to the water just before cooking is completed. Drain, add butter or bacon fat, salt and pepper.

A little milk or cream may be added or it may be creamed or scalloped or served au gratin.

SCALLOPED CABBAGE WITH CHEESE

1 small head cabbage
2 cups grated cheese

1½ cups medium white sauce
½ to ¾ cup bread crumbs

Cook the cabbage as directed for boiled cabbage. Into a greased baking dish, put a layer of cabbage, then a layer of cheese, then a layer of white sauce, and continue to add layers until the ingredients are all used. Cover the top of the mixture with the crumbs, which may be mixed with a little melted butter, and bake in a moderate oven (350°-400° F.) for about twenty minutes, or until the crumbs are brown.

CARROTS, TOASTED

To serve carrots as a separate vegetable, scrape, and wash; leave young carrots whole and cut old carrots in slices lengthwise or crosswise. Boil them until tender (15-30 minutes) in water containing one teaspoon sugar. Just before cooking is completed, salt the water Drain, add butter, and seasoning or roll in butter, then in corn flakes and brown in oven at 350°F.

CARROTS AND PEAS

No. 1.

2 cups cubed, cooked carrots
1 cup cooked peas, fresh or
  canned

3 tablespoons butter or
  other fat or
  Medium white sauce

Combine the carrots and peas, reheat and serve with melted butter or any savory fat such as bacon fat; or combine with a white sauce. Season to taste with salt and pepper.

No. 2—With Green Mint—Combine the carrots and peas, as directed above, add one-half cup mint leaves and a little boiling water and boil for five minutes. Drain, add salt and pepper, a generous amount of butter, and a sprinkle of sugar. Set in the oven until the sugar melts. Serve with a garnish of fresh mint leaves.

CARROT MOLDS

2 cups grated raw carrot
½ cup bread crumbs
2 eggs

1 teaspoon salt
2 teaspoons melted fat
½ cup milk

Wash, scrape, and grate the carrots and mix with the crumbs. Beat the eggs and add to them the salt, fat, and milk. Add this mixture to the carrot and crumb mixture. Fill a greased ring mold or popover cups, set in a pan of hot water and bake in a slow oven (250°-325° F.) until firm.

BOILED CAULIFLOWER

Remove the green leaves from the cauliflower and cut off any bruised or dirty spots. Place it, top downward, in a deep bowl of cold, salted water and allow it to stay there about half an hour to draw out dust and other imprities. Cook it, whole or broken into flowerets, in boiling water, uncovered. Just before cooking is completed (15-30 minutes) salt the water. Lift out the cauliflower carefully and allow it to drain in a warm place. Pour medium white sauce over it or send the sauce to the table in a sauce boat, or serve it with melted butter and paprika.

Sometimes hot boiled cauliflower is sprinkled with grated cheese and then with buttered crumbs and baked to a light brown in a moderate oven (400° F.), or it may be sprinkled with the grated cheese and served without baking.

SCALLOPED CAULIFLOWER

1 medium cauliflower	1½ cups medium white
2 hard-cooked eggs or	sauce
4 tablespoons grated cheese	Bread crumbs

Break the cauliflower into flowerets before boiling. Drain. Place a layer of the cooked cauliflower in a greased baking-dish, then a layer of egg slices or of grated cheese, then a layer of white sauce. Repeat until all the cauliflower is used. Put a layer of crumbs over the top and bake in a moderate oven (350°-400° F.) from fifteen to thirty minutes. A bit of cayenne pepper or paprika may be added for additional seasoning.

CREAMED CELERY

2 cups celery cut into	2 tablespoons flour
1-inch pieces	2 tablespoons butter
½ cup milk	Salt and pepper

Wash the stalks clean and cut them into pieces. Place the celery in a saucepan, cover with boiling water and boil until tender (about half an hour), by which time the water should be reduced to about one-half cup. Make a sauce with the celery water, milk, flour and butter. Add the cooked celery and season with salt and pepper.

SCALLOPED CELERY

Boil celery, as directed in the preceding recipe, using all milk in the sauce instead of part celery water. Turn the creamed celery into a greased ramekin, sprinkle with grated cheese and buttered crumbs and bake in a moderate oven (350°-400° F.) until it is a golden brown (15-30 minutes).

CELERIAC

Not every housewife knows celeriac, but it is well worth adding to her list of vegetable acquaintances. It is a variety of celery grown for its turnip-like root instead of for the blanched stalks. The flavor is similar to that of celery.

To prepare celeriac, trim off the tops, and pare the bulb, drop it into boiling water and cook about one-half hour, or until tender. Add the salt just before cooking is completed It may then be prepared in the same way as creamed or scalloped celery, or may be used cold, sliced or diced, in salads.

BOILED GREEN CORN

To have this vegetable in perfection, the husks should be on until just before it is to be served. Drop the ears into boiling water and cook 3 to 7 minutes, according to the size of the corn. (Do not salt the water, as this toughens the corn.) Or fit ears with only the clinging water into a closely-covered Dutch oven. Allow to steam at medium heat 15-20 minutes.

Lay a napkin on the serving-plate, pile the corn upon this, cover it with the corners of the napkin and serve.

CORN SOUFFLÉ

1 tablespoon fat	Pepper
1 tablespoon flour	1 boiled pimiento
½ cup milk	2 cups corn pulp
1 teaspoon salt	2 eggs
¼ teaspoon paprika	

Made a white sauce, using the fat, flour, milk, and seasoning. Press the pimiento through a sieve and add it to the sauce. Add the corn to the mixture. Cool slightly, then add the well-beaten egg yolks and fold in the stiffly beaten egg whites. Turn into a greased baking dish, set the dish in a pan of hot water, and bake in a moderate oven (375° F.) until the egg is set, about thirty minutes.

CORN OYSTERS

2 cups corn pulp	2 tablespoons fat
2 eggs	Salt and pepper
2 tablespoons flour	

If fresh corn is used, grate it from the cob with a coarse grater. If canned corn is used, select one of the sieved varieties. Beat the egg yolks and whites separately and add to the grated corn, with flour and fat, salt, and pepper. Drop the batter from a spoon into hot fat (360°-370° F.) and fry light brown (2-3 minutes). Drain on soft paper. Serve hot.

CORN PUDDING OR DEVILED CORN

2 tablespoons fat	2 cups corn pulp
2 tablespoons flour	1 egg
1½ cups milk	1 tablespoon Worcestershire
1 teaspoon salt	sauce
¼ teaspoon mustard	Buttered crumbs
Paprika	

Make a sauce of fat, flour, milk, and seasonings, add corn, egg slightly beaten, and Worcestershire sauce. Pour into a baking dish, cover with buttered crumbs and bake in a moderate oven (350°-400° F.) fifteen to thirty minutes.

BAKED CORN AND TOMATOES

2 cups cooked corn	1 teaspoon sugar
2 cups tomatoes	1 cup fresh bread crumbs
1 teaspoon salt	3 tablespoons fat
Pepper	

Mix seasonings with the corn and tomatoes and pour all into a greased baking dish. Spread the crumbs over the top, dot them with the fat, and bake in a moderate oven (350°-400° F.) for one-half hour. This is a satisfactory way of utilizing leftover corn or tomatoes.

CUCUMBER CUPS

This makes a dainty dish for luncheon. Cut the unpared vegetables into sections two inches long and cook until tender in water salted just before cooking is completed. Scoop out the center of each section, leaving one-half-inch thickness all around the sides, as well as on the bottom, thus making green cups of the vegetable. These cups may be filled with creamed chicken, sweetbreads, mushrooms or any other filling held together with white sauce.

STEWED CUCUMBERS

3 cucumbers	1 cup boiling water
6 slices toast	½ teaspoon salt
2 tablespoons fat	Pepper
2 tablespoons flour	1½ tablespoons lemon juice

Peel medium-sized cucumbers and cut them into quarters lengthwise. Place in a shallow pan, cover with the boiling water and cook gently for ten to twenty minutes. Add salt just before cooking is completed. When done, lay them carefully on toasted bread, make a sauce of the flour, fat, water in which cucumbers were cooked, and seasonings; cook until smooth, and pour the sauce over the cucumbers.

CUCUMBER SAUTÉ

4 cucumbers	Salt and pepper
Butter	Minced parsley or chives
Flour	

Pare and quarter the cucumbers and boil them, without any water, for three minutes. Drain; season with salt and pepper; roll in flour and sauté in a little butter until tender. Sprinkle with parsley or chives just before the cooking is completed.

DANDELION GREENS

2 pounds dandelion greens	1 tablespoon butter
Salt and pepper	

Dandelions should be used before they blossom, as they become bitter after that time. Cut off the roots, pick the greens over carefully, and wash them well in several waters. Place them in a kettle, add a little boiling water, and boil until tender. Salt the water just before cooking is completed. When done, lift them into a colander, press them to drain off all the water, and chop. Add butter, salt, and pepper.

FRIED EGGPLANT

1 eggplant   Cracker meal or bread crumbs
Salt   Egg

Cut the eggplant into one-half-inch slices, pare and sprinkle each slice with salt. Lay slice upon slice and place a plate upon the top. Let stand two hours. The salt will draw out the disagreeably bitter flavor. Half an hour before serving, wipe each slice dry, dip in beaten egg, then in cracker meal or fine bread crumbs, and saute in hot fat. Put a pan in the oven or in some other place where it can be kept hot; lay a piece of absorbent paper in the pan, and upon it place the slices as they come crisp and brown from the frying pan. Serve on a hot platter with the slices overlapping.

STUFFED EGGPLANT

1 eggplant   ½ cup water
2 tablespoons butter   2 cups crumbs
Salt and pepper

Cut the eggplant in half lengthwise and scoop out the center pulp, leaving the rind about one-half inch thick so that the shape may be firm. Cover the shells with cold water. Chop the pulp fine, season it with salt, pepper, and butter, and cook in a frying pan for ten minutes, stirring well, then add water and one cup of bread crumbs. Drain the shells, sprinkle the interior of each with salt and pepper and fill them with the mixture. Spread the remaining crumbs over the tops. Place the halves in a baking dish or deep pan, and pour enough hot water into the pan to come one-third up the sides of the plant. Bake in a moderate oven (350°-375° F.) one-half hour, and serve hot.

CREAMED CHICORY OR ENDIVE

Wash the plant carefully and pick off the outer green leaves, leaving only the white part. Boil until tender, drain well, return it to the kettle, and nearly cover with medium white sauce, which should be well seasoned.

FRIED PARSNIPS

12 medium-sized parsnips   Salt and pepper
Flour or fine crumbs

Scrape and boil the parsnips until tender. If mature, re-move the woody centers. Drain, and when cold, cut them in long, thin slices about one-third of an inch thick, and sea son each slice with salt and pepper. Dip the slices in flour or fine crumbs and sauté in fat or oil until both sides are thoroughly browned. Drain well and serve very hot.

BOILED PEAS

2 quarts peas in the shell   2 tablespoons butter
Salt and pepper

Fresh peas should not be shelled until just before they are needed for cooking. Look them over carefully after shelling, taking out any tendrils that may be mixed with them. Wash and cook until tender in a covered pan in just enough boil-ing water to prevent scorching. Add salt just before cooking is completed. Young peas will cook in ten to twenty min-utes but those that are more mature require a longer time. Most of the water should have cooked away. If any remains, drain carefully. Let the peas stand in the drainer over hot water. Melt the butter, add salt and pepper and the drained peas. Mix well, reheat, and serve.

CREAMED PEAS

2 cups cooked peas   1 cup medium white sauce

Mix peas with white sauce. Reheat and serve.

BHUGIA

2 cups peas   2 tablespoons oil or
4 medium potatoes   melted fat
Chopped green peppers   Salt

This is a popular dish in India and is usually served with the dinner roast. Boil the peas and potatoes separately. When the potatoes are thoroughly done, drain and let them cool enough to be easily handled. Drain the peas. Heat the oil in a frying pan. Slice the potatoes and sauté potatoes and peas together in the oil. Season with salt and sprinkle with chopped green peppers.

RICE AND PEAS

1 cup rice   2 onions   2 cups green peas

Boil the rice and peas separately. Chop the onions fine and fry them in oil until tender. Add the cooked rice and peas.

BOILED POTATOES

Select potatoes of uniform size. Wash, pare, if you wish, and dip into cold water. Cook in boiling water until tender when pierced with a fork. Just before cooking is completed, add the salt. The water should be kept boiling constantly. When done, drain and shake the pan over the heat to dry the potatoes. Serve in an uncovered dish or cover with a folded napkin. Old potatoes should be soaked in cold water for an hour or so before boiling. When they are pared, potatoes lose much vitamin and mineral content in boiling. It is better, therefore, from the nutritional standpoint, to wash them thoroughly, scrubbing with a brush, and boil them with the skins on. They may be peeled quickly before they are served, or served with the skins on.

RICED POTATOES

Force hot, freshly boiled potatoes through a ricer or coarse strainer. Sprinkle with salt and pile lightly into the serving-dish. Serve at once in an uncovered dish.

BAKED POTATOES

Select smooth, medium-sized potatoes, scrub, remove the eyes and any blemishes, place in a baking pan or on the rack in a very hot oven (450°-500° F.) and bake until tender (30-60 minutes). Be sure to have the oven hot before the potatoes are put in. To test the potatoes, do not pierce them with a fork, but squeeze them with the hand wrapped in a towel. When soft, break the skin to keep them from being soggy, and serve.

STUFFED POTATOES ON THE HALF SHELL

Select large potatoes; scrub and bake. Remove from oven and cut potatoes in two lengthwise. Scoop out the inside, being careful not to break the shell. Mash very thoroughly or put them through the ricer—add butter, salt and milk, and beat well. Pile the mixture lightly back into the shells, Do not smooth down the top. Stand the filled shells in a shallow pan, return to the oven (400° F.) and brown lightly on top. Tuck in small wieners before serving if desired, or add ½ cup peanut butter and 2 egg whites to the potato mixture.

POTATO SALMON PIE

1 No. 1 can salmon   1 cup cooked peas
2 cups Thick White Sauce   2 cups mashed potatoes
1 tablespoon butter

Bone and flake salmon; add hot sauce and drained peas. Place in baking dish; top with potatoes. Dot with butter; brown in hot oven (450° F.) 15 minutes. Serves 6.

POTATOES SUZETTE

6 medium-sized potatoes   Salt and pepper
½ cup hot milk   6 tablespoon buttered
2 tablespoons melted fat   crumbs
6 eggs   1 tablespoon grated cheese

Prepare as for potatoes on the half shell. Refill the shell almost to the top, break an egg into each opening, season with salt and pepper and sprinkle with buttered crumbs that have been mixed with grated cheese and bake in a slow oven (250°-350° F.) long enough to set the egg and brown lightly.

SCALLOPED POTATOES

6 medium-sized potatoes   4 tablespoons butter
Salt and pepper   Milk
2 tablespoons flour

Pare raw potatoes and cut them into thin slices. Place in a baking dish a layer of the potato one inch deep, season with salt and pepper, sprinkle a portion of the flour over each layer, add a part of the butter in bits. Repeat and continue until required amount is used. It is best not to have more than two or three layers because of difficulty in cooking. Add milk until it can be seen between the slices of potato, cover and bake (350°-400° F.) until potatoes are tender when pierced with a fork (1-1½ hours). Remove the cover during the last fifteen minutes to brown the top. Serve from the baking dish.

FRANCONIA POTATOES

Select medium-sized potatoes, pare and place them in the baking pan with the roast, allowing an hour and a quarter for their cooking. Turn them often and baste with the gravy from the roast. Serve them arranged about the meat on the platter. If you wish to shorten the cooking time, parboil them for fifteen minutes before putting them into the roasting pan, and allow forty-five minutes for the roasting.

DUTCH POTATOES

6 potatoes	6 slices fat salt pork or bacon
6 frankfurter sausages	Pepper

Scrub medium-sized potatoes; pare or leave the skins on as preferred. With an apple-corer cut a tunnel through the center of each, lengthwise. Draw through each cavity one of the frankfurters. Place in a dripping pan and lay a blanket of fat salt pork or a thick slice of bacon on each potato. Pepper lightly and bake in a very hot oven (450°-500° F.) until the potatoes are tender, basting occasionally with the drippings and a little hot water.

POTATO PUFF OR SOUFFLÉ

2 cups hot mashed potatoes	2 tablespoons butter or
2 eggs	other fat
1 cup milk	

To the mashed potatoes add the fat, the egg yolks which have been beaten until very light, and the milk. Stir until well blended and then fold in the stiffly beaten egg whites. Mix lightly and pile the mass in a well-greased baking dish. Set in a pan containing hot water and bake in a moderate oven (375° F.) twenty to thirty minutes. Serve at once.

MASHED POTATOES AU GRATIN

6 potatoes, riced
3 tablespoons fat
½ teaspoon salt
½ teaspoon paprika

2 eggs
¼ cup grated cheese
½ cup buttered crumbs

Add fat, seasoning, and eggs to the hot riced potatoes. Beat until light and mound on a baking dish. Cover with grated cheese and then with buttered crumbs. Bake (400° F.) ten minutes, or until the crumbs are brown.

DUCHESS POTATOES

2 cups riced potatoes
2 tablespoons fat

2 egg yolks
Salt and paprika

Mix riced potato, fat, and beaten yolks of eggs, reserving a little of the yolk for brushing the cakes. Add a little salt and paprika. Shape by means of a pastry bag and tube into leaves, crowns, pyramids, etc. Brush over with beaten egg yolk to which one teaspoon of water has been added. Brown in a hot oven (400°-450° F.).

FRENCH FRIED POTATOES

No. 1—Wash and pare potatoes and cut into eighths lengthwise. Dry between towels and fry in deep fat (395° F.). Drain on soft paper, sprinkle with salt and serve in an uncovered dish.

No. 2—Cut uncooked potatoes into blocks measuring about three-fourths of an inch each way, and place them in boiling water. Cook until almost done, ten or eleven minutes being usually required. Then drain off all the water and allow five minutes for the escape of steam. Fry them a few at a time in deep fat (395° F.). Drain on soft paper placed on a hot plate. Sprinkle with salt and pepper.

BELGIAN BAKED POTATOES

Prepare potatoes as for French fried. Dip them in melted fat and lay them in a shallow pan, being sure that the pieces do not overlap. Bake in a quick oven (400°-450° F.) until brown on top, turn carefully and continue baking until they resemble French fried potatoes. Baste them with more fat during baking, if necessary. When done, sprinkle with salt and serve piping hot.

POTATO CHIPS OR SARATOGA POTATOES

Wash and pare potatoes and shave into very thin slices. Soak them for one hour in cold water, then drain and dry on a towel. Fry in deep fat (395° F.) a few slices at a time until light brown, keeping them in motion with a skimmer. Lay them on soft paper to drain. Sprinkle lightly with salt, and serve.

In cool weather, enough potato chips may be cooked at one time to last a week or ten days. They should be kept in a cool dry place and should always be reheated in the oven until crisp, before serving.

AMERICAN FRIED OR BROWNED POTATOES

No. 1—Cut boiled potatoes into slices one-fourth of an inch thick. Heat a very little fat in a frying pan and sauté the slices, browning on both sides. Season with salt and pepper.

No. 2—Chop the potatoes in a chopping bowl until the pieces measure one-half inch or less, and add them to the hot fat in the frying pan. Season with salt and pepper and sauté, stirring constantly, until the potatoes look yellow and are cooking well. Then cover the pan, set it in a slow heat for five minutes, and serve in a heated dish.

HASHED BROWN POTATOES

2 tablespoons oil or drippings	6 boiled potatoes
	Salt and pepper

Chop the potatoes, adding salt, and a dash of pepper. Heat the fat in a frying pan, and add the chopped potatoes to the depth of one inch. Press the potatoes down in the pan, packing them firmly. Cook slowly, without stirring, until the potato is brown. Then begin at one side of the pan and fold the potatoes over on the other like an omelet, packing closely together. Turn out on to a hot serving platter and serve.

CREAMED POTATOES

2 cups diced cold cooked potatoes

1½ cups medium white sauce
Salt and pepper

Combine potatoes and white sauce and heat thoroughly. Season with salt and pepper. Serves 6.

Or use milk instead of white sauce. Dice potatoes into skillet in which 2 tablespoons butter have been melted. Season with salt and pepper and almost cover with milk. Simmer, uncovered, until milk is absorbed, tilting pan occasionally and basting top of potatoes with milk.

CREAMED NEW POTATOES

Scrape new potatoes and cook in a small amount of boiling salted water, closely covered, until tender. Place in serving dish and pour hot seasoned white sauce over them. Sprinkle with paprika or minced parsley.

POTATO PANCAKES

3 cups grated potatoes
2 eggs, well beaten
1½ tablespoons flour

⅛ teaspoon baking powder
1 teaspoon salt
½ teaspoon onion juice

Pare large potatoes and cover with cold water. Let stand 12 hours. Pour off water and grate potatoes. Drain well. Add eggs and mix lightly. Stir in remaining ingredients. Drop from tablespoon onto hot well-greased skillet and brown on both sides. Serve with applesauce. Makes 12 pancakes.

FLUFFY—Use 6 eggs. Add beaten egg yolks to grated potatoes, add remaining ingredients and fold in stiffly beaten egg whites last. Fry as above.

DELMONICO POTATOES

2 cups cooked potatoes, diced
2 cups Medium White Sauce

Salt and pepper
Buttered crumbs

Mix potatoes and sauce, add salt and pepper, and pour into a buttered baking dish; cover with crumbs and bake ten minutes in a hot oven (400° F.). Serves 6.

Add ¼ cup diced cooked pimiento to white sauce. The crumbs may be omitted and the potatoes sprinkled with grated cheese or grated cheese may be mixed with crumbs.

POTATOES AU GRATIN

Creamed potatoes No. 1
1 teaspoon minced parsley
1 cup buttered crumbs

2 to 4 tablespoons grated cheese

Follow directions for creamed potatoes No. 1 adding the parsley. Turn into greased baking dish, sprinkle with cheese, cover with buttered crumbs and bake in a hot oven (400° F.) until crumbs are brown.

POTATO DROPS

2 cups mashed potatoes
   (without any milk)

2 eggs
Salt and pepper

Mix the mashed, seasoned potato and the beaten eggs. Drop the mixture from a spoon into the hot fat (375°-390° F.) and fry until a golden brown, (2-3 minutes) then drain on brown paper and serve with a garnish of parsley. If the spoon is dipped into boiling water after every using, each drop will retain the shape of the spoon.

POTATO O'BRIEN

6 medium-sized potatoes
Salt

Chopped pimientos
Onion juice

Wash, pare and cut potatoes into half-inch dice. Dry between towels. Fry in hot fat (395° F.) until a delicate brown. Drain on soft paper, sprinkle with salt, then sauté them in just enough fat to keep them from burning, adding minced pimientos and a few drops of onion juice. They should be tossed frequently during cooking, and not pressed close to the pan.

POTATOES PERSILLADE

12 small new potatoes
   or 6 medium-sized old
   potatoes

Butter
Juice of one-half lemon
½ cup minced parsley

These are dependent upon parsley, not only for their name but for their attractive appearance. Scrape new potatoes. Pare old potatoes and cut the size of a small egg or, with a vegetable scoop, cut them into balls. Boil until tender.

Add salt just before cooking is completed. Drain, place in a saucepan with sufficient butter to coat all the potatoes, add the lemon juice and sprinkle with minced parsley. The potatoes should be well coated with parsley when served.

LYONNAISE POTATOES

2 cups boiled potatoes, diced
Salt and pepper
1 tablespoon minced onion
2 tablespoons fat
1 tablespoon chopped parsley

The potatoes should be rather underdone to produce the best results. Season with salt and pepper. Sauté the onion in fat until yellow, add the diced potato and stir with a fork until all sides are brown, being careful not to break the potatoes. Add more fat if necessary. When done, turn the potatoes out upon a hot dish, sprinkle parsley over the top, and serve hot.

SPANISH POTATOES

1 tablespoon minced onion
2 tablespoons chopped green pepper
2 tablespoons chopped pimiento
4 tablespoons oil or cooking fat
2 cups cold boiled potatoes, diced
½ cup cold cooked ham, chopped
1 teaspoon salt
½ teaspoon paprika

Sauté the onion, pepper and pimiento in the fat until light brown, add the diced potatoes, the chopped ham and seasonings and cook until thoroughly heated through.

MASHED POTATO BALLS

2 cups cold mashed potatoes
1 egg yolk
Salt and pepper
Butter

Mix cold mashed potato with the beaten egg yolk, salt and pepper and shape the mixture into balls. Place the balls in a greased pan and make a depression on the top of each, put a bit of butter in each depression and brown in the oven (400°-450° F.).

PRINCESS POTATOES

2 cups cold mashed potatoes
1 egg
Melted fat

If the potato is cold and firm, cut into strips two inches long, one inch wide and one-half inch thick, otherwise shape into flat cakes one-half inch thick. Dip the strips or cakes first into the melted fat and then into the egg, which has been slightly beaten, and lay them carefully on a greased pan. Cook in a hot oven (400°-450° F.) until brown.

BOILED SWEET POTATOES

Follow directions for boiled white potatoes (See Index).

BAKED SWEET POTATOES

Follow directions for boiled white potatoes (See Index).

GLAZED OR CANDIED SWEET POTATOES

No. 1.

6 sweet potatoes	1 cup brown or maple sugar
Salt and pepper	¼ cup water
Butter	

Boil the potatoes without paring them, and when tender drain and strip off the skins. Make a sirup by boiling together the sugar and water. Cut each potato in half or in thick slices, dip each piece into the sirup and lay it in a greased baking dish. Season with salt and pepper and bits of butter. When all the potato is in the dish, pour over it any sirup that remains and bake in a quick oven (400°-450° F.) until the potatoes are brown. They will brown quickly.

No. 2—Use the same quantities as for No. 1. Pare the potatoes and boil until about half done. Drain, cut in lengthwise slices, and lay in a shallow greased pan. Spread generously with butter and pour over all the sirup. Bake in a moderate oven (350°-400° F.) basting frequently with the sirup until the potatoes are transparent. It may be necessary to add more sirup during the baking. An hour or more is usually required for these potatoes.

SWEET POTATO PUFF

2 cups mashed sweet potato	Salt and pepper
2 tablespoons fat	¼ cup milk or cream
1 egg	

To the mashed sweet potatoes add the melted fat, seasonings and milk. Beat the egg yolk and egg white separately, add the yolk to the potato mixture, and then fold in the white. Put into a baking dish or individual molds, set in a pan containing hot water and bake (375° F.) until puffy and brown.

SWEET POTATO WITH PINEAPPLE

6 small sweet potatoes
⅓ as much pineapple as potato

⅓ cup honey
¼ cup water

Boil the potatoes with the skins on. When cool, peel and cut them in pieces one-quarter of an inch thick. Mix honey and hot water. Just cover the bottom of a baking dish with the mixture, add the sweet potatoes and sliced pineapple. Pour the remaining honey mixture over them and bake for ten minutes in the oven (400° F.).

CREOLE SWEET POTATOES

6 large sweet potatoes
Salt
Celery salt
White pepper

Grated nutmeg
1 cup rich brown stock
Few drops of caramel

Prepare potatoes by parboiling them for twenty minutes. Remove skins and cut potatoes in halves. Place the pieces in a shallow baking pan, sprinkle with salt, celery salt, white pepper and grated nutmeg. Pour into the pan the stock, to which a few drops of caramel have been added, and bake in a quick oven (400°-450° F.) until tender and slightly browned. Baste frequently with the stock. Serve around planked fish.

MASHED SWEET POTATO CARAMEL

2 cups mashed sweet potato
Milk
Pepper and salt

½ cup maple sirup
¼ cup butter

Leftover sweet potatoes, either baked or boiled, may be used for this dish. Mash potatoes and add sufficient milk or cream to make a smooth, soft paste. Season with pepper and salt. Put into a well-greased casserole. Pour in thick maple sirup heated with butter. Bake at 400° F. until the top is caramelized.

SWEET POTATO CASSEROLE—Omit maple sirup and butter. Cover potatoes with marshmallows and bake in a moderate oven (350° F.) until browned.

SWEET POTATO WAFFLES

4 tablespoons fat	¾ cup flour
1 tablespoon sugar	2 teaspoons baking powder
1 egg	1 cup milk
1 cup mashed sweet potato	Salt, cayenne, nutmeg

Mix the fat and sugar to a cream, stir in the well-beaten egg yolk, potato, flour, baking powder, milk and seasonings, and beat well until smooth. Fold in the stiffly beaten egg white. Bake in a heated waffle iron until golden brown. Serve, sprinkled with sugar and cinnamon, as an accompaniment to roast duck or turkey.

CREAMED RADISHES

1½ cups large, strongly flavored radishes	1 cup milk
2 tablespoons flour	2 tablespoons fat
	Salt and pepper

Wash, pare, and slice the radishes. Boil until tender. Make a white sauce of the flour, fat, milk, and seasonings. Combine radishes and sauce and serve. The flavor is not unlike spicy turnips and they make a pleasant novelty served with steak or chops.

BOILED RICE

1 cup rice	3 quarts water or more	1 tablespoon salt

Wash the rice; drop it into the salted boiling water; and boil rapidly, uncovered, for fifteen or twenty minutes, or until the kernels are soft when pressed between the thumb and finger. Place in a colander (saving the water for soup) and pour boiling water over the rice to remove the loose starch and separate the grains. Drain and place in the oven with the door open for a few minutes, to allow the cereal to dry out. The grains should be separate and distinct.

CURRY OF RICE

1 cup rice	1 to 2 tablespoons curry
2 tablespoons fat	powder
1 teaspoon chopped onion	2 teaspoons salt
2½ cups boiling water	¼ teaspoon pepper

Wash the rice well. Place fat and onion in a saucepan and cook them until the onion is yellow, add the rice and stir the whole over high heat for five minutes. Remove from heat, season with the curry powder, salt and pepper, stir well and pour in the boiling water. Cover the pan and boil rapidly for ten minutes, then cook for forty minutes over a double boiler.

Curry of rice is appropriate with any kind of meat dish that has been prepared with a sauce.

RICE À LA CREOLE

1 onion	2 cups cooked tomatoes
1 sliced cooked ham	Salt
1 tablespoon fat	Paprika
1 cup boiled rice	Bread crumbs

Chop onion and ham very fine. Add fat, boiled rice, and tomatoes seasoned with salt and paprika. Mix thoroughly, put into a baking dish, cover with bread crumbs and bake (400° F.) for fifteen minutes.

CREAMED SALSIFY OR OYSTER PLANT

Wash and scrape the salsify, drop it immediately into cold water to which a little vinegar or lemon juice has been added, to prevent discoloration. Cut in 1-inch slices and cook in boiling water until tender, adding salt just before cooking is completed. When tender, drain and combine with Medium White Sauce. Serve with tiny fried Beef Balls.

FRIED SALSIFY

Follow directions for fried parsnips (see index).

STEAMED OR BAKED SUMMER SQUASH

Cut the squash into pieces of medium size, remove the seeds and the soft mesh surrounding them. Steam or bake until tender. Serve in the shell or scrape from shell, mash, and place, uncovered, for ten minutes in a good heat to dry, stirring frequently. Season with butter, salt, and pepper.

FRIED SQUASH

2 white squash   Egg and crumbs   Salt and pepper

The white "button" squash, about four inches in diameter, is best when fried. Pare and cut the squash into thin slices, dip in seasoned crumbs, then in beaten egg, then in more crumbs, and fry in deep fat (395° F.) from four to five minutes. When the slices are brown, drain on soft paper. Serve on a platter or other flat dish. Fried squash makes an excellent luncheon dish.

SQUASH IN THE SHELL

1 squash
3 tablespoons butter
Salt and pepper
Egg
Milk

Cut off the top of a small squash, remove the seeds and stringy portion, place in a pan and boil, steam, or bake about two hours until tender. Remove the pulp from the shell being careful to keep the large shell intact. Mash the pulp and season it with salt, pepper, and butter.

Return the mixture to the shell, smooth the surface to a dome shape, score with a knife, brush over with milk and beaten egg, add bits of butter and place in a quick oven (400° F.) for a few minutes to brown. Or leave the pulp in the squash, season well and fill center with ham à la king, chicken à la king, creamed salmon, or sausage mixtures.

BOILED SPINACH

No. 1—AMERICAN STYLE

2 pounds spinach
Salt and pepper
3 tablespoons butter

Remove roots and wilted leaves of the spinach. Wash in several waters, until all trace of sand has disappeared. Place in a large kettle without additional water the water which clings to the leaves is sufficient. Cover the kettle and cook with low heat until the spinach is tender. The time of cooking depends on the age of the spinach. Long cooking darkens it. Salt the water just before cooking is completed. When done, drain, chop, season with salt, pepper, and butter and one tablespoon lemon juice, if desired.

SPINACH MOLD—

1 peck spinach, cooked
    and chopped
3 unbeaten eggs
¼ cup milk
¼ cup butter
1½ cups bread crumbs
¼ teaspoon pepper
1 teaspoon salt

Combine all ingredients, turn into a buttered ring mold and steam 2 hours. Unmold and garnish with hard-cooked eggs and carrots. Fill center of mold with mashed potatoes or creamed mushrooms.

CREAMED SPINACH

2 pounds spinach	Salt and pepper
1 tablespoon butter	2 tablespoons cream
2 hard-cooked egg yolks	

Cook spinach according to directions for boiled spinach No. 1, drain well, and chop fine. Return to heat, add butter, salt, and pepper, and stir until the butter is melted, then add cream and chopped yolks and mix well.

SPINACH SOUFFLÉ

2 cups cooked spinach, fresh or canned   2 eggs

This is a satisfactory way to dispose of leftover cooked spinach. To the spinach add egg yolks beaten; place in a saucepan, heat and stir over the heat until the egg sets, then remove from the heat and when cold add the beaten egg whites. Fill individual baking dishes one-half full of this mixture. Set the dishes in a pan of hot water and bake in a moderate oven (375° F.) from twenty to thirty minutes. Serve at once to prevent falling.

SPINACH IN EGGS

2 cups boiled spinach	Mustard
6 eggs	Butter
Salt	Vinegar
Red pepper	

While the spinach is cooking, cook the eggs hard. Cut eggs in halves crosswise and remove the yolks. Cut a slice from the bottom of each cooked egg white so that it will stand on a platter. Season the yolks with red pepper, mustard, butter, and salt. Mix thoroughly with vinegar to taste. Fill the egg cups with the spinach, mounding it high, and put the rest around the egg. Put the prepared yolks in a ricer and squeeze over all.

SUCCOTASH

2 cus green corn or
1 cup dried corn
2 cups fresh lima, string
or butter beans, or 1
cup dried lima beans

Salt and pepper
1 cup milk
4 tablespoons butter

If fresh vegetables are used, cut the corn from the cob. Cover the beans with the least possible amount of boiling water to prevent scorching, and cook until tender. Drain off the water, add the corn and the milk and cook slowly until the corn is tender. Add the butter and other seasoning.

When dried corn and beans are used, soak both separately over night. In the morning, cover the beans with fresh water, and boil them very gently until tender. Do not drain the water from the corn, but reduce heat so it will cook slowly. When the beans are tender, drain and add them to the corn, allowing only water enough to cover. Cook slowly until tender and drain off water to save for soup. Add the milk and seasoning.

STEWED TOMATOES

6 tomatoes, fresh or canned
2 tablespoons butter

Salt and pepper
Crumbs or flour

Pour boiling water on fresh tomatoes, and after they have remained covered one minute drain them and plunge them into cold water. Slip off the skins, remove the hard stem ends, and cut the tomatoes in pieces. Cook them in their own juice in a saucepan until tender; add butter, salt, and pepper. Bread crumbs or cracker crumbs, or a little flour blended with the butter, may be added for thickening.

FRIED TOMATOES

6 tomatoes   Crumbs   Salt and pepper

Select firm, ripe tomatoes, wash them and cut in half-inch slices without removing the skins. Season fine crumbs with salt and pepper, dip each slice of tomato in the crumbs, and sauté in hot fat. Serve hot.

STUFFED TOMATOES

No. 1.

6 tomatoes	2 tablespoons fat
1½ cups soft bread crumbs	1 teaspoon salt
¼ teaspoon pepper	

The tomatoes should be very firm, smooth, and of equal size. Cut a piece from the stem end of each tomato and remove the centers without breaking the walls. Make a stuffing of the centers of the tomatoes, crumbs, seasonings, and melted fat and mix well. Sprinkle each tomato well with salt and pepper and fill with the stuffing, packing it in quite firmly.

Place a small piece of butter on the top of each, arrange the tomatoes in a baking dish and bake in a moderate oven (350°-400° F.) until tender. Serve hot in the baking dish.

No 2—INDIAN STYLE.

6 tomatoes	⅛ teaspoon pepper
3 tablespoons rice	⅛ teaspoon garlic clove
1 tablespoon fat	1 teaspoon chopped celery
1 slice bread	A little chopped parsley
2 tablespoons milk	Thyme
2 hard-cooked egg yolks	½ teaspoon curry powder
½ teaspoon salt	

Cut the tops from the tomatoes and remove the pulp. Put rice into a saucepan with one-half cup salted boiling water and the tomato pulp and cook until the rice is soft. Add the fat, the bread soaked in the milk, the mashed egg yolk, and seasonings. Stuff the tomato shells with this mixture, replace the tops and place in a baking dish.

Bake in a moderate oven (350°-400° F.) until the tomatoes are soft (about twenty minutes). The curry powder gives an unusual flavor to the tomatoes, but may be omitted.

MASHED TURNIPS

1 pound white or yellow turnips	3 tablespoons butter
	Salt and pepper

Wash, pare, and slice the turnips and cook in boiling water until soft, adding salt just before the cooking is completed. Drain and mash the turnips in the saucepan and place the pan, uncovered, over low heat for ten minutes to dry the turnips well, stirring them frequently. Add butter and pepper and more salt of needed.

TURNIPS IN CREAM

1 pound white or yellow turnips	4 tablespoons flour
	4 tablespoons fat
2 cups milk	Salt and pepper

Pare the turnips, cut them in cubes; cook until tender. Make a white sauce of the flour, fat, milk, and seasonings. Pour sauce over turnip cubes and serve.

TURNIP SHELLS OR CUPS

Pare the turnip and remove the center, leaving a shell one-half inch in thickness. Cook shell in boiling water until tender. Just before cooking is completed, add the salt. Cook the center in the same way and use for stuffing cup or serve as mashed turnips.

The turnip cups may be used as cases for creamed or buttered peas, carrots, beets, or any suitable vegetable or meat.

VEGETABE MARROW, FRIED

Wash and pare a vegetable marrow, and scoop out the inside. Cook in boiling water for about fifteen minutes, and then drain and slice in inch slices, or cut in pieces of any desired size. Roll in flour, dip in beaten egg which has been diluted with water, roll in fine crumbs and fry in deep fat (395° F.). After frying, drain the pieces on absorbent paper, sprinkle with salt and pepper and serve hot.

To BAKE VEGETABLE MARROW, cut in half between the ends; peel each half, scoop out seeds and loose pulp. Fill each half with seasoned fresh ground beef, diced onion, and bread crumbs (beef loaf p. 133) or chopped leftover meats, chopped onion, green or red peppers, and cooked rice. Fit halves together and truss with string or use skewers in opposite directions. Bake or simmer in deep pot or baking dish, covered with heavy seasoned tomato sauce, until marrow is transparent but not too well done. Serve by slicing through so each serving is a complete circle.

SAUCES FOR FISH, MEAT, POULTRY, GAME, AND VEGETABLES

Sauces add variety to the diet, make foods more attractive to the eye and to the palate, and thus stimulate appetite, aid digestion, and improve nutrition.

WHITE AND BROWN SAUCES

Methods of combining flour or cornstarch with liquids are given in the front of the book. The simplest method of thickening sauces is by means of a roux. Equal parts of fat and flour make the best roux. If much more fat than flour is used, the fat rises to the top of the mixture. If less fat than flour is used, the paste may burn. Therefore, if more fat than flour is required in the sauce, it should be beaten in in small pieces after the liquid is added and just before the sauce is served; if less fat than flour is required, it is better not to make it into a roux but to use another method of thickening the sauce.

All sauces thickened with cornstarch should be cooked for at least fifteen minutes. Standing over hot water in a double boiler for an hour or longer improves the flavor. Sauces thickened with flour are better if cooked for at least five minutes after thickening. The seasonings should be added just before the sauce is served.

To Make a Roux

For a White Sauce—The American method of making a roux for white sauce is to melt the fat, add the flour and cook only until the mixture bubbles before adding the liquid. This saves time, but at the expense of the flavor of the sauce. The French method is to melt the fat, add the flour and cook, with constant stirring, for five minutes before adding any liquid. This removes the raw taste of the flour.

For a Brown Sauce—Melt the fat and allow it to brown

before adding flour, then stir in the flour and stir constantly until the flour is brown. The color depends on this browning, but care must be taken not to scorch. This long preliminary cooking is the secret of a successful brown sauce. Tomato juice or sauce may be used as liquid.

STANDARD RECIPE FOR WHITE SAUCE

THIN WHITE SAUCE.
For cream soups

1 tablespoon butter or other fat	1 cup milk
	¼ teaspoon salt
1 tablespoon flour	⅛ teaspoon pepper

MEDIUM WHITE SAUCE.
For gravies, sauces, creamed and scalloped dishes

2 tablespoons butter or other fat	1 cup milk
	¼ teaspoon salt
2 tablespoons flour	⅛ teaspoon pepper

THICK WHITE SAUCE.
For cutlets, croquettes, and soufflés

4 tablespoons butter or other fat	1 cup milk
	¼ teaspoon salt
4 tablespoons flour	⅛ teaspoon pepper

Use method 1 or 2 for making these sauces.

METHOD 1—Melt butter, blend in flour until smooth. Add milk gradually, stirring constantly until boiling point is reached. Reduce heat and cook for 3 minutes longer; add seasonings and blend. Place over hot water to keep hot and cover tightly to prevent film from forming.

METHOD 2—Heat milk. Blend butter or other fat and flour together and add to hot milk, stirring constantly until mixture thickens. Cook for 3 minutes longer, add seasonings and blend.

METHOD 3—When less butter than flour is used, heat ¾ of the milk; mix remaining milk with flour to make a smooth paste; stir into hot milk, heat to boiling and cook until thickened, stirring constantly. Add butter or other fat and seasonings and cook for 3 minutes.

VARIATIONS OF WHITE SAUCE

USE 1 cup medium white sauce as the basis for each sauce.

CAPER SAUCE—Add 2 to 4 tablespoons chopped capers.

CELERY SAUCE—Add ½ cup chopped cooked celery.

CHEESE SAUCE—Add 2 to 4 ounces grated cheese. Set over hot water and stir until the cheese is blended with sauce. Season to taste with mustard and paprika.

CREAM GRAVY—Use 2 tablespoons meat drippings for butter in white sauce recipe.

CREAM SAUCE—Use cream instead of milk in white sauce.

EGG SAUCE, No. 1—Add 1 hard-cooked egg, chopped.

No. 2—Beat an uncooked egg, dilute with 1 tablespoon of hot thin white sauce, then beat this into the remainder of a cup of sauce. If the egg white is beaten separately, the sauce will be foamy.

LOBSTER SAUCE—Add ½ cup finely flaked cooked lobster.

MOCK HOLLANDAISE SAUCE—Pour sauce over 2 slightly beaten egg yolks, 2 tablespoons each of butter and lemon juice, beat thoroughly and serve immediately.

MUSHROOM SAUCE—Add ⅓ to ½ cup chopped or sliced cooked mushrooms to sauce.

OLIVE SAUCE—Add ¼ cup chopped ripe or stuffed olives.

OYSTER SAUCE—Heat 1 pint small oysters in their own liquor to boiling point. Remove from heat after they have cooked ½ minute and combine with sauce. Season to taste.

PARSLEY SAUCE—Add 2 to 4 tablespoons chopped parsley.

PIMIENTO SAUCE—Add 2 tablespoons minced onion and 6 tablespoons minced pimiento. Onion may be browned in fat when making white sauce if desired.

SHRIMP SAUCE—Add ½ cup chopped cooked shrimp.

SOUBISE SAUCE—Rub 4 boiled onions and 2 sprigs parsley through a coarse sieve. Combine with sauce.

TOMATO CREAM SAUCE—Cook 1 cup fresh or canned tomatoes, 1 stalk celery, 1 slice onion, ½ teaspoon salt, and a few grains cayenne together for 20 minutes. Press through a sieve. Add gradually, stirring constantly, to white sauce.

VELOUTÉ SAUCE—Use 1 cup well-seasoned white stock for milk in thin or medium white sauce.

YELLOW SAUCE—Add hot sauce to 1 or 2 slightly beaten egg yolks and beat thoroughly.

BECHAMEL SAUCE

No. 1.

Use one-half cup of meat stock instead of half of the milk in medium or thin white sauce. If an acid flavor is desired, add one teaspoon of lemon juice to each cup of sauce.

No. 2.

1 small onion	4 tablespoons flour
2 tablespoons fat	1 pint milk
¼ cup chopped lean raw ham	Salt and pepper

Slice the onion, place the fat in a saucepan and slightly brown the onion and ham in it. Add the flour and, when well mixed, the milk. Stir until it boils, then cook over hot water for ten minutes or longer. Add seasonings, strain and use.

CHAUD-FROID SAUCE

WHITE—Soak one tablespoon gelatin in cold water and add to one cup of hot velouté sauce. Mix well; strain, if necessary; let cool and use to coat cold meats.

BROWN—Use a brown roux and brown stock in making the velouté.

YELLOW—Add the beaten yolks of two eggs to white chaud-froid sauce just before removing from the heat.

PINEAPPLE-ORANGE SAUCE

6 tablespoons sugar	1 cup orange juice
½ tablespoon cornstarch	Grated rind 1 orange
1 cup water	⅓ cup crushed pineapple

Combine ingredients in the order listed. Heat to boiling and cook for 3 minutes. Serve with ham or tongue.

Brown sugar may be used in place of granulated.

Add ¼ cup raisins and cook until they puff.

POULETTE SAUCE

1 cup velouté sauce	2 egg yolks
1 cup cream	

Slowly add, with constant stirring, the velouté to the egg yolks, beat in the cream and reheat over hot water. Beat well and serve at once. It is improved by adding, a little at a time, one tablespoon butter, the juice of half a lemon, a tablespoon of chopped parsley and a dash of nutmeg.

BUTTER SAUCE A LA CREOLE

1 cup cold water   ½ tablespoon flour
4½ tablespoons butter   Juice of 1 lemon

Make a sauce of one-half cup cold water, one-half table-spoon butter and the flour. When the mixture boils, stir in quickly four tablespoons butter and add, a small amount at a time, another one-half cup of cold water to keep the mixture from boiling. Stir in the juice of a lemon and strain. It must be served at once and hot. It becomes oily if kept long. One tablespoon of chopped parsley may be added.

DRAWN BUTTER SAUCE

⅓ cup butter   1 pint boiling water
4 tablespoons flour   ¼ teaspoon salt

Make a roux of four tablespoons of the butter and all of the flour. Gradually add the boiling water, stirring constantly over hot water, until the sauce comes to the boiling point. Simmer until it is thick and smooth. When ready to serve, add salt and remaining butter in small pieces, beating constantly.

MAÎTRE D'HÔTEL SAUCE

2 cups drawn-butter sauce   2 egg yolks
1 tablespoon lemon juice   Salt and pepper
1 tablespoon chopped parsley

Add the lemon juice and chopped parsley to the drawn-butter sauce. Let it cool slightly, add the beaten yolks, and season with salt and pepper. Do not permit the sauce to boil after the addition of the egg yolk.

CAPER SAUCE

Follow the recipe for maître d'hôtel sauce, omitting the parsley and adding three tablespoons capers. This is excellent with fish.

(For another recipe for caper sauce, see Variations of White Sauce, page 291.)

IMITATION CAPER SAUCE

½ cup chopped pickles   2 cups drawn butter sauce

To the drawn butter sauce add pickles, cut into tiny cubes of a uniform size and well drained. Boil for one minute. Serve with fish or chops.

HOLLANDAISE SAUCE

2 egg yolks   ¼ teaspoon salt
½ cup butter   Dash cayenne
1 tablespoon lemon juice

Place egg yolks with ⅓ of the butter in top of a double boiler. Keep water in bottom of boiler hot but not boiling. Stir eggs and butter constantly; when butter melts add another portion and as it melts and the mixture begins to thicken add remaining butter. Keep stirring all the time. As soon as mixture is thick, remove from heat and add seasonings. The sauce is delicious served over vegetables. Should sauce separate, beat in 2 tablespoons boiling water, drop by drop. Makes 1 cup sauce.

Increase lemon juice to 1½ tablespoons.

WITH WATER—Cream butter, add egg yolks 1 at a time, blending each one in thoroughly. Add remaining ingredients and beat. Just before serving add ½ cup boiling water gradually, beating constantly. Cook over hot water, stirring constantly until thickened. Serve at once.

WITH ANCHOVY—Season sauce with anchovy paste.

WITH SHERRY—Just before serving sauce, add 2 tablespoons sherry, drop by drop, beating constantly.

BÉARNAISE SAUCE

4 tablespoons fat   1 teaspoon tarragon vinegar
Yolks 4 eggs   1 teaspoon onion juice
½ teaspoon salt   1 teaspoon chopped tarragon
½ teaspoon pepper   1 teaspoon chopped parsley

Stir the fat until perfectly soft and creamy. Place the egg yolks and the salt and pepper in the top of a double boiler and beat light with rotary beater, then add one-third of the fat and beat until smooth, add another third and beat again, and then add the remainder and beat until all is perfectly smooth. Add the vinegar and onion juice and beat again.

Place over boiling water and cook for three minutes, beating constantly with the rotary beater. Remove from the heat, put in the chopped parsley and tarragon and use immediately.

VICTOR HUGO SAUCE

½ teaspoon fine chopped shallot
1 tablespoon tarragon vinegar
⅓ cup butter
Yolks of two eggs

1 teaspoon lemon juice
1 teaspoon meat extract or one meat cube
1 tablespoon grated horseradish

Cook the shallot in the vinegar for five minutes. Wash the butter and divide it into thirds. Add one of the thirds to the vinegar, with the egg-yolks, lemon juice and meat extract. Cook over hot water, stirring constantly. As soon as the butter is melted, add the second piece, and then the third piece. When the sauce thickens, add the grated horseradish.

GIBLET GRAVY

Giblets and neck of fowl
2 tablespoons chicken fat

2 tablespoons flour
Salt and pepper

Place the giblets (liver, heart, and gizzard) and the neck in a saucepan and cover them with cold water. Simmer slowly and when they are tender remove the flesh from the neck and chop it fine with the giblets. Save the stock in which the giblets and neck were cooked. Heat the fat in a small saucepan on top of the stove and when it is hot stir in the flour. Cook two minutes, then add one cup of the stock, pouring it in gradually so that it will not thin the gravy too much. If the gravy seems too thick, add a little hot water. Lastly, put in the chopped giblets and season to taste with salt and pepper.

BREAD SAUCE

1 cup dry bread crumbs
2 cups milk
Salt

1 onion
3 tablespoons butter
Pepper

This sauce is generally served with small birds. It may be served with roast chicken or duck. The crumbs must be entirely white. Sift them through a coarse sieve, place the ones that pass through in the milk, add the onion and place in a saucepan on the heat to cook. Cook for twelve minutes, remove the onion and add one tablespoon of butter with salt and pepper to taste.

BROWNED CRUMBS—Place the remaining butter on the fire in a frying-pan, add the coarse bread crumbs and fry them until brown, being careful to have the fat very hot before putting in the crumbs. Stir vigorously for two or three minutes, but do not allow the crumbs to burn. Serve the sauce in a gravy dish and sprinkle with the browned crumbs.

No. 1.   **BROWN SAUCE**
1 tablespoon chopped onion   2 tablespoons flour
2 tablespoons fat   1 cup brown meat stock
Pepper   Salt

Brown the onion and fat. Add the flour and make a brown roux (See Index). Pour in the brown stock and cook with constant stirring until the sauce thickens. Strain to remove the particles of onion, and season with pepper and salt. If the roux was not sufficiently brown to make the sauce a desirable color, a few drops of vegetable flavoring or of Worcestershire sauce may be added. If a more highly flavored sauce is desired, add a slice of carrot, a sprig of parsley, a little thyme and a few peppercorns to the onion, and brown in the fat.

No.2—In making brown sauce for a roast, the simplest way is to use the fat and juice of the roast. Add two tablespoons of flour to two tablespoons of the hot drippings, stir and cook well. Then add one cup of boiling water, stir well to avoid lumps, and season to taste with salt and pepper. If liked, add a tablespoon or two of catchup or a flavoring of Worcestershire or other sauce.

GRAVY
2 small onions   Butter or other fat
1 carrot   Flour
Small piece of lean beef,   Pepper
   size of egg, or 1 beef   Salt
   cube or 1 teaspoon   Catchup
   beef extract

Cut up onions and carrot, place them with the lean beef or extract in a saucepan with the fat and brown all together. Add enough water to cover the mixture and stir slowly until the vegetables are cooked. Strain, thicken with flour, using two tablespoons to each cup of liquid, and add pepper, salt and catchup. Color brown with caramel or vegetable flavoring if necessary.

CUCUMBER CREAM DRESSING

2 tablespoons vinegar	1 cup diced cucumber
2 tablespoons sugar	1 cup heavy cream, whipped

Add vinegar and sugar to cucumbers; fold into cream.

CURRANT JELLY SAUCE

1 onion	2 tablespoons vinegar
1 tablespoon fat	2 cups stock
1 tablespoon flour	1 bay leaf
1 stalk celery, chopped	½ cup currant jelly

Slice the onion and cook in the fat till it begins to brown, then add the flour and celery and stir until brown. Add the vinegar, stock, and bay leaf; simmer twenty minutes. Strain, skim off all the fat, add jelly and stir until it is melted. This sauce is used with game.

MUSHROOM SAUCE

4 tablespoons fat	Salt and pepper
4 tablespoons flour	1 cup mushrooms, fresh
2 cups stock	or canned

Make a brown sauce of fat, flour, and stock. Season, add mushrooms and cook 4 minutes for canned and 5 or 6 minutes for fresh ones.

ONION SAUCE

½ cup minced onion	1½ cups beef stock
3 tablespoon fat	1 tablespoon minced parsley
3 tablespoons flour	

Cook the onion with the fat until slightly browned. Stir in the flour, then add the stock and parsley, stirring constantly. Serve with beef.

SAUCE SUPREME

2 tablespoons fat
2 tablespoons flour
1 cup chicken stock
2 tablespoons lemon juice
2 teaspoons chopped parsley

Place the fat in a frying-pan, over the fire, and when it is hot, add the flour. Stir well. When it is turning brown, add the chicken stock and boil for several minutes, stirring constantly. Then add the lemon juice and the parsley. After the sauce has boiled up once, it is ready to serve.

OLIVE SAUCE

2 dozen olives
2 tablespoons salad oil
1 slice onion
1 lemon
2 tablespoons flour
1 pint stock
Salt and pepper

Place the olives in an earthenware bowl, cover with hot water and let them remain for half an hour to draw out the brine. Place the oil in a skillet, and add the onion; when this commences to brown, add the flour. Stir until smooth. After it has cooked for two minutes, add the stock, and regulate the heat so that the sauce will simmer gently. Pare the olives from the stones, round and round as though paring an apple, leaving the pulp in a single strip. If this is done carefully, the olives will coil back into shape. Place them in the sauce, add the seasoning and the juice of the lemon and simmer for twenty minutes. Skim carefully and serve.

SPANISH SAUCE

1 tablespoon minced lean
raw ham
1 tablespoon chopped celery
1 tablespoon chopped carrot
1 tablespoon chopped onion
2 tablespoons fat
2 tablespoons flour
½ cup stock
½ cup tomato juice
½ teaspoon salt
⅛ teaspoon pepper

Melt the fat. Add the ham and vegetables and cook until they are brown. Make a sauce of this mixture and the flour, salt, pepper, and liquid.

CHATEAUBRIAND SAUCE

3 tablespoons fat
1 tablespoon lemon juice
1 teaspoon salt

Pepper
1 teaspoon minced parsley
2 cups Spanish sauce

Whip together the fat, lemon juice, salt, a pinch of pepper, and minced parsley. Add the Spanish sauce, reheat, stir for a moment and serve.

TOMATO SAUCE

1 quart fresh or canned
  tomatoes
1 slice onion
8 cloves

3 tablespoons fat
3 tablespoons flour
Salt and pepper

Set the tomatoes, onion and cloves on the fire and cook for twenty minutes. Brown the fat in the frying-pan, add the flour, and cook until smooth and brown, stirring constantly, Add the tomatoes, cook for three minutes, season with salt and pepper and pass through a strainer fine enough to hold back the seeds. This makes a very thin sauce. Use more flour if you prefer a thick sauce.

TOMATO AND MUSHROOM SAUCE

2 slices bacon or small
  quantity uncooked ham
1 slice onion
6 slices carrot
Bay leaf
2 sprigs thyme
Sprig parsley
½ No. 1 can mushooms

2 cloves
½ teaspoon peppercorns
Few gratings nutmeg
½ No. 2 can tomatoes
5 tablespoons flour
1½ cups brown stock
Salt and pepper

Chop the bacon or ham, and cook with onion and carrot for five minutes. Add bay leaf, thyme, parsley, cloves. peppercorns, nutmeg, and tomatoes, and cook five minutes. Mix the flour with five tablespoons of cold water and rub out all the lumps; then add enough water so that the batter can be poured in a thin stream. Add to the sauce, stirring constantly. As the sauce thickens, dilute it with the stock. Cover, set in the oven (300° F.) and cook one hour. Strain, add salt and pepper to taste, and the mushrooms, drained and cut in quarters. Then cook two minutes over direct heat.

RAVIGOTE SAUCE

1 cup thin white sauce	1 tablespoon minced chervil
1/4 cup lemon juice	1 tablespoon minced tarragon
1 tablespoon tarragon	leaves
vinegar	1 tablespoon minced chives
1 tablespoon minced shallot	1 tablespoon butter

While sauce is hot, add other ingredients, except butter. Keep hot five minutes, strain, beat in butter. Serve hot or cold.

BROWNED BUTTER

Place a piece of butter in a hot frying-pan and toss about until it browns. Stir browned flour into it until it is smooth and commences to boil. This is used for coloring gravies, sauces, etc.

BROWNED FLOUR

Spread flour on a pie pan and place over heat or in a very hot oven (450°-500° F.). When it begins to brown, stir constantly until it is evenly browned throughout. When cold, store in covered jars.

GLAZES FOR MEAT

No. 1—Boil one quart of consommé until it is reduced to one cup. For half-glaze, reduce it to one pint.

No. 2—Simmer a small amount of jellied stock with burnt sugar until it becomes sirupy.

No. 3—To one cup brown stock, add one-half tablespoon gelatin soaked in four tablespoons water. The glaze should be melted over hot water and applied to meat, fish, game, or poultry.

No. 1. **CRANBERRY SAUCE**

1 quart cranberries   2 cups boiling water
2 cups sugar

Boil the sugar and water together for five minutes. Remove any scum that may have formed. Add the cranberries and cook without stirring until they are thick and clear.

No. 2—Cook the cranberries and water together until the skins of the berries are broken. Add the sugar and simmer for five or ten minutes. Chill before using.

No. 3—If a strained sauce is desired, cook the cranberries and water as in No. 2 and press through a sieve. Return the strained portion to the heat, add the sugar and simmer for five or ten minutes.

SPICED CRANBERRIES

4 cups cranberries   5 allspice
5 cloves   2 sticks cinnamon
3 cups sugar   2 blades mace

Pickup over and wash the berries. Place in a saucepan and cover with cold water. Tie spices in a cheesecloth bag and drop in with the berries. Cook until the berries burst. Remove spices, add sugar, and cook until the mixture is clear. Chill.

MOCK WILD CHERRY SAUCE

1 quart cranberries   2¼ cups sugar
1 cup water   1 teaspoon almond flavoring

Add cranberries to boiling water, cover and cook until the berries burst. Add sugar and boil a few minutes longer. Add flavoring.

No. 1. **APPLE SAUCE**

4 quarts sweet cider   2 quarts apples

By boiling it uncovered reduce four quarts of new cider to two quarts. Pare quarter and core the apples and simmer with the cider for four hours. Flavor with cinnamon if desired.

No. 2.

1 quart apples	1 cup water
1 cup sugar	

Pare, chop and place apples in a deep pudding dish; sprinkle with sugar and pour water over them. Bake in a slow oven (250°-350° F) two hours or more, until they are a rich red-brown. Serve with goose, pork or game.

MINT SAUCE

1 tablespoon powdered sugar	½ cup vinegar
	¼ cup minced mint leaves

Dissolve sugar in vinegar. Pour this over minced mint leaves and set where it will keep warm but not hot. Allow it to infuse for half an hour. If vinegar is very strong dilute with water.

CURRANT MINT SAUCE

⅔ cup currant jelly	1 to 2 tablespoons chopped mint leaves
Shavings from orange rind	

Separate jelly into pieces, but do not beat it. Add chopped mint leaves and orange rind shavings. Serve around roast.

SOUTHERN BARBECUE SAUCE

½ cup butter or other fat	2 tablespoons chili sauce
1 sour pickle, finely chopped	4 slices lemon
	1 teaspoon brown sugar
2 tablespoons Worcestershire sauce	1 green pepper, chopped fine
2 tablespoons chopped onion	1 cup vinegar

Combine all ingredients and mix thoroughly. Place in a saucepan and simmer until butter or other fat melts, stirring constantly. Place in the top of a double boiler and keep warm until ready to use on barbecued meats or as a sauce for barbecued sandwiches. Make 1¾ cups sauce.

BARBECUED MEATS, beef, lamb, veal, and pork in the form of roasts, chops, or steaks are braised in this sauce. Chickens may also be used.

CUCUMBER SAUCE

2 cucumbers
½ cup stock
½ tablespoon vinegar

Salt and cayenne
Celery essence

Cut peeled cucumbers into very small pieces. Simmer until tender in a saucepan with stock, vinegar, salt, cayenne, and a little celery essence. Celery-salt may be used instead of plain salt, if preferred. A bit of boiled onion and a little butter may be added also, if desired. Strain through a sieve.

ANCHOVY SAUCE

¼ cup fresh butter
1 teaspoon anchovy paste

Cayenne pepper

Melt the butter and stir in the anchovy paste and the cayenne pepper. Warm and stir thoroughly and serve with either boiled or fried fish.

BEURRE NOIR

2 tablespoons butter
1 tablespoon vinegar
1 teaspoon lemon juice

1 tablespoon chopped parsley
½ teaspoon salt
¼ teaspoon pepper

Place the butter in a skillet and when it is browned add the other ingredients. Bring to boil and serve. This sauce is poured over fried fish or boiled fish just before serving.

PARSLEY BUTTER

3 tablespoons butter
½ to 1 tablespoon lemon
juice

1 tablespoon chopped parsley
½ teaspoon salt
⅛ teaspoon pepper

Cream butter and add lemon juice, chopped parsley, salt, and pepper. This may be used to spread on fried or boiled fish, or over potato balls. When intended for potato balls, one-half tablespoon of lemon juice will be enough.

LOBSTER BUTTER

1 lobster coral
3 tablespoons chopped lobster

3 tablespoons butter
Seasoning

Lobster butter is used in lobster soups and sauces to give color and richness. Pound the coral of a lobster to a smooth paste with two tablespoons of butter, add chopped lobster and remaining tablespoon of butter and pound again until all is reduced to a smooth paste, then rub through a fine sieve. If coral is not obtainable, the small claws may be pounded with the butter.

MUSTARD SAUCE

1 tablespoon dry mustard
½ teaspoon sugar
¼ teaspoon salt

1 tablespoon vinegar
1 tablespoon melted butter
⅛ cup boiling water

Mix dry ingredients, add liquids, mix well and serve.

MARMALADE SAUCE

1 glass orange or grapefruit
marmalade

1 teaspoon dry mustard
1 teaspoon salt

Turn the marmalade out into a deep plate and beat it to a foam. Then add dry mustard and salt and beat again thoroughly.

ORANGE RAISIN SAUCE

1 cup boiling water
Juice and grated rind
   of one orange
¼ cup sugar

1 tablespoon flour
1 tablespoon butter
⅓ cup seeded raisins

Mix the dry ingredients, add boiling water and cook until clear. Add the orange juice and rind, the raisins, and the butter.

REMOULADE SAUCE

2 hard-cooked egg yolks
1 uncooked egg yolk
3 tablespoons tarragon vinegar
3 tablespoons cider vinegar

2 cups oil
1 teaspoon mustard
½ teaspoon salt
1 teaspoon parsley

Put the cooked yolks of eggs through a coarse wire sieve, and then put them in a dish with the raw yolk and the seasoning. Add two tablespoons of the vinegar and beat thoroughly five minutes. Next add the oil, one teaspoon at a time, beating the mixture two or three minutes at a time after each addition of oil. When five teaspoons have thus been added, the rest of the oil may be put in in larger quantities, three or four teaspoons at a time. Whenever the sauce becomes so thick that the beater turns hard, put in one-half tablespoon of vinegar. This sauce may be used for meat, for salads, or for such vegetables as asparagus, broccoli and artichokes. It may be varied by adding capers, minced gherkins, and a dash of cayenne. There is not a great deal of difference between remoulade sauce and mayonnaise.

TARTAR SAUCE

1 cup mayonnaise dressing
1 teaspoon onion juice
1 tablespoon capers
1 tablespoon chopped cucumber pickle

Make the mayonnaise rather more tart and with a little more mustard than for salad, and mix into it the capers, pickle, and onion juice. Set in the refrigerator until needed. It should be quite thick when served.

HORSERADISH SAUCE

No. 1.
1 teaspoon mustard
3 tablespoons cream
1 tablespoon vinegar
Salt
Horseradish

Mix the first four ingredients and add as much grated horseradish as needed to make it the desired thickness.

No. 2.
¼ cup heavy cream
3 tablespoons grated horseradish
1 tablespoon vinegar
¼ teaspoon salt
Sprinkle of cayenne or pepper

Whip the cream stiff. Mix the other ingredients and beat them gradually into the whipped cream. Serve on baked ham.

BUTTER-ORANGE FLUFF

¼ pound butter
1 teaspoon grated orange rind
½ cup brown sugar

Cream the butter until light and fluffy. Add brown sugar gradually beating the mixture to a light, fluffy mass. Stir in the grated orange rind. Use for waffles and pancakes.

VINAIGRETTE SAUCE

1 teaspoon salt
¼ teaspoon paprika
Few grains pepper
1 tablespoon tarragon
vinegar
2 tablespoons cider vinegar

6 tablespoons olive oil
1 tablespoon chopped pickle
1 tablespoon chopped green
pepper
1 teaspoon chopped parsley
1 teaspoon chopped chives

Mix the ingredients in the order given.

CREOLE SAUCE

2 tablespoons chopped
onion
4 tablespoons minced green
pepper
2 tablespoons butter
3 tablespoons flour

Salt and pepper
2 tomatoes or ½ cup
canned tomatoes
1 cup bouillon
¼ cup sliced mushrooms

Sauté onion and pepper in butter 5 minutes; add flour and
seasonings and stir until browned; add tomatoes and mushrooms gradually and cook 2 minutes; then add bouillon and
heat to boiling. Serve with omelet, spaghetti and fish. Yield:
2 cups.

FRONTIER SAUCE

3 tablespoons flour
2 tablespoons butter
½ teaspoon salt
½ teaspoon paprika
Dash of tabasco

¾ cup tomato juice
¼ cup liquid drained from
stewed or canned mush-
rooms
2 tablespoons heavy cream

Stir flour into melted butter; add seasonings and tabasco,
then add tomato juice and mushroom liquor gradually and
cook 5 minutes, stirring constantly until smooth and thick.
Add cream and blend. Serve on macaroni or spaghetti. Yield:
1¼ cups sauce.

SALADS

FRUITS, nuts, uncooked and cooked vegetables and some cooked meats, fish and fowl, served cold and dressed with condiments, oils and acids, are known as salads.

Utensils Needed for Salad Making

A chilled earthenware bowl is excellent for mixing salad ingredients. Two forks or a fork and a spoon are better to use in folding together the ingredients than a spoon alone, because they do not crush the materials so much as a single utensil.

A sharp edged knife or vegetable cutter is necessary for slicing vegetables or fruits. Where fruit pulp is to be removed from the thin white membrane enclosing it, a thin narrow knife slightly curved at the tip is useful. A pair of shears can be used for many of the processes of salad making, such as shredding lettuce, clipping off wilted or discolored edges, etc.

Various fancy shapes for molding individual salads may be bought, or tea-cups or small bowls may be used as molds. Gelatin salads may be put into pans and cut in square or fancy shapes after they have hardened. The cube trays of mechanical refrigerators are excellent for molding gelatin.

Materials for Salads

VEGETABLES—Leaf vegetables, such as head lettuce, curly lettuce, endive, chicory, romaine, water cress, celery and cabbage, make very attractive salads served alone with a dressing or in combination with other materials.

Tomatoes, cucumbers, celery, cabbage and ground carrots are excellent uncooked materials for salad, as are also Bermuda or Spanish onions in thin wafer-like slices or young spring onions marinated in French dressing.

Many cooked vegetables, such as peas, carrots, beans, beets, cauliflower, spinach, asparagus, and potatoes, are used in salad making, alone or in combination.

FRUITS—The fruits most commonly used in the preparation of salads are oranges, bananas, apples, cherries, grapefruit, grapes, peaches, pears and pineapple. Watermelon or cantaloupe adds a delicious flavor to a fruit salad.

DRIED FRUITS—Dates, figs and raisins give variety to fruit salads.

MEATS—Chicken always makes a delicious salad. Veal and pork may be combined with chicken and it is difficult to detect their use. They may be used alone in salads, also

Crab, lobster, shrimp, oysters, salmon, tuna fish and sardines are most commonly used in fish salads. Any firm-fleshed cooked fish may be diced and combined with other materials.

CHEESE—Cream cheese or cottage cheese, served in mounds on lettuce leaves, makes an attractive salad, with bar-le-duc or other jelly or jam as a garnish. It can also be mixed with green peppers or pimientoes, rolled in nuts, served with pineapple or molded in a loaf and sliced.

EGGS—The most common egg salad is the "deviled egg," or salad egg. Hard-cooked eggs can be cut in slices or quarters or fancy shapes and served on a bed of lettuce leaves with a dressing or used with other ingredients in a vegetable or fish salad.

HERBS—Such herbs as chervil, mint, parsley, peppergrass, sorrel and tarragon may be added to salad to give a pungent flavor.

Fennel (finochio) tops, or root and stem of anise flavor, dandelion, chard, escarole, celery cabbage, or cooked zucchini are used both as body of the salad and as flavoring. Those who have a garden will find dill, nasturtium leaves and seeds, catnip and rose geranium leaves usable.

Important Points in Salad Making

WASHING INGREDIENTS—Wash salad greens, drain thoroughly, and gently pat dry with a soft, clean towel or absorbent paper. If necessary, crisp greens by placing them for a short time in ice and water.

CHILLING INGREDIENTS—All ingredients, fruits, vegetables, and dressing, should be chilled (see directions on next page for keeping materials) before being folded together. The bowl used should be chilled; also the plates upon which the salad is served.

FROZEN SALADS—This name may seem misleading because pieces of fruit or vegetable in salads should never be actually frozen. Combined with whipped cream and mayonnaise, the mixture is frozen like mousse, but it should not be frozen long enough to harden the fruit or vegetable. Salads made of vegetable or fruit pulp may be frozen. The freezing can be done by packing in ice and salt or by placing the mixture in the trays of the refrigerator.

KEEPING MATERIALS—To prevent lettuce and other salad greens from wilting, they should be stored in the refrigerator in closely covered vegetable drawers, plastic bags, or other moisture-vapor proof material. Most other vegetables and fruits should be stored in this manner also.

ARRANGEMENT OF SALAD—A salad should have a carefree look, not too carefully arranged to look overhandled nor too carelessly prepared to look untidy. A salad should fit the serving dish, not skimpily, nor too full.

MARINATING SALADS—A marinade is used to give flavor to salad materials and is made by mixing oil, salt, and lemon juice or vinegar (sometimes onion juice). The vegetables, fish or meat may stand an hour or so in the marinade before using. When several vegetables are to be used, each one should be marinated separately. For serving, these vegetables may be combined, or placed on lettuce leaves in small individual mounds, as preferred.

ADDITION OF SALAD DRESSING—A salad is complemented by the dressing, so suit it to the salad. Dressings should coat the greens, not drown them; they should accompany the salad, not hide it. Usually the dressing is added to the mixture just before serving, except in the case of a salad such as potato salad when the dressing is sometimes added several hours before serving to allow it to permeate the vegetables.

GELATIN SALAD MOLDS—Lightly oil molds with a flavorless salad or cooking oil (not olive oil). Invert mold to drain excess oil.

Chill gelatin mixtures in the refrigerator, stirring occasionally, or over ice and water, stirring frequently until of desired consistency. Chill until slightly thicker than consistency of thick, unbeaten egg white before adding remainder of ingredients, such as chopped or whole foods which would sink to bottom of mold.

Garnishes for Salads

Chives, mint, chervil, parsley and similar small greens may be minced and sprinkled over a green salad.

Strips of pimiento and green pepper, or a dash of paprika may be used to give life to a colorless salad.

A chapon is a small piece of bread rubbed with garlic. When placed in a salad bowl it gives a delicious flavor to the salad.

The outside leaves of a head of lettuce may be used as garnish for a salad, reserving the heart for heart-of-lettuce salad.

MOLDED SALADS

Among the most decorative ways to serve jellied salad are the form mold and the ring mold. The latter lends itself to many additional touches since the center may be used for decorative vegetables, a pile of cut jelly of contrasting color or the bowl of salad dressing. Of exact size to fit, the bowl may be of glass, china or silver. Be sure the plate onto which the ring is unmolded is large enough for the decoration planned.

COLD MARINADE

3 tablespoons oil
6 tablespoons lemon juice or vinegar
1 teaspoon salt
½ teaspoon pepper
½ teaspoon onion juice

For fish, use three tablespoons vinegar and three tablespoons lemon juice. Mix ingredients in order given.

Vegetable Salads

ASPARAGUS SALAD

6 rings cut from green pepper or lemon
24 stalks cold boiled asparagus, fresh or canned
Lettuce leaves
French dressing
½ tablespoon tomato catchup

Cut rings about one-third inch wide. If lemon is used, remove the pulp, leaving only the peel. Slip four stalks of cold asparagus through each ring and arrange each serving on crisp lettuce on salad plates or all on a platter. Serve with French dressing mixed with catchup. Serves 6.

GREEN BEAN SALAD

2 cups cooked green beans,   Lettuce
   cut or whole   1 hard-cooked egg yolk,
1 tablespoon minced onion   minced
½ cup French Dressing

Marinate green beans and onion in French dressing for 1 hour or longer. Drain beans and arrange on lettuce. Sprinkle minced hard-cooked egg yolk over beans. Serves 4.

CABBAGE SALAD

Select a small firm head of cabbage. Cut into halves and slice it from the cut edge with a sharp knife or slaw cutter. Combine with any desired dressing and serve immediately.

To retain the vitamins, cabbage should be sliced as near serving time as possible and should never be soaked in water.

IN ASPIC—Fold cut cabbage into one package lemon gelatin made as directed on the package, chill and unmold. Garnish.

CALIFORNIA SLAW

1 small head of cabbage   1 tablespoon sugar
2 tart apples, chopped   1 teaspoon dry mustard
1 medium onion, minced   1 tablespoon melted butter
2 pimientos, minced   ⅓ cup lemon juice
3 hard-cooked eggs   ½ cup cream, whipped
¼ teaspoon salt   Parsley

Shred cabbage and combine with apples, onion and pimientos. Rub yolks of hard-cooked eggs to a paste and add salt, sugar, mustard and butter and mix thoroughly until smooth. Stir in lemon juice and mix. Add whipped cream. Combine with shredded cabbage mixture and garnish with the whites of cooked eggs and bits of parsley. Serves 6.

PENNSYLVANIA CABBAGE SALAD

2 cups shredded cabbage   1 teaspoon salt
1 green or red pepper,   ½ cup Sour Cream Salad
   cut fine   Dressing (page 333)

Mix shredded cabbage, pepper and salt; pour dressing over cabbage and mix well. Serve at once. Makes 6 portions.

CARDINAL SALAD

2 large beets
2 tablespoons vinegar
½ cup wax beans
½ cup peas
½ cup asparagus tips

Mayonnaise made with vinegar from beets
Lettuce
Radishes for a garnish

Boil beets until tender, slice, cover with vinegar and let stand until the following day. Drain off the vinegar and use it in making the mayonnaise. Arrange beans, peas, asparagus tips and mayonnaise in little rose-like nests of lettuce leaves, and garnish with radishes.

CARROT SALAD

1 cup grated raw carrot
1 cup chopped raw cabbage or celery, or cabbage and celery combined

1 tablespoon lemon juice
½ teaspoon salt
Mayonnaise or boiled dressing
Lettuce leaves

Mix the ingredients well and serve on crisp lettuce leaves. The grated carrot may be served alone on lettuce or may be combined with cold boiled peas, with chopped nuts and apples, or with onions and radishes.

CAULIFLOWER AND SHRIMP SALAD

1 cauliflower
Mayonnaise dressing

Lettuce
Cooked shrimps

Cook the cauliflower in boiling water, drain, and put it, head down, into a bowl. When cold, place it, stem down, on a shallow dish and cover with mayonnaise. Garnish with lettuce arranged to resemble the leaves of the cauliflower, and add little clusters of shrimps.

CELERY SALAD

2 cups celery
½ cup mayonnaise

Strips of pimiento or green pepper and celery curls

After thoroughly washing the celery allow it to crisp in cold water. Then wipe it dry, cut it into inch lengths and these into lengthwise strips. Place them in a salad-bowl, and add sufficient mayonnaise dressing to moisten the whole. Garnish with the pimiento or pepper and the celery curls. Serve at once. Celery salad admits of a wide range of additions, any cold meat, fish or fowl left from a previous meal being palatable served in it.

CELERY CURLS— These are made from the tender inner stalks. Cut in lengths of two or three inches and slit in narrow strips almost to the end. Place in water with plenty of ice. As the slit stalks chill, the ends curl.

CRESS SALAD

1 pint water cress   1 onion   French dressing

Pick over the leaves of the cress carefully, removing all bruised or wilted ones, wash and drain, and with the fingers break the stems into two-inch lengths. Lay the cress in a salad bowl, chop the onion very fine, strew it over the cress, add French dressing and serve.

CRESS AND DANDELION SALAD

1 cup water cress   6 thin slices raw onion
1 cup dandelion greens   French dressing

The dandelion should be fresh and young. Wash the leaves carefully and drain well. Arrange them in a salad bowl with the cress. Add the slices of onion and pour the French dressing over all.

CRESS AND WALNUT SALAD

½ cup walnut meats   1 pint water cress
1 lemon   French dressing

Crack walnuts and remove their meats as nearly as possible in halves. Squeeze over them the juice of the lemon and let them stand for a short time. Pick over the water cress and wash it carefully. Drain it on a napkin and at the last moment drench it with French dressing. Spread the nuts over it and give them also a generous sprinkling of the dressing.

CUCUMBER SALAD

3 cucumbers   Salt   French dressing

Cut about an inch off the point of each cucumber, and pare carefully. Slice very thin, sprinkle with a little salt, and let stand ten minutes. Serve with French dressing.

No. 1.   **POTATO SALAD**

1 quart potatoes   2 tablespoons grated onion
2 tablespons chopped parsley French dressing to moisten

Boil the potatoes with skins on and allow them to cool before peeling, as it is considered a good thing to have potatoes waxy rather than mealy for salad. Peel potatoes, cut into small pieces or thin slices, and mix with parsley, onion, and French dressing. Set in a cool place for two hours before serving.

No. 2.

1 quart new potatoes   1 tablespoon chopped parsley
1 tablespoon oil   Salt and pepper
2 tablespoons vinegar   Thin mayonnaise or boiled
1 onion   dressing
2 stalks celery   Cut beets
1 tablespoon capers   Lettuce, lemon

Boil potatoes until done, but not too soft, slice them when cooled and add oil and vinegar. Chop onion and celery very fine, and add, with capers, parsley, and salt and pepper to taste. Pour a thin mayonnaise over all, mixing thoroughly with a wooden spoon and fork. Garnish with lettuce, a few pieces of lemon and cut beets.

POTATO AND PEA SALAD

2 cups boiled potatoes, diced   ½ cup French dressing
1 cup boiled peas   Lettuce, mayonnaise

Pour two-thirds of the French dressing over the diced potatoes, and the other third over the cold peas, and set where they will be chilled. After an hour, combine them and arrange on lettuce leaves. Garnish with mayonnaise.

SPINACH SALAD

1 pint spinach   2 hard-cooked eggs   French dressing

Wash spinach carefully. Select only thick, tender leaves (save others and stems for cooking). If too large, tear to size. Shake off excess water. Chop whites and yolks of eggs, separately and turn into bowl with leaves. Moisten with tart French dressing. Add any mild-flavored vegetable.

No. 1.   **TOMATO AND LETTUCE SALAD**

3 tomatoes   Lettuce leaves   6 tablespoons French dressing

Scald the tomatoes, remove the skins and chill the tomatoes. Just before serving time, cut them in halves, crosswise, and place one piece, with the outside upward, on each serving-plate with one or two leaves of white, crisp lettuce underneath. Pour over each portion a tablespoon of French dressing.

No. 2.

3 tomatoes   ⅓ to ½ cup French dressing
Lettuce   1 tablespoon capers

Select smooth tomatoes about two inches in diameter. Scald, peel and chill. Cut in quarters or in slices and arrange on a plate with lettuce leaves or sections of lettuce hearts. Add the capers to the dressing.

TOMATO AND CELERY SALAD

6 tomatoes   ⅓ to ½ cup mayonnaise
2 cups celery, diced   Lettuce leaves

Select firm tomatoes of a good size, scald, peel and chill, cut a slice from the top of each, and scoop out all the seeds and soft pulp, being careful not to break the sides. Cut celery into small dice, mix it with mayonnaise dressing, fill the shells with mixture, place one teaspoon of the dressing on top of each tomato and serve individually on a bed of lettuce leaves, placing three or four small leaves on each plate and the tomato in the center.

TOMATO SURPRISE SALAD

6 tomatoes   ¼ cup chopped nuts
¾ cup diced cucumber   ¼ cup mayonnaise dressing
½ cup diced, cooked   Lettuce
  chicken   Parsley, cauliflower buds

Select medium-sized smooth tomatoes. Scald, peel and chill. Carefully scoop the inside out of the tomatoes. Remove the seeds from the pulp. Chill all ingredients, and when ready to serve, mix the chicken, cucumber, tomato pulp, and nuts with the mayonnaise dressing. Add more salt if needed. Fill the tomatoes. Arrange on lettuce leaves. Garnish with mayonnaise and decorate each tomato top with parsley and cauliflower buds.

TOMATO JELLY SALAD

3 cups stewed tomatoes,
fresh or canned
¼ cup chopped onion
½ cup chopped celery
1 bay leaf   1 clove
¼ green pepper

1 teaspoon sugar
Salt
1 tablespoon gelatin
½ cup cold water
Lettuce
Mayonnaise

Cook tomatoes with seasonings. Soak gelatin in cold water, add to boiling tomatoes, strain and pour into cups about the size of a tomato. Make a nest of small green lettuce leaves for each mold when serving, and place one tablespoon of mayonnaise on top of each tomato as it is turned from the mold.

TOMATO ASPIC RING SALAD—Pour into ring mold and fill center with crisp greens, cottage cheese, chicken or fish salad.

TOMATO ROSE SALAD

Firm Tomatoes
Cream cheese
Milk

Hard-cooked egg yolk
Watercress or lettuce
French dressing

Peel tomatoes and chill them. Slightly soften cream cheese with milk. Form two rows of petals on each tomato by pressing level teaspoons of the softened cheese against the side of the tomato, then drawing the teaspoon down with a curving motion. Sprinkle center of each tomato with hard-cooked egg yolk pressed through a strainer. Serve on crisp watercress or lettuce with French dressing.

FROZEN FRUIT SALAD

1 teaspoon unflavored
gelatin
2 tablespoons cold water
¾ cup mayonnaise
1 teaspoon sugar

2 cups heavy cream
1½ cups cut fruit (fresh
canned or candied cherries,
peaches, pineapple, etc.)
Lettuce

Soften gelatin in the cold water, melt it over steam and beat it into the mayonnaise. Add the sugar to the cream and whip it, then combine with mayonnaise. Stir in fruit. Freeze as directed on page 308. Serve on lettuce. The mayonnaise may be omitted and served separately.

AVOCADO PEAR SALAD

2 avocado pears	French dressing
Lettuce leaves	

The alligator pear, or avocado, is now available in all markets at very reasonable prices throughout the greater part of the year. Cut each pear into six pieces, giving wedge-shaped sections, and if these are too large, cut each section again lengthwise. Peel and arrange wedges on beds of lettuce leaves. Either French dressing or Russian dressing may be used, but the fruit is so rich that French dressing is preferred by most people.

APRICOT AND BANANA SALAD

2 cups lettuce leaves, shredded	6 stewed apricots
1 cup sliced bananas	Whipped cream or boiled dressing

On each plate arrange a bed of shredded lettuce, and on it place a layer of sliced ripe bananas, topped by the halves of an apricot. Serve with whipped cream or boiled dressing.

BANANA AND NUT SALAD

3 well ripened bananas	½ cup mayonnaise or boiled dressing
½ cup chopped nuts	
6 leaves lettuce	

Peel bananas and cut in two lengthwise. Roll each half in nut meats. Place on lettuce leaf and garnish with dressing. Equal parts of dressing and whipped cream may be used.

COCONUT, CELERY AND APPLE SALAD

1½ cups mixed diced tart apples and celery	4 tablespoons orange juice
½ cup shredded coconut	Salt
1 tablespoon lemon juice	Paprika
4 tablespoons oil	Lettuce leaves
	Currant or plum jelly

Mix the apples, celery, and coconut. Sprinkle with the lemon juice. Add a French dressing made from the oil and orange juice, with salt and paprika to taste. Line a salad-bowl with lettuce leaves and pile chilled salad in center. Dot with currant or plum jelly.

FRENCH FRUIT SALAD

1 orange	1 dozen walnuts
1 banana	Lettuce
½ pound Malaga grapes	French dressing

Peel the orange and cut the sections from the membrane with a sharp knife or a pair of shears. If the fruit is allowed to stand in cold water after peeling, the bitter membrane will come off easily.

Peel the banana and cut in quarter-inch slices. Remove the skins and seeds from the grapes. Break walnuts into small pieces, but do not chop. Mix these ingredients thoroughly and place on ice. Serve on lettuce leaves with French dressing.

GRAPEFRUIT SALAD

Peel grapefruit and free the sections from all membrane and seeds. Cut sections in half, crosswise; lay on bed of lettuce leaves and serve with French dressing. Sprinkle with tarragon leaves or with mint if desired.

GRAPEFRUIT AND GRAPE SALAD

2 cups grapefruit sections	2 tablespoons French dressing
2 tablespoons grape juice	½ cup Malaga grapes, peeled and seeded

Peel fine large grapefruit and separate the sections, removing every particle of the bitter white inner skin. Peel and seed the grapes and mix with the grapefruit. Set, covered, in the refrigerator until very cold. Pour over them the grape juice and French dressing.

WHITE GRAPE SALAD

1 pound Malaga grapes	French dressing
Lettuce	or mayonnaise

Peel grapes and remove the seeds by cutting the grapes almost in two, with a thin sharp knife. Arrange on lettuce leaves and serve with French dressing or mayonnaise.

FRESH AS THE DEW ON YOUR
GARDEN FLOWERS IS THIS DE-
LICIOUS SALAD BOWL

SIMPLIFY YOUR SERVING WITH THESE
LUSCIOUS INDIVIDUAL SALADS OF
RAW AND COOKED VEGETABLES

PEELED MELON FILLED WITH
TOMATO ASPIC AND FROSTED
WITH CREAM CHEESE

NATURE IN THE RAW IS EN-
TICING WHEN IT'S A SALAD
OF SUN-RIPENED FRUITS

ORANGE SALAD

Peel oranges and free the sections entirely from the membrane. Remove seeds, cut sections in halves crosswise, lay on bed of lettuce leaves, and serve with French dressing. Sprinkle with tarragon or with minced green pepper, if desired. Minced celery may be added.

LIME FRUIT SALAD IN MOLD

1 package lime gelatin	½ cup canned white cherries
1 cup boiling water	¼ cup red seeded grapes, cut
1 cup cold water	into fancy shapes
4 slices canned pineapple	4 pears, halved

Dissolve gelatin in boiling water and add cold water. Set aside to cool slightly. Add fruit and pour into mold. Chill until firm. Serves 12.

GARNISH

Head lettuce and endive	Raisins
Pimiento cream cheese	Nuts
1 No. 2½ can pears	Preserved ginger
Cream cheese	Sliced pineapple

Mix cream cheese with chopped nuts, raisins and ginger and stuff pears. Use as garnish around lime mold. Top with pimiento cream cheese flower. Place slices of pineapple topped with pimiento cream cheese between pears. Garnish with endive. Serve with mayonnaise.

PEAR AND CHERRY SALAD

6 halves of stewed pears,	36 white cherries
fresh	French dressing or
or canned	mayonnaise
Lettuce leaves	

Place the half pears on crisp lettuce leaves. Stone the cherries and arrange them around the pears. Serve with preferred dressing. Omit cherries and garnish pear halves with pimiento.

PINEAPPLE AND NUT SALAD IN TOMATO BASKETS

1 cup crushed pineapple   6 tomatoes
1 cup broken nut meats   Mayonnaise
French dressing

Mix pineapple with nut meats and stand in French dressing in the refrigerator. Peel and cut off the top of each tomato leaving a strip to form a handle. Carefully scoop out the center and fill with the pineapple and nuts. Place one teaspoon of mayonnaise on top of each basket.

PINEAPPLE AND CREAM CHEESE SALAD

6 slices canned pineapple   French dressing
1 cup cream cheese   Lettuce leaves
Purple grape juice

Work enough grape juice into the cream cheese to soften it so that it can be made into balls with the hands or with butter paddles. Place a slice of pineapple on a lettuce leaf, put a cheese ball on top and pour grape juice and French dressing over all.

TROPICAL SALAD

1 cup cantaloup balls   Any desired dressing
6 slices tomatoes   Lettuce leaves
Garnish of red pepper

With a vegetable cutter, cut small balls from a cantaloup that is fairly firm in texture. Arrange several balls on a slice of tomato which has been placed on a nest of lettuce leaves. Garnish with pieces of red pepper or green pepper cut in diamond shapes. Serve with any desired dressing.

WALDORF SALAD

1 cup diced apple   French dressing
1 cup diced celery   Lettuce leaves
½ cup broken walnut meats   Mayonnaise

Fold together the apple, celery, and nuts with French dressing and serve on lettuce leaves with mayonnaise. Do not allow this to stand long before serving, as the nuts will discolor the fruit.

WASHINGTON SALAD

¾ cup chopped celery
¾ cup bottoms of
artichokes, chopped

¾ cup canned cherries
¾ cup diced grapefruit pulp
Cheese straws

Pile cheese straws in log-cabin style on a large plate leaving a center space sufficient to hold the salad. Mix celery, artichokes, cherries and grapefruit pulp with French dressing and decorate with a large spoon of mayonnaise. Serve two cheese straws with each portion of salad.

FROZEN CHEESE SALAD

½ pound cream cheese
1 green pepper, chopped
1 cup crushed pineapple
½ cup mayonnaise

½ cup cream, whipped
2 to 4 teaspoons salt, celery
salt, mustard, paprika,
mixed according to taste

Soften the cheese. Add pepper, mayonnaise, pineapple and seasonings and fold in with whipped cream. Freeze.

SANTA CLARA SALAD

24 prunes in sirup
6 ounces cream cheese
Maraschino cherries

8 slices pineapple
Head lettuce

Stone prunes. Soften cream cheese with evaporated milk, if necessary, and stuff prunes. Place pineapple on lettuce and arrange three stuffed prunes on each slice. Garnish prunes with bits of maraschino cherries. Serves 8.

COMBINATION CREAM CHEESE BALL SALAD

¾ cup cream cheese
¾ cup chopped celery
2 tablespoons chopped olives
Lettuce leaves

¼ cup chopped nut meats
or chopped parsley
French dressing

Mix cream cheese with chopped celery and olives and form into balls about the size of a large hickory nut. Roll each ball in chopped nut meats or chopped parsley. Arrange on lettuce leaves and serve with French dressing.

PEAR-GRAPE SALAD—Frost the curved surface of one-half pear with cream cheese, stud with one-half grapes and garnish with chicory and watercress, or other attractive greens.

LETTUCE AND CHEESE SALAD

4 oz. cheddar cheese	½ cup shredded lettuce
Milk or cream	½ cup pimiento strips
Pepper and salt	Lettuce leaves
6 chopped olives	Boiled or mayonnaise dressing

Put the cheese through a food-grinder and moisten slightly with milk or cream. Add pepper and salt to taste. Add chopped olives, shredded lettuce, and pimiento strips. Press this mixture into the form of a brick and, when cool and firm, cut in slices. Place on lettuce leaves and serve with boiled or mayonnaise dressing.

FROSTED MELON MOLD

Melon	Milk
Fruit gelatin	Curly endive or chicory
Cream cheese	French or mayonnaise dressing

Peel a whole melon. Cut a slice from end and remove seeds. Fill center with fruit gelatin and refrigerate until gelatin is firm. Slightly soften cheese with milk and frost the entire outside of melon. Serve in slices on crisp chicory, with dressing.

EGG AND PEANUT SALAD WITH CELERY

6 hard-cooked eggs	Mayonnaise
¼ to ½ cup chopped	Celery curls
peanuts or peanut butter	Garnish of peanut halves

Cut eggs in half lengthwise, remove the yolks and combine with chopped peanuts or peanut butter and mayonnaise to moisten. Fill the whites with this mixture. Put two halves of egg on a plate, surround with curls of celery. Put two tablespoons of mayonnaise dressing over each egg and garnish with peanut halves. Lay a halved peanut on each celery curl.

SALAD EGGS

6 hard-cooked eggs
1 tablespoon butter
1 tablespoon cream
½ teaspoon mustard
Pinch cayenne

1 teaspoon salt
1 tablespoon anchovy paste
Lettuce or cress
Garnish of radishes and
  small onions

Remove the shells from the cold, hard-cooked eggs and cut a large piece from the top of each, take out the yolks and mix them to form a paste with butter, cream, mustard, cayenne, salt, and anchovy paste. Put this mixture back into the hollows and lay the eggs on a dish of lettuce or cress. Garnish with radishes and small onions.

DAISY SALAD

6 hard-cooked eggs
12 lettuce leaves

½ cup mayonnaise

Cut the whites of eggs into rings and mix the yolks with the mayonnaise. On a platter arrange lettuce leaves to form cups. On these cups arrange the egg rings to simulate daisy petals and heap the yolks in the center. Cold string beans, boiled whole, may be used to simulate foliage if desired.

MISCELLANEOUS COMBINATIONS FOR FRUIT AND VEGETABLE SALADS

1. Avocado, grapefruit, romaine
2. Avocado, orange, and cress
3. Avocado, peeled white grapes, and chicory
4. Avocado, tangerine, pecans, and lettuce
5. Avocado, tart apple, and romaine
6. Chicory, escarole, and grapefruit
7. Chicory, shredded cabbage, and lettuce
8. Escarole, Chinese cabbage, and cress
9. Chinese cabbage, tomato slice, radish, olive, in a pagoda
10. Endive, carrot sticks, and grapefruit
11. Shredded carrot, Chinese cabbage, and romaine
12. Orange, Bermuda onion, and romaine
13. Tomato, cucumber, celery, and onion
14. Potato diced, celery, cucumber, green pepper, and pimiento
15. Green peas, peanuts, mint leaves, and lettuce
16. Dandelion, escarole, pimiento, and onion

Meat and Fish Salads
CHICKEN SALAD

2 cups diced chicken
1 cup diced celery
Mayonnaise
Lettuce

Garnish of celery tops, beets cut into dice, capers, egg yolks, etc.

Left-over chicken makes a very good salad. To prepare a chicken especially for salad, rub well with salt and pepper, place one small onion and one bay-leaf inside, wrap with a napkin, tie securely and steam for three hours, or until a fork can be easily turned around in the meat. When the chicken is cold, cut the meat into pieces of convenient size for eating. The most carefully made salads contain only white meat, but the dark meat has a juiciness and flavor not possessed by the breast. If dark meat is used, cut it into smaller cubes than the white meat and the white will predominate in appearance. Marinate the cut up chicken and let it stand. Make a mayonnaise dressing, stir part of it into the celery, place the celery on a thin layer of lettuce or arrange it directly upon the salad-dish and garnish the edge with the tips of the celery. Heap the chicken mixture in the center, pour over it the remainder of the mayonnaise, and garnish with white celery tops, boiled beets cut in dice, capers, cold hard-cooked egg yolks that have been pressed through a sieve, or any other garnish that pleases the fancy.

CRAB SALAD

1 cup crab meat
1 cup chopped celery
French dressing
Mayonnaise

Garnish of crab claws, hard-cooked eggs, parsley, celery tops, etc.

If fresh crabs are used, prepare as directed. (See Index.) Combine crab meat and celery and then marinate with French dressing. Place the mixture in the salad bowl, toss with mayonnaise and garnish with crab claws and hard-cooked eggs in alternation with bits of green such as parsley and the leaves of the celery.

Canned crabs make very good salad. If there is any oil in the can, drain it off; sprinkle the crabs well with salt and vinegar, and drain again before adding the dressing.

FISH SALAD

1 pound flaked, cooked fish	1 cup chopped celery
2 tablespoons oil	Lettuce
1 tablespoon vinegar	Mayonnaise

The remains of almost any cold fish may be used in salad very satisfactorily, but the salad is more successful when made of fish that will flake nicely, such as salmon, cod, haddock, or halibut. Remove the bones, pick the fish into flakes, pour over it a mixture of oil and vinegar and set in a cold place. When about to serve, chop celery and add to the fish. Arrange crisp white leaves of lettuce in cup shapes on a platter, using one or two leaves for each, then lay one spoonful of the mixture in each cup and pour over it one spoonful of mayonnaise.

LOBSTER SALAD

1½ cups diced lobster meat	Mayonnaise
½ cup diced celery	Lettuce
Vinegar	

Prepare lobster as directed (see Index). Remove the meat and the coral. Cut the meat into pieces of convenient size for eating. Sprinkle a very little vinegar over the lobster, but keep the celery crisp until it is time to make the salad. Then mix the lobster meat and celery together, stir in enough mayonnaise to moisten and flavor the whole. Arrange the salad on the center of a bed of crisp white lettuce bordered with green lettuce leaves laid under the outer edges. Top with additional mayonnaise and sprinkle over it the coral, well pounded, and, if desired, a few capers. Garnish with the claws. Sometimes lettuce leaves are arranged on a platter in cup-like clusters of two or three each, and the salad is divided equally among the clusters. The salad may be served in the cleaned lobster shells.

OYSTER SALAD

1 quart oysters	2 tablespoons vinegar
1 tablespoon oil	1 tablespoon lemon juice
½ teaspoon salt	1 pint celery
⅛ teaspoon pepper	½ cup mayonnaise

Clean the oysters (see Index) and place them in a saucepan over the heat, adding no water. When they are boiling, drain them in a colander; place them in an earthenware dish, and add the oil, salt, pepper, vinegar and lemon juice. When cold, set in the refrigerator for at least two hours. Cut the white part of the celery into very thin slices, and place it in a bowl in the refrigerator. When ready to serve, drain the celery, mix with the oysters and half of the mayonnaise. Turn the whole into a salad-bowl, and pour over it the rest of the dressing. Garnish with white celery leaves and serve at once.

If preferred, lettuce leaves may be arranged on a large platter in groups of two or three to form cups and in each cup may be dropped four or five oysters with one spoonful of mayonnaise poured over them. A tiny sprig of parsley may be thrust into the sauce at the center of each cup.

SALMON SALAD

1 cup cold cooked salmon, fresh or canned	1 cup shredded cabbage or chopped celery
Mayonnaise	Lettuce leaves

Combine salmon (flaked), and shredded cabbage or celery. Serve with mayonnaise on lettuce leaves.

SARDINE SALAD

¾ cup sardines	1 cucumber
¾ cup hard-cooked egg	Lettuce leaves
Mayonnaise or French dressing	

Remove the skin and bones from sardines and mix with chopped hard-cooked eggs. Cut cucumber in thin slices and arrange on lettuce leaves. Add sardine and egg mixture. Serve with mayonnaise or French dressing.

SHRIMP SALAD

1 pint cooked shrimps or prawns	Lettuce, shredded celery, or shaved cabbage
Marinade	Mayonnaise or other dressing

Marinate the shrimps and serve whole on lettuce, shredded celery, or shaved cabbage, and cover well with a mayonnaise or other dressing. Canned shrimps are excellent for salads.

SALAD DRESSINGS

THERE are three kinds of salad dressings which are the foundation for practically all others used: French dressing, mayonnaise dressing and boiled dressing.

French Dressing

French dressing, made from oil and acid, is the most widely used dressing. Vinegar is the acid generally used with the oil in vegetable and meat salads, while in fruit salads the juice of lemons, grapefruit or oranges is used.

The choice of oils to be used in dressing is an individual matter. Olive oil has the most distinct flavor. With cottonseed or corn oil the amount of condiments used may be slightly increased if desired.

Serve French dressing with chicken fish, meat, vegetable, and fruit salads.

FRENCH DRESSING

1 clove garlic (optional)	1 tablespoon paprika
1 cup vinegar	½ teaspoon pepper
2 teaspoons dry mustard	2 cups salad oil
1 tablespoon sugar	1 tablespoon salt

If using garlic, soak it in vinegar ½ hour before mixing the dressing. Mix dry ingredients together and place in a covered jar or bottle. Remove garlic from vinegar and add vinegar to dry ingredients. Pour on the oil slowly. Place in refrigerator until ready for use. Just before serving, shake vigorously for 2 minutes. Makes 3 cups dressing.

VARIATIONS—TARRAGON DRESSING: Tarragon vinegar may be used. Mustard, sugar and paprika may be omitted.

FOR FRUIT SALADS: Use ¼ cup each of lemon or lime and orange juice in place of half the vinegar. Reduce mustard to ½ teaspoon, salt to 1 teaspoon and paprika to ½ teaspoon. Increase sugar to ¾ cup. Add ½ teaspoon Worcestershire sauce and omit pepper and garlic.

VARIATIONS using ½ recipe French Dressing as foundation—

ANCHOVY: Cream 2 tablespoons anchovy paste with seasonings. Add 1 tablespoon each of minced onion and parsley.

CHIFFONADE: Add 2 tablespoons each of chopped green pepper, olives, parsley, pimiento and 1 hard-cooked egg, chopped. Add chopped red peppers and cooked beets, if desired.

CURRY: Add ½ teaspoon curry powder and a few drops onion juice.

HORSE-RADISH: Add 4 tablespoons grated horse-radish (juice pressed out) ½ clove garlic, crushed and a dash of cayenne.

MINT: Add 2 tablespoons chopped mint.

OLIVE: Add ½ cup chopped ripe or stuffed olives.

PARMESAN: Add 4 tablespoons grated Parmesan cheese.

PICKLE: Add ¼ cup minced pickles.

ROQUEFORT: Add 4 tablespoons crushed Roquefort cheese, 1 to 1½ teaspoons onion juice or finely chopped chives and a dash of Tabasco sauce or cayenne pepper.

LEMON FRENCH DRESSING

½ cup lemon juice
½ cup salad oil
1 teaspoon salt

1 teaspoon paprika
2 tablespoons sugar or honey

Combine ingredients in the order listed. Shake well before serving. If desired, add ½ teaspoon celery seed and clove of garlic. Makes 1 cup dressing.

If a clear dressing is desired, omit paprika and substitute a dash of pepper.

HAWAII FRENCH DRESSING

¼ cup pineapple juice
2 tablespoons lemon juice
½ cup salad oil

1 teaspoon sugar
½ teaspoon salt
½ teaspoon paprika

Combine ingredients, chill. Shake or beat thoroughly before serving. This recipe is adapted for use with mixed fruit salads. Makes ⅞ cup.

VARIATIONS—BANANA FRENCH DRESSING: Add 2 thoroughly mashed ripe bananas and ¼ teaspoon nutmeg.

RUBY FRENCH DRESSING: Add 1 to 1½ teaspoons grenadine or maraschino cherry juice.

No. 1. **MAYONNAISE DRESSING**

2 uncooked egg yolks	⅛ teaspoon mustard
½ teaspoon salt	3 tablespoons vinegar or
¼ teaspoon pepper	lemon juice
¼ teaspoon paprika	2 cups salad oil

To yolks, add dry seasonings, beat thoroughly, add vinegar or lemon juice and beat again. Add oil gradually (drop by drop at first) beating hard between additions. The mixture should be thick and creamy. Should mayonnaise curdle, begin with a third egg yolk, add a small quantity of oil to the egg, and then by very small quantities, add the curdled dressing. At times a dressing may be quite firm when left, only to be found curdled and disappointing when the time comes to use it. This third egg process will, however, usually restore it. Equal proportions of vinegar and lemon juice may be used. Tarragon vinegar is sometimes used to give an interesting flavor.

1 egg yolk, hard cooked	¼ teaspoon Worcestershire
1 egg yolk, uncooked	sauce
½ teaspoon sugar	1 cup salad oil
½ teaspoon salt	3 tablespoons vinegar
¼ teaspoon pepper	or lemon juice
½ teaspoon prepared mustard	

Place hard-cooked egg yolk in a bowl and mash it fine. When the yolk is like powder, add uncooked yolk and stir until mixture is smooth, then add sugar, salt pepper, mustard, and sauce. When the whole is well mixed, stirring constantly, gradually add oil, then vinegar or lemon juice to thin as necessary. Chill for 1 hour before using.

Originally, only a spoon was used in beating this dressing, however, now a wire whisk, small wooden spoon, rotary beater, or a four-tined fork may be used.

COLORED MAYONNAISE: To color mayonnaise red, add lobster paste, raspberry or cooked beet pulp or juice from raspberries or beets; for green color add chopped fresh spinach, parsley, or concentrated liquor from boiled artichokes.

MAYONNAISE VARIATIONS—Foundation 1 cup mayonnaise.

APPETIZER MAYONNAISE: Rub bowl with garlic and beat in 2 cups French Dressing *(page 329)*.

CHILI SAUCE MAYONNAISE: Add ½ teaspoon lemon juice, 2 teaspoons chili sauce ½ teaspoon confectioners' sugar and 1 teaspoon horse-radish.

CORONATION MAYONNAISE: Add 1 tablespoon each of lemon juice and red Bar-le-Duc and a dash of paprika.

FRUIT JUICE MAYONNAISE: Add 3 tablespoons fruit juice, ½ cup confectioners' sugar and 1 cup heavy cream, whipped.

LEMON CREAM MAYONNAISE: Add ½ cup confectioners' sugar, ¼ cup lemon juice, a few grains salt, and 1 cup heavy cream, whipped.

ROQUEFORT MAYONNAISE: Add 2 tablespoons Roquefort cheese, mashed, 1 teaspoon lemon juice, and ¼ teaspoon salt.

SOUR CREAM MAYONNAISE: Add ⅓ cup confectioners' sugar, 2 tablespoons lemon juice, and 1 cup sour cream, whipped.

THOUSAND ISLAND DRESSING: Add ⅓ cup chili sauce, 1 tablespoon each chopped olives and pimientos, and 1 hard-cooked egg yolk, chopped or pressed through a sieve.

WHIPPED CREAM MAYONNAISE: Add 4 teaspoons confectioners' sugar and 1 cup cream, whipped.

RUSSIAN DRESSING

1½ tablespoons lemon juice
2 tablespoons thick chili sauce
1 tablespoon Worcestershire sauce
½ cup mayonnaise

Mix the lemon juice, chili, sauce, and Worcestershire thoroughly and add the mayonnaise.

THOUSAND ISLAND DRESSING

1 cup mayonnaise
4 tablespoons chili sauce
1 tablespoon chives
3 tablespoons catchup
1 teaspoon tarragon vinegar
1 tablespoon chopped green pepper
3 tablespoons chopped red pepper
1 teaspoon paprika

Add chili sauce, chives, catchup, peppers, paprika, and vinegar to mayonnaise.

BOILED DRESSING

1½ tablespoons sugar
¼ teaspoon salt
1 tablespoon flour
1 teaspoon dry mustard

3 egg yolks
¾ cup cold water
¼ cup vinegar
2 tablespoons butter

Mix sugar, salt, flour, and mustard together. Beat egg yolks slightly; add dry ingredients, water and vinegar, and mix to a smooth paste. Cook over low heat, stirring constantly, until thickened. Remove from heat and blend in butter. When ready to use thin with cream or fold in whipped cream. Makes 1 cup dressing.

CREAMY EGGLESS MAYONNAISE

1 tablespoon sugar
½ teaspoon paprika
½ teaspoon salt
Few grains white pepper
½ teaspoon dry mustard

½ cup evaporated milk, undiluted
2½ tablespoons vinegar
1¼ to 1½ cups salad oil

Mix dry ingredients with milk; beat in vinegar, add oil gradually, beating thoroughly. Use less oil for a thinner mixture or thin with evaporated milk before serving. Makes 1 pint.

SOUR CREAM SALAD DRESSING

1 teaspoon salt
1 tablespoon sugar
⅛ teaspoon cayenne

1 tablespoon lemon juice
2 tablespoons vinegar
1 cup sour cream

Combine all ingredients and mix thoroughly. Makes 1 cup.

WHIPPED CREAM FRUIT DRESSING

⅔ cup sugar
2 tablespoons flour
2 eggs beaten
2 tablespoons salad oil

3 tablespoons lemon juice
4 tablespoons orange juice
1 cup pineapple juice
½ cup heavy cream, whipped

Mix sugar and flour; add remaining ingredients except cream and cook over low heat until thickened, stirring constantly. When cold fold in whipped cream. Makes 2 cups.

CAKES

CAKES are of two general types depending upon the basic ingredients they contain. In one group are the cakes made with shortening—the various butter cakes, pound cakes, fruit cakes, and the chiffon-type cakes; and in the other group are those made without shortening—sponge and angel food cakes. Butter cakes are most frequently baked in layers and sheets, pound cakes in loaves, and sponge and angel food cakes in tubed pans.

For success in cake-making, follow recipe directions exactly. Use the type and size of baking pans specified in the recipe and fill them half to two-thirds full. Bake cakes in a preheated oven at the temperature specified. Place oven rack so top of cake will be almost at middle of oven. For layer cakes, stagger pans so no pan is directly over another and they do not touch each other or walls of oven. Test cakes for doneness at end of minimum baking time. Cool cakes completely before frosting.

Materials Used in Cake Making

For best results, have all ingredients at room temperature unless recipe directs otherwise.

SUGAR—Granulated beet and cane sugar give equal results. Some recipes specify the use of brown sugar because of its distinct flavor. When measuring brown sugar, pack it firmly into the cup.

SHORTENING—Any hydrogenated shortening, butter, margarine, or lard may be used for the shortening, except for the quick method cakes which have been developed especially for emulsifier-type shortenings. Use oil or melted shortening only when stated in the recipe. Melted shortening should be cooled before being added to the batter. Solid shortenings should be creamed with the sugar, except in the quick method cakes.

EGGS—Eggs for cakes should be of finest quality.

FLOUR—In the cake recipes in this book, cake flour has been used most generally. Although cake flour is preferred for cake-making, successful cakes are made with all-purpose flour. If all-purpose flour is substituted, reduce the amount used by 2 tablespoons per cup of flour. Always sift flour before measuring. Spoon flour lightly into measuring cup and level with straight-edged knife or spatula. Resift with dry ingredients as directed. (In some southern areas where a blend of soft wheats is used, better products may result when minor adjustments are made in recipes. A little less liquid or more flour may be needed.)

LEAVENING AGENTS—The most usual leavening agents in cake-making are eggs and baking powder. No baking powder is used in true sponge cakes. The air incorporated by beating the eggs to the proper stage, and the steam generated in baking, make the cake rise as it bakes.

LIQUIDS—The usual liquid in cake batters is milk, either sweet or soured. Buttermilk may be substituted for soured milk. Cream, water, coffee beverage, or fruit juices are used in some recipes.

FLAVORINGS—Vanilla is used most commonly but lemon, almond, orange, pineapple, and rose extracts give a variety in flavors. Sometimes the juices of fresh fruits such as lemons or oranges, or their grated rinds, are used in special cakes.

Mixing Shortening Cakes

Methods of mixing shortening cakes that are in common use are the Conventional, Conventional-Sponge, and Quick Methods.

CONVENTIONAL METHOD:

CREAM THE SHORTENING until plastic. This can be done by rubbing the shortening against the sides of the bowl with a wooden spoon, or it may be done with an electric mixer. Flavoring extract or spices may be creamed with the shortening.

ADD THE SUGAR gradually and cream with shortening until graininess disappears and the mixture is light and fluffy.

BEAT WHOLE EGGS until thick and piled softly. Add in thirds to the creamed mixture, beating about 100 strokes after each addition. The mixture should hold its shape.

SIFT THE FLOUR with the remaining dry ingredients such as salt and baking powder.

ADD DRY INGREDIENTS AND LIQUID alternately to creamed mixture. The flavorings may be added to the liquid. Add dry ingredients in fourths, liquid in thirds, beginning and ending with dry. Stir the batter after each addition only until blended (about 25 strokes). After the last flour has been mixed in stir about 150 strokes with a spoon or 1 minute with electric mixer at medium speed. Scrape spoon or beater and bottom and sides of bowl during mixing.

BLEND IN FRUITS or nuts, if used, with the final stirring.

MELT CHOCOLATE OVER SIMMERING WATER, cool, and add to creamed mixture after whole egg has been beaten in, unless otherwise directed.

CONVENTIONAL-SPONGE METHOD:

CREAM THE SHORTENING, flavoring and half the sugar as directed in the Conventional Method.

SEPARATE EGG WHITES AND YOLKS. Add yolks one at a time to creamed mixture and beat well after each addition.

SIFT FLOUR with remaining dry ingredients, except sugar.

ADD DRY INGREDIENTS AND LIQUIDS alternately to creamed mixture. Add dry ingredients in fourths, liquid in thirds, beginning and ending with dry. Stir batter after each addition only until blended (about 25 strokes). After the last flour has been mixed in stir about 150 strokes with a spoon or 1 minute with electric mixer at medium speed. Scrape spoon or beater and bottom and sides of bowl during mixing.

BEAT EGG WHITES just until soft peaks form. Gradually add remaining sugar and beat until peaks round over gently when beater is slowly lifted upright.

USING SPATULA, FOLD meringue gently into batter with about 35 folding strokes or until blended.

BLEND LN FRUITS or nuts, if used, with the final 10 folding strokes.

MELT CHOCOLATE OVER SIMMERING WATER, cool, and add to creamed mixture after egg yolks have been beaten in, unless otherwise directed.

QUICK METHOD:

Use only recipes especially developed for the Quick Method as their proportion of ingredients is carefully balanced. Be sure to use emulsifier-type shortening. All ingredients must be at room temperature. Follow the recipe exactly for method of mixing and beating. The batter tends to be thinner than that of most other cakes.

Baking Shortening Cakes

For any cake made with shortening, except chiffon-types, grease bottom of baking pan, line pan with waxed paper cut to fit bottom exactly, and grease paper. Batter should fill pan half to two-thirds full. Spread batter well into corners and against sides of pan, leaving a slight depression in center. Tap bottom of cake pan sharply with hand to release air bubbles before placing in oven.

The time and temperature for baking vary with the proportion of ingredients in the cake, the depth of the batter, and the type of pan used.

BAKE CAKE in preheated oven at temperature specified. Use a portable oven thermometer to check accuracy of oven temperatures.

TEST CAKE at end of minimum baking time. Touch lightly at center; if it springs back, the cake is done. Or, insert a cake tester or wooden pick in center; if it comes out clean, the cake is done.

COOL CAKES in pan 10 minutes on cooling rack. Then, with a spatula or knife, loosen the edges from the pan. Remove cake from pan by inverting on cooling rack. Turn right side up immediately after peeling off waxed paper. Cool cake completely before frosting.

Mixing Cakes Without Shortening

Cakes without shortening depend for leavening largely upon the air beaten into the eggs. The whites and yolks of the eggs may or may not be separated, depending upon the kind of cake. If using the whole egg, beat it until light and foamy. Add the sugar gradually, then any liquid or flavoring used, and the salt. Beat until thick and piled softly. Sift a portion of the flour over the top of the egg mixture and fold in with spatula. Continue until all the flour is used.

If the whites and yolks are separated, beat the yolks, flavoring and half the sugar together until very thick and lemon-colored. Sift one-fourth of the flour over mixture, fold with about 10 strokes with a spatula; repeat until all flour is folded in. Beat egg white until foamy. Add remaining half of the sugar a tablespoon at a time, and beat well after each addition. Beat until whites stand up in peaks with only the tips folding over slightly when the beater is slowly lifted upright. Spread yolk mixture over beaten whites. Fold together gently with spatula until well blended.

Baking Cakes Without Shortening

Use an ungreased baking pan (preferably tubed) for sponge and angel food cakes. If pans are greased the batter cannot cling to the sides of the pan as it bakes and thus the cake does not reach full volume. Push batter gently into pan. Cut through batter several times with a spatula to release air bubbles.

BAKE AT ONCE in preheated oven at temperature specified.

TEST CAKE at end of minimum baking time. If the cake springs back when lightly pressed with the finger, it is done. The cake should be inverted and allowed to cool in the pan. For a tubed pan, rest the tube part on the neck of a funnel; rest the edges of square or loaf pans on the edges of two other pans. Let cake hang until cold. To remove cold cake from pan loosen it from sides and tube of pan with a spatula and gently shake it out of pan.

Mixing Chiffon-Type Cakes

Chiffon-type cakes are distinguished by the use of oil for shortening. Sift flour, baking powder, part of the sugar, and salt together into bowl. Make a well in center and add the oil, unbeaten egg yolks, liquid and flavorings, in that order. Beat together until smooth.

Beat egg whites until frothy, add cream of tartar and continue to beat slightly. Gradually add the remaining sugar, beating well after each addition. Beat until rounded peaks are formed and whites do not slide when bowl is inverted. Do not underbeat.

Slowly pour yolk mixture over entire surface of whites. Fold together gently with a spatula just until blended. Do not stir.

Baking Chiffon-Type Cakes

Pour batter into ungreased pan and bake at once. Follow exact directions with specific recipes for size of baking pans, baking times and temperatures. The cake is done if the top springs back when lightly touched. Remove from oven and immediately turn pan upside down. Cool in pan as directed in recipes.

FOUNDATION OR PLAIN CAKE

1½ cups sifted cake flour	¾ cup sugar
2 teaspoons baking powder	2 eggs, well beaten
¼ teaspoon salt	½ cup milk
⅓ cup shortening	1 teaspoon vanilla

Sift flour, baking powder, and salt together. Cream shortening, add sugar gradually and cream until light and fluffy. Add eggs in thirds, beating well after each addition. Then stir in dry ingredients alternately with milk and vanilla. Pour into greased and lined pans and bake at 350° F. about 25 minutes. Frost as desired. Make 2- (8-inch) round layers.

CHEESE CAKE

2 cups fine zwieback crumbs	1½ teaspoons lemon juice
1½ cups sugar	1½ teaspoons grated lemon rind
1 teaspoon cinnamon	
½ cup melted butter or other shortening	1 cup cream
4 eggs	1½ pounds cottage cheese
⅛ teaspoon salt	3 tablespoons flour
	¼ cup chopped nut meats

Mix zwieback with ½ cup sugar, cinnamon, and butter or shortening. Set aside ¾ cup to sprinkle over top, press remainder of crumbs into a 9-inch spring form pan, lining bottom and sides. Beat eggs until light and foamy, then gradually beat in remaining 1 cup sugar; beat until light. Beat in salt, lemon juice and rind, cheese, and flour. Strain through a fine sieve. Pour into lined pan, sprinkle with remaining crumbs and nut meats. Bake at 350° F. about 1 hour or until center is firm. Turn off heat, open oven door, and leave in oven 1 hour or until cooled. Serves 10 to 12. (If desired, use 1 teaspoon vanilla instead of lemon juice and rind.)

ONE-EGG CAKE

¼ cup shortening
1 cup sugar
1 egg, unbeaten
2 cups sifted cake flour

¼ teaspoon salt
2½ teaspoons baking powder
¾ cup milk
1 teaspoon vanilla

Cream shortening, add sugar gradually and cream until fluffy. Add egg and beat thoroughly. Sift dry ingredients together 3 times and add alternately with milk and vanilla. Pour into greased pans. Bake in a moderate oven (350° F.) 25 minutes. Makes 2 (9-inch) layers.

CARAMEL OR BURNT SUGAR CAKE

1¾ cups sugar
⅓ cup hot water
3 cups sifted cake flour
3 teaspoons baking powder
½ teaspoon salt

¾ cup butter or other shortening
3 eggs, well beaten
1 teaspoon vanilla
⅔ cup milk

Heat ½ cup sugar in heavy skillet over low heat, stirring constantly as sugar melts. When a golden brown color, remove from heat and graudally stir in hot water; stir until dissolved; cool. Sift flour, baking powder and salt together 3 times. Cream shortening, add remaining sugar (1¼ cups) gradually; cream until light and fluffy. Add well-beaten eggs in thirds, beating well after each addition. Beat in 3 tablespoons of the caramel sirup. Stir in sifted dry ingredients and milk and vanilla alternately. Pour into greased and lined pans. Bake at 350° F. 25 to 30 minutes. Makes 2 (9-inch) round layers.

IN-A-JIFFY CAKE

1½ cups sifted cake flour
¾ cup sugar
¼ teaspoon salt
2 teaspoons baking powder

¾ cup milk
1 teaspoon vanilla
¼ cup melted shortening
1 egg, beaten

Sift dry ingredients together 3 times. Combine remaining ingredients and add gradually to dry ingredients. Beat mixture 2 minutes. Pour into greased cake pan. Bake in moderate oven (350° F.) 30 minutes. Makes 1 (8 x 8 x 2 inch) cake.

ONE-TWO-THREE-FOUR CAKE (Measure Cake)

1 cup butter or other shortening
2 cups sugar
4 eggs, separated
3 cups sifted cake flour
¼ teaspoon salt
3 teaspoons baking powder
1 cup milk
1 teaspoon vanilla

Cream shortening, gradually add 1 cup of the sugar; cream until fluffy. Add egg yolks 1 at a time, beating well after each. Sift dry ingredients (except sugar) together 3 times; stir in alternately with liquid. Beat egg whites until soft peaks form; gradually add rest of sugar and beat until peaks round over gently; fold into batter. Pour into 3 (9-inch) round layer pans, greased and lined. Bake at 350° F. about 25 min.

MAPLE SIRUP CAKE

½ cup sugar
⅓ cup shortening
¾ cup maple sirup
½ cup milk
Salt
2¼ cups flour
3 tablespoons baking powder
3 egg whites

Cream shortening, gradually add half the sugar; cream until fluffy; beat in the sirup. Stir in sifted dry ingredients (except sugar) alternately with milk. Beat egg whites until soft peaks form; gradually add rest of sugar and beat until peaks round over gently; fold into batter. Bake in 13x9½x2-inch pan at 350° F. 45 to 60 minutes. When cool, frost with Caramel Frosting, *(page 367)*.

DEVIL'S FOOD CAKE

¾ cup butter or other shortening
1⅞ cups brown sugar
3 eggs, well beaten
¾ cup boiling water
3 ounces (3 squares) un-
sweetened chocolate
2¼ cups sifted cake flour
1½ teaspoons baking soda
¾ teaspoon baking powder
¾ cup sour milk
1½ teaspoons vanilla

Cream shortening, gradually add sugar; cream until light and fluffy. Add well beaten eggs in thirds, beating well after each addition. Pour boiling water over chocolate; stir over low heat until smooth and thick; cool and stir into egg mixture. Sift dry ingredients together 3 times; stir into chocolate mixture alternately with combined milk and vanilla, until blended. Pour into 3 (8-inch) round layer pans, greased and lined. Bake at 350° F. 25 to 30 minutes. Cool and spread with Boiled Frosting (*page 367*).

CHOCOLATE NUT CAKE

¾ cup butter or other shortening
1½ cups sugar
4 eggs, separated
1¾ cups sifted cake flour
2 teaspoons baking powder
½ teaspoon cloves
½ teaspoon cinnamon
½ teaspoon allspice
1 cup milk
4 ounces (4 squares) unsweetened chocolate (melted)
1 cup walnuts, chopped
1 teaspoon vanilla

Cream shortening, gradually add half the sugar; cream until fluffy. Add egg yolks 1 at a time, beating well after each. Sift dry ingredients (except sugar) together 3 times; stir in alternately with milk. Beat egg whites until soft peaks form; gradually add rest of sugar and beat until peaks round over gently; fold into batter. With last few strokes, fold in the chocolate, nuts, and vanilla. Pour into 8½x4½x2½-inch loaf pan, greased and lined. Bake at 325° F. about 50 minutes. When cool, frost with Marshmallow-Cream Frosting (*page 369*).

SOUR CREAM COCOA CAKE

½ cup coca
¾ cup boiling water
½ cup shortening
2 cups sugar
2 cups sifted cake flour
½ teaspon salt
½ cup sour cream
½ teaspoon baking soda
1 teaspoon vanilla
3 egg whites

Mix cocoa with boiling water; stir until smooth; cool. Cream shortening, gradually add half the sugar; cream until light and fluffy; add cocoa mixture. Sift dry ingredients (except sugar) together 3 times; stir into cocoa mixture alternately with combined cream and vanilla. Beat egg whites until soft peaks form; gradually add rest of sugar and beat until peaks round over gently; fold into batter. Pour into 2 (9-inch) round layer pans, greased and lined. Bake at 350° F. about 30 minutes. When cool, frost with Mocha Frosting (*page 369*).

COFFEE CAKE

2 tablespoons shortening
½ cup sugar
1 egg

¾ cup flour
1 teaspoon baking powder
¼ cup milk

½ teaspoon vanilla

Cream shortening, gradually add sugar; cream until fluffy. Add well beaten egg in thirds, beating well after each addition. Stir in sifted dry ingredients alternately with liquid. Spread half of mixture in greased 8-inch pie pan. FILLING—

½ cup brown sugar
2 teaspoons cinnamon

1 cup chopped walnuts
2 tablespoons flour

2 tablespoons melted fat

Mix all the ingredients thoroughly and spread one half over the batter in the pan. Add the rest of the cake batter and spread the remainder of the filling over the top. Bake in a moderate oven (350° F.) about 20 minutes.

SOUR MILK CHOCOLATE CAKE

½ cup shortening
1½ cups sugar
1 teaspoon vanilla
3 eggs separated

2 ounces (2 squares) unsweetened chocolate, melted
2 cups sifted cake flour
1 teaspoon baking soda
½ teaspoon salt

1 cup soured milk

Cream shortening, add half the sugar gradually; cream until fluffy; beat in yolks 1 at a time; stir in chocolate. Sift flour, soda, and salt together; stir in alternately with milk. Beat egg whites until soft peaks form; gradually beat in rest of sugar; fold into batter. Pour into 2 (9-inch) round layer pans, greased and lined. Bake at 350° F. about 25 minutes.

GINGER COCONUT CAKE

⅔ cup molasses
½ cup sugar
½ cup butter or other
    shortening
1 teaspoon ginger

1 teaspoon cinnamon
1 teaspoon baking soda
2 cups sifted cake flour
1 cup soured milk
2 eggs, beaten

Heat first 5 ingredients to boiling, stirring constantly. Cool.

to lukewarm. Stir in sifted dry ingredients alternately with combined milk and eggs, until blended. Pour into greased muffin pans. Bake in a 350° F. oven 15 minutes. Makes 16 cakes.

NUT CAKE

½ cup shortening
1 cup sugar
2 eggs, separated
1½ cups sifted cake flour

2 teaspoons baking powder
½ cup milk
1 teaspoon vanilla
1 cup chopped nut meats

Cream shortening, add half the sugar gradually; cream until fluffy; beat in yolks 1 at a time. Sift flour and baking powder; stir in alternately with liquid. Beat egg whites until soft peaks form; gradually beat in rest of sugar; fold into batter with nuts. Pour into 8½x4½x2½-inch loaf pan, greased and lined. Bake at 350° F. about 50 minutes.

WHITE MOUNTAIN CAKE

½ cup shortening
1½ cups sugar
2½ cups sifted cake flour
3 teaspoons baking powder

¼ teaspoon salt
1 cup milk
1 teaspoon vanilla
4 egg whites

Cream shortening, add half the sugar gradually; cream until fluffy. Stir in sifted dry ingredients (except sugar) alternately with liquid, until blended. Beat egg whites until soft peaks form; gradually add rest of sugar; beat until peaks round over gently; fold into batter. Pour into 2 (9-inch) round layer pans, greased and lined. Bake at 350° F. 25 to 30 minutes.

WHITE CAKE

⅔ cup shortening
2 cups sugar
3 cups sifted cake flour
3 teaspoons baking powder

½ teaspoon salt
1 cup milk
1 teaspoon vanilla
5 egg whites

Cream shortening, add half the sugar gradually; cream until fluffy. Stir in sifted dry ingredients alternately with liquid. Beat whites until soft peaks form; gradually beat in rest of sugar; fold into batter. Pour into 3 (9-inch) round layer pans, greased and lined. Bake at 350° F. about 30 minutes.

GOLD CAKE

¾ cup butter or other shortening
1¼ cups sugar
8 egg yolks, beaten

2½ cups sifted cake flour
3 tablespoons baking powder
¼ teaspoon salt
¾ cup milk
1 teaspoon vanilla

Cream shortening, add sugar gradually; cream until fluffy; add yolks in thirds, beating well after each addition. Stir in sifted dry ingredients alternately with liquids, until blended. Pour into 3 (9-inch) round layer pans, greased and lined. Bake at 350° F. about 20 minutes.

ORANGE CAKE

¾ cup shortening
1½ cups sugar
3 eggs
Grated rind of 1 orange
3 cups sifted cake flour

4 teaspoons baking powder
¾ teaspoon salt
½ cup orange juice
1 tablespoon lemon juice
½ cup water

Cream shortening, add sugar gradually, creaming until light and fluffy. Add well-beaten eggs in thirds, beating well after each addition. Add orange rind. Sift dry ingredients together 3 times and add alternately with liquids to creamed mixture. Pour into cake pans lined with waxed paper. Bake in a moderate oven (350° F.) 25 to 30 minutes. Makes 2 (9-inch) layers. When cold spread Orange Filling (*page 365*) between layers and Twice Cooked Frosting or Seven Minute Frosting (*page 367*) on top and sides.

LAYER CAKE

½ cup shortening
1 cup sugar
2 eggs, separated
2 cups sifted cake flour

¼ teaspoon salt
2½ teaspoons baking powder
⅔ cup milk
1 teaspoon vanilla

Cream shortening, add half the sugar gradually; cream until fluffy; beat in egg yolks 1 at a time. Stir in sifted dry ingredients alternately with liquid. Beat egg whites until soft peaks form; gradually beat in rest of sugar; fold into batter. Pour into 2 (9-inch) round layer pans, greased and lined. Bake at 350° F. 20 to 25 minutes.

LADY BALTIMORE CAKE

¾ cup butter or other
  shortening
2 cups sugar
3 cups sifted cake flour
3 teaspoons baking powder

½ teaspoon salt
½ cup milk
½ cup water
1 teaspoon vanilla
6 egg whites

Cream shortening, add half the sugar gradually; cream until fluffy. Sift flour, baking powder, and salt together; combine milk, water and vanilla; stir alternately into creamed mixture, blending well. Beat egg whites until soft peaks form; gradually add rest of sugar; beat until peaks round over gently; fold into batter. Pour into 3 (9-inch) round layer pans, greased and lined. Bake at 350° F. about 25 minutes.

LADY BALTIMORE FROSTING AND FILLING—

3 cups sugar
1 cup water
¼ teaspoon cream of tartar
3 egg whites, stiffly beaten

1 teaspoon vanilla
½ cup chopped figs
1 cup chopped raisins
1 cup chopped nut meats

Boil sugar, water, and cream of tartar together to 238° F. or until a small amount of sirup will form a soft ball when tested in cold water. Pour hot sirup gradually over beaten egg whites, beating constantly and continuing to beat until mixture is of spreading consistency. Add vanilla. Divide mixture in half. Add fruit and nuts to 1 portion and spread between layers of cake. Frost top and sides with remaining frosting.

MARBLE CAKE

⅓ cup butter or other
  shortening
1 cup sugar
2 eggs, well beaten
½ teaspoon vanilla
1¾ cups sifted cake flour

2 teaspoons baking powder
½ teaspoon salt
½ cup milk
1 ounce (1 square) un-
  sweetened chocolate,
  melted

Cream shortening; gradually add sugar; cream until light and fluffy. Add eggs in thirds and vanilla, beating well after each addition. Sift dry ingredients together and stir into creamed mixture alternately with milk, until blended. Add chocolate to ⅓ of the batter and blend thoroughly. Place batter by spoonfuls in a greased 2-quart ring mold, alternating light and dark mixtures. Bake at 350° F. 35 to 40 minutes.

BLITZ TORTE

½ cup shortening
½ cup sugar
⅛ teaspoon salt
4 egg yolks
1 teaspoon vanilla
3 tablespoons milk
1 cup sifted cake flour

1 teaspoon baking powder
4 egg whites
¾ cup sugar
½ cup sliced blanched
  almonds
1 tablespoon sugar
½ teaspoon cinnamon

Cream shortening, gradually add sugar and salt; cream until fluffy. Add egg yolks 1 at a time, beating well. Sift flour and baking powder and stir into creamed mixture with milk and vanilla. Spread in 2 (9-inch) round layer pans. Beat egg whites until soft peaks form; gradually add sugar; beat until peaks round over gently; spread on batter in pans. Sprinkle with almonds, 1 tablespoon sugar and cinnamon. Bake at 350° F. about 30 minutes. When cool, put together with cream filling.

CREAM FILLING—
⅓ cup sugar
3 tablespoons cornstarch
¼ teaspoon salt

2 egg yolks
2 tablespoons butter
2 cups milk, scalded

1 teaspoon vanilla

Combine sugar, cornstarch, salt and egg yolks; beat thoroughly. Add butter and enough milk to make a smooth paste. Add paste to remaining hot milk and cook over boiling water, stirring constantly until mixture is thickened. Cool and add vanilla. If desired add ½ cup chopped nut meats.

OLD-FASHIONED POUNDCAKE

1 pound butter (2 cups)
1 pound sifted cake flour
  (4 cups)

10 eggs, separated
1 pound sugar (2 cups
1 teaspoon vanilla

Cream butter, work in flour until mixture is mealy. Beat egg yolks, vanilla, and half the sugar until thick and lemon colored; beat thoroughly into first mixture. Beat egg whites until soft peaks form; gradually beat in rest of sugar; fold into batter; stir until blended. Pour into 2 (8½x4½x2½-inch) loaf pans, greased and lined. Bake at 325° F. about 1¼ hours.

SPICECAKE

½ cup shortening
2 cups brown sugar
3 eggs, well beaten
2 cups sifted cake flour
¼ teaspoon salt

1 teaspoon baking soda
2 teaspoons cinnamon
1 teaspoon cloves
½ teaspoon nutmeg
1 cup thick sour cream

Cream shortening, gradually add sugar; cream until fluffy. Add eggs in thirds, beating well after each addition. Sift dry ingredients together and stir in alternately with cream. Pour into 9x9x2-inch pan, greased and lined. Bake at 350° F. about 50 minutes. Frost with Caramel Frosting *(page 367)* or Boiled Frosting *(page 367)*.

FIG LOAF CAKE

1 cup shortening
2 cups brown sugar
4 eggs, well beaten
3 cups sifted cake flour
3 teaspoons baking powder
¼ teaspoon salt

1 teaspoon cinnamon
½ teaspoon ground cloves
1 teaspoon nutmeg
1 cup water
½ pound figs, finely cut
2 cups chopped raisins

Cream shortening, add sugar gradually and cream until fluffy. Add eggs in thirds, beating well after each addition. Sift dry ingredients together and stir in alternately with water. Blend in fruits. Pour into 10x5x3-inch loaf pan, greased and lined. Bake at 300° F. about 2 hours.

DELICIOUS FRUITCAKE

4 cups sifted cake flour
1 teaspoon mace
¼ teaspoon nutmeg
2 teaspoons cinnamon
½ teaspoon baking soda
3 pounds currants
2 pounds seeded raisins

1 pound citron, sliced
2 cups blanched almonds, sliced
1 pound butter
2 cups light brown sugar
9 eggs, well beaten
1 cup cold coffee beverage

Sift flour, spices, and soda together 3 times. Mix with nuts and fruits. Cream butter, gradually add sugar; cream until fluffy; add eggs in thirds, beating well after each addition. Stir in flour-fruit mixture alternately with coffee beverage. Pour into 3 (9½x5¼x2¾-inch) loaf pans, greased and lined. Bake at 275° F. 3 to 4 hours. Rich fruitcake can be steamed 1 hour, then baked for remaining time.

WEDDING CAKE

2 pounds butter
1 pound granulated sugar
¾ pound brown sugar
20 eggs
2 oranges, juice and grated rind
1 lemon, juice and grated rind
1 teaspoon baking soda
½ cup molasses
1 cup cold coffee beverage
½ cup honey
2 pounds flour

1½ teaspoons salt
1 teaspoon cloves
2 teaspoons cinnamon
2 tablespoons nutmeg
2 tablespoons mace
1 cup tart jelly
3 pounds seeded raisins
2 pounds seedless raisins
5 pounds currants
1 pound almonds
2 pounds citron
2 cups flour (for the fruit)

Look over raisins and currants carefully; wash, drain and dry. Blanch and slice the almonds; save half the almonds to sprinkle on the bottom and top of batter in baking pans. Cut citron in thin strips. Mix the 2 cups flour thoroughly with this fruit so that pieces will not stick together. Candied orange or grapefruit peel may be substituted for the citron. Some markets, especially at holiday time, sell fruit already prepared for fruit cakes.

Cream butter, gradually add the white sugar and sifted brown sugar and cream until fluffy. Beat eggs until thick and piled softly; add in thirds to creamed mixture, beating well after each addition; stir in grated rinds.

Sift flour, soda, salt, and spices together; stir into egg mixture alternating with the orange juice, lemon juice, molasses, coffee beverage, honey, and fruit-flour mixture. Break the jelly into pieces and stir into batter.

This amount makes about twenty-four pounds of cake, and can be baked in 8 (9½x5¼x2¾-inch) loaf pans. Grease pans lightly; line bottom and sides of each pan with three layers of crossed strips of waxed paper cut to fit; grease the top layer of paper.

Sprinkle bottoms of pans with about one-third of reserved almonds; put batter into pans, making sure that the corners are well filled and that the top is level and smooth. Sprinkle the remaining almonds on top of the batter in pans. Bake at 275° F. for 2 hours. Let cool in the pans, but rest the pans on wire racks so air can circulate around them.

Turn out and remove the paper. Cool and store in a cool dry place tightly covered. A few sound apples placed in the container where cake is stored will help keep the cake moist if it must be kept long, but they must be watched and replaced if they begin to show decay, or if they become shriveled.

As there is so much preparation involved, the fruits and nuts can be gotten ready several days before the cake is to be baked. Even after the cake is entirely mixed and in the pan or pans it can stand overnight if kept in a cool place.

CHRISTMAS FRUITCAKE

1 pound butter	1 pound citron, sliced
1½ pounds brown sugar	1 pound dates, sliced
1½ pounds flour	10 eggs, well beaten
2 teaspoons nutmeg	1 cup molasses
1 teaspoon mace	1 cup cold coffee beverage
1 teaspoon cloves	Puice and grated rind of
2 teaspoons cinnamon	2 oranges
1 teaspoon baking soda	Juice and grated rind of
3 teaspoons baking powder	1 lemon
3 pounds raisins	1 cup tart jelly
2 pounds currants	¼ pound almonds, sliced

Cream butter, gradually add sugar; cream until fluffy. Sift dry ingredients together; mix with fruit. Add eggs in thirds to creamed mixture, beating well. Stir in fruit mixture alternately with next 5 ingredients; blend well. Pour into 4 (9½x 5¼x2¾-inch) loaf pans, greased and lined; sprinkle with almonds. Cover cakes with greased paper. Steam 2 hours, then bake at 300° F. 1½ to 2 hours; remove paper last ½ hour.

DRIED APRICOT CAKE

1 cup dried apricots	1 teaspoon vanilla
2 cups water	1¾ cups sifted cake flour
6 tablespoons sugar	½ teaspoon salt
½ cup shortening	½ teaspoon baking soda
1 cup sugar	1 teaspoon baking powder
2 egg yolks	¼ cup water

Simmer first 3 ingredients together ½ hour; mash; measure ½ cup pulp. Cream shortening, gradually add sugar; cream until fluffy; beat in yolks 1 at a time; add vanilla. Sift dry ingredients; stir in alternately with water and pulp. Bake in greased and lined 8x8x2-inch pan 350°F. about 45 min.

APPLESAUCE SPICECAKE

½ cup butter or other
  shortening
1 cup sugar
2 eggs, well beaten
½ cup chopped nuts
1 cup chopped raisins

2 cups sifted cake flour
1 teaspoon baking soda
½ teaspoon nutmeg
1 teaspoon cinnamon
1 cup unsweetened
  applesauce

Cream shortening, gradually add sugar; cream until fluffy. Add eggs in thirds, beating well after each addition. Stir in nuts and raisins. Sift dry ingredients together; stir in alternately with applesauce, blending well. Pour into greased and lined 8½x4½x2½-inch loaf pan. Bake at 350° F. about 1 hour. This may also be baked in 2 (9-inch) round layer pans about 25 minutes.

PINEAPPLE CAKE

½ cup butter
1⅓ cups sugar
2½ cups sifted cake flour
½ teaspoon salt
3 teaspoons baking powder
3 egg whites

¼ cup evaporated milk
¼ cup water
½ cup sirup drained from
  pineapple
1½ teaspoons vanilla

Cream butter, gradually add half the sugar; cream until fluffy. Sift dry ingredients. Combine liquids and vanilla. Stir dry ingredients alternately into creamed mixture with liquids. Beat egg whites until soft peaks form; gradually beat in rest of sugar; fold into batter. Pour into 2 (9-inch) round layer pans, greased and lined. Bake at 350° F. about 35 minutes.

TRUE SPONGECAKE

1 cup sifted cake flour
¼ teaspoon salt
Grated rind ½ lemon
1½ tablespoons lemon juice

5 egg yolks
5 egg whites
1 cup sugar

Add lemon rind, juice and ½ cup sugar to yolks; beat until thick and lemon colored. Sift ¼ of flour plus salt over mixture and fold in; repeat until all flour is folded in. Beat whites until foamy; gradually beat in remaining sugar; beat until tips of peaks fold over only slightly. Spread yolk mixture over whites; fold together gently. Bake in ungreased 9-inch tubed pan at 350° F. about 1 hour. Invert and allow to cool in pan. FOR MARTHA WASHINGTON CREAM PIE, bake in 2 (8-inch) round layer pans. Use the filling *page 362;* top with whipped cream. Cut in pie wedges to serve.

HOT WATER SPONGECAKE

1 cup sifted cake flour
1½ teaspoons baking powder
¼ teaspoon salt
1½ teaspoons lemon juice

2 eggs, separated
1 cup sugar
6 tablespoons hot water

Proceed as for True Spongecake *(page 351),* adding water to egg and sugar mixture before adding dry ingredients.

MERINGUE SPONGECAKE

½ cup water
1¼ cups sugar
¾ cup egg whites (6)
1 teaspoon cream of tartar

1 tablespoon lemon juice
6 egg yolks, beaten thick
1⅛ cups sifted cake flour
¼ teaspoon salt

Cook water and sugar to soft ball stage (238° F.). Beat egg whites until frothy; add cream of tartar; beat until soft peaks form; gradually pour in sirup while beating whites; cool. Add juice and salt to yolks; fold into whites; fold in flour in fourths. Bake in ungreased 10-inch tubed pan at 350° F. 45 minutes.

ANGEL CAKE

1¼ cups sugar
1 cup sifted cake flour
1 cup egg whites
  (7 to 8 eggs)

1 teaspoon cream of tartar
½ teaspoon salt
¾ teaspoon vanilla
¼ teaspoon almond extract

Sift flour and ¼ cup sugar together 4 times. Beat egg whites until frothy; beat in cream of tartar and flavorings; beat until tips of peaks fold over slightly; sprinkle remaining sugar over surface 2 tablespoons at a time and fold in. Sift 4 tablespoons flour over surface and fold in; repeat until all flour is added. Slide gently into 9-inch tubed pan; cut through batter with spatula to break large air bubbles. Bake at 375° F. about 30 minutes. Invert and allow to cool in pan.

WHIPPED CREAM CAKE

1 cup whipping cream
2 eggs, beaten until thick
and piled softly
1 cup sugar

1 teaspoon vanilla
1½ cups sifted cake flour
¼ teaspoon salt
2 teaspoons baking powder

Whip chilled cream until it stands in peaks; add beaten eggs and fold together; add vanilla. Sift sugar, flour, salt, and baking powder together and fold into egg mixture a portion at a time. Pour into 2 (8-inch) round layer pans, greased and lined. Bake at 350° F. about 25 minutes. When cool, spread Seven Minute Icing *(page 367)* or whipped cream between layers and on top.

SOUR CREAM CAKE

2 eggs
1 cup sugar
1 cup thick sour cream
1 teaspoon vanilla
2 cups sifted cake flour

1½ teaspoons baking
powder
½ teaspoon baking soda
¼ teaspoon salt

Beat eggs until thick and piled softly; beat in sugar gradually. Sift flour, baking powder, soda, and salt together; stir in alternately with combined cream and vanilla. Pour into 8x8x 2-inch pan, greased and lined. Bake at 350° F. about 35 minutes.

PRUNE AND APRICOT UPSIDE-DOWN CAKE

¼ cup butter
½ cup brown sugar
½ teaspoon lemon rind
Stewed apricot halves
Stewed prune halves
5 tablespoons shortening

⅔ cup sugar
1 egg, beaten
1 cup milk
2¼ cups flour
4 teaspoons baking powder
½ teaspoon salt

Cream butter and lemon rind, add sugar gradually; cream until fluffy. Spread in 8x8x2-inch pan; arrange apricots and prunes on top. Cream shortening, gradually add sugar; cream until fluffy; add egg in thirds, beating well after each additon. Sift dry ingredients together and stir into creamed mixture alternately with milk. Pour batter carefully over fruit. Bake at 350° F. about 50 min. Invert; remove from pan.

CHIFFON CHOCOLATE CHIP CAKE

1⅛ cups sifted cake flour
¾ cup plus 2 tablespoons sugar
1½ teaspoons baking powder
½ teaspoon salt
¼ cup cooking (salad) oil
3 egg yolks, unbeaten

⅓ cup cold water
1 teaspoon almond extract
½ cup (4 to 5) egg whites
¼ teaspoon cream of tartar
1½ ounces (1½ squares)
    chocolate, grated

Sift flour, ½ cup sugar, baking powder, and salt together into bowl. Make a well in center and add in order, the oil, egg yolks, water, and extract; beat until smooth and set aside. Beat egg whites until frothy in a large, wide bowl; add cream of tartar and continue to beat slightly. Gradually add remaining sugar, beating well after each addition; beat until rounded peaks are formed and egg whites do not slide when bowl is inverted. Slowly pour egg-yolk mixture over entire surface of egg whites. Fold gently until completely blended; sprinkle grated chocolate over top and gently fold in with a few strokes. Pour into ungreased 9x9x2-inch pan. Bake at 350° F. 30 to 35 minutes, or until cake tests done. Invert and rest edges of pan on the edges of two other pans; let hang until cold.

CHIFFON BANANA CAKE

1⅛ cups sifted cake flour
¾ cup sugar
1½ teaspoons baking powder
½ teaspoon salt
¼ cup cooking (salad) oil
¼ teaspoon cream of tartar

2 egg yolks, unbeaten
½ cup mashed ripe bananas
 (1 to 2 bananas)
1½ teaspoons lemon juice
1½ cup (4 to 5) egg whites

Sift flour, ½ cup of the sugar, baking powder, and salt together into bowl; make a well in center and add in order, the oil, egg yolks, bananas, and lemon juice; beat until smooth and set aside. Beat egg whites until frothy in a large, wide bowl; add cream of tartar and continue to beat slightly; gradually add remaining ¼ cup sugar, beating well after each addition; beat until rounded peaks are formed and egg whites do not slide when bowl is inverted; slowly pour yolk mixture over entire surface of whites; fold gently until completely blended. Pour into ungreased 9¼x5¼x2¾-inch loaf pan. Bake at 325° F. 50 to 55 minutes. Invert and rest edges of pan on the edges of two other pans; let hang until cold.

CHIFFON ORANGE CAKE

1⅛ cups sifted cake flour
¾ cup sugar
1½ teaspoons baking powder
¼ teaspoon salt
¼ cup cooking (salad) oil
2 egg yolks, unbeaten

⅓ cup orange juice
1 tablespoon grated orange rind
½ cup (4 to 5) egg whites
¼ teaspoon cream of tartar

Sift flour, ½ cup sugar, baking powder, and salt together into bowl. Make a well in center and add in order, the oil, egg yolks, orange juice and rind; beat until smooth and set aside. Beat egg whites until frothy in a large, wide bowl. Add cream of tartar and continue to beat slightly. Gradually add the remaining ¼ cup sugar, beating well after each addition. Beat until rounded peaks are formed and whites do not slide when bowl is inverted. Slowly pour yolk mixture over entire surface of whites. Fold gently until completely blended. Pour into ungreased 9-inch tubed pan or 9¼x5¼x2¾-inch loaf pan. Bake at 325° F. 50 to 55 minutes, or until cake tests done. Invert; rest tubed pan on neck of funnel, rest edges of loaf pan on the edges of two other pans; let hang until cold.

CHIFFON COCOA CAKE

½ cup cocoa
¾ cup boiling water
1¾ cups sifted cake flour
1¾ cups sugar
1 tablespoon baking powder
½ teaspoon cream of tartar

¾ teaspoon salt
½ cup cooking (salad) oil
5 egg yolks, unbeaten
2 teaspoons vanilla
1 cup (7 or 8) egg whites

Mix cocoa and boiling water and set aside to cool. Sift cake flour, 1 cup sugar, baking powder, and salt together into a large bowl. Make a well in center and add in order, the oil, egg yolks, cooled cocoa mixture, and vanilla. Beat until smooth and set aside. Beat egg whites until frothy in a large wide bowl. Add cream of tartar and continue to beat slightly. Gradually add the remaining ¾ cup sugar, beating well after each addition. Beat until rounded peaks are formed and whites do not slide when bowl is inverted. Slowly pour yolk mixture over entire surface of whites. Fold gently until completely blended. Pour into ungreased 10-inch tubed pan. Bake at 325° F. 55 minutes, then at 350° F. 10 to 15 minutes, or until cake tests done. Invert until cold.

CHOCOLATE CHIP CUPCAKES

2 cups sifted cake flour
3 teaspoons baking powder
¾ teaspoon salt
½ cup shortening
1 cup sugar

1½ teaspoons vanilla
2 eggs
1 cup chocolate pieces
⅔ cup milk

Sift flour, baking powder, and salt together. Cream shortening with sugar and vanilla. Add eggs one at a time, beating well after each addition. Mix chocolate pieces with part of flour mixture and add to creamed mixture. Add flour alternately with milk in small amounts. Bake in greased muffin pans in moderate oven (350° F.) 25 minutes. Makes 18.

LITTLE BALTIMORE CAKES

1 cup sifted cake flour
1½ teaspoons baking powder
¼ teaspoon salt
1 tablespoon grated orange
   rind

4 tablespoons shortening
½ cup sugar
4 egg yolks, well beaten
¼ cup milk

Sift flour with baking powder and salt. Cream orange rind, shortening and sugar until fluffy. Add egg yolks and beat well. Add sifted ingredients alternately with milk in small amounts. Bake in greased cupcake pans in moderate oven (375° F.) about 18 minutes. Cool. Makes 18.

PETITS FOURS

2 cups sifted cake flour
3 teaspoons baking powder
¼ teaspoon salt
½ cup shortening
½ teaspoon vanilla

1 cup sugar
½ cup milk
4 egg whites, stiffly beaten
2 recipes Fondant

Sift flour, baking powder, and salt together. Cream shortening, vanilla, and sugar together until fluffy. Add sifted ingredients and milk alternately. Fold in stiffly beaten egg whites. Pour into 2 greased (9-inch) pans. Bake in moderate oven (375° F.) about 25 minutes. Cool, then cut into 2-inch squares or triangles or use cookie cutters. Brush off crumbs, arrange on wire racks and place racks on waxed paper. Melt fondant slowly over hot water, tint with food coloring, if desired, and pour slowly over cakes. Decorate with nuts, candied fruit, small candies, coconut, or ornamental frosting formed into flower shapes with a pastry tube. Makes about 30.

LITTLE CHOCOLATE CAKES

1½ cups sifted cake flour
2 teaspoons baking powder
½ teaspoon salt
½ cup shortening
1 cup sugar

2 eggs, well beaten
3 ounces (squares) chocolate, melted
¾ cup milk
1 teaspoon vanilla

Sift flour with baking powder and salt. Cream shortening with sugar until fluffy. Add eggs and beat well; then add chocolate. Blend. Add sifted ingredients alternately with milk. Add vanilla. Fill greased cupcake pans ⅔ full and bake in moderate oven (350° F.) about 20 minutes. Makes 20.

FIG CUPCAKES

1 cup dried figs
2 cups sifted flour
3 teaspoons baking powder
1 teaspoon salt
1 teaspoon ginger

1 teaspoon cinnamon
½ cup shortening
1 cup sugar
2 eggs, beaten
½ cup milk

Pour boiling water over figs; cover, let stand 5 minutes, drain and dry. Clip stems and put through food chopper. Sift flour, baking powder, salt, and spices together. Cream shortening and sugar until fluffy. Add eggs; beat well. Add sifted ingredients alternately with milk in small amounts. Add figs. Fill greased muffin pans about ⅔ full. Bake in hot oven (400° F.) about 20 minutes. Makes 15.

SPICE MARBLE CAKES

2 cups sifted cake flour
3 teaspoons baking powder
¼ teaspoon salt
½ cup shortening
1 cup sugar

2 eggs, well beaten
⅔ cup milk
1 teaspoon cinnamon
½ teaspoon cloves
½ teaspoon nutmeg

2 tablespoons molasses

Sift flour with baking powder and salt. Cream shortening and sugar until fluffy. Add eggs and beat thoroughly. Add sifted dry ingredients and milk alternately in small amounts, beating well after each addition. Divide batter into 2 parts. To one part add spices and molasses. Drop by tablespoons into fluted paper baking cups, alternating light and dark mixtures. Bake in moderate oven (350° F.) 25 minutes. Cool and frost. Makes 1½ dozen.

No. 1   **GINGERBREAD**

2 cups sifted cake flour   ⅓ cup shortening
2 teaspoons baking powder   ½ cup sugar
¼ teaspoon baking soda   1 egg, well beaten
2 teaspoons ginger   ⅔ cup molasses
1 teaspoon cinnamon   ¾ cup soured milk
½ teaspoon salt   or buttermilk

Sift flour with baking powder, soda, spices, and salt 3 times. Cream shortening with sugar until fluffy. Add egg and molasses; then add sifted ingredients alternately with milk in small amounts. Bake in greased (8-inch) pan in moderate oven (350° F.) about 50 minutes.

No. 2
2½ cups sifted flour   ½ cup shortening
1½ teaspoons ginger   ½ cup boiling water
1 teaspoon baking soda   1 cup molasses
½ teaspoon salt

Sift dry ingredients together. Melt shortening in boiling water. Add molasses. Add sifted dry ingredients and mix well. Place in greased (8-inch) baking pan and bake in moderate oven (350° F.) 30 to 40 minutes.

TEA CAKES

1⅔ cups sifted cake flour   1 cup sugar
1½ teaspoons baking powder   2 eggs, well beaten
¼ teaspoon salt   ⅔ cup milk
⅓ cup shortening   1 teaspoon vanilla

Sift flour, baking powder, and salt together. Cream shortening with sugar until fluffy. Add eggs. Add flour alternately with milk in small amounts. Add flavoring. Fill greased cupcake pans ⅔ full. Bake in hot oven (400° F.) 15 to 18 minutes. Makes 2 dozen.

SPICED TEA CAKES—Sift 1 teaspoon cinnamon, ¼ teaspoon cloves and ¼ teaspoon nutmeg with flour.

SNOWBALLS—Bake plain or spiced tea cakes in tiny pans. When cool spread on all sides with boiled frosting and roll in moist coconut.

CREAM PUFFS

½ cup shortening
⅛ teaspoon salt
1 cup boiling water

1 cup sifted flour
4 eggs, unbeaten

Add shortening and salt to boiling water and heat to boiling. Reduce heat, add flour all at once and stir vigorously until mixture forms ball around spoon, leaving pan clean. Remove from heat. Add 1 egg at a time, beating very thoroughly after each addition. Continue beating until mixture is thick and shiny and breaks from spoon. Shape on ungreased cookie sheet, using 1 teaspoon or 1 tablespoon of pastry for one puff (depending upon size desired). Bake in very hot oven (450° F.) 20 minutes. Reduce heat to moderate (350° F.) and bake about 20 minutes longer. Cool. Make slit on one side of each puff and fill with whipped cream or Cream Pie Filling *(page 398)*. Makes 1 dozen large or 4 dozen small puffs.

CREAM PUFF SWANS—Press part of batter through a paper funnel onto baking sheet into form of figure 2. Bake these with the other puffs to form heads and necks of the swans. The necks should be removed as soon as delicately browned. When puffs are filled, make eyes on each side of the head, using dots of chocolate and insert into base of puff.

ÉCLAIRS—Shape cream puff paste into strips 1 inch wide and 4 inches long. Bake as for cream puffs. When cool split, fill with custard or sweetened whipped cream and frost with uncooked chocolate frosting. Makes about 12.

LADYFINGERS

3 eggs, separated
½ cup sifted confectioners'
  sugar

½ teaspoon vanilla
½ cup sifted cake flour
⅛ teaspoon salt

Beat egg whites until stiff but not dry. Beat in sugar gradually. Beat egg yolks until thick, fold into egg whites, then fold in vanilla, flour and salt. Shape into (4½-inch) fingers on baking sheet covered with heavy paper. Sprinkle with additional confectioners' sugar and bake in moderate oven (350° F.) 10 to 12 minutes. Press together in pairs. Makes 12.

CAKE FILLINGS AND FROSTINGS

A TABLE giving the temperatures of boiling sugar sirup at various stages will be found on page 10.

FILLINGS—A filling is defined as "something that serves to fill up a space or cavity." In connection with cakes, the word is used to designate a soft, sweetened, cooked, or uncooked mixture that will spread easily. It is usually put between layers to hold them together or is put into a cavity in a cake, but occasionally it is spread over the top and sides of a cake. Sometimes a frosting is used between the layers instead of a filling.

FROSTING AND ICING—A frosting is a preparation of sugar and a liquid, which may or may not be combined with egg, and may be cooked or uncooked. The term is derived from the fact that the first sugar decorations of this sort were uncolored and gave the effect of hoarfrost. The word is now used to mean any sweet covering applied to cakes, whether white or colored.

Icing has been used interchangeably with the word frosting but more often in reference to the uncooked frostings. In the beginning the word was probably used because the substance looked like ice, being translucently white instead of frostily white. Therefore, it may be desirable to use the word icing to mean a thin mixture of confectioners' sugar and a liquid, spread on to give a glazed surface; and to keep the term frosting for a thicker, more opaque coating.

Applying Fillings and Frostings

Cakes should be cooled, and the surface should be free from loose crumbs before a filling or frosting is applied, and the filling or frosting should be cool enough so that it will not soak in. Either the top or the bottom crust may be frosted, but the bottom crust is likely to be softer and more level than the top crust. This point should be considered also when fillings are to be put between layers. Fillings usually hold layers together better when the bottom crusts are placed together. A very soft filling should not be used for a cake that is to be kept any considerable time before it is eaten because the filling will soak into the cake and make it soggy. Sometimes the shape of a loaf cake makes it desirable to put the frosting on the bottom crust. The frosting may extend over the top of a cake only or may be spread over the sides. A well-made boiled frosting should be soft, but not soft enough to run. A frosting may be put on with a very smooth surface, may be left rough, or may be scored in ridges or designs.

Fillings
APPLE FILLING

2 apples   1 lemon   1 cup sugar

Pare two large, sour apples and grate them into a suacepan, add the juice and grated rind of the lemon, and the sugar. Cook for five minutes, stirring constantly. Cool before spreading on cake.

CARAMEL FILLING

1½ cups brown sugar   1 cup milk
1 tablespoon butter   1½ teaspoons vanilla
2 teaspoons cornstarch

Cook the sugar, corn-starch, milk and butter together in a double boiler until thick. Remove from the fire and beat vigorously until the mixture is stiff. Add flavoring. Cool before spreading on cake.

CHOCOLATE FILLING
No. 1.

1½ squares chocolate   1 egg yolk
¼ cup milk   ½ teaspoon butter
1 cup brown sugar   1 teaspoon vanilla

Melt the chocolate over hot water, in a double boiler; add the milk, and cook together, stirring until the mixture is thick and creamy. Add sugar and beaten egg-yolk, stir until smooth and cook five minutes. Add the butter. Beat well. Remove from heat and add flavoring. Cool before spreading on cake.

No. 2.

1½ squares chocolate	1 cup powdered sugar
⅓ cup cream	½ teaspoon butter
1 egg yolk	½ teaspoon vanilla

Melt the chocolate over hot water, in a double boiler. Mix the cream and beaten yolk and add gradually, then the butter. Stir in the sugar and cook until thick. Remove from heat. Add flavoring. Cool before spreading on cake.

COCONUT FILLING

No.1.

1 teaspoon gelatin	½ cup sugar
⅓ cup cold water	3 egg whites
½ cup boiling water	1½ cups moist coconut

Soak gelatin in the cold water until soft; then disslove it in the boiling water. Add sugar and stir until it is dissolved. Allow gelatin to cool partly. When it begins to set, beat the egg-whites until stiff and beat in the gelatin. Fold in the coconut and spread upon the layers.

No. 2.

1½ cups moist coconut	4 tablespoons confectioners'
2 egg whites	sugar

Beat the egg-whites stiff and add the sugar and coconut gradually. Spread the mixture thickly over the cake. If you like, sprinkle the surface with dry shredded coconut.

MARTHA WASHINGTON FILLING

1½ cups milk	¼ cup cold water
1 cup sugar	¼ cup rum, brandy or whisky
2 tablespoons flour	½ cup candied cherries, chopped
3 egg yolks	½ cup citron, chopped
2 tablespoons gelatin	1 cup whipped cream

Scald milk. Add sugar and flour to beaten egg yolks. Add to scalded milk and cook over hot water until eggs are done. Remove from heat. Add gelatin which has been soaked in the cold water. Chill. Add liquor, beat with rotary beater and chill again. Fold the fruit and cream into the mixture. Pile between layers of sponge cake. Top with whipped cream.

CHOCOLATE—Use 2 squares unsweetened chocolate, melted over hot water, omit liquor, add ⅛ teaspoon salt, dash cinnamon, and increase sugar to 1½ cups.

COFFEE—Scald milk with two tablespoons ground coffee, strain, and make same as cream filling, omitting liquor.

ORANGE—Use half orange juice and half milk and add two tablespoons grated orange rind to ingredients above, omitting the liquor. If you like, add one tablespoon lemon juice.

WHIPPED CREAM FILLING

½ tablespoon gelatin
¼ cup cold water
2 cups cream
½ cup powdered sugar
1 teaspoon vanilla
¼ cup boiling water

Soak the gelatin in the cold water until softened. Whip the cream in a pan set in ice-water and sift the sugar over it. Add the vanilla. Pour the boiling water upon the gelatin and, when it is dissolved and cooled, strain it over the whipped cream. Then beat rapidly with a flat whip, turning the pan with the left hand while beating with the right. Beat until the gelatin is thoroughly blended with the cream. Set in a cool place. When the filling is nearly stiff, spread it on the cake layers.

WHIPPED CREAM MOCHA FILLING

½ pint cream
2 tablespoons sugar
1½ tablespoons Mocha extract or strong coffee

Whip the cream in a bowl set in ice-water; add the extract or coffee and the sugar. Beat well.

If the top of the cake is spread with this filling, three-fourths cup of chopped nut-meats may be sprinkled over it.

FRUIT FILLING

½ pound single or mixed fruit
1 cup water
1 cup sugar
1 teaspoon vanilla

Chop the fruit fine and boil in the water, if necessary, until tender. Add sugar and cook slowly until smooth and thick. Remove from the heat, add vanilla and cool.

MIXTURE FOR UPSIDE-DOWN CAKES

2 tablespoons butter   Fresh or canned fruit
    4 tablespoons sugar (white, brown or maple)

In a deep cake pan or heavy skillet, melt 2 tablespoons butter. Sprinkle 4 tablespoons sugar over bottom of pan and cover with well-drained sour cherries (or other canned or fresh fruit). Pour batter or light yeast dough over this layer and bake at 425° F. for 30 minutes.

FRUIT AND NUT FILLING

1 cup chopped raisins   1 egg white
½ cup chopped nuts   Currant jelly
½ cup shredded coconut

Mix the raisins, nuts and coconut and add them to the stiffly beaten egg-white. Spread the layers of cake with a thin layer of currant jelly, then with a thick layer of the filling, and put together.

TUTTI-FRUITTI FILLING

¼ pound seeded or   Chopped walnuts
    seedless raisins   ¼ pound   maraschino cherries
¼ pound figs   ¼ pound maple sugar
½ pound dates   ½ cup water

Put raisins and figs in colander over a kettle of hot water and allow them to steam for about one hour. Then add dates, which have been pitted, and steam for fifteen minutes longer. Remove from steamer, add cherries, and chop all the fruit fine. Bring the maple sugar and water to a boil and pour it over the fruit. Mix well. When cool, spread between layers and on top of the cake and sprinkle with chopped walnuts.

LEMON FILLING

No. 1.   ½ cup sugar
2 tablespoons flour   Juice and grated rind
¾ cup cold water   of 1 lemon
1 egg white   2 teaspoons butter

Make a smooth paste of the flour and two tablespoons of the cold water. Cook the rest of the water, the sugar, grated lemon rind and butter. When the sugar is dissolved and mixture boiling, stir in the flour mixture slowly. Cook until clear and smooth, about fifteen minutes. Add lemon juice and beaten egg yolk and cook two minutes. Cool before spreading on cake.

MAPLE CREAM FILLING

2 cups maple sirup   1 tablespoon butter
¾ cup milk   Salt

Cook sirup, milk, butter, and salt together to the soft-ball stage (238° F.). Cool and beat until creamy. Use as a filling for cakes, cream-puffs or tarts.

ORANGE FILLING

2 tablespoons butter   1 tablespoon grated orange
¼ cup granulated sugar   rind
2 eggs beaten   1 tablespoon lemon juice
½ cup orange juice

Combine all ingredients and mix well. Cook over hot water, stirring constantly, until well thickened, about ten minutes. Chill well before spreading on cake.

PINEAPPLE FILLING

2 tablespoons cornstarch   2½ cups drained crushed
¼ cup sugar   pineapple
            4 tablespoons orange juice

Mix cornstarch and sugar. Add pineapple and cook until smooth and thickened. Add orange juice.

PRUNE FILLING

¼ pound prunes   ½ cup rhubarb juice or
½ tablespoon gelatin   pineapple juice
4 tablespoons cold water   ½ cup whipped cream
½ cup sugar

Wash the prunes, soak over night in water to cover, and cook slowly until soft. Remove pits and rub pulp through a coarse sieve. Soak the gelatin in cold water. When soft, add it to the hot prune plup and stir until the gelatin dissolves. Add sugar and fruit juice. When the filling has cooled, fold in the whipped cream.

WALNUT FILLING

2 cups brown sugar
½ cup water
2 egg whites

½ teaspoon vanilla
½ cup chopped walnut meats

Cook the sugar and water, stirring occasionally until the sugar is dissolved. Boil without stirring until sirup will form a thread when dropped from the tip of the spoon (234° F.). Remove from the heat and cool while beating the egg whites stiff, then pour the sirup in a thin stream on the egg whites, beating the mixture constantly until it is thick enough to spread. Add flavoring and nuts. Cool before spreading on cake. Chopped nut meats may be sprinkled over the top of the cake.

Frostings
CONFECTIONERS' FROSTING

1 egg white   ½ cup confectioners'   ½ teaspoon vanilla
                sugar

Beat the egg white stiff and add the sugar gradually; continue beating until the mixture is smooth and light. Add flavoring.

EGGLESS CONFECTIONERS' FROSTING

2 tablespoons milk or   1 cup confectioners' sugar
water   ½ teaspoon vanilla

Stir the sugar gradually into the milk or water. Add vanilla. More sugar may be added if the frosting is not thick enough.

Any fruit juice or flavored liquid such as strong coffee or maple sirup may be used instead of milk or water.

Crushed berries mixed with the sugar give a pleasing frosting.

Two tablespoons cocoa may be mixed with the sugar.

One-half square of melted chocolate may be added.

BOILED FROSTING

1 cup sugar
½ cup water

1, 2, or 3 egg whites
½ teaspoon vanilla

Cook the sugar and water together, stirring until the sugar has dissolved. Then cook without stirring. For one egg white, cook to 238° F.; for two egg whites, cook to 244° F.; and for three egg whites, cook to 254° F. Remove from the heat and allow it to cool while you are beating the egg white stiff, then pour the sirup in a thin stream over the stiff white, beating the mixture constantly until thick enough to spread. Add vanilla.

ORNAMENTAL OR TWICE-COOKED FROSTING

1½ cups granulated sugar
½ cup water
2 egg whites

1 teaspoon flavoring extract
⅛ teaspoon cream of tartar

Boil sugar and water without stirring until the sirup will form a soft ball in cold water (234° F.); add very slowly to beaten egg whites; add flavoring and cream of tartar and beat until smooth and stiff enough to spread. Put over boiling water, stirring continually until icing grates slightly on bottom of bowl.

SEVEN-MINUTE ICING

1 unbeaten egg white
⅞ cup granulated sugar

3 tablespoons cold water
½ teaspoon flavoring extract

Place all the ingredients in the top of a double boiler. Place over boiling water and beat with beater for seven minutes. Add flavoring, beat, and spread on cake.

CHOCOLATE—Add to above one and one-half ounces melted unsweetened chocolate two minutes before taking from heat.

COFFEE—Use cold boiled coffee in place of water.

CARAMEL FROSTING

1 cup brown sugar
½ cup water
2 egg whites

1 teaspoon vanilla or
½ teaspoon lemon extract

Make a sirup of the sugar and water and cook to the soft-ball stage (238° F.). Remove from the heat and cool while the egg whites are beaten. then pour the sirup in a thin stream on to the stiff whites, beating the mixture constantly until thick enough to spread. Add the flavoring.

Chopped nuts may be stirred into the frosting just before spreading.

CHOCOLATE FROSTING

1 square chocolate	1 egg white
3 tablespoons granulated sugar	2 tablespoons confectioners' sugar
1 tablespoon water	½ tablespoon vanilla

Cook the chocolate, granulated sugar, and water together, stirring until the mixture is smooth and glossy. Beat the white of the egg enough to thin it, but not to make it frothy; add the confectioners' sugar, stir until smooth and light, then add the chocolate mixture and vanilla. Cool before spreading on the cake.

COFFEE-BUTTER FROSTING

1½ cups confectioners' sugar	⅓ cup butter
1 tablespoon dry cocoa	1 tablespoon strong coffee

Cream the butter and add gradually the sugar and cocoa mixed together. Beat well. Stir in the coffee. Ornamental designs may be made by forcing the frosting through a pastry-bag or syringe, using the various tips to produce the desired designs.

FUDGE FROSTING

2 cups sugar	1 teaspoon vanilla
½ cup milk	6 marshmallows or 2
1½ tablespoons butter	heaping tablespoons
2 squares chocolate	marshmallow whip
1 tablespoon corn sirup	

Put first five ingredients into a saucepan and boil to soft ball stage (234° F.). Remove from heat and stir in the marshmallows just until they dissolve. Cool and add vanilla and beat until right consistency to spread on cake.

MAPLE MARSHMALLOW FROSTING

1 cup maple sugar
½ cup boiling water
2 egg whites

6 marshmallows or 2 tablespoons marshmallow cream
½ teaspoon vanilla

Cook the sugar and water together, stirring until the sugar is dissolved; then cook without stirring to the soft-ball stage (238° F.) add the marshmallow to the hot sirup, pressing it under the surface so that it will melt. If marshmallow candies are used, cut them into small pieces. Pour the sirup in a thin stream on to the stiffly beaten egg whites, beating the mixture constantly with a spoon. Add vanilla. Cool before spreading.

MARSHMALLOW-CREAM FROSTING

¾ cup sugar
¼ cup milk
2 tablespoons hot water

6 marshmallows or 2 tablespoons marshmallow cream
½ teaspoon vanilla

Put the milk and sugar into a saucepan, bring slowly to the boiling-point and boil for five minutes. Place the marshmallow in a double boiler with hot water and vanilla. Stir until the mixture is smooth, then add the milk and sugar sirup gradually, stirring constantly. Beat until cool, then spread.

MILK FROSTING

1 teaspoon butter
1½ cups sugar

½ cup milk
½ teaspoon vanilla

Put the butter into a saucepan and, when it is melted, add the sugar and milk. Stir until the boiling-point is reached and then boil for ten minutes without stirring (235° F.). Remove from the heat, add vanilla, and beat until of spreading consistency.

MOCHA FROSTING

1½ teaspoons Mocha extract
or strong coffee

1 cup confectioners' sugar
2 tablespoons water

Mix the extract or coffee with the sugar and stir into the water, gradually, rubbing out all lumps. After the frosting is spread on the cake, three-fourths of a cup of chopped nut-meats may be sprinkled over the top.

COOKIES

Cookie doughs range from those soft enough to drop to those stiff enough to shape into a roll and slice for baking. Between these extremes are doughs which are spread in the pan and cut after baking, doughs just stiff enough to roll and those which are molded with a cookie press or pastry tube.

Shaping Cookies

Cookie doughs for rolling or slicing are more easily handled if they are well chilled; others may be chilled if time allows.

ROLLED COOKIES—Have dough as soft as it can be handled. Use only as much of the chilled dough as can be handled at one time and keep the remainder cold. Shape a portion of dough quickly into a smooth ball and place on lightly floured board or on board covered with canvas or heavy towel. Roll out from center to edges with light deft strokes of floured rolling pin, keeping the edges the same thickness as the center. Shift the dough frequently to be sure it is not sticking to board but do not turn dough over. Keep rolling pin and board free from any particles of dough. Work rapidly and lightly. Dust additional flour on board or pin when necessary but use as little as possible. Excess flour makes cookies tough.

Dip cutter into flour, shake to remove excess flour and cut cookies as close together as possible. Place on baking sheet with spatula, leaving 1-inch space between cookies. Save scraps from each rolling and combine all for chilling and rerolling. Cookies made from rerolled dough will be less tender.

Shortcut Methods—Shape cookie dough into small balls and place on cookie sheet. Flatten out with tines of fork, spatula or bottom of a tumbler, covered with waxed paper.

Roll dough on bottom of inverted baking sheet and cut into desired shape. Remove scraps between cookies. This method is especially useful when dough is a little too soft to handle well or if cookies are being cut into large shapes which would be difficult to move.

Cut cookies into squares, triangles or diamonds with knife or pastry wheel to eliminate rerolling of scraps.

Refrigerator Cookies—Press ½ the dough into a roll about 1½ inches in diameter and wrap tightly in waxed paper. Roll dough lightly back and forth to smooth outside and chill several hours or overnight. Make second roll in same way. Slice cookies very thin with very sharp knife, using very light pressure.

Molded Cookies—Pack dough firmly in cookie press or pastry tube, being careful to leave no air spaces. Shape on cold baking sheet. Make cookies small and dainty.

Rolled Wafers—Bake only a few at a time. Shape at once into scrolls over rolling pin or handle of wooden spoon or roll into cornucopias. If last of cookies become too crisp to shape, warm in oven until softened.

Baking Cookies

Bake cookies on sheets with no sides or with very low ones. Or bake on inverted pans so that warm air can circulate freely over cookies and brown the tops.

Storing Cookies

Cool cookies thoroughly before storing. To keep soft cookies moist and crisp cookies dry, store each separately in tightly covered jars. If crisp cookies become soft they may be reheated until crisp.

Drop Cookies
ROLLED OAT COOKIES

2 cups sifted flour	1½ cups brown sugar
½ teaspoon salt	2 eggs, beaten
½ teaspoon baking soda	⅔ cup soured milk
2 teaspoons baking powder	1½ cups rolled oats
1 teaspoon cinnamon	1 cup raisins or chopped
½ teaspoon cloves	dates
1 cup shortening	1 cup chopped nuts

Sift flour, salt, soda, baking powder, and spices together. Cream shortening with brown sugar until fluffy. Add beaten eggs and mix well. Add sifted ingredients alternately with sour milk in small amounts. Add rolled oats, raisins, and nuts. Drop from teaspoon onto greased baking sheet and bake in moderate oven (350° F.) until browned. Makes about 48.

DROP HERMITS

4½ cups sifted cake flour
2½ teaspoons baking powder
1 teaspoon salt
½ teaspoon baking soda
1 teaspoon cinnamon
½ teaspoon allspice

1 cup shortening
2 cups brown sugar
1 cup milk
2 eggs, beaten
1 cup nuts, chopped
1 cup raisins

Sift first 6 ingredients together. Cream shortening and sugar together. Add milk to beaten eggs. Add dry ingredients alternately with liquid to creamed mixture. Add nuts and raisins. Drop from teaspoon onto greased baking sheet and bake in moderate oven (350° F.) until browned. Makes 3 dozen (2-inch) hermits.

HONEY HERMITS

2¼ cups sifted flour
1 teaspoon baking soda
¼ teaspoon salt
½ teaspoon allspice
½ teaspoon cinnamon
½ cup shortening
1 cup honey

½ cup brown sugar
2 eggs, well beaten
3 tablespoons milk
1 cup seedless raisins
1 cup dried currants
1 cup chopped dates
½ cup chopped nuts

Sift flour, soda, salt, and spices together 3 times. Cream shortening with honey and sugar. Add eggs. Add milk, dry ingredients, fruit, and nuts and mix thoroughly. Drop from teaspoon onto greased baking sheet and bake in hot oven (400° F.) 10 to 12 minutes. Makes about 4 dozen.

RAISIN ROCKS

3 cups sifted cake flour
½ teaspoon salt
2 teaspoons baking soda
½ teaspoon cloves
½ teaspoon cinnamon
1 cup shortening

2 cups brown sugar
2 eggs, beaten
1 cup soured milk or
   buttermilk
1 cup nuts, chopped
1 cup raisins, chopped

Sift flour, salt, soda, and spices together. Cream shortening and sugar until fluffy. Add eggs. Add sifted ingredients alternately with sour milk in small amounts. Add nuts and raisins and mix thoroughly. Drop from teaspoon onto greased baking sheet and bake in moderate oven (350° F.) about 12 minutes or until brown. Makes 100.

SOUR CREAM SPICE COOKIES

3 cups sifted cake flour
1 teaspoon baking soda
1 teaspoon cinnamon
½ teaspoon cloves
½ teaspoon nutmeg
½ teaspoon salt

⅓ cup shortening
2 cups brown sugar
2 eggs, well beaten
1 teaspoon vanilla
⅔ cup thick sour cream

Sift flour, soda, spices, and salt together 3 times. Cream shortening with sugar until light and fluffy. Add eggs and vanilla and mix well. Add dry ingredients alternately with sour cream in small amounts. Mix well. Drop from teaspoon onto greased baking sheet and bake in moderate oven (350° F.) 12 minutes. Makes 40.

ALMOND COOKIES

¾ cup butter
¾ cup sugar
1 egg, unbeaten
½ teaspoon vanilla

¼ teaspoon salt
½ cup blanched almonds,
  ground fine
1½ cups sifted flour

Cream butter with sugar until fluffy. Add egg, vanilla, salt, and almonds and beat thoroughly. Add flour, a small amount at a time. Blend thoroughly. Drop from teaspoon onto greased baking sheet and bake in moderate oven (375° F.) about 15 minutes. Makes 45 cookies.

SPONGE DROPS

2 eggs, separated
½ cup sugar
1½ tablespoons cold water
½ teaspoon lemon extract

2 teaspoons cornstarch
½ cup sifted flour
½ teaspoon baking powder
⅛ teaspoon salt

Beat egg whites until stiff but not dry; then fold in ¼ cup sugar gradually. Beat egg yolks together with cold water and flavoring until thick and lemon colored. Beat in remaining ¼ cup sugar, then fold lightly into beaten egg whites. Sift dry ingredients together and fold into egg mixture. Drop from tablespoon onto greased baking sheet. Bake in moderate (350° F.) 12 minutes. Remove from oven and roll into cones, securing each with a wooden pick. When cool, remove wooden picks and fill cones with whipped cream. Makes 12.

LACE COOKIES

½ cup butter
¾ cup sugar
2 eggs
1 teaspoon cinnamon

½ teaspoon soda
½ cup flour
1 cup chopped pecans
½ cup raisins

Cream butter with sugar; add eggs, well beaten; sift in cinnamon and soda with flour. Add pecans and then raisins. Drop very small amounts on warm metal sheets and bake in a moderate oven (350° F.) 10 to 12 minutes. Makes 4 dozen.

GINGERSNAPS

1½ cups shortening
2 cups sugar
2 eggs
½ cup molasses
4 cups sifted flour

2 teaspoons baking soda
2 teaspoons cinnamon
2 teaspoons cloves
2 teaspoons ginger

Cream shortening and sugar together. Beat in eggs, add molasses and sifted dry ingredients. Roll into 1-inch balls. Dsip in sugar. Place on baking sheet 2 inches apart. Bake in moderate oven (375° F.) 15 to 18 minutes. Makes 5 dozen.

Rolled Cookies
FILLED OAT CRISPS

2½ cups sifted cake flour
½ teaspoon baking powder
½ teaspoon salt
2½ cups rolled oats,
  ground fine

1 cup butter
1 cup light brown sugar
½ cup water
1 recipe Raisin Filling

Sift flour with baking powder and salt and add rolled oats. Cream butter with sugar until fluffy. Add dry ingredients alternately with water. Chill. Roll out a portion of dough ut ⅛ inch thick on lightly floured board and cut into h rounds. Bake on greased baking sheet in moderate (350° F.) about 10 minutes or until browned. Cool ore. When ready to use, spread filling on one cookie with another. Makes about 2½ dozen.

A GLAMOROUS CREAM-FILLED TORTE COMES FORTH IN A BLAZE OF GLORY TO SHED ITS RADIANCE ON YOUR ANNIVERSARY OR JUNIOR'S BIRTHDAY

GAY LITTLE PLUM PUDDINGS TO SPREAD HOLIDAY SPIRITS AND CHEER

USE THE PASTRY TUBE FOR MERINGUES AND GAY LITTLE CAKES FOR GALA OCCASIONS

FOR THAT CLEVER TOUCH, COOKIE CUTOUTS TO MATCH THE MOOD OF YOUR PARTY

SUGAR COOKIES

2¼ cups sifted flour　　　　1 cup sugar
¼ teaspoon salt　　　　　　2 eggs, beaten
2 teaspoons baking powder　½ teaspoon vanilla
½ cup shortening　　　　　　1 tablespoon milk

Sift flour, salt, and baking powder together. Cream shortening and sugar together, add eggs and vanilla, then add sifted ingredients and milk. Roll and cut. Sprinkle with sugar and bake on baking sheet in moderate oven (375° F.) 12 minutes. Makes 2½ dozen cookies.

BROWN SUGAR—Use brown sugar, firmly packed, instead of white.

CARAWAY—Sprinkle cookies with caraway seed.

CHOCOLATE—Add 2 ounces (squares) unsweetened chocolate, melted, to creamed mixture.

LEMON—Use lemon extract instead of vanilla.

MAPLE SUGAR—Use maple sugar instead of granulated.

SAND TARTS—Omit 1 egg and reduce flour to 1¾ cups. Brush cut cookies with egg white and sprinkle with sugar, cinnamon, and blanched slivered almonds. Bake as above.

SPICE—Sift ¼ teaspoon each cinnamon, allspice, and cloves with flour.

FILLED COOKIES

1 recipe Sugar Cookies　　　1 recipe Fig or Raisin Filling

Roll out dough and cut into circles. Place a teaspoon of filling on half the circles, keeping it away from the edges. Cover with remaining circles and press together around edges with tines of fork. Bake as for sugar cookies.

FIG FILLING
½ cup chopped figs　　　　¼ cup sugar
½ cup water　　　　　　　1 tablespoon flour
Juice ½ lemon　　　　　　Dash salt
Combine ingredients and cook until thick. Cool.

RAISIN FILLING
⅓ cup sugar　　　　　　　1½ teaspoons butter
⅓ cup hot water　　　　　Dash salt
1 cup raisins
Combine ingredients and cook until thick. Cool.

SOFT MOLASSES COOKIES

3 cups sifted flour
1½ teaspoons baking powder
¼ teapsoon salt
½ teaspoon baking soda
½ teaspoon ginger

1½ teaspoons cinnamon
½ cup shortening, melted
1 cup molasses
2 tablespoons warm water
1 egg, beaten

Sift dry ingredients together. Combine remaining ingredients. Add sifted ingredients, mix thoroughly and let stand about 10 minutes. Roll out on floured board, cut and bake in hot oven (400° F.) about 15 minutes. Makes 4 dozen.

SCOTCH SHORTBREAD

1 cup butter
¾ cup brown sugar

2¼ cups sifted cake flour

Cream butter and sugar together and work in flour. Chill. Roll out about ¼ inch thick on lightly floured board. Cut with pastry wheel, small fancy cutters or cut into diamonds. Bake in slow oven (325° F.) Makes 70.

Molded Cookies
RICH CINNAMON COOKIES

2 cups sifted cake flour
¼ teaspoon salt
2 teaspoons baking powder
2 teaspoons cinnamon

½ cup butter
1 cup sugar
1 teaspoon vanilla
2 eggs, beaten

Sift first 4 ingredients together. Cream butter, sugar and vanilla together. Add sifted ingredients alternately with beaten eggs. Mold with cookie press on cold ungreased baking sheet. Bake in hot oven (400° F.) 10 minutes. Makes 3 dozen.

SPRITZ COOKIES

2½ cups sifted flour
½ teaspoon baking powder
1 cup butter
¾ cup sugar

Dash salt
1 egg, unbeaten
1 teaspoon vanilla

Sift flour with baking powder. Cream butter, sugar, and salt, add egg and vanilla and mix well. Add sifted ingredients in small amounts. Mold with cookie press on cold ungreased baking sheet. Bake in 375° F. oven 12 to 15 minutes. Makes 45.

CHOCOLATE STARS

2½ cups shortening
1¾ cups confectioners' sugar
2½ ounces (squares) unsweetened chocolate, melted

6 cups sifted cake flour
7 teaspoons cocoa
6 egg whites, stiffly beaten
⅔ cup raspberry jam

Cream shortening with sugar until fluffy. Add chocolate
and beat thoroughly. Sift flour with cocoa. Add to creamed
mixture, a small amount at a time, blending well after each
addition. Add egg whites and blend well. Press dough through
cookie press, using star tip. Make tiny flat stars approximately ¾ inch in diameter on ungreased cookie sheet and bake in
moderate oven (375° F.) about 8 minutes. Spread bottom of
½ of cookies with thick raspberry jam, cover with remaining
cookies and dust with confectioners' sugar. Makes 100.

Refrigerator Cookies

STANDARD REFRIGERATOR COOKIES

6 cups sifted flour
4 teaspoons baking powder
½ teaspoon salt
1½ cups shortening

3 cups brown sugar
2 eggs, well beaten
2 teaspoons vanilla

Sift flour, baking powder, and salt together. Cream shortening and sugar until fluffy. Add eggs and flavoring and mix
well. Add dry ingredients. Divide dough into 6 equal portions. Leave 1 plain and make the following variations of
remaining dough. Shape each piece of dough into a roll. Chill.
When firm slice very thin and bake in moderate oven (375°
F.) 10 to 12 minutes. Makes 10 dozen.

CHOCOLATE—Add 2 ounces (squares) unsweetened chocolate, melted, to 1 portion of the dough. Blend well.

COCONUT—Add ⅓ cup shredded coconut to 1 portion.

FRUIT—Add ⅓ cup chopped dates, raisins, currants, dried
apricots, prunes, or figs to 1 portion. Mix well.

NUT—Add ⅓ cup finely chopped almonds, pecans, pe
nuts, Brazil nuts, or walnuts to 1 portion of dough. Mix we

SPICE—Add ½ teaspoon cinnamon and ¼ teaspoon nutm
to 1 portion of the dough. Mix well.

BUTTERSCOTCH SLICES

3½ cups sifted cake flour
2½ teaspoons baking powder
½ teaspoon salt
1 cup butter

1½ cups brown sugar
2 eggs
1 cup broken walnut meats
1½ teaspoons vanilla

1½ teaspoons milk

Sift flour, baking powder, and salt together. Cream butter with sugar until fluffy. Add eggs, 1 at a time, beating thoroughly after each is added. Add nuts, vanilla, and milk, then add flour, mixing well. Shape into rolls. Chill and slice. Bake on ungreased baking sheet in hot oven (425° F.) 5 to 6 minutes. Makes about 8 dozen.

Bar Cookies

DATE BARS

2 eggs
1 cup confectioners' sugar
1 tablespoon shortening, melted
¼ cup sifted cake flour

¼ teaspoon salt
½ teaspoon baking powder
1 cup chopped dates
¾ cup nuts, chopped
1 teaspoon vanilla

Beat eggs until light. Add sugar and shortening. Blend well. Sift dry ingredients together and add. Add dates, nuts and vanilla. Blend well and pour into greased shallow cake pan. Bake in slow oven (300° F.) about 25 minutes. Cut into bars and roll in confectioners' sugar. Makes about 24.

FROSTED DELIGHTS

1½ cups sifted cake flour
½ teaspoon salt
1 teaspoon baking powder
½ cup shortening
1 cup granulated sugar

2 eggs, beaten
½ teaspoon vanilla
1 cup brown sugar, sifted
1 egg white, stiffly beaten
1 cup nut meats, chopped

Sift flour, salt, and baking powder together. Cream shortening with granulated sugar until fluffy. Add eggs, vanilla, and sifted ingredients and mix well. Spread batter very thin on baking sheet. Fold brown sugar into egg white, spread over cookie batter and sprinkle with nuts. Bake in slow oven (325° F.) 30 minutes. Cut into squares. Makes 30.

FUDGE SQUARES

¾ cup sifted cake flour
½ teaspoon baking powder
⅛ teaspoon salt
⅓ cup shortening
2 ounces (squares) chocolate

1 cup sugar
2 eggs, well beaten
½ cup chopped walnut
  meats
1 teaspoon vanilla

Sift flour with baking powder and salt. Melt shortening with chocolate. Beat sugar into eggs, add chocolate mixture and blend. Add sifted ingredients, nuts, and vanilla and mix well. Bake in greased (8-inch) pan in moderate oven (350° F.) about 35 minutes. Cool and cut into squares. Makes 2 dozen.

BROWNIES

½ cup sifted cake flour
Dash salt
¼ teaspoon baking powder
3 tablespoons shortening
½ cup sugar
2 tablespoons strained honey
2 tablespoons corn sirup

1 egg, beaten
1 ounce (square) chocolate,
  melted
1 tablespoon hot water
1 teaspoon vanilla
½ cup pecans, chopped

Sift flour, salt, and baking powder together. Cream shortening with sugar until fluffy. Add honey and sirup and continue creaming. Add egg and mix well. Add melted chocolate. Add dry ingredients, hot water, and vanilla and blend well. Mix in pecans and spread mixture in 1 (8-inch) pan. Bake in moderate oven (350° F.) about 20 minutes. Makes 36.

MINCEMEAT BARS

Rolled oats
1¾ cups sifted flour
½ teaspoon baking soda

1 cup brown sugar (packed)
1 cup shortening
1½ cups moist mincemeat

Put rolled oats through food chopper, using coarse blade, and measure 2 cups. Add flour, soda, and sugar and mix thoroughly. Cut in shortening until mixture is crumbly. Divide into 2 parts. Pack ½ firmly in bottom of oiled 7½x11 inc baking pan. Spread mincemeat evenly on top, then add re maining dough and pack firmly. Bake in moderate oven (35 F.) 40 minutes. Cool thoroughly and cut into 14 to 16 bar

ALMOND BARS

½ cup shortening
1½ cups brown sugar
1 cup sifted cake flour
2 eggs, unbeaten
1 teaspoon vanilla
2 tablespoons sifted cake flour

1 teaspoon baking powder
½ teaspoon salt
1 cup shredded coconut
1 cup toasted almonds, chopped

Cream shortening with ½ cup brown sugar and work in 1 cup flour. Spread in very thin layer in square baking pan. Bake in moderate oven (350° F.) 10 minutes. Cool slightly. Beat eggs until light, then beat in vanilla and remaining sugar. Add remaining ingredients in order listed and blend well. Spread over partly cooled mixture. Return to oven and bake until browned, about 25 minutes. Cool slightly and cut into bars. Makes 24.

WALNUT STICKS

1 cup brown sugar
½ cup sifted flour
¼ teaspoon salt

½ teaspoon vanilla
2 eggs, well beaten
1 cup chopped walnuts

Add sugar, flour, salt, and vanilla to eggs and mix well. Add walnuts. Spread in greased shallow (9x12½ inch) baking pan and bake in moderate oven (375° F.) 20 to 25 minutes. Cut into strips and remove from pan while warm. Makes 24.

FIG COOKIE SQUARES

½ cup dried figs
⅓ cup butter
1 cup sugar
1 teaspoon mace
1 teaspoon cinnamon
1 teaspoon nutmeg
¼ teaspoon salt

1 egg, beaten
⅓ cup drained crushed pineapple
1¾ cups sifted flour
¾ teaspoon baking soda
1½ tablespoons heavy cream

Pour boiling water over figs, cover and let stand about 5 minutes. Drain, dry on a towel, clip stems and slice fine. Cream butter with ⅔ cup sugar, spices, and salt until fluffy. Add egg and beat well. Add pineapple and figs. Sift flour with soda and add, mixing well. Pour into greased (11x7 inch) pan. Smooth top with spatula and spread with mixture of remaining sugar and cream. Bake in hot oven (400° F.) 20 to 25 minutes. Cut into squares. Serve hot or cold. Makes 20 squares.

MERINGUES

2 egg whites   ½ cup sugar
⅛ teaspoon cream of tartar   ½ teaspoon vanilla
Dash salt

Beat egg whites with cream of tartar and salt until stiff but not dry. Add sugar, 1 tablespoon at a time, beating until stiff after each addition. Fold in vanilla. Heap in rounds or press through a pastry bag onto baking sheet covered with heavy ungreased paper. Bake in slow oven (275° F.) 40 to 60 minutes or until lightly browned. Remove at once from paper. Makes 18 large meringues.

BROWN SUGAR—Use brown sugar instead of white, fol . in one-half cup chopped nuts.

PEANUT—Add ⅔ cup finely chopped peanuts.

COCONUT KISSES

1⅓ cups (1 can) sweetened   3 cups (¾ pound) shredded
  condensed milk   coconut
1 teaspoon vanilla   ⅛ teaspoon salt

Combine ingredients and drop from teaspoon onto greased baking sheet. Bake in moderate oven (375° F.) about 10 minutes. Remove from sheet while hot. Makes about 30.

CEREAL-FLAKE—Use 2 cups prepared cereal flakes with 1 cup shredded coconut.

CHOCOLATE—Add 2 ounces (squares) chocolate, melted.

FRUIT—Use 2 cups chopped dried fruit such as raisins, dates, or figs and only 1 cup coconut.

NUT—Add 1 cup chopped peanuts, walnuts, or pecans. Omit 1 cup coconut.

PEANUT-BUTTER—Add ½ cup peanut butter.

CHOCOLATE CHIP KISSES

½ cup sweetened condensed   ½ teaspoon baking powder
  milk   1 cup chocolate pieces
1½ cups shredded coconut

Combine condensed milk, coconut, and baking powder. Add chocolate pieces and drop from teaspoon onto greased baking sheet. Bake in slow oven (325° F.) 25 minutes or until browned around edges. Makes 2 dozen

CEREAL-FLAKE KISSES

3 egg whites
½ teaspoon salt
1½ cups sugar

½ teaspoon vanilla or almond extract
1½ cups shredded coconut
3 cups cereal flakes

Beat egg whites with salt until stiff but not dry, add sugar in small amounts, beating after each addition until stiff. Mixture should be stiff enough to hold its shape by the time all sugar has been added. Beat in flavoring and fold in coconut and cereal flakes. Drop from teaspoon onto greased baking sheet and bake in slow oven (325° F.) 15 to 25 minutes, depending on size. Remove from pan as soon as taken from oven. Makes 4½ dozen.

ALMOND MACAROONS

½ pound almond paste
3 egg whites, slightly beaten
¼ cup sifted flour

½ cup granulated sugar
½ cup confectioners' sugar
⅛ teaspoon salt

Work almond paste with a wooden spoon until smooth. Add slightly beaten egg whites and blend thoroughly. Add flour, sugars, and salt sifted together. Drop from teaspoon or press through a cookie press onto baking sheets covered with heavy paper. Bake in slow oven (300° F.) about 30 minutes. Remove from paper while still warm. If paper sticks to cookies, moisten it on the underside. Makes about 4 dozen.

CHOCOLATE MACAROONS

4 egg whites
¼ cup water
⅔ cup sugar
2 teaspoons vanilla
½ teaspoon salt

1 tablespoon flour
2 ounces (squares) chocolate, melted
2½ cups shredded coconut

Beat egg whites with cold water until stiff but not dry. Beat in sugar and vanilla. Add salt and flour and blend carefully. Fold in melted chocolate and coconut. Drop from teaspoon onto heavy paper on baking sheet and bake in slow oven (325° F.) 25 to 30 minutes. Makes about 2½ dozen.

PASTRY AND MERINGUES

PASTRY may be defined as a stiff dough made very short by means of some kind of shortening. It is used for pies and tarts and for some other dishes. There are two kinds of pastry; plain pastry and puff pastry.

PLAIN PASTRY is usually used for pies and tarts.

PUFF PASTRY is used for tarts of various kinds, for cases, such as patty shells, and vol-au-vents, to hold creamed mixtures, and for various shapes which are frosted or otherwise decorated for serving with afternoon tea or as desserts. It is not used for under crusts of pies because it rises or puffs up too much. It is used for rims where height is desirable, or for upper crusts of rich pies.

Pastry Making

Good pastry is flaky, tender, delicate and evenly browned. It is not crumbly, but when broken, shows layers of flat flakes, piled one above the other with air spaces between.

To achieve this result the cook must be quick and "light-handed," since pastry cannot be good if handled roughly or slowly. The flakiness of pastry is caused by many particles of shortening which are surrounded and separated by flour. During baking each shortening particle melts to form a delicate flake. However, rough, slow handling may cause these particles to melt and blend with the flour to form a solid mass, which is tough and hard after baking.

Everything Must Be Cold

Chilled ingredients are important for success and for the beginner even the flour may be chilled. A cold, solid shortening and ice water are essentials. Baking powder is sometimes used but with skillful mixing and handling of the dough it is unnecessary.

Sift flour and salt together, then add cold shortening and cut in as quickly as possible. A pastry blender is one of the best utensils to use for this purpose, although a quick job can be done with 2 knives. The fingers may be used by those able to work rapidly enough to work in the shortening before it starts to melt from the heat of the fingers. Distribute the shortening evenly through the flour, being sure not to neglect that at the bottom of the bowl. It has been mixed sufficiently when the largest pieces of shortening are the size of small peas. These particles roll out and melt into crisp flakes. The mixture may be placed in a clean jar, covered and kept in the refrigerator.

How Much Water

The greatest care is required when adding water. No definite amount can be specified since this varies with the dryness of the flour and the amount of shortening used. Usually 2 to 3 tablespoons water are required for 1 cup flour. Sprinkle the water a tablespoon at a time over the flour mixture while tossing it quickly with a fork. Avoid stirring or mixing that would crush shortening particles and blend them with the flour. Push moistened portions to one side before adding more water so a dry portion can be sprinkled each time. If allowed to do so, the shortening-flour mixture will absorb a great deal more water than should be used, so care must be taken to keep the moisture well distributed. Too much moisture makes the crust hard and brittle. Too little makes a crust which cracks at the edges while being rolled; it may crack open while baking and the pie be difficult to serve.

Be Swift and Deft

When moist enough to hold together under slight pressure, divide into halves, press each into a ball, flatten out with the hands and chill. If too little or too much water has been used, nothing can be done about it, except to profit by experience next time. Sprinkle board and rolling pin lightly with flour and rub into wood. A canvas cloth or coarse linen kitchen towel to cover the board and a "stocking" for the rolling pin are aids to the rolling out process, by preventing sticking without the use of too much flour. Excess flour on board and pin make the crust hard. Roll quickly but lightly since heavy pressure makes the pastry stick and breaks the surface. Start each stroke at center of dough and roll to edge, keeping pastry in as circular a shape as possible and keeping edges as thick as the center. Lift and turn pastry occasionally to make sure it is not sticking and rub extra flour over board if necessary. Keep all particles of dough cleaned from uncovered rolling pin since the pastry being rolled will stick to these more readily than to the wood. Roll out to ⅛-inch thickness for lower crust; roll top crust slightly thinner. Place pastry in pans and bake as directed.

Piecrust mixtures, containing all ingredients, except the water can now be purchased. They are valuable for the small family.

About the Filling

When filling for a two-crust pie is very juicy some precautions are necessary to prevent it from boiling over. The top crust should be well slashed to allow steam to escape. Some get good results by inserting paper funnels or several 3-inch lengths of uncooked macaroni through the slashes into the filling to act as "chimneys." The edge of the pie may be bound with an inch-wide strip of muslin dipped into water, or with paper pie tape used as directed on the package. A little flour paste will hold the ends together. Remove strip when pie is baked. Another method is to cut the top crust ½ inch larger than necessary and turn the excess under the moistened edge of the under crust. Or cut bottom crust ½ inch larger and turn it over the top crust. When these are firmly pressed together a tight seal is made. A little flour, cornstarch or tapioca mixed with sugar thickens the juice.

PLAIN PASTRY

2 cups sifted flour   ⅔ cup shortening
¾ teaspoon salt   4 to 6 tablespoons cold water

Sift flour and salt together and cut in shortening with 2 knives or pastry blender. Add water, using only a small portion at a time, until mixture will hold together. Divide dough into 2 parts. Roll out on floured board to desired size. Line the pie pan with one piece of dough, being careful not to stretch dough. After filling is placed in pastry, dampen edges of lower crust with cold water and cover with remaining dough which has been rolled out and slashed in several places to allow steam to escape while baking. Press edges together with prongs of fork and bake according to recipe for filling selected. Makes 2 (9-inch) shells or one 2-crust (9-inch) pie.

PASTRY SHELL—Roll ½ of the dough ⅛ inch thick, fold in half and lift into pie pan. Do not stretch dough. After crust is fitted, trim edges evenly, leaving a 1-inch overhanging border, fold dough under and back to make an upright rim, then flute edges using thumb and index finger of one hand and the index finger of the other hand. Prick crust thoroughly with a fork and use one of the following methods to prevent shrinkage of crust.

TO PREVENT SHRINKAGE OF CRUST

Place rolled dough in pan and set aside for 5 minutes, then fit into place with a ball of dough.

Line pastry shell with waxed paper and partially fill with rice or beans, remove paper after first 10 minutes of baking.

Fit a second pan inside on crust, remove pan after first 10 minutes. Bake in a very hot oven (450° F.) about 15 minutes or until delicately browned.

PASTRY FORMS

TARTS—Cut pastry into rounds to fit muffin or tart pans and proceed as for pies. Makes 4 (2-crust) or 8 single tarts.

TART SHELLS—Cut pastry into rounds to fit muffin or tart pans and proceed as for Pastry Shell, or shape pastry over the back of muffin or tart pans, trim edge and prick thoroughly with a fork. Makes 8 shells.

PASTRY WHEELS—Combine leftover scraps of dough; roll out, sprinkle with cinnamon and sugar and roll up tightly. Slice into tiny circles and bake in hot oven.

HOT WATER PASTRY

2 cups sifted flour
1/2 teaspoon baking powder
1 teaspoon salt
1/3 cup boiling water
2/3 cup shortening

Sift flour, baking powder and salt together. Pour water over shortening and mix with fork until creamy, add flour mixture and mix into a dough. Chill thoroughly and proceed as for Plain Pastry. Makes 1 (9-inch) double crust pie or 2 (9-inch) shells.

SOUTHERN PASTRY

2 cups sifted flour
1/2 teaspoon salt
1 cup shortening
6 tablespoons ice water

Mix flour and salt, cut shortening into flour; add water a tablespoon at a time, using only enough to make a workable paste; too little will leave it crumbly. This pastry, being exceedingly rich, must be handled deftly. Roll out pastry and line pie pan. Makes 2 (9-inch) pastry shells or pastry for 1 two-crust (9-inch) pie.

Thorough chilling before rolling makes pastry easier to handle.

OFF TO A GOOD START CUTTING IN THE SHORT-ENING AND ICE WATER

A LIGHT TOUCH AND NOT TOO MUCH OF IT, IN THE KNEADING AND ROLLING

FILLED WITH
JUICY FRUIT
AND COVERED
WITH A BLAN-
KET OF PAT-
TERNED CRUST

FINISHING
TOUCHES—
SNUGLY RUF-
FLED AND
LIGHTLY
BRUSHED

DECORATIONS

Roll out Plain, Southern, Cheese or Hot Water Pastry according to directions and cut out any of the following designs with cookie cutters or cardboard patterns, leave plain or decorate as suggested below. Bake in very hot oven (450° F.) about 10 minutes. Top any open-faced pie or tart.

CAT OR OTHER ANIMALS—After baking, mark to suggest features, using melted chocolate, colored sugar, nut meats, candied or dried fruits.

CHICK—After pastry is baked, mark features using a toothpick and melted chocolate.

CHRISTMAS TREE—Mark to suggest branches and decorate with green sugar.

CRESCENT—Sprinkle with colored sugar.

CROWN—Cut rounds with large scalloped cutter and cut out center with medium cutter.

FLAG—Mark to suggest stars and stripes and decorate with red, white and blue sugar.

HATCHET—Press cutting edge to make it thin and sprinkle red sugar over handle.

HEART—Sprinkle red sugar over all or only on edges. Arrange heart-shaped candies on pastry.

HEARTS, CLUBS, SPADES AND DIAMONDS—Sprinkle colored sugar over top.

PUMPKIN—Mark ribs and sprinkle stem with green sugar.

SANTA CLAUS—Mark features and decorate with red sugar.

SHAMROCK—Sprinkle green sugar over all or only on edges.

STAR—Use colored sugar.

TURKEY—Sprinkle with cinnamon and sugar.

WITCH—Mark features.

CHEESE PASTRY

½ cup butter
1 cup sifted flour

¼ pound cottage or cream cheese

Cut butter into flour; add cheese and mix to a smooth dough. Chill thoroughly. Roll and proceed as for Plain Pastry. Makes 1 (9-inch) pastry shell.

PUFF PASTE

1 cup butter   ½ cup ice water
2 cups sifted cake flour

Wash butter in cold water to remove salt. Allow ⅔ of butter to become soft. Cut remaining butter into flour with 2 knives or a pastry blender; add ice water using only enough to hold ingredients together. Roll out to ¼-inch thickness on a lightly floured board, making a square sheet. Spread ⅔ of dough with ¼ of softened butter; fold unbuttered ⅓ over center ⅓ and fold remaining ⅓ over to cover first ⅓, buttered side down, making 3 layers of dough with butter between each layer. Turn dough ¼ of way around on board and roll to about ¼-inch thickness. Spread with butter. Fold as before and chill thoroughly. Roll, spread with butter, fold and chill 2 more times. Roll, shape and bake as directed in recipes using Puff Paste. Bake at once or wrap in waxed paper and chill 12 to 24 hours. Makes 15 to 24 fancy pastries.

PATTY SHELLS

Roll puff paste ¼ inch thick, cut into 3-inch rounds with floured cutter. Cut out centers from half of rounds with a small cutter; moisten underside of each ring with cold water and place one on each remaining plain round, pressing down lightly. Bake in very hot oven (450° F.) for 10 minutes, reduce to 400° F. bake 5 minutes, then reduce to 350° F. and bake 15 minutes longer.

VOL-AU-VENT

Roll puff paste 1½ inches thick and cut a circle about 6 inches in diameter, using a cutter or, with a sharp knife, cutting around the edge of a plate placed on the paste. Place circle on a baking sheet and, with a sharp pointed knife or smaller cutter, cut a circle around the top about 1½ inches from the edge and 1 inch deep. Do not remove the center but bake entire circle in a very hot oven (450° F.) about 8 minutes, reduce temperature to 350° F. and bake 30 minutes longer. When the outer crust is baked, lift out center and remove uncooked paste from below. Place top upside down and place in oven a few minutes to dry.

Fill with any kind of sweetened fresh berries or fruit, creamed fish, fowl or meat. Replace top and sprinkle with confectioners' sugar, if using fruit.

CRUMB PIE SHELL

1½ cups fine crumbs   ½ cup butter, melted
¼ cup sugar

Mix crumbs and sugar together; stir in butter. Line pie pan with mixture by pressing it firmly into place. Chill for 20 minutes or bake in moderate oven (350° F.) 10 minutes. Cool. Makes 1 (9-inch) shell.

CINNAMON—Add ½ teaspoon cinnamon to bread or graham cracker crumbs.

Use crumbs of the following: Chocolate Cookies; Cereal Flakes; Gingersnaps; Graham Crackers; Toasted Bread; Vanilla Wafers; Zwieback.

BRAZIL-NUT—Omit crumbs and butter and use 1⅔ cups ground Brazil nuts. Proceed as above.

ALMOND PASTRY

1½ cups sifted flour   ½ cup shortening
¼ cup ground almonds   1 egg, beaten
¼ cup sugar   Cold water
½ teaspoon salt

Mix first 4 ingredients and cut in shortening. Add egg and cold water to make stiff dough. Chill, roll and bake as for plain pastry.

MÜRBE TEIG FOR PIES

1 cup sifted flour   ¼ cup butter
⅛ teaspoon salt   1 egg yolk, slightly beaten
1 tablespoon sugar

Combine flour, salt, and sugar. Cut in butter with 2 knives or a pastry blender. Add egg yolk and mix thoroughly. Press into a pie plate or spring-form pan to ¼-inch thickness. Fill with a fruit filling. Bake in hot oven (425° F.) 10 minutes, reduce temperature to 350° F. and bake until fruit is cooked. Makes 1 (9-inch) shell.

CHEESE STICKS

Use ½ recipe Plain Pastry. Roll out ¼ inch thick, sprinkle half with ⅓ cup grated cheese and fold over other half. Roll out 2 more times, sprinkle with cheese each time. Cut into strips and bake on an ungreased baking sheet in a hot oven, (425° F.) about 10 minutes or until delicately browned.

SUET PASTRY

1 teaspoon baking powder	1 cup chopped suet
2 cups sifted flour	1 cup cold water
½ teaspoon salt	

This pastry is excellent for boiled fruit pudding and dumplings or for baked or boiled meat pies. All the ingredients must be very cold. Sift baking powder with flour, add salt, suet, and water and mix into a smooth, firm dough. Chill and roll out. Makes one 2-crust (9-inch) pie or 2 (9-inch) shells.

APPLE PIE

6 apples	2 tablespoons flour
½ to ⅔ cup sugar	1 recipe Plain Pastry
¼ teaspoon salt	1 tablespoon butter

Pare and slice apples. Sift dry ingredients together and mix with apples. Line pie pan with pastry, fill with apple mixture, dot with butter and cover with top crust. Bake in very hot oven (450° F.) 15 minutes; reduce temperature to moderate (350° F.) and bake 45 minutes longer. Makes 1 (9-inch) pie.

VARIATION—Add 1 teaspoon cinnamon to dry ingredients.

ENGLISH DEEP-DISH APPLE PIE

1 recipe Plain Pastry	1 teaspoon cinnamon or
6 to 8 tart apples	nutmeg
⅔ cup sugar	¼ cup water
	1 teaspoon butter

Invert a heavy china cup or custard cup in the center of a baking dish, 2 or 3 inches deep. Line sides of dish with pastry, letting it extend a little above the dish. Do not line the bottom with pastry. Pare and core apples and cut into slices. Add sugar, spice, and water and dot with butter. Cover apples with pastry, slash the top to let steam escape and pinch edges of pastry together. Bake in very hot oven (450° F.) for 10 minutes; reduce temperature to 350° F. and bake 45 minutes longer. When serving, slip the knife under cup to let the confined juice mix with apples. Serve in wedges with hard sauce. Serves 6.

VARIATION—Use 2 recipes Cheese Pastry or 2 recipes Murbe Teig for Pies instead of Plain Pastry.

Use fresh peaches, apricots or pears instead of apples.

BLUEBERRY PIE

4 cups blueberries
1 cup sugar
4 tablespoons flour
⅛ teaspoon salt
1½ tablespoons lemon juice
1 recipe Plain Pastry

Mix berries with sugar, flour, salt, and lemon juice. Line pie pan with pastry, pour in filling and cover with top crust. Bake in very hot oven (450° F.) 10 minutes; reduce temperature to moderate (350° F.) and bake 20 to 30 minutes longer. Makes 1 (9-inch) pie.

FRESH CHERRY PIE

1¼ cups sugar
2½ tablespoons flour
¼ teaspoon salt
1 quart tart red cherries, washed and pitted
1 recipe Plain Pastry

Mix sugar, flour, salt, and cherries together. Line pie pan with pastry, add cherry mixture and cover with top crust. Bake in very hot oven (450° F.) 10 minutes; reduce temperature to moderate (350° F.); bake 25 minutes longer. Makes 1 (9-inch) pie.

VARIATIONS—Decrease flour to 1 tablespoon and add 2 tablespoons quick-cooking tapioca. Dot cherries with 1 tablespoon butter.

For a pie with a clearer filling use 1¼ tablespoons cornstarch instead of the flour listed.

Use 2 recipes Cheese Pastry instead of Plain Pastry.

CRANBERRY PIE

4 cups cranberries
1½ cups sugar
2 tablespoons flour
¼ teaspoon salt
3 tablespoons water
1 tablespoon melted butter
1 recipe Plain Pastry

Wash berries, chop and mix with next 5 ingredients. Line pie pan with pastry, pour in filling and arrange strips of pastry over top in lattice design. Bake in very hot oven (450° F.) 15 minutes; reduce temperature to moderate (350° F.) and bake about 30 minutes longer. Makes 1 (9-inch) pie.

CRANBERRY AND APPLE—Use 2 cups cranberries and 1½ cups chopped apples instead of 4 cups cranberries.

PEACH PIE

1 cup sugar
2 tablespoons flour
¼ teaspoon salt

8 peaches, silced
1 recipe Plain Pastry

Sift dry ingredients together and mix with peaches. Line pie pan with pastry, fill with peach mixture and cover with top crust. Bake in very hot oven (450° F.) 15 minutes; reduce temperature to moderate (350° F.) and bake 35 minutes longer. Makes 1 (9-inch) pie.

PINEAPPLE PIE

2 eggs
1⅓ cups sugar
1 tablespoon lemon juice

2 cups shredded fresh
pineapple
1 recipe Plain Pastry
1 tablespoon butter

Beat eggs slightly, add sugar, lemon juice, and pineapple. Line pie pan with pastry, pour in filling, dot with butter and cover with top crust. Bake in very hot oven (450° F.) 10 minutes; reduce temperature to moderate (350° F.) and bake 35 minutes longer or until pineapple is tender. Makes 1 (9-inch pie.

CANNED PINEAPPLE—Use 2 cups canned shredded pineapple instead of fresh and only ½ cup sugar.

PINEAPPLE AND STRAWBERRY—Use 1 cup grated fresh pineapple and 1 cup sliced strawberries.

PLUM PIE

3 cups pitted fresh plums
1¼ cups sugar
2 tablespoons flour
2 tablespoons lemon juice

⅛ teaspoon salt
1 recipe Plain Pastry
1 tablespoon butter

Combine plums, sugar, flour, lemon juice, and salt. Line pie pan with pastry, add filling, dot with butter and cover with top crust. Bake in very hot oven (450° F.) 10 minutes; reduce temperature to moderate (350° F.) and bake 35 minutes longer or until plums are tender. Makes 1 (9-inch) pie.

PRUNE—Use 2½ cups quartered cooked prunes for plums. Reduce sugar to ½ cup. Omit flour and add 1½ tablespoons prune juice. Proceed as for plum pie.

RAISIN PIE

⅓ cup lemon juice
1 teaspoon grated lemon rind
½ cup orange juice
2 teaspoons grated orange rind
1 cup brown sugar

2 cups seeded raisins
1¾ cups water
6 tablespoons flour
1 recipe Hot Water Pastry

Combine lemon juice and rind, orange juice and rind, sugar, raisins, and 1¼ cups water and heat to boiling. Mix flour and remaining ½ cup water to a smooth paste and add to mixture gradually, stirring constantly. Cook 5 minutes. Line pie pan with pastry, pour in filling and cover with top crust. Bake in hot oven (400° F.) 40 minutes. Makes 1 (9-inch) pie.

RHUBARB PIE

3 tablespoons flour
1 cup sugar
1 egg, beaten

2 cups rhubarb cut into
    small pieces
1 recipe Plain Pastry

Sift flour and sugar together, add egg, beat thoroughly and add rhubarb. Line pie pan with pastry and pour in filling. Cover with top crust or lattice and bake in very hot oven (425° F.) 10 minutes; reduce temperature to moderate (350° F.) and bake 35 minutes longer. Makes 1 (9-inch) pie.

FRUIT SALAD PIE

Soften 2 teaspoons gelatin in 3 tablespoons orange juice; dissolve over hot water. Mix with 3 cups diced, sweetened fresh fruits. Pour into chilled Crumb Pie Shell; cover with sweetened whipped cream. Makes 1 (9-inch) pie.

STRAWBERRY PIE

1 cup sugar
1 tablespoon cornstarch
⅛ teaspoon salt

3 cups fresh strawberries
1 recipe Plain Pastry
1 tablespoon butter

Mix sugar, cornstarch and salt together and add to berries. Line pie pan with pastry, add filling, dot with butter and cover with top crust. Bake in very hot oven (450° F.) 10 minutes; reduce temperature to moderate (350° F.) and bake 30 minutes longer. Makes 1 (9-inch) pie.

RASPBERRY—Use fresh raspberries intead of strawberries.

BUTTERSCOTCH PIE

¾ cup brown sugar
5 tablespoons flour
½ teaspoon salt
2 cups milk
2 egg yolks, slightly beaten

2 tablespoons butter
1 teaspoon vanilla
1 baked Pastry Shell
Whipped cream

Combine sugar, flour, and salt and stir in milk slowly. Cook over boiling water until thickened, stirring constantly. Cover and cook 10 minutes longer, stirring occasionally. Add mixture to egg yolks, stirring vigorously; cook 1 minute longer. Add butter and vanilla and cool. Place filling in pastry shell and cover with whipped cream. Makes 1 (8-inch) pie.

BANANA BUTTERSCOTCH—Peel and slice 3 bananas and arrange in layers with filling in butterscotch pie.

CREAM PIE

1½ cups milk
¼ cup sugar
¼ teaspoon salt
3 tablespoons flour
1 egg yolk

1 tablespoon butter
½ teaspoon vanilla
1 baked Pastry Shell
Whipped cream

Scald 1 cup milk over boiling water. Mix sugar, salt, flour, and remaining milk together. Stir into hot milk and cook slowly until thickened, stirring constantly. Cover and cook over boiling water for 5 minutes. Add mixture slowly to egg yolk and cook 1 minute longer. Add butter and vanilla. Cool. Pour into pastry shell and spread with whipped cream. Makes 1 (8-inch) pie.

VARIATIONS—Any crumb pie shell may be used instead of baked pastry shell. For 9-inch pie use 2 cups milk and 3 egg yolks, or 1 of the following variations:

BANANA—Use 4 ripe bananas. Fill pastry shell with alternate layers of sliced bananas and cooled filling.

CHOCOLATE—Add 1 ounce (square) chocolate, melted, and 2 tablespoons sugar.

COCONUT—Stir 1½ cups moist shredded coconut into filling.

FRUIT—Stir 1½ cups drained canned fruit salad and a few slices of banana into filling.

CUSTARD PIE

4 eggs, slightly beaten
¼ teaspoon salt
½ cup sugar
3 cups milk, scalded

½ teaspoon vanilla
½ recipe Plain Pastry
Nutmeg

Combine eggs, salt, and sugar; add milk and vanilla slowly. Line pie pan with pastry, pour in filling and sprinkle with nutmeg. Bake in very hot oven (450° F.) 10 minutes. Reduce temperature to slow (325° F.) and bake 30 to 40 minutes longer, or until a knife inserted comes out clean. Makes 1 (9-inch) pie.

CARAMEL—Carmelize sugar and add to scalded milk before combining milk with egg mixture.

COCONUT—Add 1 cup shredded coconut to custard before baking.

MODERN CUSTARD—Use 1 baked Pastry Shell in place of pastry. Pour custard into well-greased pie pan of same size as used for pastry shell. Bake in slow oven (325° F.) 45 to 55 minutes, or until knife inserted in center comes out clean. Chill thoroughly. Place waxed paper on top of custard, a cookie sheet on paper and turn upside down, leaving custard on sheet. Remove pie pan and invert pastry shell and its pie pan over custard. Turn right-side up. This method keeps crust crisp.

BARBARA FRIETCHIE PIE

½ recipe Southern Pastry
¾ cup granulated sugar
¾ cup brown sugar
½ cup heavy cream or
evaporated milk
2 egg yolks, beaten

2 tablespoons butter
½ teaspoon vanilla
⅛ teaspoon salt
2 egg whites, beaten
Nutmeg

Line pie pan with pastry. Cook next 5 ingredients in top of double boiler until thickened, stirring constantly. Remove from heat, add vanilla, salt, and egg whites. Pour into pastry shell, sprinkle with nutmeg. Bake in hot oven (425° F.) 10 minutes, reduce temperature to slow (300° F.) and bake about 45 minutes longer or until knife inserted in center comes out clean. Serve very cold. Makes 1 (9-inch) pie.

Omit pastry and use Brazil-nut Pie Shell.

ORANGE CHIFFON PIE

1 tablespoon unflavored
  gelatin
¼ cup cold water
4 eggs, separated
1 cup sugar
½ cup orange juice

1 tablespoon lemon juice
½ teaspoon salt
1 tablespoon grated orange
  rind
1 Cereal Flake Pie Shell
Whipped cream

Soften gelatin in water 5 minutes. Beat egg yolks and add ½ cup sugar, orange juice, lemon juice, and salt. Cook over boiling water until of custard consistency. Add grated orange rind and softened gelatin and stir thoroughly. Cool. When mixture begins to thicken fold in stiffly beaten egg whites to which remaining ½ cup sugar has been added. Fill crumb shell and chill. Spread with whipped cream. Makes 1 (9-inch) pie.

GRAPEFRUIT AND ORANGE—Use ⅓ cup grapefruit juice and ¼ cup orange juice instead of orange juice and lemon juice.

LEMON—Use ½ cup lemon juice and 1 teaspoon grated lemon rind instead of orange juice and rind.

LIME—Use ½ cup lime juice instead of orange juice.

PINEAPPLE—Use ⅔ cup canned pineapple juice and only ½ cup sugar. Omit orange rind.

STRAWBERRY—Omit orange juice and rind. Combine 1 cup diced strawberries with the first ½ cup sugar and allow to stand 1 hour. Strain juice and use instead of orange juice.

PINEAPPLE FLUFF PIE

2½ tablespoons cornstarch
½ cup water
1 cup pineapple juice
¾ cup sugar
1 cup drained crushed
  pineapple

3 egg whites
¼ teaspoon salt
1 Chocolate Cookie Shell
Whipped cream

Blend cornstarch and water. Add pineapple juice and ½ cup sugar and cook slowly until thickened, stirring constantly. Add pineapple and cook a few minutes longer. Combine egg whites and salt and beat until foamy; add remaining sugar gradually, beating until stiff. Fold into pineapple mixture and pour into crumb shell. Cool. Spread with whipped cream. Makes 1 (9-inch) pie.

RHUBARB WHIPPED CREAM PIE

2 tablespoons unflavored
gelatin
½ cup cold water
2½ cups stewed rhubarb

1 cup sugar
1 cup heavy cream, whipped
1 Cereal Flake Pie Shell

Soften gelatin in water. Heat rhubarb and sugar to boiling, add gelatin and stir until dissolved. Cool; when mixture begins to thicken fold in whipped cream. Pour into pie shell and chill. Makes 1 (9-inch) pie.

TOFFEE CHIFFON PIE

1 tablespoon unflavored
gelatin
¼ cup cold water
2 cups hot milk
⅛ teaspoon salt
⅓ cup sugar

2 eggs, separated
½ teaspoon vanilla
¾ cup crushed pecan
toffee
1 Zwieback Pie Shell
Pecan toffee shavings

Soften gelatin in water 5 minutes. Combine milk, salt, and 4 tablespoons sugar; stir until dissolved. Add to slightly beaten egg yolks and cook over boiling water until thickened, stirring constantly. Add gelatin and stir until dissolved. Cool. Add vanilla and toffee when custard begins to thicken. Beat egg whites until stiff, add remaining sugar and fold into custard. Fill crumb shell and chill. Sprinkle with toffee shavings. Makes 1 (9-inch) pie.

SHERRY—Use almond extract instead of vanilla; add 2 tablespoons sherry and use ¼ cup chopped almonds instead of toffee and toffee shavings.

PRUNE CHIFFON PIE

1 tablespoon unflavored
gelatin
¼ cup cold water
1 cup chopped cooked
prunes
¾ cup prune juice

½ cup sugar
¼ teaspoon salt
2 tablespoons lemon juice
1 teaspoon grated lemon rind
2 egg whites, stiffly beaten
1 baked Pastry Shell

Soften gelatin in water 5 minutes. Combine prunes, juice, sugar, salt, lemon juice, and rind, and heat to boiling. Remove from heat, add gelatin and stir until dissolved. Cool. When slightly thickened, fold in egg whites. Pour into pastry shell and chill. Makes 1 (9-inch) pie.

PUMPKIN PIE

⅛ teaspoon salt
⅔ cup sugar
2 teaspoons pumpkin pie spice
2 eggs, slightly beaten

1⅔ cups milk
1½ cups mashed cooked
pumpkin
½ recipe Plain Pastry

Sift dry ingredients together and stir into eggs. Add milk and pumpkin. Line pie pan with pastry and pour in filling Bake in very hot oven (450° F.) 10 minutes; reduce temperature to slow (325° F.) and bake 35 minutes longer or until knife inserted in center comes out clean. Cool. Makes 1 (9-inch) pie.

VARIATION—Use 1 teaspoon cinnamon, ¼ teaspoon nutmeg and ½ teaspoon ginger instead of pumpkin pie spice.

SQUASH PIE

1 cup sugar
¾ teaspoon salt
1 teaspoon cinnamon
1 teaspoon nutmeg
¾ teaspoon ginger
¼ teaspoon mace

1 cup steamed squash,
strained
3 eggs
1 cup heavy cream or
evaporated milk
½ recipe Plain Pastry

Add sugar, salt, and spices to squash and mix thoroughly. Beat eggs, add cream and mix with squash. Line pie pan with pastry and pour in filling. Bake in very hot oven (450° F.) 10 minutes, then reduce temperature to moderate (350° F.) and bake 40 minutes longer or until knife inserted in center comes out clean. Makes 1 (9-inch) pie.

SWEET POTATO PIE

½ cup sugar
¼ teaspoon salt
1 teaspoon cinnamon
1 teaspoon nutmeg
½ teaspoon ginger

2 cups steamed sweet
potato, strained
1 cup milk
2 eggs, slightly beaten
½ recipe Plain Pastry

Combine dry ingredients and mix with sweet potato. Mix milk and eggs and combine with sweet potato mixture. Line pie pan with pastry and pour in filling. Bake in a very hot oven (450° F.) 10 minutes, then reduce temperature to 350° F. and bake 35 minutes longer. Makes 1 (9-inch) pie.

CHEESE PIE

1½ recipes Zwieback Pie
  Shell
4 eggs
1 cup sugar
⅛ teaspoon salt
1½ tablespoons lemon juice

1½ teaspoons grated lemon
  rind
¾ cup cream
3 cups cottage cheese
4 tablespoons flour
¼ cup chopped nut meats

Line a deep dish or pie pan with zwieback mixture, reserving ½ cup for the top. Beat eggs, add sugar and continue beating until light. Add salt, lemon juice and rind, cream, cheese, and flour; beat thoroughly and strain through a fine sieve. Pour into pastry shell, sprinkle remaining crumbs and nuts on top and bake in moderate oven (350° F.) about 1 hour or until center is firm. Turn off heat, open oven door and let stand in oven 1 hour, or until cooled. Serves 10 to 12.

STRAWBERRY ICE CREAM PIE

10 marshmallows
2 tablespoons crushed
  strawberries
Few drops red food
  coloring
2 egg whites

¼ cup sugar
¼ teaspoon salt
⅔ quart vanilla ice cream
1 Cereal Flake Pie Shell
1 cup fresh strawberries, sliced
8 or 10 unstemmed berries

Heat marshmallows with crushed strawberries slowly, folding over and over until marshmallows are half melted. Remove from heat and continue folding until mixture is smooth and fluffy. Add coloring and cool. Beat egg whites until they hold a peak; add sugar slowly, beating constantly. Add salt. Blend lightly with marshmallow mixture. Place ice cream in crumb shell, cover with sliced strawberries and top with marshmallow meringue, swirled attractively. Brown quickly in broiler or very hot oven (450° F.) ½ minute, or until tips of the meringue swirls are browned. Remove pie from oven, tuck unstemmed strawberries into the swirls and serve immediately. Makes 1 (9-inch) pie.

PEACH—Use sliced peaches instead of strawberries. Heat marshmallows with 2 tablespoons hot water instead of with crushed strawberries. Use baked Almond Pie Shell.

RED RASPBERRY—Use fresh red raspberries instead of strawberries. Use mint ice cream instead of vanilla ice cream. Do not slice berries. Garnish baked meringue with whole berries and mint leaves.

CHEESE PASTRIES

4 eggs
1 tablespoon cream
3 ounces cream cheese

⅔ cup sugar
Puff Paste

Beat eggs until light, add next 3 ingredients and beat until mixed. Line shallow muffin pans with puff pastry and bake in very hot oven (450° F.) 10 minutes. Remove from oven, fill with cheese filling, and bake again in slow oven (325° F.) 30 minutes. Makes 4 to 6 pastries.

DUTCH APPLE PIE

2 cups sifted flour
3 teaspoons baking powder
½ teaspoon salt
2 tablespoons butter
1 egg, beaten

⅔ cup milk (about)
6 to 8 juicy apples
1 teaspoon cinnamon
¼ cup molasses
3 tablespoons sugar

Sift flour, baking powder, and salt together; cut in butter. Add egg and enough milk to make a soft dough. Roll ½ inch thick and line greased baking pan with it. Cover dough with sliced apples and sprinkle with cinnamon and molasses. Bake in hot oven (400° F.) 30 minutes or until browned. Sprinkle with sugar and bake 5 minutes. Serve hot. Makes 1 (9-inch) pie.

BANBURY TARTS

¼ cup chopped raisins
¼ cup chopped dates
¼ cup chopped figs
¼ cup chopped nut meats
1 cup brown sugar
1 tablespoon flour

1 egg, slightly beaten
3 tablespoons lemon juice
1 tablespoon grated lemon rind
1 recipe Plain Pastry

Combine first 7 ingredients and cook slowly for 10 minutes, stirring constantly. Remove from heat and stir in lemon juice and rind. Cool. Roll pastry to ⅛-inch thickness and cut into 3-inch squares. Place 2 teaspoons of filling on each square, moisten edges and fold over, making 3-cornered tart. Pinch edges together, make 3 short slits in top. Bake in hot oven (425° F.) about 20 minutes. Makes 12 tarts.

Use Puff Paste instead of plain pastry. Add ¼ cup each chopped candied cherries and pineapple to filling.

CHESS PIES

1 recipe Southern Pastry
½ cup butter
1¼ cups sugar
3 eggs, separated

1 cup chopped raisins
1 cup chopped nut meats
1 teaspoon vanilla

Line individual pie plates with pastry. Cream butter with 1 cup sugar; add beaten egg yolks and 1 egg white, stiffly beaten. Blend well, add fruits, nuts, and ½ teaspoon vanilla; pour into pastry shells and bake in a hot oven (400° F.) about 15 minutes or until fillings are set. Reduce temperature to 325° F. Beat remaining egg whites until stiff, fold in remaining sugar and vanilla. Cover pies with meringue and return to oven. Bake about 15 minutes longer until meringues brown. Makes 6 pies.

VARIATION—Instead of topping with meringues, bake pies as above, cool and top with whipped cream.

COVENTRY TARTLETS

½ pound cream cheese
½ cup sugar
¼ cup butter
2 egg yolks

½ teaspoon salt
¼ teaspoon nutmeg
1 tablespoon orange juice
1 recipe Plain Pastry

Mix cheese with next 6 ingredients until creamy. Line 12 tart pans with pastry. Prick and fill with cheese mixture. Bake in a hot oven (450° F.) 10 minutes. Then reduce temperature to 325° F. and bake 15 minutes longer or until brown and firm. When done, turn upside down on sheet of paper to cool. Spread each tartlet with apricot or currant marmalade, quince or apple jelly, or greengage plum jam. Makes 12.

DAINTY TARTS

1 cup sweetened rhubarb
  sauce
½ cup diced pineapple
½ cup sliced strawberries

8 small baked Tart Shells
Whipped cream
Pineapple wedges and
  strawberries

Combine first 3 ingredients. Pile into tart shells, cover with whipped cream and garnish with pineapple wedges and whole strawberries. Makes 8 tarts.

Fill tart shells half full with Cream Pie filling. Cover with fruit and whipped cream as described above.

FRENCH PASTRY SANDWICHES

1 recipe Puff Paste   1 cup sugar
1 lemon   1 egg

Roll puff paste about ¼ inch thick and cut into circles. Dip in ice water and bake. Serve 2 of these put together with filling made as follows: Remove rind and seeds from lemon and chop lemon fine. Add sugar and egg and beat together thoroughly. Cook until thickened. This filling is sufficient for 12 pastries.

GLAZED STRAWBERRY TARTS

1 quart strawberries   1 tablespoon cornstarch
½ cup confectioners' sugar   Red food coloring
1 cup water   8 baked Tart Shells
½ to ¾ cup granulated   Whipped cream
  sugar

Wash and stem berries, mix 3 cups of them with confectioners' sugar and let stand at least 1 hour. Cook remaining cup of berries with water until tender and rub through a sieve. Mix granulated sugar and cornstarch, add to strained strawberry juice and cook until clear. If not red enough, add food coloring. Arrange whole berries in tart shells and pour hot glaze over top. Cool. Garnish with whipped cream. Makes 8 tarts.

VARIATIONS—Use 1 quart cherries, ground cherries, or gooseberries instead of strawberries. Omit coloring.

Fill tart shell ⅓ full with Cream Pie filling, cool and add berries and glaze.

GOOSEBERRY TARTS

Combine 2 cups cleaned gooseberries, a few grains salt, ¾ cup sugar, mixed with 1 tablespoon flour, and 3 tablespoons water. Heat slowly until berries break, then cool. Line tart pans with pastry, fill with cooled mixture, cover with pastry and bake in very hot oven (425° F.) 15 minutes. Makes 6 tarts.

MACAROON TARTS

Mix yolks of 2 eggs with ½ cup sugar and beat until light. Add 1 cup macaroon crumbs, 3 tablespoons lemon juice and 1 tablespoon butter. Fold in stiffly beaten egg whites. Place a teaspoon of marmalade in bottom of baked tart shells, cover with mixture and brown in a moderate oven (350° F.).

SWEET RISSOLES

Cut circles of Puff or Plain Pastry 3 inches in diameter from a sheet rolled not more than ¼ inch thick. Wet the edges of each circle for ½ inch all around, place teaspoon of any thick stewed fruit or marmalade on one side of the circle and fold the other half over upon this until edges meet. Pinch edges together, brush over with beaten egg and fry in hot deep fat at 365° F. Sprinkle with sugar and serve.

PASTRY ROLLOVERS

Roll Plain Pastry ¼ inch thick and cut into 5-inch circles. Prick thoroughly, spread with jelly and sprinkle with chopped nuts. Roll closely over and over. Place on a baking sheet with the lapped side underneath. Bake in hot oven (400° F.) 10 minutes. Brush with milk before removing from oven.

MERINGUES

A meringue is a very light, delicate preparation consisting of stiffly beaten egg whites, sweetened and generally flavored, then baked to a delicate brown.

EGG WHITES FOR MERINGUES—Use good quality egg whites so that they have no tendency to be too liquid to beat up well.

VARIETIES OF SUGAR FOR MERINGUES—The sugar for meringues may be confectioners', granulated or brown. It should be free of lumps.

PROPORTION OF SUGAR TO EGG WHITE—For pie and pudding meringues, use 1 to 3 tablespoons sugar to each egg white. For kisses and meringue shells, use from 4 to 5 tablespoons sugar to each egg white.

IN SPREADING MERINGUES over the surface of a pie, tarts, or a pudding be sure that it touches the pastry rim or baking dish all around or it will shrink away from it while the meringue is baking.

TEMPERATURES FOR BAKING—All meringues should be baked in a slow oven. For meringues on pies, tarts and puddings the temperature should be 325° F. for 12 to 18 minutes, depending upon the thickness of the meringue. The meringue for kisses or shells should be baked in a very slow oven (250° to 275° F.) 40 to 60 minutes, depending upon the size.

PIE OR PUDDING MERINGUE

2 egg whites
4 tablespoons sugar
Few grains salt

½ teaspoon vanilla or ¼ teaspoon lemon extract

Method 1.

Beat egg whites until stiff, add sugar gradually and continue beating until the mixture is fine grained and will hold its shape. Add salt and vanilla and bake as directed.

Method 2.

Add sugar to unbeaten egg whites and beat mixture until stiff. Add salt and vanilla and bake as directed.

Methods of Using Meringues on Pies, Tarts, and Puddings

These may be used in any of the following ways:

No. 1—Spread the meringue evenly over the surface, using a knife or the back of a spoon.

No. 2—Make the surface uneven by spreading in ridges or by making points.

No. 3—Make fancy shapes by using a pastry bag and tube.

No. 4—Put the meringue on by the spoonful. This is desirable for some puddings, for then it is easy when serving the pudding to have a nicely shaped meringue for each serving.

No. 5—Bake the meringue for puddings by itself. To do this, float spoonfuls of the mixture upon hot water in a shallow pan. Set the pan in a slow oven (325° F.) and bake until the meringues are lightly browned. Skim them off immediately and place upon the prepared pudding.

CHOCOLATE MERINGUES

4 egg whites
1 cup sugar

1½ ounces chocolate, melted
½ teaspoon vanilla

Beat egg whites until frothy and add sugar gradually, beating well after each addition. Fold in chocolate and vanilla. Drop from spoon onto baking sheet covered with wet unglazed paper. Bake in slow oven (275° F.) 50 to 60 minutes. Makes 12 large meringues.

BAKED ALASKA, A TOOTHSOME
TREASUURE WORTH PROSPECT-
ING FOR IN ANY COUNTRY

PATTERNS OR ME-
RINGUE MOLDS —
FLAVORED WITH
CHOCOLATE OR
FRUIT — HOWEVER
YOU SERVE IT, ICE
CREAM IS AMERI-
CA'S FAVORITE
DESSERT

AN IRRESISTI-
BLE SUMMER
SYMPHONY OF
FRUIT AND ICE
CREAM

FRENCH MERINGUES

2 cups sugar	¼ teaspoon salt
¾ cup water	¼ teaspoon cream of tartar
5 egg whites	1 teaspoon vanilla

Cook sugar and water to 238° F., or until a soft ball forms when a small amount of sirup is dropped into cold water. Beat egg whites until stiff, adding salt and cream of tartar when frothy. Pour sugar sirup over stiffly beaten egg whites gradually, beating constantly. Continue beating until cool. Fold in vanilla. Wet sheets of unglazed paper and arrange on baking sheets. Shape meringues with a pastry tube or a spoon on wet paper and bake in a slow oven (275° F.) 1 hour or longer, depending upon the size. The soft inner portion may be removed and center filled with ice cream or fresh fruit or fruit sauce may be served over the ice cream filled meringues. Makes 15 meringues. These are often called MERINGUE GLACES.

NUT MERINGUE

1 recipe French Meringues or 2 recipes Meringues (page 383)	1 cup finely chopped nut meats (walnuts, pecans, or toasted blanched almonds)

Prepare meringues and fold in nut meats. Shape into one large or several small meringues and bake as directed for each.

NUT BRITTLE MERINGUES—Use 1 cup crushed peanut brittle instead of nut meats.

DATE AND NUT MERINGUES—Add 1 cup finely chopped dates to Nut Meringues and drop from teaspoon onto wet unglazed paper. Bake as directed.

MARRON MERINGUES—Use ⅔ cup marrons instead of nut meats and use only 3 tablespoons sugar for each egg in meringue.

FRUIT FILLED MERINGUES

1 recipe French Meringues or 2 recipes Meringues (page 383)	Sweetened fresh fruit (sliced peaches, strawberries, or apricots)

Prepare meringues and bake in muffin pans, lined with unglazed ungreased paper. Bake in a slow oven (275° F.) 1 hour and 15 minutes. Remove from pans while warm and take out soft center from underside. Cool. Just before serving fill center uith fruit and top with whipped cream. Serves 15.

CUSTARDS, GELATIN AND CREAM DESSERTS

MOST desserts made with eggs, cream and gelatin, or with any one or two of these ingredients, are best served very cold. These desserts should be kept in the refrigerator when prepared in advance.

Custards

A custard is a mixture of cooked egg and milk, flavored. Starchy material is sometimes used to replace part of the eggs. Custards are classified according to the method used in cooking them; those cooked over hot water and stirred throughout the cooking process are known as soft or stirred custards—erroneously, as boiled custards; those set in hot water and cooked in the oven (oven-poaching) are firm or baked custards.

The firmness of a custard depends on the proportion of eggs to milk. The finest-grained custards are those in which the yolks predominate.

If fresh milk is not available, diluted evaporated milk or milk powder may be used with excellent results.

PLAIN SOFT CUSTARD

No. 1

2 cups milk	⅛ teaspoon salt
2 whole eggs or	4 tablespoons sugar
4 egg yolks	½ teaspoon vanilla

Scald the milk in the top of the double boiler. Beat together slightly the eggs, sugar, and salt. Add the hot milk to the egg mixture, mix thoroughly and return to the top of the double boiler. Cook over hot water, stirring constantly until the egg coats the spoon. Add vanilla.

No. 2—If eggs are expensive, modify the recipe for soft custard by substituting one teaspoon of cornstarch for one egg yolk or two teaspoons for two egg yolks or one whole egg. Make the milk and starch into a sauce and cook over hot water twenty to thirty minutes before adding any eggs.

VARIATIONS OF PLAIN SOFT CUSTARD

COFFEE—Use recipe for soft custard, substituting one cup of very strong coffee for one of the cups of milk.

CARAMEL—Caramelize one-fourth cup sugar and add to one cup scalded milk.

Follow recipe for soft custard, using this milk with caramel as part of the milk, and using in addition the full amount of sugar called for in the recipe.

CHOCOLATE—Melt one ounce of chocolate and add to it two tablespoons of sugar dissolved in two tablespoons of boiling water. Mix thoroughly. Add this chocolate mixture to two cups of scalded milk and use as the milk in a plain soft custard.

WAYS OF SERVING SOFT CUSTARD

Soft custard may be served in sherbet cups, frappe' glasses, or deep sauce dishes, garnished with whipped cream and pieces of tart jelly.

It may be poured over fresh fruit.

It may be poured over ladyfingers or sponge cake and may then be garnished with meringue or whipped cream.

It may be served as a sauce for most gelatin dishes.

It is an excellent foundation for ice creams.

FLOATING ISLAND

2 cups milk	6 to 8 tablespoons sugar
3 eggs	½ teaspoon vanilla
⅛ teaspoon salt	

Follow directions for soft custard, using two egg yolks and one whole egg. Cool and turn the custard into a glass dish or into custard cups. Beat the two egg whites until stiff and beat into them two to four tablespoons of fine granulated or powdered sugar. Drop this meringue by spoonfuls on the custard and chill thoroughly. A candied cherry or a small bit of red jelly placed on each spoonful of meringue adds to the attractive appearance of the dish.

CARAMEL PUDDING

1 cup brown sugar	¼ cup flour
2 cups milk	2 eggs

Mix sugar and one and one-half cups of milk. Scald in double boiler until sugar is dissolved. Mix flour with beaten egg yolks and the remaining half cup of milk and add to the hot milk, stirring constantly until it thickens. Remove from heat and fold in stiffly beaten egg whites. Chill and serve with whipped cream.

ORANGE FOOL

6 oranges	Sugar
3 eggs	Nutmeg
2 cups cream	Cinnamon

Squeeze and strain the juice from the oranges. Beat the eggs and add to them the cream and the orange juice. Sweeten to taste. Add a sprinkle of grated nutmeg and powdered cinnamon, and cook in a double boiler, stirring constantly until the mixture coats the spoon. Pour into glass dishes and chill thoroughly before serving.

PLAIN BAKED CUSTARD

2 cups scalded milk	⅛ teaspoon salt
3 eggs	½ teaspoon vanilla
4 tablespoons sugar	

Scald the milk. Mix sugar, eggs, salt, and flavoring and combine with scalded milk. Pour into custard cups or baking dish set in pan of hot water and poach in a slow oven (300° F.) until firm. A knife blade run into the center of the custard will come out clean.

VARIATIONS OF BAKED CUSTARD

CARAMEL.

No. 1—Caramelize one-fourth cup of sugar and add to two cups of scalded milk. Use as the liquid in a plain baked custard.

No. 2—Caramelize one-half cup of sugar. Pour into a mold or pour a little into each of six custard cups. Before it hardens, move the mold about so that the caramel will coat the sides. When the caramel is hard, fill the molds with plain baked custard mixture and bake as directed for baked custard. These custards are unmolded and served either hot or cold. The caramel melts during the cooking process and when the custard is turned into a dish forms a sauce around it.

CocoA—Substitute cocoa, made as for drinking, for scalded milk in baked custard recipe.

CHOCOLATE—Melt one and one-half ounces of chocolate and add to milk. Use in a plain baked custard.

COFFEE—Substitute one cup of strong coffee for one cup of milk in baked custard recipe.

Gelatin and Cream Desserts
ONE QUART STANDARD GELATIN JELLY

1 ounce (2 tablespoons) unflavored gelatin
½ cup cold water
½ cup boiling water
3 cups other liquid or fruit juice

¼ cup to 1 cup sugar (lemon juice requires more sugar than orange juice, and orange juice more than coffee or cream)

Soak gelatin in cold water until soft. Add to boiling water and stir over hot water until thoroughly dissolved. The object of heating only part of the water is to hasten the cooling and solidifying of the gelatin mixture. Add sugar and stir until dissolved. Remove from heat. Add remaining liquids or fruit pulp and mix thoroughly. Pour into molds that have been rinsed with cold water.

STANDARD FORMULA FOR WHIPS

Use recipe for standard gelatin jelly but leave the mixture in the bowl in which it was mixed until it begins to congeal. Then whip until it becomes light and frothy. Fold in 1½ cups fruit pulp, as prune or apricot. Turn into molds and chill.

STANDARD FORMULA FOR SPONGES

Use recipe for standard gelatin jelly with these exceptions: use three-eighths cup instead of one-half cup cold liquid; whip the congealing jelly and add beaten whites of two eggs after jelly begins to congeal.

ANY FRUIT SPONGE may be made into a delicious semi-frozen dessert by substituting cream for egg white and chilling two to three hours. Three tablespoons cream should be substituted for each egg white in the recipe, the other quantities remaining the same. Whip the cream and fold in, following directions given for egg white.

STANDARD FORMULA FOR CHARLOTTE OR BAVARIAN CREAM

Use recipe for standard gelatin jelly with these exceptions: Use one-quarter cup instead of one-half cup cold liquid and add one-quarter cup cream, which should be beaten and folded in after the mixture begins to congeal. Part cream and part whipped egg white may be used if you prefer.

LEMON JELLY

1 ounce (2 tablespoons) unflavored gelatin	2¼ cups ice water
½ cup cold water	1 cup sugar
½ cup boiling water	¾ cup lemon juice
	A little lemon rind

Combine as directed for standard gelatin jelly. Serve with cream or soft custard.

SNOW PUDDING OR LEMON WHIP

When lemon jelly begins to congeal, beat it thoroughly with an egg beater. Mold. When cold and jellied, serve with soft custard.

LEMON SPONGE

Reduce the ice water in lemon jelly to two cups. When the jelly begins to congeal, whip until light and frothy and fold in the stiffly beaten whites of two eggs. Serve with cream or soft custard.

ORANGE JELLY

1 ounce (2 tablespoons) unflavored gelatin	1 cup ice water
½ cup cold water	1½ cups orange juice
½ cup boiling water	3 to 4 tablespoons lemon juice
1 cup sugar	A little grated orange rind (may be omitted)

Combine as directed for standard gelatin jelly.

ORANGE WHIP

When orange jelly begins to congeal, whip until light and frothy. Mold.

ORANGE SPONGE

Reduce the ice water in orange jelly to one-half cup. When the jelly begins to congeal, whip until light and fold in the stiffly beaten whites of two eggs.

ORANGE CHARLOTTE OR BAVARIAN CREAM

Omit the ice water in orange jelly. When the jelly begins to congeal, fold in one cup of whipping cream beaten to a stiff froth. The jelly may be whipped before adding the cream, if desired. It makes a more delicate product.

FRUIT JELLIES, WHIPS, SPONGES, CHARLOTTES, OR BAVARIAN CREAMS

Use recipe for orange jelly, orange sponge, or orange charlotte or Bavarian cream, substituting one and one-half cups of any other fruit pulp or juice for one and one-half cups of orange-juice. If stewed sweetened fruit pulp is used, reduce the amount of sugar proportionately. Fresh raspberries, strawberries, and peaches make particularly good sponges and Bavarian creams.

COFFEE JELLY

1 ounce (2 tablespoons)
unflavored gelatin
½ cup cold water
½ cup boiling water
1 cup sugar
3 cups strong coffee

Combine as directed for standard gelatin jelly. Particularly good served with whipped cream.

FIG AND GINGER PUDDING

½ pound crystallized ginger
1½ pounds figs
2 cups sugar
5 cups water
½ teaspoon powdered ginger
½ ounce (1 tablespoon)
unflavored gelatin
½ cup cold water
Whipped cream

Cut the crystallized ginger and figs into tiny pieces. Dissolve the granulated sugar in the water, and add the powdered ginger, the crystallized ginger, and the figs. Place all in a double boiler and simmer slowly all day. The entire mass must form a soft pulp so that the ingredients will scarcely be recognized. Soften the gelatin in the cold water and stir into the mixture while hot. Turn into long-stemmed glasses and serve ice cold with whipped cream.

GRAPEFRUIT À LA ST. PATRICK

1 ounce (2 tablespoons)	¾ cup sugar
unflavored gelatin	1 cup ice water
½ cup cold water	2 cups grapefruit pulp
½ cup boiling water	and juice
Fresh mint	Maraschino cherries

Cut the grapefruit in half, crosswise, and scoop out the pulp being careful not to cut the skins. Drop the shells into cold water until needed. Simmer a few sprigs of fresh mint in the boiling water until the flavor is extracted. Follow the standard directions for making jelly. When jelly is firm, cut it into cubes, pile the cubes in the grapefruit shells, and garnish with sprigs of mint and cherries.

PINEAPPLE SQUARES

1 package lemon gelatin	1 drop oil of peppermint
2 cups boiling water	½ cup drained crushed
2 cups cold water	canned pineapple
1 package lime gelatin	1 cup dry cake crumbs
1 cup heavy cream, whipped	

Dissolve lemon gelatin in 1 cup boiling water, add 1 cup cold water and chill. Do the same with lime gelatin, adding peppermint with cold water. When lemon gelatin is slightly thickened, fold in pineapple. Pour into shallow pan; chill until firm. Fold cake crumbs into whipped cream and spread on lemon gelatin. When lime gelatin is slightly thickened, place in bowl of cracked ice and whip until thick. Pour on cream mixture. Chill until firm, cut into squares. Serves 10.

Decorating Jelly

Have the mold thoroughly chilled. Pour in a layer of jelly about one-half inch deep. Chill. When firm, arrange a design of fruit or nuts or both, dripping a few drops of jelly on each piece to hold the design while the jelly hardens. When the jelly holding the design in place has congealed, add enough jelly to cover the design and let this harden. A single design may serve or alternate layers of fruit and jelly may be arranged in this way. Each layer must congeal before the next is added.

REFRIGERATOR CHEESE CAKE

½ cup melted butter
¾ cup sugar
2 cups fine zwieback crumbs
2 teaspoons cinnamon
2 tablespoons gelatin
1 cup cold water

3 eggs, separated
3 cups cream cheese
3 tablespoons lemon juice
1 tablespoon grated lemon rind
¼ teaspoon salt
½ cup whipping cream

Blend butter, ¼ cup sugar, crumbs, and cinnamon. Press ¾ of this mixture on the bottom of a 9-inch spring form pan. Soak gelatin in ½ cup cold water for 5 minutes. Cook egg yolks, remaining sugar (½ cup) and water (½ cup) in a double boiler, stirring constantly, until mixture coats a metal spoon. Add gelatin and stir until dissolved. Add gradually to cream cheese, add lemon juice, rind, and salt, beat thoroughly. Cool, when beginning to congeal, beat several minutes with rotary beater. Whip cream and fold in with stiffly beaten egg-whites, blend thoroughly. Pour onto crumbs. Sprinkle remaining crumbs over top. Chill until firm. Serves 10 to 12.

For variety use crumbs made from graham crackers, vanilla wafers, gingersnaps, chocolate cookies, browned dried bread crumbs, crushed cornflakes or other suitably prepared breakfast foods in place of zwieback.

GELATIN BLANC MANGE

1 pint milk
1½ teaspoons unflavored gelatin

1 tablespoon water
¼ cup sugar
1 teaspoon vanilla

Heat the milk in the top of a double boiler. Add the gelatin softened in the cold water. Stir constantly, adding the sugar a little at a time. Cook over hot water for fifteen min-

utes stirring frequently. Add vanilla. Strain into molds that
have been rinsed with cold water and chill. Serve with cream.

CHOCOLATE—Dissolve one square unsweetened chocolate,
add the milk and sugar, using one-third cup sugar, before
adding the gelatin.

CHOCOLATE CREAM

6 tablespoons cocoa   3 tablespoons water
⅓ cup sugar   1 pint heavy cream
½ teaspoon salt   1 egg

Mix cocoa, sugar, salt, and water, and cook, stirring until
thick and smooth. Cool slightly and pour over stiffly whipped
cream, and beat thoroughly with a spoon. Add egg and again
beat well. Chill in refrigerator, allowing an hour and a half
or two hours for an electric or gas refrigerator and longer
for an ice-cooled refrigerator.

VELVET CREAM

No. 1

½ ounce (1 tablespoon)   4 tablespoons powdered
  unflavored gelatin   sugar
¼ cup cold water   1 pint cream
¼ cup boiling water   1 teaspoon vanilla

Follow standard directions for making the jelly. As soon
as it begins to congeal, add the cream. Flavor with vanilla.
Turn into a mold and place on ice to harden. Serve with
maple sauce.

No. 2—Use same ingredients as for preceding recipe. Whip
the cream and fold into it the dissolved gelatin and sugar
mixture. Mold.

SPANISH CREAM

1 ounce (2 tablespoons)   ¼ teaspoon salt
  unflavored gelatin   2 eggs
½ cup cold water   2¼ cups cold milk
½ cup hot milk   1 teaspoon vanilla
⅓ cup sugar

Make a custard of the egg yolks, sugar and hot milk. Add
the softened gelatin. Proceed as for standard sponge mixtures. Mold, chill and serve with whipped cream.

PLAIN BAVARIAN CREAM

1 ounce (2 tablespoons)   ½ cup sugar
    unflavored gelatin   Salt
½ cup cold water   1 teaspoon vanilla
1 pint scalded milk   1 pint heavy cream
4 egg yolks

Soak the gelatin in cold water until soft. Make a soft custard of the milk, egg yolks, sugar, and flavoring. Stir the softened gelatin into the hot custard. When the gelatin has dissolved, strain and cool. Whip the cream and fold it in as the mixture congeals.

RICE BAVARIAN

1½ pints milk   1 ounce (2 tablespoons)
Lemon peel   unflavored gelatin
½ cup rice   ½ cup cold water
¼ teaspoon salt   1 cup heavy cream
½ cup sugar   Strawberries
1 teaspoon flavoring

Put the milk and a few thin cuts of lemon peel into a double boiler. When it is hot, stir in the well-washed rice and salt. Cook until the rice is perfectly tender. The milk should be nearly absorbed, leaving the rice very moist. Add to the hot cooked rice the flavoring, the sugar, and the gelatin, which has been soaked in the cold water, and mix carefully. When the mixture is beginning to set, fold in the cream, whipped stiff. Pour into a mold and chill. Serve with sweetened crushed strawberries. The white mold with red sauce makes a charming combination.

MONT BLANC

1 pound large chestnuts   ¾ cup sugar
½ teaspoon salt   Whipped cream

Put the chestnuts into the oven for a moment, until the shell and inner skin can be easily removed. Boil the skinned chestnuts in water with the salt and three tablespoons of the sugar, until they are very tender. Add one-half cup sugar to the water and chestnuts and let stand until thoroughly cold. Remove chestnuts from this sirup and run them through a potato-ricer on to a platter, mounding it high. Save a few of the finest whole pieces to decorate the dish. Top the mound with a spoonful of sweetened whipped cream, and put a border of whipped cream around the edge of the dish, dotting it with the whole nuts here and there.

MACAROON BISQUE

1 cup heavy cream
Powdered sugar
Vanilla

18 macaroons
6 maraschino cherries

Whip a cup of cream until stiff, sweeten with powdered sugar and flavor lightly with vanilla. Stir in six macaroons broken in small pieces, but not powdered. Pile in sherbet glasses with a border of the whole macaroons and decorate with marshmallows or maraschino cherries. This is an excellent emergency dessert.

PINEAPPLE AMBROSIA

1 fresh pineapple or
  1 can crushed pineapple
½ pound marshmallows

1 cup heavy cream
2 tablespoons sugar
1½ tablespoons lemon juice

Shred the pineapple with a fork. Cut the marshmallows into small pieces, using a pair of scissors. Mix the pineapple and marshmallows and let stand on ice until thoroughly chilled. Just before serving, whip the cream and add the sugar to it. Add lemon juice to the pineapple mixture and then fold in the whipped cream. Serve immediately in individual glasses or in a large dessert dish.

FRUIT FLUFF

1 cup powdered sugar
1 cup thick cream
2 egg whites

4 cups sliced peaches or
  applesauce or berries

Add half the sugar to the cream, stir until the sugar is dissolved, and then add the whites of the eggs, beaten stiff. Place the sliced peaches in a dish, sprinkle them with the remainder of the sugar, pour on the cream mixture, and serve at once. The success of this depends upon its being thoroughly chilled when served. The cream, egg whites and fruit should be chilled for at least two hours before the dish is to be prepared, and the finished dessert should be kept in the refrigerator until needed.

FIG PUFF

1 cup cream	2 tablespoons powdered sugar
1 egg white	Chopped figs
1 tablespoon grapefruit	Maraschino cherries
marmalade	Shredded almonds

Whip the cream until thick. Beat the egg white until stiff, then combine with the cream and add the sugar and marmalade. Stir chopped figs into the mixture until it becomes very thick. Pack in long-stemmed glasses. This may be garnished by sprinkling the top with macaroon crumbs. Arrange a half maraschino cherry with radiating strips of almonds in the center of each.

CHARLOTTE RUSSE

No. 1—Line a number of small molds, or one large deep mold, with a thin layer of cake. Thin sponge cake that has been cut with a sharp knife, when cold, into two layers of equal thickness is considered attractive, but halved ladyfingers or pieces of any plain cake cut one-half inch thick may be used. Charlottes are made with and without tops, according to taste or convenience.

Fill the forms with whipped cream sweetened with powdered sugar and any desired flavoring. To make sure that the cream is sufficiently stiff, fold into it lightly the stiffly beaten whites of two eggs to each pint of cream. Keep the charlottes on ice until needed, and serve on chilled plates.

No. 2—Substitute velvet cream (See Index) for the whipped cream mixture in the preceding recipe.

MAPLE CHARLOTTE RUSSE

½ ounce (1 tablespoon) unflavored gelatin	½ cup maple sirup
½ cup cold water	1 teaspoon vanilla
½ cup scalded milk	1 pint heavy cream
¼ cup brown sugar	Ladyfingers

Follow standard formula for charlotte or Bavarian cream (See Index). Line molds with ladyfingers and fill with the cream mixture. Chill, unmold and serve.

REFRIGERATOR CAKES

GENERAL DIRECTIONS—Line the bottom and sides of a spring form melon mold or deep cake form with ladyfingers, separated and placed with the rounded side toward the pan. Place them as close together as possible. Prepare any of the fillings and proceed as follows:

Place a layer of the filling on the ladyfingers at the bottom of the form. On top of this arrange another layer of ladyfingers, then another layer of filling, and so on, placing ladyfingers on top like the spokes of a wheel.

Set in the refrigerator or other cold place and let it stand twenty to twenty-four hours. When ready to serve, remove the rim of the form, place the cake with the tin bottom on a platter, cover the top with sweetened and flavored whipped cream. Decorate, if desired, with pistachio or other nut meats, with candied cherries or fresh strawberries.

QUANTITIES REQUIRED—To encase and garnish the fillings given below, unless an exception is noted, the quantities required are as follows:

2½ dozen ladyfingers   ½ cup confectioners' sugar
½ pint thick cream   ½ teaspoon vanilla

CHOCOLATE FILLING

4 eggs   3 tablespoons water
½ pound sweet chocolate   3 tablespoons sugar

Melt the chocolate in a double boiler, add the sugar and the water with the yolks of the eggs, well beaten. Cook slowly until thick and smooth, stirring constantly. When cool, add the stiffly beaten egg whites.

MOCHA FILLING

1 cup hot milk   ½ cup sugar
¼ cup ground coffee   3 eggs
2 tablespoons cornstarch   1 teaspoon vanilla
⅛ teaspoon salt

Pour the hot milk over the coffee and let stand where it will keep hot for ten minutes. Strain. Mix cornstarch, salt, and sugar in a double boiler, add the egg yolks, well beaten, stir in the coffee infusion gradually. Cook slowly until thick and smooth, stirring constantly. Remove from heat and cool slightly. While warm, fold in vanilla and stiffly beaten egg whites.

ALMOND OR PECAN FILLING—With this filling macaroons are combined with the ladyfingers usually used.

1 cup unsalted butter
1⅓ cups powdered sugar
½ pounds blanched and grated almonds

6 eggs
18 ladyfingers
30 macaroons

Line the bottom of the mold with stout waxed paper. Separate the ladyfingers and place the halves close together on the sides of the pan, rounded ends cut off and rounded sides toward the pan. Lay macaroons close together on the bottom, flat side down. Fill the small spaces between macaroons with the ends cut from the ladyfingers.

Cream butter and sugar, add three eggs, one at a time, and stir well. Add the yolks of the remaining eggs, well beaten, then the nuts, then fold in the beaten whites. Place one-half of this mixture over the macaroons. Add another layer of macaroons and top with the rest of the filling.

Set in the refrigerator and leave for thirty hours. Serve as outlined in General Directions.

LEMON FILLING.

1 cup rich milk
1 tablespoon butter
1 teaspoon cornstarch

½ cup sugar
3 eggs
Juice of 1 lemon

Place cornstarch, sugar, egg yolks, slightly beaten, milk and butter in a double boiler. Cook slowly until thick and smooth, stirring constantly. Add the lemon juice. Remove from the heat and cool slightly. While still warm, fold in the stiffly beaten egg whites.

RICH LEMON CREAM.

5 eggs, separated   1 cup powdered sugar
½ cup lemon juice

Mix egg yolks, sugar, and lemon juice and cook over hot water 5 minutes, stirring constantly until mixture thickens. Fold gently into stiffly beaten egg whites. Chill.

PUDDINGS

THE temperature at which a pudding is served depends somewhat upon the nature of the pudding. However, soufflés must be served hot because they begin to fall as soon as they are taken from the oven; and certain others, such as the steamed puddings and baked batters or doughs, become soggy when cold.

Some puddings may be chilled almost to the point of freezing, and for these the automatic refrigerator is excellent.

Puddings That May Be Served Either Hot or Cold

BREAD PUDDING

2 cups dry bread crumbs	¼ teaspoon salt
4 cups milk, scalded	¼ teaspoon nutmeg
2 eggs	1 teaspoon vanilla
½ cup sugar	½ cup raisins, if desired

Soak bread crumbs in milk until soft. Beat eggs until light; add sugar, salt, nutmeg, vanilla, and raisins. Mix thoroughly with bread mixture. Pour into greased baking dish and set in pan of hot water. Bake in moderate oven (350° F.) 1 hour or until a knife inserted in center comes out clean. Serve warm or cold with any desired sauce. Serves 6 to 8.

Chopped dates, figs, or nuts may be added if desired.

CHOCOLATE BREAD PUDDING—Melt 2 ounces of chocolate over hot water and add this to the soaked bread and milk.

COCONUT PUDDING

½ cup bread crumbs	3 tablespoons sugar
½ cup moist coconut	½ teaspoon salt
2 cups milk	1 tablespoon butter, melted
1 egg, separated	

Soak bread crumbs and coconut in milk. Beat egg yolk and add sugar, salt, and butter. Add to milk mixture. Fold in beaten egg white. Pour into greased baking dish; set in pan of hot water; bake in moderate oven (350° F.) 45 minutes. Serves 6.

ORANGE AND RICE

1 cup rice
8 cups boiling water
1 tablespoon salt
2 cups sugar

2 cups water
1 tablespoon lemon juice
3 oranges

Wash rice thoroughly and add slowly to boiling, salted water. Boil 20 minutes, or until rice is tender when pressed between the fingers. Drain, rinse with hot water, cover with clean cloth and let stand in warm place to separate grains. Boil sugar, water, and lemon juice together for 10 minutes to make a sirup. Peel oranges, cut into halves crosswise and remove core. Add oranges to sirup and cook until tender but not broken. Place rice in a mound on serving dish. Arrange oranges around rice and pour sirup over the whole. Serve with plain or whipped cream or Custard Sauce. Serve hot or cold. Serves 6.

QUEEN OF PUDDINGS

1 cup fine bread crumbs
2 cups milk, scalded
2 eggs, separated

½ cup sugar
¼ teaspoon salt
Currant jelly or jam

Soak crumbs in milk. Beat egg yolks; add ¼ cup of the sugar and salt and add to milk mixture. Pour into greased baking dish, set in pan of hot water and bake in moderate oven (350° F.) 1 hour, or until firm. Spread a thick layer of jelly over top. Beat egg whites with remaining ¼ cup sugar until stiff. Spread meringue over top of pudding. Bake 10 minutes longer or until browned. Serve hot or cold. Serves 6.

SPICE PUDDING

1 egg, beaten
½ cup sugar
2 cups milk, scalded
1½ cups bread crumbs
1 teaspoon cinnamon
½ teaspoon cloves

½ teaspoon allspice
¼ teaspoon nutmeg
⅛ teaspoon salt
1 cup raisins
1 tablespoon melted butter

Combine ingredients in order given; mix thoroughly. Pour into greased baking dish; set in pan of hot water. Bake in moderate oven (350° F.) 45 minutes or until firm. Serve hot with Coffee or Raisin Sauce. Serves 6.

SCALLOPED PEACHES

1 cup sliced peaches   ¼ cup brown sugar
4 cups sliced apples   ¼ cup bread or cake crumbs
¼ teaspoon salt   ¼ cup water

Arrange a layer of peaches on bottom of greased baking dish. Place half of apples over the peaches. Sprinkle with salt. Add remainder of peaches and apples and sprinkle again with salt. Spread sugar over the top, then crumbs, and add water last. Cover baking dish first 30 minutes so crumbs will not brown too rapidly. Bake in moderate oven (350° F.) 45 minutes. Serve hot or cold. Serves 6.

Other fruits may be used such as rhubarb, apricots, etc.

Puddings That Should Be Served Hot
SOUFFLÉS

FRUIT—

1 cup fruit pulp   Sugar
1 tablespoon lemon juice   3 egg whites, stiffly beaten
⅛ teaspoon salt

Any kind of fruit, fresh, canned, or preserved may be used. If canned fruit is used, first drain sirup. Press fruit through a sieve; add lemon juice, salt and sweeten if necessary; heat. Fold stiffly beaten egg whites into hot fruit pulp. Pour into greased baking dish or individual molds, filling them only ¾ full. Set in pan of hot water. Bake in moderately hot oven (375° F.) 20 minutes if a soft soufflé is desired. If a firmer soufflé is preferred, bake in slow oven (325° F.) 40 minutes. Serve as soon as baked or mixture will fall. Serve plain or with whipped cream or a pudding sauce. Serves 6.

VANILLA—

¼ cup butter, melted   ¼ cup sugar
¼ cup flour   3 eggs, separated
1 cup milk, scalded   1 teaspoon vanilla

Make a white sauce of butter, flour, milk, and sugar. Add to beaten egg yolks and vanilla. Mix thoroughly. Fold in stiffly beaten egg whites, pour into greased baking dish. set in pan of hot water and bake in moderate oven (350° F.) 45 to 50 minutes or until soufflé is firm to the touch. Serve immediately with Lemon Sauce or Cream. Serves 6.

CHOCOLATE—

1 tablespoon butter	⅓ cup sugar
3 tablespoons flour	2 ounces chocolate
1 cup milk, scalded	3 eggs, separated

Make a sauce of butter, flour, milk, sugar, and chocolate. Proceed as for vanilla soufflé. Serves 6.

COFFEE—

Substitute coffee for milk in vanilla soufflé and omit vanilla.

CUSTARD—

2 tablespoons butter	2 tablespoons sugar
2 tablespoons flour	½ cup crumbled macaroons
1 cup milk	4 eggs, separated

Make white sauce of butter, flour, and milk. Stir in sugar and macaroons; allow mixture to cool slightly. Add egg yolks which have been beaten until thick; mix thoroughly. Fold in stiffly beaten egg whites. Pour into greased baking dish and bake as directed for vanilla soufflé. Serve at once. Serves 6.

LEMON—

5 eggs, separated	3 tablespoons lemon juice
⅔ cup sugar	¼ teaspoon salt
Grated rind of ½ lemon	

Beat egg yolks until light. Add sugar and beat again; add lemon rind and juice. Beat egg whites with salt until stiff. Fold lemon mixture into beaten whites and bake as directed for vanilla soufflé. Serve at once. Serves 6.

OMELET—

6 eggs, separated	½ teaspoon salt
½ cup confectioners' sugar	1 teaspoon vanilla

Beat egg yolks until thick, add sugar, salt, and vanilla. Beat whites until stiff. Fold whites into yolk mixture. Pile the mass as high as possible in a greased baking dish. Smooth the top and bake as directed for vanilla soufflé. The top may be sprinkled with additional confectioners' sugar before or after baking. Serve at once. Serves 6.

INDIAN PUDDING

No. 1

4 cups milk, scalded   ⅓ cup sugar
⅓ cup corn meal   2 tablespoons butter
½ cup molasses   ¾ teaspoon cinnamon
1 teaspoon salt   ½ teaspoon nutmeg

Scald milk in double boiler, slowly add corn meal and cook 25 minutes. Add remaining ingredients. Pour into greased baking dish and bake in slow oven (275° F.) 2 hours. Serves 6.

No. 2

6 thick slices whole-   ¼ teaspoon salt
  wheat bread   4 cups milk
½ cup butter   ½ cup molasses

Remove crusts from bread and spread generously with butter. Place bread in greased baking dish. Add salt, milk, and molasses. Bake in slow oven (275° F.) 2 hours. Serve hot with plain, whipped or ice cream. Serves 6.

Dates, raisins, figs, or nuts may be added.

OLD FASHIONED STRAWBERRY OR OTHER FRUIT SHORTCAKE

2 cups sifted flour   ⅓ cup shortening
4 teaspoons baking powder   ¾ cup milk (about)
½ teaspoon salt   Butter
1 tablespoon sugar   3 cups crushed strawberries

Mix and sift dry ingredients; cut in shortening with knife or pastry blender. Add milk gradually to make a soft dough. Turn out on lightly floured board and knead just enough to shape into smooth ball. Roll or pat lightly ½ inch thick. Cut with floured biscuit cutter or bake in large sheets or bake in muffin pans. Brush tops with butter and bake in hot oven (450° F.) 15 minutes. Split hot biscuits. Butter generously and put together again with filling of sweetened strawberries. Top with more fruit. Serve at once with plain or whipped cream. Serves 6.

Some delicious and tempting shortcake fillings are: crushed raspberries with diced oranges, sliced bananas with strawberries, raspberries and pineapple, applesauce, peaches, blackberries, cooked blueberries, apricots, etc.

COTTAGE PUDDING

1¾ cups sifted flour 1 cup sugar
2½ teaspoons baking powder 1 egg
½ teaspoon salt 1 teaspoon vanilla
¼ cup shortening ⅔ cup milk

Sift flour, baking powder, and salt together. Cream shortening and add sugar gradually. Beat in egg and vanilla. Alternately add flour and milk to sugar mixture, beating after each addition until smooth. Pour into 8 x 8 x 2-inch greased pan and bake in moderate oven (350° F.) 30 to 45 minutes. Serve with Lemon Sauce or jelly. Serves 6.

BLUEBERRY PUDDING

Add 1 cup blueberries to cottage pudding batter and bake in greased baking dish or muffin pans.

FRUIT BATTER PUDDING

Place a thick layer of fruit in bottom of greased baking dish and pour vanilla soufflé or cottage pudding batter over it. Bake in moderate oven (350° F.) 45 minutes, or until done. Any fresh, dried, or canned fruit that is not too juicy many be used. Serve hot. Serves 6.

BROWN BETTY

This pudding is usually made with apples, but almost any other fruit may be used instead of, or in combination with, them. Serve hot with cream or with any preferred sauce.

No. 1

⅓ cup butter melted ¼ teaspoon nutmeg
2 cups bread crumbs ½ cup sugar
2 cups sliced apples ½ cup water
¼ teaspoon cinnamon 1 lemon, rind and juice

Mix butter and crumbs. Arrange layers of crumbs and apples in greased baking dish. Sprinkle each layer with spices and sugar. Add water mixed with lemon rind and juice. Sprinkle top with crumbs; cover dish. Bake in moderate oven (350° F.) 30 minutes, remove cover and bake 45 minutes longer. Serves 6.

No. 2

1 cup bread crumbs	1 cup water
4 cups chopped apples	2 tablespoons lemon juice
¾ cup honey	1 apple

Mix crumbs and chopped apples and place in greased baking dish. Heat honey and water to boiling, add lemon juice and pour over fruit mixture. Sprinkle a few dry crumbs over top. Wash, core, and slice apple. Arrange apple rings over top. Bake as directed for No. 1. Serves 6.

APPLE CHARLOTTE

2 recipes Mürbe Teig	½ cup sugar
4 cups diced apples	1 teaspoon cinnamon
¾ cup chopped almonds	1 lemon, rind and juice
½ cup raisins	¼ cup fruit juice

Line greased baking dish with ⅔ of mürbe teig. Mix remaining ingredients and pour into shell. Cover with remaining mürbe teig. Bake in hot oven (425° F.) 10 minutes, reduce temperature to moderate (350° F.) and continue baking about 35 minutes, or until fruit is tender and top browned. Serves 6.

Raisins may be omitted and currants used.

Red or white wine may be used and fruit juice omitted.

PEACH PUDDING

¼ cup sugar	3 eggs, beaten
½ teaspoon salt	Sliced dry bread
½ teaspoon vanilla	6 peaches, sliced
2 cups milk	

Mix sugar, salt, and vanilla with milk and stir in well beaten eggs. Dip slices of bread into egg mixture. Line greased baking dish with bread slices. Arrange alternating layers of bread and sliced peaches to fill dish. Pour any remaining liquid over the top. Set dish in pan of hot water and bake in moderate oven (350° F.) about 30 minutes or until firm. Serve hot with any desired pudding sauce. Serves 6.

Use canned or cooked dried peaches. Or other fruits may be used if desired.

Omit bread and use dry cake slices or ladyfingers.

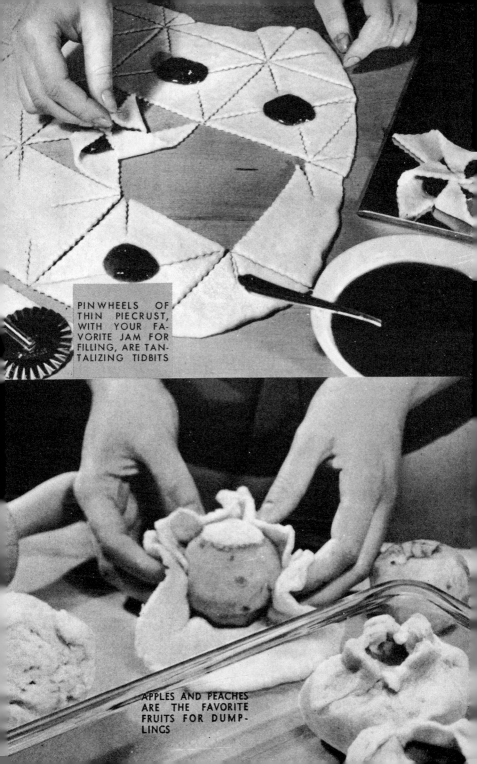

PIN WHEELS OF
THIN PIECRUST,
WITH YOUR FA-
VORITE JAM FOR
FILLING, ARE TAN-
TALIZING TIDBITS

APPLES AND PEACHES
ARE THE FAVORITE
FRUITS FOR DUMP-
LINGS

ALL DATED UP
AND DRESSED IN
WHIPPED CREAM
RUCHING, THIS
DATE PUDDING IS
READY FOR DINNER

MONARCH OF ENGLISH
COOKERY, THIS PLUM
PUDDING ALSO HOLDS
COURT IN MANY AMERI-
CAN HOMES

APPLE DUMPLINGS

6 large apples
¾ cup brown sugar
¼ teaspoon salt
4 tablespoons butter
¾ teaspoon cinnamon
1 teaspoon grated lemon rind
1 recipe Plain Pastry

Pare and core apples. Combine next 5 ingredients. Roll pastry ⅛ inch thick and cut into squares large enough to cover apples. Place apples on pastry squares and fill each cavity of apple with sugar mixture. Bring corners of pastry together at top; moisten edges and pinch together to hold apple in place. Place in greased baking pan and bake in a moderate oven (350° F.) 30 minutes or until apples are tender. Serve with pudding sauce or cream. Serves 6.

Baking powder biscuit dough may be used instead of pastry.

APRICOT—Omit cinnamon and prepare as above.

PEACH—Prepare as apple dumplings.

ENGLISH PLUM PUDDING

¾ cup sifted flour
1 teaspoons salt
¾ teaspoon baking soda
1 teaspoon cinnamon
¼ teaspoon nutmeg
½ teaspoon mace
½ pound raisins, chopped
½ pound dried currants, chopped
⅛ pound lemon peel, chopped
¼ pound citron, chopped
⅛ pound orange peel, chopped
⅛ pound blanched almonds, chopped
¾ cup hot milk
½ cup fine bread crumbs
½ pound brown sugar
4 eggs, separated
½ pound suet, chopped
¼ cup fruit juice
½ cup jelly

Sift flour, salt, soda, and spices together; stir in fruit and almonds. Pour milk over bread crumbs and let stand 10 minutes. Beat sugar with egg yolks until light and fluffy. Add suet and crumbs to egg yolk mixture; stir into flour-fruit mixture. Add fruit juice and jelly and mix thoroughly; fold in stiffly beaten egg whites. Fill greased mold, ⅔ full, cover tightly and steam for 3½ hours. Serves 12.

Use grape, plum, or currant jelly.

Steamed Puddings

To steam puddings: generously grease molds and covers. Use steamer or deep covered kettle with rack. Have water, to half the depth of the mold, boiling rapidly. Keep water boiling constantly and add more boiling water as needed. If desired, place in oven 5 minutes to dry top.

APPLE, OR OTHER FRUIT ROLY-POLY

2 cups sliced apples
¾ cup sugar
½ teaspoon cinnamon
2 teaspoons grated lemon rind

1 recipe Baking Powder Biscuits
2 tablespoons melted butter

Combine apples, sugar, cinnamon, and lemon rind. Roll dough into a rectangle ¼ inch thick. Spread with butter and apple mixture; roll up like jelly roll. Wet edges and press together so that juice will not escape. Place roll in a cloth and tie loosely. Steam 1½ hours. Remove from cloth, slice, and serve with a pudding sauce. Serves 6.

Cherries, peaches or other fruit may be used for apples.

CARROT PUDDING

1½ cups bread crumbs
¼ teaspoon salt
1 teaspoon baking powder
1 tablespoon shortening
½ cup grated carrots
1 cup molasses

½ cup chopped dates
½ cup raisins
½ cup shopped figs
½ cup ground nuts
2 tablespoons lemon juice
1 teaspoon grated lemon

Mix crumbs, salt, and baking powder together very well. Add remaining ingreditents and mix thoroughly. Fill greased mold ⅔ full and steam 3 to 4 hours. Serve with Lemon or Raisin Sauce. Serves 6.

FRUIT PUDDING

½ cup brown sugar
Cooked fruit, drained
1¼ cups sifted flour
¾ cup granulated sugar
3 teaspoons baking powder

¼ cup shortening
2 eggs
⅓ cup milk (about)
1 teaspoon vanilla

Grease a small pudding mold. Add brown sugar and arrange fruit over sugar. Sift dry ingredients. Melt shortening in a cup; add unbeaten eggs and milk to fill the cup. Add to dry ingredients and beat until smooth. Add vanilla. Pour over fruit. Steam 45 to 60 minutes. Serves 6.

STEAMED CHOCOLATE PUDDING

1½ ounces (1½ squares) unsweetened chocolate
1 tablespoon butter
1 cup sifted flour
1½ teaspoons baking powder

⅛ teaspoon salt
1 egg
½ cup sugar
½ cup milk
1 teaspoon vanilla

Melt chocolate and butter together. Sift flour, baking powder, and salt together. Beat egg; add sugar gradually and continue beating until mixture is creamy. Add melted chocolate and mix thoroughly. Add dry ingredients alternately with milk and vanilla, beating until smooth after each addition. Fill greased pudding mold ⅔ full, cover tightly, and steam 1 hour. Serve hot with Coffee, Hard, Foamy, or Marshmallow Mint Sauce. Serves 4 to 6.

STEAMED DATE PUDDING

1 pound dates
½ pounds suet
3 cups bread crumbs
¾ cup sugar

1 egg, beaten
½ cup milk
4 tablespoons flour
2 teaspoons baking powder

Grind dates and suet very fine. Mix with bread crumbs and add sugar. Add remaining ingredients and mix thoroughly. Fill greased pudding mold ⅔ full, cover tightly and steam 2½ to 3 hours. Serve hot with Caramel, Custard, Orange, or Vanilla Sauce. Serves 8 to 10.

STEAMED WHOLEWHEAT PUDDING

½ cup raisins
1 tablespoon white flour
1 cup wholewheat flour
¼ cup corn meal
2 teaspoons baking powder
¼ teaspoon baking soda
½ teaspoon salt

½ teaspoon cinnamon
¼ teaspoon each: mace. cloves, allspice, ginger
½ cup molasses
½ cup soured milk
¼ cup ground cracklings

Mix raisins and white flour. Mix dry ingredients thoroughly. Add molasses, milk, cracklings, and raisins; mix well. Fill a greased mold ⅔ full, cover tightly and steam 3 hours. Serve with Caramel or Lemon Sauce. Serves 6.

STEAMED SUET PUDDING

1 cup raisins	½ teaspoon grated nutmeg
3 cups sifted flour	1 teaspoon salt
1 teaspoon baking soda	1 cup ground suet
1 teaspoon cinnamon	1 cup soured milk
1 teaspoon cloves	1 cup molasses

Mix raisins with ½ cup of the flour. Sift remaining flour with dry ingredients. Combine suet, milk, and molasses and add to dry ingredients. Add raisins and mix thoroughly. Fill greased pudding mold ⅔ full, cover tightly and steam 3 hours. Serve with Hard Sauce or any desired pudding sauce. Serves 8 to 10.

Cold Puddings

RICE PUDDING

½ cup raisins	½ cup sugar
2 cups milk, scalded	1¼ cups cooked rice
2 eggs, separated	⅛ teaspoon cinnamon or
¼ teaspoon salt	nutmeg

Add raisins to hot milk and let stand 15 minutes. Beat egg yolks, salt and sugar until thick. Add hot milk, raisins, rice and cinnamon and cook in double boiler until thickened. Fold in stiffly beaten egg whites. Chill. If desired, serve garnished with sections of fruit. Serves 6.

RICE AND APPLE PUDDING

6 tart apples	¼ teaspoon salt
⅔ cup water	1½ cups cooked rice
4 tablespoons butter	½ cup marmalade
⅓ cup sugar	

Pare apples, core, and slice. Add water, butter, sugar, and salt; simmer until tender. Line bottom and sides of a greased baking dish with part of rice, fill with cooked apples, and spread marmalade over top. Cover with remaining rice. Bake in a moderate oven (350° F.) 15 to 20 minutes. Let stand until cold, then unmold and turn onto a serving plate. Serve with any desired pudding sauce. Serves 6.

Apricots or other fruit may be used instead of the apples.

FRUIT CHARLOTTE

Line cups with alternating triangular pieces of spongecake and chocolate cake. Fill center with slices of oranges and peaches. Chill, turn out on serving plate and surround with whipped cream and blackberries. Serve very cold topped with whipped cream.

SWEET STRAWBERRY OR OTHER FRUIT SHORTCAKE

1½ cups sifted cake flour 　　¾ cup sugar
2½ teaspoons baking powder 2 eggs, beaten
¼ teaspoon salt 　　　　　　½ cup milk or water
¼ cup shortening 　　　　　Strawberries or other fruit

Sift flour, baking powder, and salt together 3 times. Cream shortening and sugar until light and fluffy. Beat in eggs. Add dry ingredients and milk alternately, beating until smooth after each addition. Pour into 2 greased cake pans and bake in a moderate oven (350° F.) 25 minutes. Turn out and cool. Cover one layer with sweetened crushed fruit. Cover with other layer and cover with whole sweetened fruit. Top with whipped cream, if desired. Serves 6 to 8.

RENNET-CUSTARDS

1 rennet tablet 　　　　　　3 tablespoons sugar
1 pint milk (not evaporated 1 teaspoon vanilla
　or soft curd)

Set out 4 or 5 dessert glasses. Dissolve rennet tablet in 1 tablespoon cold water. Warm milk, sugar, and vanilla slowly, stirring constantly, until lukewarm (120° F.)—not hot. A few drops of milk on the inside of the wrist should feel only comfortably warm. Remove from heat. If desired, add few grains of salt. Add dissolved rennet tablet and stir quickly for a few seconds only. Pour at once, while still liquid, into dessert glasses. Let set until it thickens—about 10 minutes. Chill rennet-custards in refrigerator. Serve in same glasses. Rennet-custards may be garnished in many attractive ways by the use of whipped cream with nuts, jams, or coconut.

FROZEN DESSERTS

Ice Creams

ICE CREAMS are generally classified as cooked or uncooked. All ice creams are stirred or beaten while freezing.

PLAIN OR PHILADELPHIA ICE CREAM—This is cream, or cream diluted with milk, sweetened, flavored, and frozen. Plain ice cream may be flavored with extracts or may have crushed nuts or fruits added. Rich, oily nuts do not combine well with ice cream. Walnuts, almonds, pecans, and pistachio nuts are most often used, and crushed peaches, pineapple, apricots, or berries are particularly good for flavoring.

BISQUE ICE CREAM—This is made by adding to plain ice cream such material as pulverized macaroons, ground nuts, and stale sponge cake crumbs, to give variety in texture and flavor.

FRENCH AND AMERICAN ICE CREAMS—In these, the foundation is a custard made with cream, milk, eggs, sugar, and flavoring, cooked, chilled and then frozen. In French ice cream the custard mixture contains many eggs. In American ice cream a plain custard is used.

NEAPOLITAN ICE CREAM—This may be made of any variety of ice cream tinted in three colors and variously flavored. It is packed in layers after it is frozen. Sometimes it is made of a combination of ice cream and water ice.

FROZEN PUDDING—This is plain ice cream plus a combination of fruit and nuts with bread crumbs, cake crumbs, or powdered macaroons.

Mousses, Parfaits, and Biscuits

MOUSSES—A mousse is whipped cream, sweetened, flavored, packed, and frozen without stirring. Gelatin is often used to give body to a mousse. In that case it is sometimes spoken of as a frozen soufflé. Chocolate, coffee, maple, and fruit flavors of various kinds are used.

PARFAITS—A parfait is made by pouring a hot, thick sirup over beaten egg yolks or beaten egg whites, adding whipped cream, and packing and freezing the mixture without stirring.

Chocolate, maple and coffee are the most popular flavors for parfaits.

Biscuits—A biscuit is a yellow parfait mixture to which beaten egg whites are added. It is stirred until it is partly frozen and then packed in small paper serving cases. The cases are laid in the trays of the refrigerator or in containers which are placed in a freezing mixture.

Water Ices, Sherbets, Bombes and Punches

All these mixtures are stirred while being frozen.

Ices—A plain ice is a sweetened fruit juice which may or may not be diluted with water.

Sherbets—A sherbet is a plain ice plus egg whites. Gelatin is sometimes used in sherbets. In milk sherbets, milk, instead of water, is used with the fruit juice.

Bombes—A bombe is a combination of two or more frozen mixtures, packed in layers in a covered mold.

Punches—A punch is a water ice frozen to a mush with some highly spiced fruit juice or other flavoring added.

Sorbets—A sorbet is a sherbet made of several kinds of fruit.

Equipment for Making Frozen Desserts
The Crank Freezer

This type of freezer consists of a bucket of wood or metal for holding the freezing mixture, ice and salt, and a non-rusting metal container with a closely fitting cover for holding the mixture to be frozen. The mixture in the container is stirred by a paddle attached through the cover to a crank which is operated by hand or which may be attached to a small electric motor.

Ice Crusher—A bag of heavy muslin, burlap, canvas, or sail-cloth is required to hold the ice while it is broken into small pieces. Some implement is necessary for pounding the ice in the bag. A wooden mallet is generally preferred because it crushes the ice more thoroughly and quickly than a smaller implement. Very satisfactory mallets and bags for breaking ice can be bought.

The Freezing Mixture—One part salt to eight parts crushed ice, by measure, is a good proportion for home use. The ice should be crushed fine, to expose as much surface as possible to the action of the salt. Snow may be used instead of ice, but it is advisable to mix a small amount of water with the snow to hasten the melting process. Rock salt is best for use in freezing. Mix the ice and salt before putting them into the freezer, and fill the freezer well above the line of the mixture in the ice-cream container.

The Automatic Freezer

This variety of freezer requires no turning. The wall of the outer compartment is constructed with an air-space which helps to keep the warm air from entering and the cold air about the ice from escaping. The ice cream is placed in the smaller container, covered and packed in ice and salt in the larger container. At intervals the cover is removed and the contents scraped from the side and beaten well with a spoon or paddle. It requires the minimum amount of ice and work to do the freezing and the frozen product is of a satisfactory quality, although not so smooth as that made by the freezer in which the mixture is stirred while freezing.

The Automatic Refrigerator

For speedy freezing, the temperature in the ice-making drawer of the refrigerator must be under twenty degrees. Your refrigerator is designed to keep foods at an even low temperature, and the freezing of desserts is an extra service. If yours will not freeze them, it is possible to have a switch added which will keep the motor operating continuously during the freezing period, or the valves may be readjusted to give the whole box a lower temperature.

No one, however, should be allowed to make adjustments or tamper with the valves except the electrician sent out by the salesman.

Preparation of Ingredients

Use More Flavoring in all mixtures that are to be frozen than in mixtures that are to be served unfrozen, because the flavor freezes out to some extent. Stir well and thoroughly dissolve sugar before freezing.

Crush Fruit for fruited creams or put it through a food chopper. Large pieces of icy fruit are difficult to eat. Partly freeze the mixture before adding the fruit, otherwise the milk or cream may curdle and the fruit may settle to the bottom.

SCALDING (not boiling) at least part of the cream and milk will give greater body and finer grain to ice cream than it will have if the cream and milk are used without this preparation.

CHILL THE MIXTURE before beginning to freeze. The best temperature is about 40° F. It should never be over 60° F. If it is too warm the cream may curdle before freezing.

Freezing Ice Cream

TO FREEZE ICE CREAM IN A CRANK FREEZER, have the ice-cream container not more than three-fourths full. The turning of the crank incorporates air in the mixture and the freezing causes expansion, so allow plenty of room for "swell." Place the can containing the mixture in the freezer pail. Cover the can and adjust the top. Turn the crank to be sure that the cover fits tight. Add the ice and salt mixture as directed. Turn the freezer slowly until the mixture begins to freeze; then turn it more rapidly. This beats up the cream and produces a swell.

Ice cream takes from twelve to twenty minutes to freeze in a crank freezer. Ice and sherbets take from twenty to thirty minutes.

TO FREEZE ICE CREAM IN A VACUUM FREEZER, pack in the same manner as when a crank freezer is used. Several times during the two hours that are necessary for freezing, remove enough ice so that you can uncover the can without danger of salting the cream; scrape the mixture from the sides of the can with a spoon or paddle and beat thoroughly.

FOR QUICK RESULTS WITH THE AUTOMATIC REFRIGERATOR, take these precautions:

1. Chill your mixture well before freezing.

2. Do not try to freeze pans of water at the same time with desserts.

3. Do not open and close your refrigerator doors often or place warm, steamy foods in the refrigerator while freezing desserts.

4. Do not have the mixture too sweet or it will not freeze.

Ice cream mixtures having a heavy custard base respond very well to the automatic refrigerator. It is best to cook only the yolks of the eggs, then chill, and finally fold in the beaten whites just before freezing. This method not only gives a better texture but a greater volume to the finished product.

Refreshing and palatable sherbets may be frozen in the automatic referigerator, but they are likely to be granular even when gelatin and beaten egg whites are added.

Ice creams and sherbets, and all other frozen desserts having a custard or gelatin foundation should be very vigorously stirred one hour after being placed in the refrigerator to freeze, and several times subsequently at half to three-quarter-hour intervals.

The addition of whipped cream does much to make the texture fine and smooth. Crushed fruit, marshmallows, grape nuts, and crumbled graham crackers will also make desirable textures.

Recipes which are especially good for refrigerator freezing are: rennet-custard ice cream, maple-fruit ice cream, peach ice cream—No. 2, prune ice cream, raspberry ice cream, chocolate ice cream, frozen pudding, peach meringue, maple mousse, strawberry mousse, maple parfait, biscuit glacé, charlotte glacé, and marshmallow mousse.

In all of these recipes, except the rennet-custard ice cream, the cream must be whipped. In making chocolate ice cream, add the whipped cream when the mixture is half frozen.

Packing and Molding Frozen Desserts

Ice cream is ready for packing when it has a dull appearance, adheres to a spoon and retains its shape for some time. By thermometer test it should be about 27° F. It should be firm and mellow, smooth and velvety, free from grains or lumps and neither tough nor mushy. Ice creams and ices that are to be molded should be packed into the molds at this time.

To PACK ICE CREAM IN THE FREEZER, drain off the brine and pack the can in coarse cracked ice and salt. Use one part salt to four of ice by measure. Cover the top of the can with a layer of ice about six inches thick. Cover the top of the can with a layer of ice about six inches thick. Cover the top of the freezer with newspapers or burlap or any other covering that will exclude air. Set the freezer in a cool place and let it stand two or three hours, for the ice cream to ripen.

WHEN FROZEN MIXTURES ARE TO BE MOLDED, have the mold chilled and ready when the mixture is frozen to the point where it is ready for packing. If it is allowed to freeze too hard before it is packed into the molds, it is difficult to handle. PACK THE MIXTURE INTO THE MOLD CAREFULLY, so that all curves and corners are filled compactly without air spaces; fill the mold to overflowing with the frozen mixture and cover with a sheet of white paper.

PRESS THE COVER DOWN TIGHT and seal the crack with a thick layer of some fat that is hard when it is cold. The crack must be completely covered. Bury the mold in cracked ice and salt, using four parts of ice to one part of salt, by measure.

IN PACKING A MOUSSE OR PARFAIT, use equal measures of salt and ice and let the mold stand from three to five hours, depending on its size.

WHEN USING THE AUTOMATIC REFRIGERATOR, pack the mixture into the trays. Allow four hours for freezing until you find that your refrigerator will freeze more quickly.

PAPER CASES MAY BE FILLED with chilled or partly frozen mixtures. These may be placed in a closely covered receptacle and packed in ice and salt or placed in the trays of the automatic refrigerator.

DOUBLE MOLDING—Line the mold with a frozen mixture, making the layer equally thick in all parts. Fill the center with a mixture of contrasting color or texture or both. This mixture may or may not have been frozen first.

Unmolding Frozen Desserts

To unmold a frozen dessert, remove the mold from the ice mixture, rinse off the salt with cold water, break the seal, remove the cover and run a knife around the edge of the mold to a depth of not more than one-half inch. Invert the mold on a serving-plate. Let it stand for a few minutes and the contents will soon slip out. If it does not come out easily, dip a cloth into lukewarm (not hot) water, wring as dry as possible and wipe quickly over the outside of the mold.

Suggestions Concerning Flavor and Texture

THE AMOUNT AND QUALITY OF FLAVORING EXTRACTS used are very apparent in the finished product. Some of the flavor freezes out, so an allowance must be made for this. The flavor should be delicately suggested rather than too pronounced.

THE AMOUNT OF FAT IN THE CREAM also affects the flavor. A rich cream has a better flavor than a thin cream.

SALT ADDED IN SMALL QUANTITIES—not more than one-half teaspoon to a gallon of the cream mixture—serves to give a "rounded out" or deeper flavor.

ICE CREAM SHOULD STAND SEVERAL HOURS to ripen or blend the many flavors of the eggs, sugar, fruit, nuts, chocolate, and other substances found in the product. Each flavor may be distinguished in freshly frozen ice cream.

IF A COLORED PRODUCT IS DESIRED, only a small amount of coloring should be used. A delicate tint is all that is desired.

TEXTURE IS AFFECTED BY WHOLE CREAM, egg white, gelatin, and cooked combinations such as milk and cornstarch or flour, and milk and eggs. A smooth velvety texture is desired. Other things being equal, a richer mixture gives a smoother product. A thin cream gives a coarse texture.

TEXTURE IS ALSO AFFECTED BY THE MANNER OF FREEZING. If the mixture is frozen too rapidly, it will be coarse and have a rough texture, while a slower freezing tends to improve its texture. This smoothness is not entirely due to the rate of freezing, however, but to the amount of whipping or beating which takes place before and during the freezing. If frozen without any beating, the product will be coarse even though made from a rich cream. The air that is beaten into the mixture in freezing produces a light, smooth consistency.

A CERTAIN AMOUNT OF EXPANSION IS DESIRABLE. If ice cream is properly made, the volume increases at least one-third and the product is smoother in texture and richer to the taste than in a cream containing no air. Too rapid freezing prevents this increase of volume.

Ice Creams

VANILLA ICE CREAM

PHILADELPHIA—

1 quart thin cream   ¾ cup sugar   ½ tablespoon vanilla
Dissolve the sugar in the cream, add the vanilla and freeze.

AMERICAN

1 pint milk   2 egg yolks
2 tablespoons flour   1 cup heavy cream
2 tablespoons water   1 teaspoon vanilla
¾ cup sugar

Scald the milk, stirring constantly. Mix the flour and cold

water to a smooth paste and add to it slowly the scalded milk, continuing the stirring. When thickened, cook over hot water for about fifteen minutes. Add sugar and beaten egg yolks and cook two minutes. Strain the custard through a fine sieve and, when cold, add the cream and vanilla and freeze. This makes a smooth, rich cream.

For variation, use dark-brown sugar or maple sugar instead of the white sugar.

FRENCH

6 egg yolks   ¾ cup sugar
5 cups medium cream   Vanilla bean

Scald the cream with a piece of vanilla bean. Beat the egg yolks, add the sugar and pour the cream slowly on the mixture, beating constantly. Cook in a double boiler until it thickens, watching it carefully. Cool, chill, and freeze.

APRICOT ICE CREAM

1 pint milk   2 egg yolks
2 tablespoons flour   1 cup heavy cream
2 tablespoons water   1½ cups strained apricot
1 cup sugar   pulp and juice

Make custard as directed for vanilla ice cream. When cool, add the apricot pulp and juice and freeze.

No. 2.

1 cup dried apricots   2 cups thin cream
1 cup sugar   1 cup milk

Soak the apricots overnight and stew them until tender. Put them through a sieve. Add the sugar to the hot apricots, stirring until dissolved. When cold, add the cream and then the milk, stirring constantly. Freeze.

BANANA ICE CREAM

1 pint milk   2 bananas
1 tablespoon flour   ⅛ teaspoon salt
1 tablespoon water   1 pint thin cream
½ cup sugar   ½ teaspoon lemon flavoring
1 egg

Make custard as directed for vanilla ice cream, American (page 446). Peel and scrape bananas, press through a sieve, add salt and add to the cold custard mixture. Add cream and flavoring. Freeze.

BERRY ICE CREAM

1 pint milk	2 egg yolks
2 tablespoons flour	1 cup heavy cream
2 tablespoons water	1½ cups crushed berries
1 cup sugar	

Make custard as directed for vanilla ice cream, American *(page 446)*. When it has cooled, freeze partly; add the crushed berries, and complete freezing.

CARAMEL ICE CREAM

2 cups milk	1 cup thin cream
1 egg	½ cup macaroons
½ cup sugar	

Caramelize half the sugar *(see Index)*. Combine the milk, beaten egg, sugar, and caramelized sugar. Heat the mixture to the boiling point. When cool, add the cream and the macaroons, crushed fine. Beat well and freeze.

BISQUE ICE CREAM

Add 1 cup of macaroon crumbs to caramel ice cream.

CHOCOLATE ICE CREAM

1 pint milk	1 cup heavy cream
2 tablespoons flour	1 teaspoon vanilla
2 tablespoons water	1½ squares unsweetened
1 cup sugar	chocolate
2 egg yolks	

Make custard as directed for vanilla ice cream, American *(page 446)*, adding the chocolate to the milk when scalding. Cool and freeze.

CINNAMON ICE CREAM

Use the recipe for vanilla ice cream, American *(page 446)*. When the milk is put on to scald, add a piece of stick cinnamon about 1 inch long and 1 square of chocolate, grated. Beat the custard thoroughly with an egg beater to insure smoothness of color. The cinnamon imparts a rich, spicy taste that is as elusive as it is delicious.

GENERAL DIRECTIONS FOR MAKING FRESH FRUIT ICE CREAM

Prepare any desired fruit by sprinkling sugar over it. Let it stand one hour, press through a coarse sieve and stir into vanilla ice cream, American *(page 446),* when the cream is frozen to a mush.

IF SEED FRUITS, such as currants or berries are used, strain through a fine sieve or a piece of cheesecloth and use the pulp only. This can be put into the freezer with the cream and not reserved until later, as in the case of the mashed fruits.

CRUSHED PINEAPPLE with the addition of a little lemon juice makes a particularly fine fruit cream.

VANILLA RENNET-CUSTARD ICE CREAM

2 rennet tablets	1 cup heavy cream
3 cups milk	1 cup sugar
2 tablespoons cold water	1 tablespoon vanilla

Dissolve rennet tablets in cold water. Warm the milk, cream, sugar, and vanilla until lukewarm (110° F.). Remove from range. Add dissolved tablets, stir a few seconds; pour at once into freezer can. Let set until firm and cool. Freeze.

MAPLE-FRUIT ICE CREAM

1 cup maple sirup	1 cup crushed pineapple,
2 cups cream	fresh or canned
½ cup candied cherries	

Combine all ingredients and freeze.

MARSHMALLOW ICE CREAM

1 pint milk	1 pint thin cream
1 egg	1 tablespoon vanilla
¾ cup sugar	½ cup marshmallows, diced
⅛ teaspoon salt	

Make custard of milk, egg, sugar, and salt. Add remaining ingredients. Cool and freeze.

PRUNE ICE CREAM

1 cup prune pulp
1 cup sugar
Juice of 1 lemon
Juice of 1 orange

⅛ teaspoon salt
½ cup milk
1 cup cream

Press cooked prunes through a sieve to obtain the pulp. Add the remaining ingredients, the cream, whipped last of all, mix thoroughly and freeze.

RASPBERRY ICE CREAM

1 quart raspberries
2 cups sugar

1 quart cream

Mash the berries and sugar together, and let them stand for an hour. Press through a strainer, add the cream and freeze.

ROSE ICE CREAM

4 cups light cream
3 cups heavy cream
1 cup milk
1 cup sugar

1 to 2 teaspoons rose
  extract
¼ teaspoon salt
Pink vegetable coloring

Mix all the ingredients together thoroughly and freeze.

BAKED ALASKA

1 brick ice cream
4 egg whites

4 tablespoons confectioners'
  sugar

Sponge cake

Freeze strawberry, vanilla, and chocolate ice cream into brick form very hard. At serving time, beat the egg whites until light, add confectioners' sugar and whip until stiff and dry. Turn ice cream onto a sheet of sponge cake placed on a board and cover it completely with meringue. Sprinkle well with confectioners' sugar and place in very hot oven (450° F.) to brown. Place on a serving platter and serve at once. Serves 12 to 16.

SMALL INDIVIDUAL—Cut sponge cake into thick slices and cut out the center of each slice, leaving about half an inch on each of the four sides and on the bottom. Set these cake boxes on a board, put slices of well frozen ice cream inside, and cover with meringue, piling it up at the sides. Set in a hot

A COOL CREAMY SLICE OF CHARLOTTE RUSSE RISES TO THE OCCASION ON A HOT SUMMER DAY

SMOOTH, CHILLED MELON MOLD OF BAVARIAN CREAM IS THE FITTING CLIMAX TO A WARM-WEATHER MEAL

MORE MOLD MAGIC IN THIS SUMPTUOUS BOMBE OF CHOCOLATE AND VANILLA ICE CREAM

YOU CAN BUY THE MAKINGS FOR THIS LUSCIOUS LOAF OF ICE CREAM AND DEVIL'S FOOD

oven (400°-450° F.) for a moment to brown the meringue. Remove to a serving dish and fill the hollows on top with any preserved fruit or nut mixture.

ICE CREAM SANDWICHES

Between thin slices of devil's food, angel cake, sponge cake, or butter cake, or between halves of éclair or cream-puff shells, place a serving of ice cream of a flavor to blend well with the cake. Cover with chocolate, butterscotch, marshmallow, maple, or fruit sauce, either hot or cold, and top with whipped cream and nut meats of various kinds, moist coconut, powdered or granulated chocolate, or pieces of fresh or canned fruit.

For example: (1) Between thin slices of gold or white cake, place a slice of vanilla ice cream; over the whole pour plain marshmallow sauce or whipped cream and garnish with several tablespoons of crushed strawberries. (2) Fill a cream-puff shell with peach ice cream and pour over it a peach sirup, topped with whipped cream. (3) Place chocolate or vanilla ice cream between layers of white or angel cake and cover with a thick fudge sauce.

SUNDAES

Vanilla, chocolate or any other ice cream served in a low glass, with sweetened crushed fruit or any desired sauce poured over it, is known as a sundae. Whipped cream, nuts, marshmallow cream, etc., may be added as a garnish.

NEAPOLITAN ICE CREAM

1 pint strawberry ice cream   (Any preferred combination
1 pint pistachio ice cream   of flavors may be used in-
1 pint orange ice   stead of these)

Pack a mold in salt and ice and spread the strawberry ice cream smoothly over the bottom. If it is not very firm, cover and let it stand for a few minutes. Spread a good layer of orange ice upon it, and as soon as this hardens, spread over it the pistachio ice cream. Cover and freeze.

Frozen Puddings

FROZEN PUDDING

2 eggs
1 cup sugar
Pinch salt

2½ cups milk
1 cup heavy cream
1 cup candied fruit or nuts

Make a custard of the eggs, sugar, salt, milk, and cream. Cool and freeze. Fill a mold with alternate layers of the frozen cream and candied fruit or nuts. Cover and freeze.

MOCHA BISCUIT

1 quart milk
½ cup pulverized coffee
6 eggs

½ cup sugar
2 tablespoons flour

Put the milk into a double boiler, drop into it a muslin bag containing the pulverized coffee and let it infuse for fifteen minutes, keeping the milk at the scalding point. Beat the eggs and sugar together until smooth. Remove the bag of coffee from the milk, add the flour stirred with a little cold milk or water and cook fifteen minutes. Pour over the egg mixture and return to the double boiler to cook until smooth and thick. When cold partly freeze, then fill paper cases with the mixture and complete the freezing. Serve garnished with whipped cream.

NESSELRODE PUDDING

3 cups milk
1½ cups sugar
5 egg yolks
⅛ teaspoon salt
1 pint cream

3 tablespoons pineapple sirup
1 cup almonds
1 cup French chestnuts
¼ cup seeded raisins
¼ cup assorted fruits

Make a custard of the milk, sugar, egg yolks, and salt. When cool, add the cream and pineapple sirup. Blanch the almonds and chop them fine, then pound to a paste. Shell the chestnuts, blanch, and boil until tender. Force through a sieve, and add to the custard. Freeze.

Line a two-quart melon mold with half the frozen mixture. To the remaining half, add a half-dozen large French chestnuts which have been boiled until tender, also the raisins and the assorted fruits cut in bits. Fill the mold with this mixture, cover and pack in ice and salt for two hours, or pack and freeze in the trays of the refrigerator. This is often served in individual paper cases with a bit of candied fruit on top of each.

PEACH MERINGUE

¼ teaspoon gelatin ⅔ cup cream
1 tablespoon cold water 2 egg whites
¼ cup boiling water 1 teaspoon vanilla
¼ cup sugar Peach ice cream

Soak the gelatin in the cold water and dissolve it in the boiling water. Add sugar and stir until it is dissolved. Add the cream. When it begin to thicken, pour slowly over the beaten whites of eggs and continue beating until it is the consistency of whipped cream. Add vanilla. Line a round mold with frozen peach ice cream and fill the center with the meringue. Pack in ice and salt, and let stand three to four hours, or pack and freeze in the trays of the refrigerator.

Mousses and Parfaits

STRAWBERRY OR OTHER FRUIT MOUSSE

1 pint rich cream   1 cup fruit pulp   Vanilla

Whip and drain the cream. Mix with it the pulp of any fruit drained free of juice and sprinkled well with powdered sugar. Add vanilla, mold, and pack in ice and salt for three hours, or pack and freeze in the trays of the refrigerator.

MAPLE MOUSSE

1¼ cups maple sirup 2 tablespoons gelatin
½ cup sugar ¼ cup cold water
5 cups cream

Combine maple sirup, sugar and one cup of cream and bring to a boil, stirring constantly. Add the gelatin softened in water and dissolved over heat. Strain, cool in ice-water until the mixture thickens, then add the remainder of the cream, whipped stiff. Place in a mold, pack in ice and salt and let stand for four hours, or pack and freeze in the trays of the refrigerator.

MAPLE PARFAIT

¾ cup maple sirup   3 egg whites   1 pint cream

Cook maple sirup to the light crack stage (270° F.). Pour the sirup over the beaten whites of the eggs and beat until cold. Fold into the stiffly whipped cream. Mold and pack in ice and salt for four hours, or pack and freeze in the trays of the refrigerator. Serve in parfait glasses with whipped cream.

MARSHMALLOW MOUSSE

1 pint cream
1 cup top milk
6 marshmallows
½ cup chopped nut meats
¾ cup powdered sugar

7 maraschino cherries, cut in pieces
½ teaspoon vanilla
1 egg white, beaten

Warm the milk, add marshmallows and beat well to dissolve, then chill. Beat egg white and fold in with the sugar and vanilla. Beat cream very stiff, and fold in, together with the nuts and cherries. Pack in ice and salt or freeze in the trays of the refrigerator not less than two and a half hours.

BISCUIT GLACÉ

1 cup sugar
¼ cup water
4 egg yolks

3⅓ cups cream
1 teaspoon vanilla
Pulverized macaroons

Make a thick sirup of the sugar and water. Beat the yolks of the eggs and add the sirup and one-half cup of the cream. Place all in a saucepan over a slow fire and stir constantly until it forms a thick coating on the spoon. Empty into a mixing bowl, set on ice, beat until it is cold and stiff, and then add the remainder of the cream, beaten very stiff. Flavor with vanilla or any preferred extract.

Pack the mixture in small paper boxes, sprinkle with pulverized macaroons, and set in a covered container. Pack in ice and salt and let stand for four hours, or pack and freeze in the trays of the refrigerator.

CHARLOTTE GLACÉ

¼ cup powdered sugar	½ tablespoon gelatin
1 pint thick cream	4 tablespoons cold water
1 teaspoon vanilla	

Dissolve sugar in cream. Add vanilla. Soften the gelatin in cold water, dissolve over heat and combine the two mixtures.

Fill a cylindrical mold (a baking-powder can will do very nicely) and pack in salt and ice for two hours, or pack and freeze in the trays of the mechanical refrigerator. Turn out on a platter, surround with ladyfingers, cover the top with whipped cream and serve.

Ices and Frozen Fruits
CRANBERRY ICE

1 quart water   1 quart cranberries   3 cups sugar

Make a sirup by boiling water and sugar together for five minutes. Boil the cranberries in a little water until soft, then press through a sieve. Add to the sirup, cool, and freeze.

LEMON ICE

1 quart water   2 cups sugar   ¾ cup lemon juice

Make a sirup by boiling the water with the sugar for five minutes. Add the strained lemon juice, cool and freeze.

ORANGE ICE

1 quart water	2 grated orange rinds
2 cups sugar	¼ cup lemon juice
2 cups orange juice	

Make a sirup as for lemon ice. Add the fruit juices and grated rind. Strain, cool, and freeze.

RASPBERRY AND CURRANT ICE

| 2 cups sugar | ¾ cup raspberry juice |
| 1¼ cups currant juice | 1 quart water |

At least one quart each of the berries and currants will be needed to give the required amount of juice. Sprinkle one-half cup of the sugar over them, stir well and let stand for one hour. Strain through a fine sieve or cheesecloth. Make a sirup of the remaining sugar and the water. Add the fruit juice, strain, cool, and freeze.

GRAPE ICE

⅔ cup sugar
1 cup grape juice
¼ cup orange juice

1½ cups water
2 tablespoons lemon juice

Boil the sugar and water together for 5 minutes. Mix all the ingredients together, strain and freeze.

COUPÉ SAINT JACQUES

Fruit cup
Lemon ice

Maraschino cherries
Angelica

Fill champagne glasses with diced fruits (pineapple, strawberries bananas, and oranges). Over the top spread a thick layer of lemon ice, decorating the center with one Maraschino cherry and four leaves of angelica radiating from it.

FROSTED STRAWBERRIES OR OTHER FRUIT

Strawberries, raspberries, fresh peaches, or crushed pineapple make delicious frosted fruit. Mash or crush the fruit very fine, add half as much sugar as there is fruit and allow it to stand until a sirup is formed. Freeze in a crank freezer or pack in the trays of a refrigerator and stir occasionally while it is freezing.

CANNED FRUITS, especially pears and peaches in heavy sirup, may be frozen in the can. Pack in ice and salt, allow 2 or 3 hours for freezing, open the can and serve in slices.

Sherbets Made without Gelatin

CURRANT SHERBET

3 pints red currants
1 pint red raspberries
2 cups water

1½ cups sugar
3 tablespoons lemon juice
2 egg whites

Place currants, raspberries, and a cup of the water in a kettle and simmer slowly together for a few minutes. Strain, add remaining water, sugar and lemon juice. Dissolve sugar in the fruit-juice mixture, cool and freeze to a mush. Stir in the beaten whites of eggs. Pack and let stand several hours.

LEMON SHERBET

No. 1—With Water.

1 quart water	¾ cup lemon juice
3 cups sugar	2 egg whites

Make a sirup by boiling sugar and water together for five minutes. Add lemon juice, cool and freeze to a mush. Add the beaten whites of the eggs and continue freezing.

No. 2—With Milk.

½ cup lemon juice   1½ cups sugar   1 quart milk

Mix together the lemon juice and sugar and add to the milk slowly, stirring constantly. If the ingredients are cold, and the acid is added slowly to the milk, rather than the milk to the acid, there is little danger of the mixture curdling. However, if it does curdle slightly the quality of the sherbet will not be affected. Strain and freeze.

PINEAPPLE SHERBET

1 quart water	2 cups crushed pineapple,
2 cups sugar	fresh or canned
1 lemon	2 egg whites

Boil water and sugar together for five minutes. Scald the pineapple in the boiling sirup, and press through a sieve. Cool, add lemon juice and freeze to a mush. Add the beaten whites of the eggs and continue freezing.

RASPBERRY SHERBET

1 cup sugar	1 tablespoon lemon juice
1 quart raspberries	1 egg white

Add sugar to the raspberries, and let stand in refrigerator for two hours. If the mixture does not seem sweet enough, more sugar may be added. Add lemon juice and beaten egg white and freeze. Serve in glasses garnished with whipped cream.

DESSERT SAUCES

APRICOT SAUCE

¾ cup apricot pulp   ¾ cup heavy cream   Sugar

DRAIN canned apricots from their sirup and press through a sieve. Beat cream until stiff, add to apricot pulp, and sweeten to taste.

BUTTERSCOTCH SAUCE

1½ cups light brown sugar   ½ tablespoon lemon juice
¼ cup water   ½ cup chopped nut meats
4 tablespoons butter

Boil sugar and water together to the soft ball stage (234°-240° F.). Add butter, lemon juice, and nut meats.

CARAMEL SAUCE

1 cup sugar   1 tablespoon cornstarch
1 tablespoon cold water   1 tablespoon butter
1⅓ cups hot water   1 teaspoon vanilla

Place the sugar and cold water in a pan and stir until the resulting sirup is a clear brown, but not so dark as caramel; then add the hot water and stir until the whole is well blended. Add the cornstarch mixed with a little cold water and boil for five minutes. Continue cooking over hot water for fifteen minutes, stirring all the time. Beat in the butter and vanilla.

CHERRY SAUCE

1 cup sugar   ½ cup water
½ cup butter   ½ cup cherry juice
1 tablespoon cornstarch

Cream the sugar and the butter, add the cornstarch and the liquid, and boil over hot water for five minutes, stirring constantly. Continue cooking for twenty-five minutes.

CHOCOLATE SAUCE

No. 1

1½ cups sugar	4 squares unsweetened choco-
½ cup water	late
¼ cup rich milk or water	½ teaspoon vanilla

Let sugar and water boil in a saucepan for five minutes. Cool partly and gradually stir in the chocolate which has been melted over hot water. Add the vanilla. Place in a double boiler or in a pan over hot water until ready to serve. At the last moment, add the milk. (If to be used with ice cream, use water instead of milk.)

No. 2.

1 cup sugar	1 square chocolate
½ cup water	1 tablespoon butter
½ teaspoon vanilla	

Mix together the sugar, water and grated chocolate. Boil for five minutes. Cool slightly and add the butter and vanilla.

COFFEE SAUCE

1 cup clear black coffee	⅓ cup sugar
3 egg yolks	

Make a soft custard of the three ingredients. This is delicious for vanilla or lemon ice cream.

CUSTARD SAUCE

Use recipe for soft custard *(See Index)*. If a thinner sauce is desired, the custard may be thinned with a little cream.

FOAMY SAUCE

½ cup butter	1 egg
1 cup confectioners' sugar	2 tablespoons hot water
1 teaspoon vanilla	

Cream the butter and gradually add the sugar, the egg, well beaten, and the hot water. Heat over hot water, beating continually until it thickens. Add the vanilla and serve.

HARD SAUCE

⅓ cup butter
1 cup powdered, granulated, brown, or maple sugar

1 teaspoon vanilla or other flavoring

Cream the butter until very soft, then stir in the sugar and the flavoring. Set in a cool place until required for use. A grating of lemon rind or nutmeg, or a sprinkle of powdered cinnamon may be used instead of the vanilla. Cream or milk may be added, with more sugar to make more sauce. This sauce may be used with a hot pudding of any kind.

HONEY SAUCE

1 egg
½ cup honey
1 cup hot water

1½ tablespoons butter
½ lemon, juice and grated rind

Beat the egg, and add the other ingredients in the order given. Cook over hot water for about fifteen minutes, stirring constantly.

LEMON SAUCE

½ cup sugar
1 tablespoon cornstarch
2 tablespoons lemon juice

Nutmeg   Salt
2 tablespoons butter
1 cup boiling water

Mix the sugar and cornstarch, add the boiling water and a pinch of salt and boil until thick and clear. Continue cooking over hot water for twenty minutes. Beat in the butter, the lemon juice, and nutmeg. A grating of lemon rind may be added.

MAPLE SAUCE

½ cup water
½ cup walnut meats

1 pound (2 cups) maple sugar or 2 cups brown sugar

Add the water to the maple sugar and boil until it reaches the thread stage (230°-234° F.). Add the walnut meats broken into small pieces. This sauce is good with ice cream, blanc mange, or custard. It may be used hot or cold.

MARSHMALLOW SAUCE

¾ cup sugar   ½ pound marshmallows
¼ cup milk   2 tablespoons water

Boil the sugar and milk to the thread stage (230°-234° F.). Cool and beat until thick and white. Set in boiling water and stir until thin enough to pour. Stir the marshmallows with the water in a double boiler until smooth. Pour the sirup over the melted marshmallows and beat together. Keep warm, but not hot.

FRUIT MARSHMALLOW SAUCE

Thin commercial marshmallow whip with fruit juice.

MARSHMALLOW MINT SAUCE

½ cup sugar   1 egg white, beaten stiff
¼ cup water   1 drop oil of peppermint
8 marshmallows   Green vegetable coloring

Make a thin sirup of the sugar and water (220°-230° F.). Cut the marshmallows in quarters and add to the sirup. Pour the mixture over the egg white gradually, beating vigorously. Add the flavoring and tint a delicate green. This sauce is excellent served with chocolate ice cream.

MOLASSES SAUCE

1 cup molasses   1 tablespoon lemon juice
1½ tablespoons butter   or vinegar

Boil the molasses with the butter for about five minutes. Remove from the fire and slowly stir in the lemon juice or vinegar. This sauce is especially good with brown betty or Indian pudding.

ORANGE SAUCE

5 tablespoons butter   3 egg whites
½ cup sugar   Juice of 2 oranges
½ cup boiling water   1½ tablespoons lemon juice

Cream the butter with the sugar. Put into a saucepan over hot water and add the boiling water. Then beat in the stiffly beaten whites of the eggs, the orange juice and lemon juice and continue beating until light and foamy.

PLUM PUDDING SAUCE

¼ cup butter
1 cup powdered sugar
2 tablespoons cider

2 eggs
½ cup rich milk or cream

Cream the butter and powdered sugar. Add the cider and the well-beaten yolks of the eggs. When well mixed, stir in the milk or cream. Cook in a double boiler until it is as thick as a custard and then gradually pour it into the beaten whites of the eggs, beating constantly.

RAISIN SAUCE

½ cup seeded raisins
1 cup boiling water
¾ cup sugar
½ teaspoon lemon juice

¼ cup chopped citron
1 teaspoon cornstarch
1 tablespoon butter

Simmer the raisins and citron in the water until the raisins are tender (about one hour). Sift the sugar and cornstarch together and add to the raisin mixture. Mix well and continue cooking for ten minutes. Add the butter and lemon juice.

SUGAR BRITTLE

Stir one-fourth cup of sugar without any water in a saucepan over the fire until melted and of an amber color. Turn on to an oiled pan. When cold, pound in a mortar or in several folds of cloth. This may be sprinkled over any ice cream.

STRAWBERRY OR OTHER BERRY SAUCE

No. 1.
2 cups berries
1 tablespoon butter
1½ cups powdered sugar

1 tablespoon granulated sugar
1 egg white

The small fruits such as strawberries, raspberries, and blackberries, make most satisfactory sauce for desserts. Place the berries in a bowl, add the granulated sugar and mash slightly. Refrigerate until time to serve. Beat the butter to a cream, add the powdered sugar gradually, working it in well. Then add the egg white, beaten stiff. Just before serving, combine with the mashed berries.

No. 2—Crush ripe berries in sugar.

CANDIES

When sugar and a liquid are boiled together, a sirup is formed which grows thicker as the boiling continues. The thickness of the sirup determines the general type of candy that will result.

Testing the Sirup

The simplest and most accurate method of determining whether the sirup is thick enough for your purpose is to measure its temperature, because the temperature rises steadily as the sirup thickens.

A Candy Thermometer registering up to 350° F. is not expensive, and it will not only give you a higher average of success in candy making but will save you the time and labor that must otherwise be given to testing the sirup. A table giving the various stages of sugar cookery will be found on page 10.

If You Are Not Provided With a Thermometer, the following test will help you to determine when to take your candy from the heat.

Drop a little sirup into ice-cold water and pinch it between the thumb and finger:

Soft ball stage (for fondant and fudge) the sirup forms a soft ball which loses its shape immediately when removed from the water.

Stiff ball stage (for caramels and nougat) the sirup forms a stiff ball which retains its shape for a second or two when removed from the water and then flattens out.

Hard ball stage (for molasses taffy and soft candies to be pulled) the sirup forms a hard ball which will roll about on a cold buttered plate when removed from the water.

Light to medium crack stage (for toffee and butterscotch and hard candies to be pulled) the sirup forms spirals or threads which are brittle under water but which soften when removed from the water and stick to the teeth when chewed.

Hard crack stage (for clear brittle candies) the sirup forms spirals or threads which are brittle when removed from the water and do not stick to the teeth when chewed.

CREAMY CANDIES—Creaminess is desirable in soft candies. "Creamy" means that the texture should be very smooth, not grainy at all; soft but not sticky. This means that the sugar must not remain as a sirup, but must crystallize. The crystals, however, must be very fine, so that they can not be felt by the fingers or in the mouth.

Creamy candy should not be overcooked. If it reaches too high a temperature, accidentally, a little water may be added and it may be recooked to the correct temperature. This does not give as good a result as one cooking to the correct temperature, but it improves a poor product.

Creamy candy should be cooled before it is beaten. Beating candy while it is hot causes large crystals to form and grainy candy results. If crystals that form on the side of the pan in which candy is cooked fall back into the candy, they tend to cause large crystals to form and to make grainy candy.

A small amount of corn sirup tends to prevent grainy candy. Creamy candies made with corn sirup will require longer beating before crystallization takes place than will candies made from all granulated sugar. They also soften more quickly on standing. If too much sirup is used, the candy will not crystallize at all and the best thing to do with it is to boil it until it reaches the proper stage for a pulled or brittle candy.

One-eighth teaspoon of cream of tartar or one-half teaspoon of lemon juice or acetic acid to two cups of sugar may be used instead of corn sirup or glucose. They change part of the granulated sugar to glucose during the cooking process.

Ingredients Used in Candies

SUGARS—Granulated, confectioners', brown and maple sugar, corn sirup, molasses, honey and maple and cane sirups are all used in candy, according to the flavor and texture desired. The light-brown sugar should be chosen rather than the darker brown, for a candy of delicate flavor. The same thing is true if corn sirup or molasses is used; the lighter color gives the less strong flavor.

Brown sugar and molasses contain an acid, which if used in candies with milk causes the milk to curdle. Therefore, candy containing these two ingredients should be stirred while it is cooking. Crystallization does not readily occur here because the milk tends to prevent it.

OTHER INGREDIENTS—Nuts of all sorts, chocolate or cocoa, butter, milk, cream, egg whites and fruits such as dates, figs, raisins and candied cherries give special flavor or texture.

Butter is often used because of its flavor and because it tends to make a creamy product. Other mild-flavored fats may be used instead of butter, particularly in candies containing chocolate, brown sugar or molasses.

Chocolate contributes flavor and tends to make a smooth candy because of the fat it contains. Three tablespoons of cocoa and two-thirds of a tablespoon of butter may be used instead of one square of chocolate.

Fresh milk, dried milk or canned milk, sweetened or unsweetened, may be used in candies.

CHOCOLATE FUDGE

2 cups sugar
1 or 2 squares chocolate
⅛ teaspoon cream of tartar
  or 2 tablespoons corn sirup

⅔ cup milk
1 teaspoon vanilla
2 tablespoons butter

Mix the sugar, milk, grated chocolate, cream of tartar, or corn sirup and boil rather slowly, stirring until the ingredients are well blended. Boil to the soft-ball stage (238° F.). Remove from the range, add the butter, but do not stir it in. When lukewarm, add the vanilla and beat until it creams; that is, until the shiny appearance disappears and the fudge will hold its shape when dropped from the spoon. Spread it in a buttered pan and when it hardens mark it into squares.

MARSHMALLOW FUDGE

To the recipe for Chocolate Fudge add three tablespoons of marshmallow cream just after taking it from the heat. Beat well and pour into buttered pans.

MAPLE FUDGE

2½ cups maple sugar
1 cup cream or milk

½ cup boiling water
1 cup broken nut meats

Break the maple sugar into small pieces and heat it in a saucepan with the water. When it is dissolved, add the milk. Boil to the soft-ball stage (238° F.). Remove from the heat and cool. When it is lukewarm, beat until it creams and add the nut meats. Spread it in a buttered pan and when it hardens mark it into squares.

DIVINITY FUDGE

2 cups sugar
½ cup corn sirup
½ cup water
¾ cup candied cherries

2 egg whites
¾ cup blanched almonds
1 tablespoon almond or lemon extract

Put the sugar, water, and corn sirup into a saucepan. Stir it while it dissolves over the fire, then let it boil without stirring to the light crack stage (265° F.). While it is cooking, beat the whites of eggs stiffly and when the sirup is ready pour it over them, beating constantly. Beat until creamy, add nuts, cherries, and extract, and pour into buttered pans.

MAPLE DIVINITY FUDGE

Follow preceding recipe, using in addition one-half cup maple sirup.

OTHER VARIATIONS OF FUDGE

Brown sugar may be used partly or entirely in place of white or maple sugar. If brown sugar is used, the cream of tartar or corn sirup should be omitted.

Evaporated milk may be used instead of fresh milk. It should have water added according to the directions on the can.

Peanut butter may be used instead of chocolate, using two tablespoons of the butter to each cup of sugar in the recipe. Like butter or other fat it should be added after the fudge is cooked.

Marshmallows or marshmallow cream may be added to any fudge after it has been taken from the heat. One cup of marshmallow to two cups of sugar is a good proportion.

Any kind of broken nuts, including coconut, may be added to the fudge just before it is turned into the pan.

Candied cherries, or other fruits, chopped candied orange-peel or citron may be added. Dates and raisins are often used.

Flavoring may be varied to suit. Orange extract is good with brown sugar, chocolate or molasses. Lemon extract or lemon juice is good in a white-sugar fudge from which the chocolate is omitted.

FUDGE-COVERED DATES

Cut dates in half, lengthwise; remove the pits and lay the halves at intervals on a greased dish. Make fudge according to any fudge recipe and drop a teaspoonful on each half date. This must be done quickly, to avoid letting the fudge harden in the pan. The hardening may be delayed by standing the pan in a larger one containing hot water.

PANOCHA

3 cups brown sugar
1 cup milk
2 tablespoons butter
1 teaspoon vanilla
1 cup nut meats

Put the sugar and milk into a saucepan and cook to the soft-ball stage, or 238° F. Remove from the fire, add butter and vanilla, and cool without stirring. When it is lukewarm, beat until it is creamy. Stir in the broken nut meats. Hickory nuts, walnuts, or pecans are especially nice. Pour into a buttered pan and when it hardens mark into squares.

MAPLE PRALINES

2 cups sugar
⅔ cup milk
1 cup maple sirup
2 cups pecan meats

Boil the sugar, milk and maple sirup until the mixture reaches the soft-ball stage (238° F.) Remove from the fire and cool. When it is lukewarm, beat until it is smooth and creamy. Add any kind of broken nut meats and drop on buttered paper from the tip of a spoon, making little mounds.

FONDANT

2 cups granulated sugar
1 cup water
2 tablespoons corn sirup or
⅛ teaspoon cream of tartar
1 teaspoon vanilla

Put the sugar, corn sirup and water in a saucepan and heat slowly. Do not let it begin to boil until the sugar is dissolved. Wash down the sides of the pan with a fork wrapped in a damp cloth or else cover and cook for two or three minutes so that the steam will carry down the crystals that have been thrown on the side of the pan. Remove the cover and continue to boil slowly without stirring to the soft-ball stage (238° F.). While cooking, keep the cover on part of the time so the steam can help to keep the crystals washed down.

Remove from the fire and pour at once on large platters or slabs which have been dipped into cold water, and let it stand until it is lukewarm. Add vanilla. Stir with a fork until creamy; then knead with the hands until it is smooth and free from lumps.

Fondant is better if allowed to ripen for several days before being used. It may be wrapped in waxed paper and put into a tightly covered jar. When it is to be used for centers of dipped bonbons the centers should be shaped by hand or in molds and allowed to stand in the air until the surface loses all stickiness. Then the shapes may be dipped into the coating.

HONEY FONDANT

2 cups granulated sugar   1 cup water
⅓ cup honey   Proceed as for plain fondant.

CANDIES MADE FROM FONDANT

TUTTI-FRUTTI—Knead fondant and flavor with cherry or almond extract. Knead into it one-third its amount of a mixture of raisins, dates, figs, candied cherries, citron, orange peel, or other candied fruits, which have been chopped together. Shape into a flat cake and cut after it stands for an hour.

WINTERGREEN CREAMS—Melt a portion of fondant in the upper part of a double boiler until it is soft enough to drop from a spoon. It may be necessary to add a few drops of hot water. Color it with red vegetable coloring to a delicate pink. Flavor with oil of wintergreen. Stir until it is creamy. Drop from a teaspoon on oiled paper.

PEPPERMINT CREAMS—Follow instructions given for wintergreen creams, but leave the fondant uncolored and flavor with oil of peppermint.

NUT CREAMS—Knead fondant and flavor with almond or coffee extract. Knead into it a mixture of chopped nuts or moist coconut. Shape into balls, squares, or other shapes attractive for dipping into chocolate.

STUFFED DATES, AND PRUNES—Stone dates or prunes and stuff them with fondant which has been colored pink and flavored with rose water. A whole nut meat should be inserted with the fondant.

CHOCOLATE BONBONS—Melt very slowly a good quality of specially prepared dipping chocolate, sweetened or unsweetened, in the top of a double boiler. Do not heat the water under the chocolate above 120° F., for overheating spoils chocolate for dipping. Stir it constantly while it is melting to keep an even temperature, and after it has melted, beat it thoroughly. Keep the heat very low during the dipping process. To dip centers, use a fork or confectioner's dipper. Drop centers in one at a time and when covered place on oiled paper. The room in which dipping is done should be cool, so that the chocolate may harden quickly.

MARSHMALLOWS

2 tablespoons gelatin	⅛ teaspoon salt
¼ cup cold water	1 teaspoon vanilla
¾ cup boiling water	Confectioners' sugar
2 cups sugar	

Soak the gelatin in the cold water until it has taken up all the water. Boil the sugar and water to the soft-ball stage (238° F.). Add vanilla and salt to gelatin. Pour the sirup slowly over the gelatin, beating constantly with a whisk until cool and thick. Butter a shallow pan slightly and dust with confectioners' sugar. Turn the marshmallow mixture into the pan and smooth the top evenly. Dust with confectioners' sugar. Let it stand overnight. In the morning cut it into small squares and roll in confectioners' sugar.

VARIATIONS FOR MARSHMALLOWS

Chopped nuts, dates, figs, raisins, or candied cherries may be added to the recipe for marshmallows. Plain marshmallows may be rolled in coconut before being rolled in sugar, or they may be dipped in melted chocolate. Marshmallows may be tinted any desired color.

CARAMELS

Vanilla—

2 cups sugar
½ cup corn sirup
½ cup milk
1 teaspoon vanilla

4 tablespoons butter
1 cup cream or evaporated
milk

Cook the ingredients, except the vanilla, to the stiff-ball stage, or 246° F. Remove from the fire, add the vanilla and pour into a buttered pan. When it is cold, turn it out of the pan and cut it into squares.

Chocolate—Use the same ingredients as for vanilla caramels but reduce the cream or evaporated milk to one-half cup and add three squares of chocolate. Break the chocolate in small pieces, add to the other ingredients and proceed as for vanilla caramels.

MOLASSES TAFFY

2 cups molasses
1 cup granulated sugar
¾ cup water
⅛ teaspoon soda

4 tablespoon butter or
other fat
½ teaspoon vanilla

Cook the molasses, sugar and water slowly to the hard-ball stage (260° F.) stirring during the latter part of the cooking to prevent its burning. Remove from the fire, add the fat, soda and vanilla and stir enough to mix. Pour into a greased pan and, when cool enough to handle, pull it until it becomes light in color. Stretch it into a long rope and cut with scissors into small pieces.

WHITE TAFFY

2 cups granulated sugar
½ cup water
1 teaspoon glycerin

2½ tablespoons vinegar
1 teaspoon lemon or
vanilla extract

Boil the sugar, water, glycerin, and vinegar to the hard-ball stage (260° F.). Add flavoring. Pour on to a greased platter. When cool enough to handle, pull until very white, stretch into a long rope, and cut into short pieces.

NOUGAT

2 cups sugar
⅓ cup corn sirup
1 cup water
4 egg whites

1 teaspoon vanilla
1½ cups nut meats
½ cup candied cherries

Boil together half of the sugar, half of the water and half of the corn sirup to the stiff-ball stage (246°-250° F.). Remove the sirup from the heat and pour it slowly over the well-beaten whites and continue beating until it is cool. While beating, cook the remaining half of the ingredients to the stiff-ball stage. Remove and add at once to the first mixture, beating while adding. When cool, add the vanilla, nut meats and candied cherries and pour into buttered pans. Smooth over the surface and let it stand overnight before cutting. In the morning, cut and wrap in waxed paper.

BUTTERSCOTCH

1 cup granulated sugar
1 cup brown sugar
¼ cup light corn sirup

1 cup water
⅓ cup butter
1 teaspoon vanilla

Put sugar, sirup, and water into a saucepan and set over direct heat. Stir until the sugar is dissolved, then cook without stirring to the stiff ball stage (250° F.). Add butter and cook to the medium-crack stage (280° F.), for soft butterscotch, or to the hard-crack stage (300° F.) for brittle candy. Remove from heat, add the flavoring, and pour on a greased slab. Mark while still warm and when cold break into pieces.

MAPLE SCOTCH

1 cup maple sugar
½ cup water

1 teaspoon vinegar
4 tablespoons butter

Boil together the maple sugar, water, and vinegar to the stiff-ball stage (246° F.). Then add the butter and cook to the medium-crack stage (280° F.). Turn into a well-buttered pan. Mark while still warm, and when cold break into pieces.

POPCORN BALLS

No. 1.

3 quarts popped corn	1 cup water
1 cup sugar	¼ teaspoon salt
⅓ cup white corn sirup	1 teaspoon lemon or vanilla

Discard all imperfect kernels and put the popped corn into a large pan. Cook sugar, sirup, and water to the medium-crack stage (280° F.). Add flavoring and salt. Pour over the corn, stirring with a spoon so that all kernels will be evenly coated. Shape the corn into balls, lay on waxed paper, and wrap in waxed paper.

No. 2.

3 quarts popped corn	⅔ cup water
1 cup honey	2 tablespoons butter
1 cup sugar	¼ teaspoon salt

Proceed as for No. 1.

MAPLE NUT BRITTLE

1 cup light brown sugar	1 teaspoon vanilla
1 cup maple sugar	¼ teaspoon salt
½ cup water	1 cup broken nut meats
2 tablespoons butter	

Boil the sugar and water to the stiff-ball stage (246° F.). Add butter and cook to the brittle stage (290°-300° F.). Add the vanilla and salt and pour over the nut meats, which have been placed on a buttered pan. When cold, break into pieces.

PEANUT BRITTLE

2 cups granulated sugar	1 teaspoon salt
2 cups chopped peanuts	

Put the sugar into a skillet and heat slowly, stirring constantly, until the sugar is melted and turns a light brown color (slightly above 300° F.). Spread the chopped peanuts in a buttered pan, sprinkle them with the salt, warm the pan slightly and pour the melted sugar over the peanuts.

TURKISH DELIGHT

3 tablespoons gelatin
2 cups sugar
½ cup cold water
Grated rind and juice of
  1 orange

½ cup hot water
Grated rind and juice of
  1 lemon
Red or green coloring

Soften gelatin in cold water. Combine sugar and hot water and heat to boiling. Add gelatin and simmer 20 minutes. Add citrus juice and rind and red or green coloring. Strain into loaf pan. The pan should be large enough so that mixture is ½ to 1 inch deep. Add chopped nuts if desired. Chill until firm.

When it is cold, turn it on to a board. Cut into cubes or other shapes and roll in confectioners' sugar.

If you prefer other flavors, such as peppermint, wintergreen and clove, omit the fruit juice and rind, add one-half cup of water, and flavor with a few drops of oil of peppermint, oil of wintergreen, oil of cloves, etc.

COCONUT BALLS

2 cups sugar
⅔ cup water
½ teaspoon vanilla

3 egg whites
2 cups moist coconut

Boil the sugar and water together to the soft-ball stage (238° F.). Add the vanilla and pour it slowly over the stiffly beaten whites of the eggs beating constantly until light and foamy. Stir in the coconut and drop on buttered pans by teaspoonfuls. Shape each confection like a ball. Bake in a slow oven (300° F.) for about twenty minutes.

MARZIPAN

2 egg whites
1 cup almond paste
½ teaspoon lemon or vanilla

1 cup confectioners' sugar,
more or less

Beat the egg whites and mix with the almond paste. Add the flavoring and enough sugar to make the mixture stiff enough to handle. After it has stood overnight, it may be molded into small shapes of fruits or vegetables such as pears, apples or carrots and colored with vegetable colors, or it may be cut into small pieces and dipped in chocolate or other coating, or used as the center for candied cherries, dates, prunes, etc.

The almond paste may be bought at a confectioner's, or the almonds may be blanched and pounded. Two and two-thirds cups shelled almonds make one cup of paste.

STUFFED SPICED PRUNES

½ pound prunes   ⅛ teaspoon grated nutmeg
½ cup sugar   ½ teaspoon cinnamon
⅛ cup corn sirup   5 allspice berries
⅛ cup water   ⅛ teaspoon maple flavoring
3 to 6 cloves   Chopped nut meats

Soak the prunes overnight, after washing them thoroughly. Drain off the water; add the sugar, sirup, water, spices, and flavoring and simmer slowly until the sirup is all absorbed by the prunes. Cut a slit along one side of each prune, slip out the stone and fill the cavities with chopped nut meats moistened with a little sirup or with cream. Roll in confectioners' sugar.

TUTTI-FRUTTI CANDY

1 pound raisins   1 pound figs
¾ pound walnut meats   ½ pound prunes
1 pound dates   Confectioners' sugar

Soak the prunes overnight. Steam until they are soft and remove stones. Wash the figs, and steam them twenty minutes. Wash the dates and remove the stones. Put the fruit and nuts through a food chopper. Put confectioners' sugar on the board and with the hands work the fruit and nuts until well blended. Roll to about one-quarter inch thick, using the sugar to dredge the board and rolling pin. Cut in any desired shape, roll in sugar, pack in layers in a tin box, using waxed paper between the layers.

HOLIDAY COCONUT BALLS

⅓ cup corn sirup   ¼ cup currants
¼ teaspoon maple   ½ cup raisins
flavoring   1 cup moist coconut

Stir the ingredients together to make a stiff loaf. Pack in a small cake-tin. Chill in the refrigerator and roll into small balls. Dust with confectioners' sugar.

BEVERAGES

Methods of Making Coffee

For weak coffee, use 1 level tablespoon coffee to 1 cup water.
For medium coffee, use 2 level tablespoons coffee to 1 cup water.
For strong coffee, use 3 level tablespoons coffee to 1 cup water.

FILTERED OR DRIP COFFEE—There are many coffee pots on the market for making filtered coffee. They all contain some sort of a strainer which allows the water to drip through the coffee very slowly. Pulverized coffee should be used for this method. Place the coffee in the strainer and pour boiling hot water over it. If the infusion is not strong enough, refilter it. Serve immediately. Glass tricolators of oven glass ware are excellent for making filtered coffee, as they hold the heat well.

BOILED COFFEE—Put the coffee into the pot with the white of an egg or some egg shells and a little cold water and stir all together thoroughly. Pour boiling water over it and place on the stove. Cover the spout of the coffee pot or stuff it with paper to preserve the aroma. As soon as it boils up, reduce the heat and allow it to settle. A quarter of a cup of cold water poured in will cause the coffee to settle more quickly. Do not allow it to become muddy by careless pouring. To avoid this, decant it into a hot serving pot.

PERCOLATED COFFEE—Use the correct size percolator for the number to be served. Measure fresh running cold water into pot to same number of cups. Measure coffee, finely ground or pulverized, into the basket, using 1 heaping tablespoon to cup of water. Use medium heat or flame until percolating begins, then lower flame and continue for 8 to 10 minutes, when the liquid in the glass cap is light brown or deep amber. Serve at once. Prolonged percolating dissipates the fine aroma and flavor.

AFTER-DINNER COFFEE

The best after-dinner coffee is made with a filter. If really black coffee is desired, use three tablespoons of finely ground coffee to each cup of freshly boiled water. Wet the strainer in cold water before adding the coffee. Pour the boiling water slowly upon the coffee, and leave the pot over the heat while the water is finding its way through the fine grains and absorbing their flavor. When all the liquid has dripped through, the coffee is done and should be served at once.

VIENNA COFFEE

Make after-dinner coffee and serve in demitasses topped with stiffly whipped cream. Sugar may be used if desired. This style coffee is best suited to afternoon or evening service, although it is adapted for after-dinner service as well. Serve with small cakes.

CAFE AU LAIT

Make medium or strong coffee by the drip or percolator method and while it is being prepared scald an equal amount of fresh milk. Pour the coffee and hot milk together into the cups in equal amounts, one pot in each hand.

TURKISH COFFEE

Use finely pulverized coffee. Mix one tablespoon of coffee for each demitasse with an equal amount of granulated sugar. When the water is boiling briskly, add the coffee, and when it looks frothy remove from the fire. In a moment or two, boil it up again and repeat a third time. It should be thick and foamy. Serve at once, without cream, as the last course at dinner or luncheon or as a refreshment in the evening with small cakes. It is too strong to serve in cups any larger than demitasse.

ICED COFFEE

Make coffee of desired strength—it should be fairly strong, as the ice dilutes it. Cool it and serve in tall glasses with cracked ice; or pour the hot coffee over cracked ice, in glasses, adding more ice if needed. Top the glass with whipped cream or vanilla ice cream. Cream may be poured on the ice before the coffee is added, and the coffee may then be topped with whipped cream.

Tea

A cup of tea with its delicately fascinating aroma is one of the most delicious beverages.

Storing Tea

Tea will absorb moisture and odors, and the volatile oil, to which it owes much of its flavor, will evaporate. Store tea, therefore, in tightly covered cans and in a cool place.

Best Method of Making Tea

Glass or earthenware pots are by all means to be preferred in making tea; avoid metal if the best flavor is desired.

THE QUALITY OF DRY TEA TO USE to 1 cup of water varies with the grade of tea and the strength desired. In general 1 teaspoon of tea to a cup gives good results.

THE METHOD OF MAKING is simple but important. Heat pot by filling with boiling water. Empty. Add tea leaves and freshly boiling water. Cover and allow it to brew for 3 to 5 minutes in warm place. Remove tea container or pour off the liquid into another warm pot or into cups. Serve at once. Do not boil tea while brewing or attempt to re-use leaves.

TEA MAY BE PUT IN A TEA BALL or a muslin bag and taken out when sufficiently steeped. These containers should be not more than half full, to allow the tea leaves room to swell.

MAKING TEA IN A CUP with the aid of a tea ball or strainer is not to be encouraged, as the tea does not steep long enough and the flavor and aroma are dissipated.

TEA MAY BE SERVED WITH SUGAR, cream or milk, lemon, cloves, candied cherries, orange peel, or rose leaves and mint. Black teas are best to serve with cream.

ICED TEA

METHOD 1—Make hot tea double strength by using twice as many tea leaves as usual for each cup of water. Brew as usual and pour into glasses or pitcher filled with ice cubes.

METHOD 2—Make hot tea regular strength. Brew as usual and pour over tea cubes made by freezing regular strength tea in refrigerator trays.

METHOD 3—Make hot tea regular strength. Brew as usual and cool. Add a little ice to chill and serve.

MATE

Maté is a beverage similar to tea, made from the roasted leaves of a South American tree. It has a refreshing and stimulating effect similar to that of tea and coffee but contains less caffeine and tannin and has no astringent qualities. The flavor is heavier than tea with a floral bouquet.

PREPARE MATÉ like tea, using only an earthenware or glass container for brewing. Let steep 5 minutes, then remove leaves at once. Do not boil. Strain and serve. Sugar, cream, lemon, or crushed mint leaves may be served with maté if desired.

ICED MATÉ may be prepared like iced tea.

Chocolate and Cocoa

CHOCOLATE is made from cocoa beans that are ground under pressure. It is sold in the unsweetened form, such as we commonly use for a beverage, and also sweetened and flavored. If chocolate is stored in a warm room, the fat known as cocoa butter will melt and come to the surface, and when it hardens will give the chocolate a gray look, because the fat is practically white. The cake of chocolate, however, is as good to use as ever. The instantaneous chocolates found on the market are combinations of cocoa, flavoring, sugar and often milk powder.

COCOA is the ground bean from which part of the fat has been extracted. It should be a rich reddish brown in color. If it is very dark, it is usually because it has been artificially colored or made from imperfectly cleansed beans or those of a poor quality.

Cocoa is a valuable food and is an excellent medium by which to introduce milk into the diet. Because it contains a stimulant, it is best to use a minimum of cocoa and a maximum of milk when giving it to children.

Cocoa preparations, in which cocoa, sugar, powdered milk, and malt are used, make quickly prepared beverages.

The method of making all beverages containing cocoa is based on the fact that cocoa is rich in starch; therefore cocoa boiled for five minutes has a much better flavor than that which is made by simply adding it to scalded milk, because cooking improves the flavor of all starches.

COCOA

2 to 3 tablespoons cocoa	1 to 2 tablespoons sugar
½ cup water	⅛ teaspoon salt
1 quart milk	

Stir cocoa, sugar, and either hot or cold water together and boil over the fire for five minutes; add salt. Scald the milk in a double boiler; add to the cocoa mixture and stir until well blended. Or, add cold milk to the cocoa mixture after boiling for five minutes and let it stand over hot water until hot and well blended. Beat with a rotary beater to make foamy before serving. Whipped cream or marshmallows may be served with cocoa.

CHOCOLATE

2 squares unsweetened chocolate	3 tablespoons sugar
	3 tablespoons water
4 cups milk	

Scrape the chocolate fine, mix it with the water and heat over hot water until the chocolate is melted. Bring the milk to the scalding point (in a double boiler), add the chocolate and the sugar, stir until dissolved and whip with a rotary beater until the beverage is light and frothy.

ICED CHOCOLATE

Make chocolate or cocoa as usual; cool and serve in tall glasses with chopped ice; top with sweetened whipped cream.

RECEPTION CHOCOLATE

1 quart milk	½ cup sugar
½ cup cocoa	½ teaspoon vanilla
¼ cup flour	⅛ teaspoon salt
1 quart water	

Mix dry ingredients and make a smooth paste with some of the water. Pour on the remainder of the water and boil slowly for fifteen minutes. Combine with the milk, bring to the boiling point. Add vanilla. Serve with whipped cream. This is a very thick, rich cocoa which is improved by standing over hot water an hour or more.

SUGAR SIRUP

4 cups sugar   4 cups water

Boil sugar and water together for ten minutes. Pour into clean hot jars and seal. This sirup may be kept on hand and used as needed.

LEMONADE

No. 1.

6 lemons   3 cups water   1 to 1½ cups sugar sirup

Squeeze the juice from the fruit. Mix well with the sirup and water. Serve very cold.

No. 2.

6 lemons   4 cups water   ½ to ⅔ cup sugar

Squeeze the juice from the lemons and mix with the water and sugar. See that the sugar is well dissolved.

VARIATIONS OF LEMONADE

APPLE LEMONADE—Wash apples and dice, using everything, including skin and core. Cook with enough water to cover, strain through a cloth and add one cup sugar for each cup of juice thus obtained. Dissolve sugar in the juice and cool. Fill glasses half full of this apple sirup, add to each glass the juice of half a lemon and fill up with ice and water.

BERRY LEMONADE—To each glass of lemonade add two tablespoons of crushed fresh or canned berries—strawberries, raspberries, blackberries, loganberries, or blueberries. Seedy fruits should be strained. Garnish with whole berries and serve with crushed ice.

CURRANT LEMONADE—

1 cup sugar   1 cup water
4 cups currants   Lemons

Cook the sugar with the currants until the fruit is soft. Add the water, strain and cool. Allow one-half lemon and one-half glass of currant sirup for each serving. Fill glasses with ice and water.

EGG LEMONADE, No. 1—For each glass use one beaten egg;

add the juice of one lemon and one-fourth teaspoon nutmeg. Fill glass with chilled water; shake well and serve.

No. 2—Into a tall glass half full of crushed ice put a spoonful of chopped fruit, pineapple, peaches or crushed berries. Beat in an egg, add juice of one lemon, and sugar to taste. Fill glass with plain or effervescent water and shake or stir until very cold.

LEMON FROST—Fill a tall glass one-fourth full of cracked ice, add lemonade fill the glass three-fourths full and frost the top with a spoonful of stiffly beaten egg white sweetened slightly and flavored with lemon juice.

LEMON GINGER—For each glass allow two tablespoons ginger sirup, the juice of one-half lemon and two tablespoons pineapple juice. Fill with cracked ice and water.

LEMON MINT—For each glass squeeze the juice of one lemon over six or seven crushed mint leaves. Sweeten to taste and add chopped ice, and water to fill the glass.

PINEAPPLE LEMONADE—

1 pineapple	1 cup sugar
1 quart boiling water	1 cup tea infusion
1 lemon	

Wash, slice, and pare the pineapple, and take out all the eyes. Prepare the tender part to serve. Put the core, the rind and the grated rind of the lemon in a kettle and pour on the boiling water. Cover and simmer for half an hour. Strain through cheese cloth. Add sugar, tea, and lemon juice. Serve cold. As some pineapples are much more sour than others, more sugar may be necessary.

LIMEADE

Limeade is made in the same way as lemonade, using limes instead of lemons and a little more sweetening. This is even more refreshing than lemonade in summer.

ORANGEADE

4 oranges	1 to 1½ cups sirup
1 lemon	3 cups water

Follow directions for lemonade given on the *preceding page*.

PINEAPPLE ORANGEADE

4 oranges   1 quart boiling water
1 pineapple   Sugar or sirup

Add the juicy parts of the pineapple, shredded, to the orange juice. Pour the water over the fruit and sweeten to taste. Cover and set aside to cool. Strain and serve iced. Blood oranges will give the mixture an attractive pink color.

MIXED FRUIT PUNCH

No. 1.

1 quart blue grape juice   Sugar or sirup to taste
1 pint white grape juice   2 quarts ginger ale
Juice of 12 oranges   1 pint charged water
Juice of 12 lemons

Mix fruit and sugar or sirup. Add ginger ale and charged water and serve with chopped ice. This will serve twenty-five people.

No. 2.

1½ cups water   Juice of 6 lemons
1½ cups sugar   Juice of 6 oranges
1 quart grape juice   1 pint tea
2 quarts chilled water   1 pint grated pineapple

Boil water and sugar ten minutes. Cool and add other ingredients and let stand one hour. Add chilled water and serve with chipped ice. This will serve twenty-five people.

No. 3.

2 cups water   1 cup white grapes
2 cups sugar   1 cup maraschino cherries
1 cup pineapple   Juice of 6 oranges
1 cup strawberries   Juice of 6 lemons
1 cup raspberries   2 quarts charged water
1 cup bananas

Boil water and sugar ten minutes. Cool and add crushed fruit and fruit juice. Chill. Add charged water just before serving. This will serve twenty-five people.

GINGER ALE PUNCH

Juice of 4 lemons
1 pint grape juice

Sugar or sirup to taste
1 quart ginger ale

Mix fruit juices and sugar or sirup. Just before serving, add ginger ale.

GINGER PUNCH

1 quart water
1 cup sugar
¾ cup chopped Canton ginger

¼ cup ginger sirup
1 cup orange juice
¼ cup lemon juice
1 quart charged water

Boil water, sugar, ginger, and ginger sirup for twenty minutes. Cool. Add fruit juices and charged water gradually.

GRAPE JUICE PUNCH

1 cup sugar sirup
1 pint water
Juice of 3 lemons

Juice of 1 orange
1 pint grape juice

Mix ingredients in order given. Chill and serve.

LEMON PUNCH

Juice of 6 lemons
Juice of 3 oranges
1 quart water

½ cup mashed strawberries
½ cup crushed pineapple

Mix fruit juice, sweeten to taste with sirup, add water and crushed fruit. Garnish with very thin slices of orange.

PARADISE ISLAND PUNCH

½ cup sirup
1 quart pineapple juice
Juice of 2 oranges
Juice of 1 lemon

Juice of ½ grapefruit
½ cup crushed pineapple
½ cup crushed strawberries

Proceed as for lemon punch.

RASPBERRY PUNCH

1 lemon
1 cup raspberries
1 cup currants

1 pint boiling water
1 cup sugar
1 cup tea infusion

Crush fruit and strain through a cloth. Without taking the pulp from the cloth, put it into another dish and pour the boiling water over it. Drain off, but do not squeeze or it will be muddy. Add the sugar and stir until it is dissolved. Cool thoroughly before adding the fruit juice and tea.

VERANDA PUNCH

Juice of 3 lemons   1 cup tea infusion
Juice of 2 oranges   1 pint ginger ale
½ cup sugar sirup   1 pint charged water

Mix fruit juice and sugar sirup. Add the hot tea. Cool, and, when ready to serve, add ginger ale and charged water. Thin slices of lemon and orange may be used for a garnish.

LOGANBERRY COCKTAIL

2 cups loganberry juice   1 cup water
1 cup orange juice   ¼ cup sirup
Juice of 1 lemon

Proceed as in lemon punch.

MOCK CLARET CUP

Small stick of cinnamon bark   1 cup currant juice
3 lemons   Sugar sirup
5 oranges   ¼ cup currants
1 pint water   1 cup tea infusion

Boil cinnamon, lemon rinds and orange rinds in the water for ten minutes. Strain, and when cool add other ingredients including the juice of the lemons and oranges. Serve in a tall glass and garnish with currants.

CHILLED GRAPE JUICE

Wash purple grapes and boil until skin, pulp and seeds separate. Press through jelly bag and to every pint of juice add one-half cup of sugar. Boil for twenty minutes, chill and serve with shaved ice.

GRAPE JUICE HIGHBALL

Use Niagara grapes. Proceed as for recipe for chilled grape juice. Serve in tall glasses half filled with shaved ice and add an equal quantity of charged water. Lemon is an attractive addition.

DESIGN FOR EATING . . BRUSSELS SPROUTS IN CHICKEN RING MOLD FLANKED WITH WHOLE CARROTS AND ACCENTS OF PARSLEY AND PIMIENTO

WHOLE BOILED SQUASH SERVED ON A PARSLEY BED, RINGED WITH TOMATO AND CUCUMBER SLICES

FRENCH DISHES EN CASSEROLE
—RECHAUFFE OF LAMB

OR SAUSAGES AND
CORN AU GRATIN

WINE SEASONS FINE FOOD

COURT BOUILLON

1½ cups boiling water
½ cup white wine (dry)
¼ teaspoon salt
2 slices garlic
2 small onions

1 bay leaf
6 peppercorns
⅛ teaspoon thyme
6 slices carrot
3 sprigs parsley

Cook together for 30 minutes at simmering temperature. Strain and use as a substitute for water in poaching fish. If the recipe calls for a sauce, use this bouillon for its base. Any fish is improved by the added flavor-giving qualities of a court bouillon. Be sure to poach, not boil, your fish.

HALIBUT À LA NEWBURG

1 lb. halibut
1 tablespoon brandy
¼ cup sherry wine
2 tablespoons butter

1 cup evaporated milk (undiluted)
1 teaspoon lemon juice
3 egg yolks
Dash cayenne—salt to taste

Cut the halibut in small cubes. Steam over hot water or poach in court bouillon for five minutes. Beware of long or swift cooking as the halibut easily loses its shape. When poached, put the fish, butter, wine, brandy, salt, and cayenne in a double boiler and heat smoking hot. Beat the yolks and combine with the evaporated milk (sour cream may be substituted for the milk and lemon juice) and cook with the hot fish for one minute. Remove from the fire and add the lemon juice. Serve on very hot plates. An excellent chafing dish innovation.

LOBSTER CURRY APPETIZER

½ cup fresh or canned lobster meat
2 tablespoons butter

¼ teaspoon curry powder
1 teaspoon sherry wine
⅛ teaspoon dry mustard

Sauté the lobster in the melted fat. Add the seasonings and the wine. When very hot serve on small bread croustades or packaged appetizer shells.

LOBSTER À LA NEWBURG

3 cups cooked lobster	1½ cups cream
3 tablespoons butter	3 egg yolks, beaten
1½ cups Madeira wine	¼ teaspoon salt
or sherry	Dash cayenne

Cut lobster meat into large pieces and heat slowly in butter about 5 minutes. Add wine and simmer until wine is almost all reduced. Beat cream into egg yolks, add to lobster and season. Cook, stirring constantly until thickened. Do not boil. Serve at once. Serves 8.

SOLE THERMIDOR

1 lb. sole or fillet of flounder	Salt and cayenne
2 cups court bouillon	½ cup sour cream
1 tablespoon flour	¼ cup brandy
3 tablespoons butter	4 tablespoons grated Swiss
1 teaspoon dry mustard	or Parmesan cheese

Neatly trim the fish fillets and poach in court bouillon. *(See page 489.)* Lift onto a hot baking platter. Combine the flour and melted butter and add the court bouillon in which the fish was poached. Add the seasonings, the cream, the brandy and 2 tablespoons of the cheese. Do not cook. Pour over the fish, sprinkle with the remaining cheese and put close under the flame to brown instantly. Serve as an entrée. Serves 3.

HAM PORTE MAILLOT

½ cup carrots	2 leaves lettuce
¼ cup onion	¼ cup fat
½ clove garlic	½ cup cooked lima beans
¼ cup celery	½ to ¾ cup dry white wine
½ cup cauliflower	Baked ham

Originated by a restaurant just outside the Porte Maillot, one of the gates of Paris, this dish brings a new flavor to a baked ham. We have substituted dried lima beans for the French white bean that is infrequently used in America. Cut the carrots, onion, garlic, celery, cauliflower, and lettuce in long narrow shreds. Simmer them in the cooking fat but do not brown. When cooked add the previously cooked lima beans and the white wine. Cook together one minute and serve around a hot baked ham or as a sauce for left-over ham that has been reheated over steam.

VEAL WITH OLIVES

1½ lbs. veal cutlets
⅓ cup Marsala wine
Salt and pepper to taste

¼ cup butter or cooking fat
10 green olives

The secret of the success of this delicious Italian meat is to have the veal pounded paper thin. Ask for veal scaloppini at markets in the East. Otherwise ask for veal cutlets and ask the butcher to pound the meat paper thin after cutting it ¼ inch thick. Wipe the veal, sprinkle with salt and pepper. Simmer very quickly in the melted butter, browning lightly on both sides, add the wine and the olives cut in narrow strips. Heat one minute and serve. The veal should cook in five minutes.

BURGUNDIAN BEEF

3 lbs. beef, rump or round
¼ lb. salt pork
3 cups minced onion
2 small shallots, minced
6 peppercorns
2 bay leaves
1 tablespoon tarragon
  vinegar or fresh minced
  tarragon

⅛ teaspoon thyme
2 tablespoons butter
3 tablespoons flour
½ carrot, cut in circles
1 clove garlic
2 tablespoons minced parsley
2 tablespoons minced chervil
1½ to 2 cups red wine
Salt to taste

Dice the salt pork and sauté in the butter. Cut the beef in two-inch cubes or leave in one piece as preferred. Sear thoroughly in the hot fat. Lift out. Add the onion, garlic, shallots, and carrot. Simmer them in the fat till light yellow. Add all the other ingredients and the beef. Cook on a very slow heat three hours. Remove excess fat and serve. It may be reheated with advantage.

LAMB CHOPS WITH MADEIRA

6 lamb chops	2 carrots
3 onions	4 mushrooms
2 tablespoons butter	2 tablespoons Madeira
1 teaspoon tomato paste	⅛ teaspoon pepper
½ clove garlic	½ teaspoon salt

Cut the vegetables in fine inch-length strips. Simmer them in the butter till tender. Cover during this cooking so that the zest will be preserved. Season. Add the tomato paste and Maderia. Serve on top of broiled lamb chops. Thick lamb chops boned and circled with bacon add elegance to this Madeira flavored dish.

CHICKEN BRAISED WITH WINE

(Coq au Vin)

1 frying chicken	3 tablespoons butter
8 small white onions	¼ lb. salt pork diced
4 small shallots	¼ lb. mushrooms
1 tablespoon minced parsley	1 bay leaf
1 tablespoon minced chervil	1 carrot
2 tablespoons flour	Pinch thyme
1 tablespoon brandy	1 cup red or white wine
Salt and pepper to taste	1 clove garlic

Lightly brown the salt pork in the melted butter, add the shallot, onions, garlic, and the carrot, cut in circles. Simmer till golden, but not browned. Lift out and brown the chicken. Sprinkle with the flour, seasoning, and herbs. Return the sautéed vegetables and add the wine. Cook fifteen to twenty minutes over rather high heat. During the last five minutes add the mushrooms. Skim off excess fat and serve.

Red wine is usual in making this dish, but the white one gives a more delicate flavor.

Make your dinner perfect by serving with this chicken a salad of mixed greens with a simple French dressing made with lemon juice. The acid of vinegar devitalizes the subtle details in flavor of the wine-cooked chicken.

EGGS WITH SHERRY AND ORANGE
(Oeufs au Xérès et a l'Orange)

6 eggs
1 tablespoon sherry
3 tablespoons tomato sauce
½ teaspoon salt
Cayenne
Butter
Grated orange rind

Beat eggs until no longer stringy. Blend in sherry and tomato sauce. Add seasonings. Melt butter in a frying pan and pour in the mixture. Cook slowly, stirring until it begins to set. Then sprinkle with the grated orange rind and serve immediately.

PLANTATION SWEET POTATOES

6 sweet potatoes
¾ cup butter or other fat
Paprika
6 tablespoons sherry wine
1½ teaspoons salt
¼ teaspoon pepper

Bake washed sweet potatoes at 450° F. for 40 minutes. Cut off a slice from the top of each and hollow out. Mash the potato. Whip with the melted butter or other fat, the seasoning and the sherry. Re-stuff in the potato shells and sprinkle with paprika. Brown in the oven.

MUSHROOMS WITH MADEIRA

½ lb. mushrooms
3 tablespoons bouillon
¼ cup butter
2 tablespoons Madeira
Salt, cayenne
8 small white onions
3 teaspoons flour
1 tablespoon minced parsley
1 tablespoon minced chervil
½ bay leaf

Melt the butter and cook onions in it for five minutes. Do not brown. Add the mushrooms that have been washed but not peeled. Whole mushrooms make the most attractive service, so slice only the stems. When well coated with butter, add the minced herbs, the flour, the bouillon, and the seasoning. Cook until the onions are tender—slowly of course. Add the Madeira and cook one minute. Serve garnished with croutons and minced herbs.

A delicious entrée or specialty for chafing dish parties.

WELSH RAREBIT

1 lb. grated American cheese   1 teaspoon butter
1 teaspoon paprika   ½ pint ale or beer
Salt and prepared mustard
  to taste

Melt the butter and stir so that it oils the bottom of your pan. (A chafing dish over hot water is ideal.) Add the cheese and gently stir into it one tablespoon of beer or ale. The cheese will at once thicken and another tablespoon of beer or ale should be added. Stir continuously. Add more liquid until the mixture is smooth and velvety. The exact amount of ale varies with different cheeses. Season to taste and serve on toast. Hot plates are essential. This will serve six single portions.

HOT WINE SAUCE FOR VENISON, GAME, OR TONGUE

1 tablespoon butter   ½ cup water
½ glass currant jelly   ½ cup port wine
Juice of ½ lemon   3 cloves
Pinch cayenne   1 teaspoon salt

Simmer together for five minutes all ingredients except the wine. Strain and add the port wine. Add also a little of the meat gravy. Serve hot.

BRANDIED APPLE FRITTERS

4 medium apples   4 tablespoons brandy
1 egg   ½ cup milk
1 tablespoon sugar   1 cup flour
1½ teaspoons baking powder ¼ teaspoon salt

Pare the apples, core and slice in circles or cut in segments. Pour over them the brandy; cover tightly with cooking parchment. Combine the well-beaten egg yolk with the sugar and milk. Add the flour that has been sifted with the salt and baking powder. Fold in the egg white, beaten stiff. Dip the brandied apples in this batter and fry in deep fat (360-370° F.) two to four minutes. Serve with sauce superb or powdered sugar.

SAUCE SUPERB

2 eggs	1 cup powdered sugar
1 cup whipping cream	4 teaspoons rum

Beat the eggs till thick and lemon colored. Add the sugar gradually and continue beating. Whip the cream very stiff, add the rum and combine the two mixtures. The secret of success in making this sauce is to beat it thoroughly. It will keep for hours in the refrigerator.

APRICOT RUM WHIP

1 #2½ can apricots	1 tablespoon rum
¾ cup whipping cream	3 egg whites

Drain the apricots and reserve the juice for beverages. Press the fruit through a sieve and combine with the whipped egg whites and the whipped cream. Fold in the rum and serve cold.

BRANDIED CARAMEL BANANAS

6 bananas	3 tablespoons butter
1 tablespoon brandy	3 tablespoons brown sugar

Peel the bananas; divide in halves lengthwise. Melt the butter and sauté the bananas. Turn when brown on one side. Add the sugar and, when browned on the other side, add the brandy. Serve on very hot plates with the brandied sugar atop the bananas.

CRÊPES SUZETTE

¾ cup flour	6 lumps loaf sugar
2 teaspoons sugar	1 orange
1 teaspoon salt	6 tablespoons brandy
¾ cup milk	¼ cup Grand Marnier Liqueur
3 eggs	⅛ lb. sweet butter

This very famous but really very simple dessert is not difficult. A more awe-inspiring recipe for the crêpes is common at many great Parisian restaurants, but this is excellent and simple. The successful making of crêpes depends on the thinness of the batter.

Add sugar and salt to the eggs, beaten slightly, then alternately the flour and the milk and then beat thoroughly with a rotary beater. Lightly grease a small frying pan (7 inches) and pour in about two tablespoons of batter. Move the pan so that the batter spreads to the outer edge of the pan. Brown on both sides and roll. Keep in a warm place until ready to serve.

The Suzette sauce is made by rubbing the lump sugar with the white part of the orange peel, adding one teaspoon of very finely minced outer peel and dissolving the sugar in one tablespoon brandy. Combine with one-eighth of a pound of sweet butter. At service time, in the chafing dish, or Suzette pan preferably, melt prepared butter, add the cooked crêpes and turn. Then add the remaining brandy and the liqueur. Light with a match and when the flame goes out serve your crêpes.

BRANDIED APRICOT OMELET

Make a puffy omelet in the usual manner. Before folding it spread with apricot jam to which you have added a tablespoon of brandy. Around the omelet serve a foamy brandy sauce or a sauce superb.

GEORGIA CHRISTMAS PUDDING

½ cup chopped walnuts or pecans
½ cup sugar
6 egg whites

½ cup chopped raisins
½ cup sherry wine
¼ cup rum
1 teaspoon lemon juice

Soak the nuts and raisins in the wines and lemon juice for at least six hours—overnight if possible. Beat the egg whites; add sugar gradually, beating until stiff peaks are formed. Fold in the wine-soaked fruits and nuts. Pour into a buttered baking dish. Set in a pan of hot water. Bake at 350° F. for one hour. Serve with the sauce.

Make a custard of 6 egg yolks, ¼ cup sugar and 1½ cups of scalded milk. When smoothly thickened, flavor with sherry and serve on the Christmas Pudding. This is a famous old Georgia recipe.

STRAWBERRIES CHANTILLY

Wash, stem and cut in half 1 quart ripe strawberries. Cover with powdered sugar and 2 tablespoons rum. Chill 30 minutes. Whisk two egg whites stiff, beat in gradually 4 tablespoons powdered sugar. Fold in the chilled berries. Serve in sherbet glasses and top with sweetened whipped cream.

TIPSY PUDDING

One of the choice recipes of our Grandmother's era. It appeared in the place of honor on New Year's Day. The secret for a successful outcome is to use a very stale, very porous cake. A broken, not cut, sunshine cake at least four days old, should be soaked in sherry. Allow about one cup sherry to a quarter of a good sized cake. An hour later cover the cake with a soft custard flavored with rum. Serve very cold.

OLD FASHIONED WINE JELLY

2 tablespoons unflavored gelatin	⅔ cup orange juice
	½ cup cold water
1 cup sherry or Madeira wine	1 cup boiling water
	Grated rind 1 orange
1 cup sugar	⅓ cup lemon juice

Soak the gelatin in the cold water until soft. Dissolve in the boiling water; add the sugar and other ingredients. Pour into molds that have been rinsed with cold water. Serve with whipped cream.

BRANDIED PEACHES

4 lbs. fruit	4 lbs. sugar
1 pint best white brandy	1 egg white
Cloves	3½ cups water

Pare the peaches with a silver knife. Insert 2 cloves in each whole peach. Make a syrup of the sugar and water. Add the egg white beaten to a froth. Skim. Put in fruit, one layer at a time, and boil five minutes, or until it may be pierced with a straw. Remove the fruit to a platter to partially cool. Then pack in glass jars. Return any excess juice to the syrup and boil about ten minutes more, or till well thickened. Remove from the fire, add the brandy and pour over the fruit. Seal at once. White cling stone peaches are particularly good. Six pounds of fruit will yield about seven pint jars. Improves with age.

HASTY WINE GELATIN

2 packages lemon-flavored   ½ cup Madeira wine or
  gelatin   ¼ cup sherry wine
3½ cups hot water

Dissolve the gelatin in the hot water. When perfectly clear add the wine. Pour in molds that have been rinsed with cold water. Serve with whipped cream. Garnish with grated orange peel on top the whipped cream. Orange-flavored gelatin combines well with Madeira.

CLARET LEMONADE

12 cubes ice   Sugar syrup to taste
1 bottle claret   Orange slices
Juice 3 lemons

Half fill a glass pitcher with ice cubes or cracked ice. Add the lemon juice and a few slices of orange. Fill the pitcher nearly full with claret and add sugar syrup to taste. Stand twenty to thirty minutes to blend and ripen.

MULLED CLARET

1 qt. hot claret   ½ cup sugar
1 piece stick cinnamon   8 cloves
Juice 1 lemon   ½ lemon, sliced

Heat the claret and add the other ingredients. Stir till dissolved and serve hot. Doughnuts were served with it in the nineties.

TUTTI FRUITTI

Into a stone jar put one cup of brandy, the best you own, one cup sugar and one cup ripe strawberries. Stir thoroughly. As each fruit comes to the height of its perfection, add it, with a cup of sugar for each cup of fruit. No more brandy is indicated. Be sure to stir at each addition. Large fruits like peaches should be cut in small pieces. Cherries and plums should be stoned. Atop vanilla ice cream this is an epicurean delight. Perhaps you will make enough to use it for preserves.

CHAMPAGNE CUP

½ cup Maraschino	2 qts. Champagne
½ cup Vermouth	Cucumber rind
½ cup Santa Cruz rum	Juice 4 oranges
Sugar to taste	Juice 3 lemons

Sweeten the fruit juices slightly. Combine all the ingredients. Let stand ten minutes after mixing with a large piece of ice in a punch bowl. It's well to use as large a piece of ice as possible, for it melts more slowly and adds less water to the punch.

EGGNOG, SOUTHERN

4 eggs	4 tablespoons brandy or
½ cup whipping cream	whiskey
	3 tablespoons powdered sugar

Beat the yolks till thick and lemon colored. Slowly beat in the brandy and sugar. Fold in the stiffly beaten whites and the whipped cream. This must be eaten with a spoon. Excellent.

EGGNOG—OTHER TYPE

4 eggs	4 tablespoons brandy or
4 tablespoons powdered	rum
sugar	3 cups milk
	Grating of nutmeg

Beat the egg white to a dry froth. Beat into the egg white the sugar and then the yolks of the eggs combined with the brandy. Add the milk and a slight grating of nutmeg. Serve at once. Famous at New Year's and Christmas.

ZABAGLIONE—

4 egg yolks	Cinnamon
3 tablespoons honey	2 tablespoons Marsala wine

Beat egg yolks with honey until thick and lemon colored in the top of a double boiler. Add wine gradually. While it heats continue to use rotary beater. Serve as drink or dessert sauce with dash of cinnamon.

HERBS, SPICES, AND FLAVORS

HERBS

BAY LEAVES—Flavor particularly good in practically all meat cooking: also in vegetable and meat soups and sauces.

BORAGE—Young tender leaves excellent for salad or pot herbs.

CHERVIL—Flavor like parsley but milder. Young leaves may be used in meat and vegetable soups, salads, and as a garnish. More attractive than parsley as a garnish but not as lasting. Used in powdered combination called *Fines Herbes*.

DILL—Both leaves and seeds of dill are used. Leaves may be used as a garnish or to cook with fish. Leaves or the whole plant may be used to flavor dill pickles.

FENNEL—Has a sweet hot flavor. Both seeds and leaves are used. Seeds may be used as a spice in very small quantity in pies and baked fruit. Leaves may be boiled with fish. Fresh leaves are valued by some people.

HOREHOUND—Used in candy making.

MARJORAM—May be used both green and dry for flavoring soups and ragouts; and in stuffing for all meats and fish.

MINT—May be used fresh in salads, fruit beverages, jellies, conserves, ices, iced tea, sauces for meats, and added minced to carrots and peas. Good with apple combinations.

PARSLEY—One of the most popular herbs, which may be used in many ways. A favorite garnish. May be used in fruit and vegetable salads, in sandwiches, in all soups and gravies, in meat sauces, minced and added just before serving to practically all vegetables, minced and added to white sauce.

PEPPER GRASS OR PEPPER CRESS—Excellent flavor. May be used in green salads and sandwiches.

SAFFRON—May be used to give pale yellow color to bread, cakes, and sauces, or to color confectionery. Has a pleasant flavor and good color.

SAGE—Used fresh and dried. May be used in poultry and meat stuffings; in sausage and practically all meat combinations; in cheese and vegetable combinations, as in vegetable loaf, or curry. The flowers are sometimes used in salads.

SAVORY—Agreeable flavor, blends well with other flavors; may be used in stuffings in meat, in vegetable soups, in sausage, with meats and with horseradish.

SORREL—Green. May be used in salads or as a pot herb.

A List of Herbs, Spices, and Flavors (Continued)

SWEET BASIL—Distinct flavor of cloves. May be used for flavoring salads, soups and meats.

TARRAGON—Leaves have a hot, pungent taste. Valuable to use in all salads and sauces. Excellent in Tartar sauce. Leaves are pickled with gherkins. Used to flavor vinegar.

THYME—Leaves, green or dried, valuable for use in stuffings, sauces, soups and meats.

SEEDS

ALLSPICE—Sold whole or ground. Better combined with other spices in fruit dishes, cakes, pies, pickles, etc.

ANISE—Leaves are used for garnishing and for flavor. Oil is extracted from the seed and used as anise extract.

CARAWAY—Seeds have a spicy smell and aromatic taste. Used in baked fruit, in cakes, breads, soups, cheese and sauerkraut.

CARDAMOM—Flavor especially good in honey combinations.

CLOVES—Should be dark brown in color. Usually used with other spices. The combination gives a better flavor than cloves used alone. Too much gives an undesirable color as well as a bitter flavor.

CORIANDER—Both leaves and seeds are used. Leaves are used in salads, soups and curry sauces. The seeds are used for flavoring pastries and confections in about the same way as caraway seeds.

CURRY POWDER—A number of spices combined in proper proportion to give a distinct flavor to such dishes as vegetables of all kinds, meat, poultry and fish.

MACE—The inner envelope of nutmegs. May be used both in "blade" and ground form in soups, sauces, pastry, pickles.

MUSTARD—Young tender leaves are used for greens and for salad. Seeds are used as a ground spice in salad dressings, pickles, sauces, in some vegetable cookery, and in some cheese dishes. Made into a paste and served with meats.

NUTMEG—Sold whole or ground. Gives good flavor used alone in small amount in various soups, meat dishes, pastry and in all dough mixtures. In combination with other spices for pickles.

PAPRIKA—A Hungarian red pepper. Bright red in color. May be used in all meat and vegetable salads. In soups, both cream and stock. As a garnish for potatoes, cream cheese, salads or eggs.

PEPPERCORN—The whole berry of the pepper plant.

PEPPER, BLACK—Reduced to proper fineness by grinding and sieving. Used in all meat and vegetable dishes where the color does not affect the product.

A List of Herbs, Spices, and Flavors (Continued)

PEPPER, CAYENNE—Usually obtained from small fruited varieties of capsicum. It should be of dull red color. May be used in very small amounts in vegetables and in some salad dressings and in cheese dishes. It must be used with care, however.

PEPPER, WHITE—Practically the same as black pepper except that the outer shell or pericarp of the berry is removed. Used where color of black pepper is undesirable.

PEPPER, WHITE CORIANDER—A product of especially attractive appearance screened to uniform size and bleached.

FLAVOR VEGETABLES

CELERY—Every part of the plant can be used to advantage. Stalks and heart may be used raw, plain or with various fillings. Other stalks may be stewed, scalloped, or used in combination to give flavor to other vegetables such as potatoes. Trimmings may be used for flavoring soups or in any cooked meat or vegetable dishes. Dried seeds may be used in pickles, soups, and salads.

CHIVES—Leaves are used in many ways. May be used in salad, in cream cheese, in sandwiches, omelet, soups, and in fish dishes. Mild flavor of onion.

GARLIC—Vegetable similar to a small onion but with the bulb divided into sections known as cloves. May be used in very small amounts in flavoring meats, soups, sauces, salads, pickles.

HORSERADISH—Valuable for its white, fleshy, pungent roots which are grated, mixed with vinegar and used as a condiment for meat, oysters, fish, sauces, and in some kinds of pickle. Young tender leaves may be used in salad or greens.

MUSHROOMS—Have a delicate characteristic flavor. May be used in meat or vegetable dishes, in sauces and soups.

ONION—Popular vegetable which combines in flavor with practically all vegetables, and some fruits—*e. g.*, apple, and orange; also with all meat and fish. Tender young tops may be minced and used as a garnish for soups and salads.

PEPPERS—All varieties of green peppers and some of the red peppers may be used to give flavor to most forms of vegetable cookery. The green peppers of mild flavor and thick-meated type are particularly good for stuffing and for salad.

SHALLOTS—A mild onion flavor used in the same way as onions.

INDEX